SERVING GOD

Dave Ness

Partnership
Publications

A Division of House to House Publications

About the Cover

"Always there, but rarely seen," would be a way of describing North America's highest peak, Denali (The Native name for Mt. McKinley means "The Great One"). When my friend, Milt, and I climbed Cathedral Mountain in Denali National Park, Alaska, it was in hopes of seeing Denali. Just as we were ready to descend, "The Great One" momentarily broke through the clouds.

The picture I took of my friend on Cathedral that day, with Denali in the distance, reminds me of what it is to serve a God whom we know is there, but whom we cannot see. It's a sometimes lonely pursuit, offset by those special times when we glimpse His majesty and goodness. When the clouds move in again, and we're back to walking by faith, not sight, we're blessed with the memory of a moment when we knew for sure that our faith is not in vain. Nothing compares with serving God. He *is* The Great One.

—*Dave Ness*

Serving God
© 2007 Dave Ness
P.O. Box 1747
Longview, WA 98632
www.PrayingforAmerica.org

ISBN 978-0-9778614-7-7

Partnership Publications
A Division of House to House Publications
www.H2HP.com

For my Mom
I followed your heart straight to God's.

Preface

I love God.

This has not been a hard thing. In fact, I guess you could say I come by it, naturally. I grew up in a maelstrom of spiritual blessings which had bounced along from generation to generation, set in motion who-knows-when by an act of faithful obedience on the part of someone now long-gone. Some people grow up rich in money; we grew up rich in spiritual blessings and in a knowledge of God. It wasn't hard to believe in God in our family; in fact, it was probably impossible not to. Faith was not reserved for Sundays or for special places; it permeated our lives.

A key figure in this heritage was my grandmother, whose spirituality was legendary. They called her, "Ma." Ma's prayer life had often found her kneeling out in a cornfield, lifting her petitions before God. If a family member back at the house listened carefully, they would often hear their own name wafting back to them over the corn rows, as Ma brought her loved ones and their needs before God's throne. Her family would say they had never known anyone so close to God.

When diagnosed with terminal cancer, her first response was to say, "Praise God! All the children are saved!" That had mattered more to her by far than life itself.

Her children fully expected her to be healed. They could think of no one more deserving, nor could they think of anything they wanted more.

Included in Ma's relentless prayers had been the boy she felt her grown son needed, to go along with the daughter they already had. She told my mother she had been asking God for a son, for them. They had been unable to conceive for five years, but it looked like, once again, Ma's prayers had been answered. Mom had not even been to the doctor to verify she was pregnant, it was so early, but she was pretty sure.

It was too late for the doctor to be able to do anything about Ma's cancer, and by now, it was a battle just to try to keep her somewhat comfortable. Grandpa had set up a bed for her in the farmhouse living room, and had strung a curtain between the living and dining rooms to provide a little privacy, plus temperature control. She was always too hot. Grandpa would sleep on the couch, nearby.

My mother was actually at another farmhouse a mile away when this dream occurred, which she tells in her own words:

I was sitting in a chair beside Ma's bed in the living room. The curtains were shut and I had been asleep. I woke to see Jesus just walking through the curtains. He didn't even look at me; he just slowly walked up to Ma's bed. I watched as He reached out His hand and touched her. Her face became a lovely pink color of health. I thought, "Oh! He's healed her! As He stood there, I thought, "Oh, if only He'd heal Dad, too, while He's here."

Dad was sleeping on the couch over on the other side of me. Jesus walked behind Ma's bed and me and went over and stood looking down at Dad Ness. He reached out and touched him. Both of them stayed asleep. Jesus looked sad.

I was afraid to ask Him to bless me while He was there. He started toward the curtains without even looking at me. I just couldn't let Him go, but I didn't have the courage to ask for myself. Then my heart cried out, "Lord, bless my baby before you go!"

Jesus stopped, turned, looked at me and smiled. It was like the sun had come out! Then He said, "Call his name David, for he's to be my servant."

He was gone. And I woke up, in my own bed, next to your Dad.

That little story has shaped my whole life. My grandmother went to be with her Lord, the following month, but not before learning of the answer to her prayers, concerning me. She had refused the efforts of those who had come to pray "the prayer of faith" over her; her mission had been accomplished, and she was going home. Soon after my mother's vision, a cure was found for Grandpa's physical afflictions, resulting in the best health of his adult life, all his remaining years.

And then there's me.

You know you're in trouble when your whole life is formed around a pregnant woman's dream!

Then again, there are advantages to having your life's purpose all laid out for you, before you were even born.

Mom told me that it wasn't even like a dream, even though she was asleep at the time. It was a very clear vision, which she was aware of at the time she was experiencing it, and which she remembered perfectly when she awoke.

Whatever it was, it was real. The vision my Mom had prior to my birth determined my name and my identity.

My purpose in life is to be a servant of God.
But is that so unique? After all, isn't that your purpose, too?

I was born rich. It wasn't money that was plentiful; it was spiritual depth–it was faith, everywhere! It would have been a daunting, lonely and fruitless task to try to grow up and rebel against God, in my family. None of us bothered. The flow was definitely toward having the wonderful kind of relationship with Jesus that each of us saw lived out every day, and we all started early. Free will? It was a technical possibility, but mostly in theory. We all took the smart route, and loved God. We haven't been disappointed!

I asked Jesus into my heart at the age of five, answered a call to the ministry when I was sixteen, and have spent my life in trying to be God's servant.

Six years ago, I decided to go on a search through the Bible to discover better what it really means to "serve God." I didn't want to know what the latest super-church pastor had to say about it; I wanted to know what God had to say about it, so I looked through every page of His Word, seeking out principles and illustrations which could be applied to my life. I was doing this purely for my own use, with no intention of trying to arrange these principles in book form, but as I neared the end of my study, I realized that there would be others who might benefit from these findings which are helping to shape my life.

I'm not a mega-church pastor. I'm not a conference speaker. All I am is a person trying to be a servant of God, just like in Mom's dream. That may well be your story, too. If it is, don't look for a promotion. Serving God is the absolute best assignment in the world!

If you are as interested in being His servant as I am, God will show you some important things through this study, as well as confirming to you and reminding you of things you already know.

God bless you, friend, as you journey with me in a consideration of what it means to "serve God."

Dave Ness
Kelso-Longview, Washington

Who's Serving Whom?

In the beginning, God created the heavens and the earth. Genesis 1:1

You would think we'd be more patient than this. If it took all those billions of years for us to evolve, you'd think we'd have emerged with a bit more patience than is generally in evidence!

It doesn't take much traffic to ruin my day. Obviously, others have about the same appreciation for it. This morning, just in the course of getting kids to school, I witnessed five cars running red lights. I'm just trying to picture modern man, irritable at having to stand in line for his caffeine, somehow putting up with the slightest improvement in his physique requiring a few million years! These are people who can't wait a few seconds for a traffic signal! If mankind got here by way of evolution, shouldn't we have picked up a little more patience along the way?

We might as well admit it—mankind did not squirm his way into existence, no matter how much time we're talking. The Bible gives us the conclusion to one of life's biggest questions in the very first sentence: We have a Creator.

If the opening statement of the Bible is true—and I believe with all my heart that it is—then God owns us. We belong to Him. We are His creation, made in His own image. Were that not true, we would be free to carve out our own identity, and free to go our own way. We're not. We belong to our Creator. It's His world, and He made the rules. We are here to serve God, not the other way around.

Know that the LORD, he is God! It is he who made us, and not we ourselves; we are his people, and the sheep of his pasture. (Psalm 100:3)

And now, Israel, what does the LORD your God require of you, but to fear the LORD your God, to walk in all his ways, to love him, to serve the LORD your God with all your heart and with all your soul, and to keep the commandments and statutes of the LORD, which I am commanding you today for your good? Behold, to the LORD your God belong heaven and the heaven of heavens, the earth with all that is in it. Yet the LORD set his heart in love on your fathers and chose their offspring after them, you above all peoples, as you are this day. Circumcise therefore the foreskin of your heart, and be no longer stubborn. (Deut 10:12-16)

I accept the mark of God's ownership on my heart. Mankind did not create God; God created us. My purpose forever is to serve Him.

Promises To Servants

God's Great Odds

"Come to me, all who labor and are heavy laden, and I will give you rest. Take my yoke upon you, and learn from me, for I am gentle and lowly in heart, and you will find rest for your souls. For my yoke is easy, and my burden is light." Matthew 11:28-30

If we confess our sins, he is faithful and just to forgive us our sins and to cleanse us from all unrighteousness. 1 John 1:9

God seems to like the word "all"—it occurs many times in the Bible. For those of us who always seem to be the exception to the rule, "all" is sweet music to our ears, when it's tied to God's promises!

One of the greatest crises in our lives occurred when our then-twelve-year-old daughter came down with what I cleverly diagnosed as the flu. Nearly a week later, a CT scan revealed that her appendix had already burst, and she underwent the first of what would eventually be three surgeries and thirty-one days in the hospital, including two days in intensive care.

She had just been transferred to the intensive care unit of a large children's hospital following her second surgery in a week, and we stood helplessly by her bed, watching a frail girl we loved more than life itself. Our daughter was under the care of the head surgeon, who came in to examine his new patient. Noting catheter bag contents that were of a color not to his liking, he simply pointed to it and said to a nearby nurse, "Fix that." His every order was obeyed without question. We watched him intently.

He saw the fear in our eyes, and directed his attention toward us for a moment.

"Calm down," he said, with a reassuring gesture. "I want you to know that 100% of our patients with this problem get better."

We liked those odds! Not only that, they proved accurate, to our joy. Those are the kinds of odds our great God gives us.

100% of those who come to Jesus Christ for help get better! 100% of those who ask forgiveness for their sins receive it. 100% of our sins are washed clean by His blood. 100% of those who come to Christ find everything they need in Him. 100% of His promises are true. I like those odds! And they are accurate, to our joy!

January 3

Return on Investment

"And everyone who has left houses or brothers or sisters or father or mother or children or lands, for my name's sake, will receive a hundredfold and will inherit eternal life. But many who are first will be last, and the last first." Matthew 19:29-30

Jesus' disciples had just watched a rich young man walk away from the call of Christ, because following Him was going to involve divesting himself of his great wealth; Jesus had just explained how difficult it is for the rich to enter the kingdom of God; Peter had blurted out, *"See, we have left everything and followed you. What then will we have?"* (Mt 19:27)

Jesus' response came in promise form. First, the promise of authority in the new world. Second, the promise of restoration—of "return on investment." Whatever we have given up for His name's sake will be restored to us a hundredfold—and along with that, eternal life! That's all Peter needed to hear. He just wanted to be sure there was a return on this investment. There is.

A tough week on Wall Street dashes the hopes of many for a good return on their investments. I wonder how hard it would be to get folks to put up $10,000 if they knew for sure that it would come back to them as $1,000,000! I'm thinking "not very hard." The trick would be getting them to believe that the promise was true. Once they believed, they would have no trouble at all in letting go. And the first hundredfold return would be the end of their hesitation!

Here is a bonafide promise from God's Son that whatever we give up for Him will be repaid to us many, many times over—plus eternal life! Why is it still difficult to give things up? It's because it's hard to believe the promise is true. But once we believe on it enough to act on it!....

A friend of mine once spent hours getting up the courage to write a check God had instructed him to write, knowing that obedience would change everything for him. It did. It resulted in a lifetime of blessings, and a passion for giving. And that's just been the down payment on the return he has coming! Others of us have given up relationships for God—and still revel in how outrageously wonderful God's plan was compared to ours! What do we get for obeying Christ? One hundred fold back, and eternal life. Beat that.

PromisesTo Servants

A God Who Wants To Give

And he said to them, "Which of you who has a friend will go to him
at midnight and say to him, 'Friend, lend me three loaves, for a friend of
mine has arrived on a journey; and I have nothing to set before him'; and
he will answer from within, 'Do not bother me; the door is now shut, and
my children are with me in bed. I cannot get up and give you anything'? I
tell you, though he will not get up and give him anything because he is his
friend, yet because of his impudence he will rise and give him whatever he
needs. And I tell you, ask and it will be given to you; seek, and you will
find; knock, and it will be opened to you. For everyone who asks receives,
and the one who seeks finds, and to the one who knocks it will be opened.
What father among you, if his son asks for a fish, will instead of a fish give
him a serpent; or if he asks for an egg, will give him a scorpion? If you
then, who are evil, know how to give good gifts to your children, how much
more will the heavenly Father give the Holy Spirit to those who ask him!"

Luke 11:5-13

God so much wants His children to ask!

"If He wants to give us things, and He already knows what we need,
why doesn't He simply provide them, then?"

Often He does. But just as my wife and I are training our children to
ask politely for things we already know they need, so our Heavenly Father
is training His children to ask Him (politely) for what it is that we need.
And we err so greatly when we assume that we won't get anything or
that we can't trust Him, so we don't ask at all! Thus the little story of the
impudent friend at midnight, and the lesson: "If someone can show up at
the home of a friend at an inconvenient time asking for a favor and come
home with exactly what he needs; if an earthly, sinful father would never
think of responding to the requests of his child by giving him something
harmful instead of something good, then why would we ever think that our
Heavenly Father would ignore our requests or punish us for asking?!"

God wants His children to *ask* Him for what we need. He wants us
to ask expectantly, confidently, and persistently until we see the answer.
He loves to give *good* gifts to His kids. He loves it when we learn to ask,
because it builds our trust in Him and our relationship with Him, which is
what this is really about, anyway. Our Father can be trusted—*completely.*
Ask.

Stubborn Belief

Therefore do not throw away your confidence, which has a great reward.
For you have need of endurance, so that when you have done the will of
God you may receive what is promised. Hebrews 10:35-36

To me, one of the greatest survival stories of all time is that of Ernest Shackleton and the crew of "Endurance." Stranded in the Antarctic for over a year, Shackleton held his men together in surviving under the harshest circumstances imaginable. When Shackleton and several others made a bold run for help across hundreds of miles of open sea in a small craft made from pieces of "Endurance," the remaining crew members daily awaited their return, holding out hope that their captain had somehow managed to miraculously survive the sea voyage and secure rescue for them.

The officer left in charge on Antarctica would tell his men the same thing each day: "Pack up your things, boys. The Boss may return today."

They held hope alive. One day their eyes were rewarded by the sight of a rescue ship. On board was a man who refused to give up, who had gone to unbelievable lengths to secure life for the band of stubborn believers who had daily awaited his return. He rescued them all, without losing a single man.

I know why I like that story so much. It's because it's so much like our story. We wait for our Savior, knowing He is our only hope of rescue. "Pack up your things, boys. The Boss may return today." We hold out stubborn belief that He will come back for us, just as He said. In fact, "stubborn belief" is a pretty good synonym for "faith," and "disciple" is another name for a "stubborn believer" who won't quit following or believing.

It takes some tenacity to be a Christian. When all the world's "odds" are against us, we still wait patiently on the beach, eyes straining for when the Boss will come back for us. We stubbornly refuse to quit, to give up, to relinquish even a little of the hope and faith we have in a Savior who promised He would return, so He *will*.

When He does, He'll find a cheering band of believers on the shore whose stubborn belief in a God worthy of their faith in Him kept them through all the long days of waiting. We kept a tight grip on our hope in Him and used it to beat off the doubts. We endured.

If we hang onto our faith, we'll be glad we did. Jesus is coming back for stubborn believers. Sometimes, that's the only kind.

Wind Sprints

It is for discipline that you have to endure. God is treating you as sons. For what son is there whom his father does not discipline? ...

For they disciplined us for a short time as it seemed best to them, but he disciplines us for our good, that we may share his holiness. For the moment all discipline seems painful rather than pleasant, but later it yields the peaceful fruit of righteousness to those who have been trained by it.

Therefore lift your drooping hands and strengthen your weak knees, and make straight paths for your feet, so that what is lame may not be put out of joint but rather be healed. Hebrews 12:7,10-13

I never cared much for wind sprints. But then, I never cared much for P.E. in general. I showed neither promise nor enthusiasm as a young athletic candidate; I was pretty much glad when the whole thing went away.

Discipline was different. In study I could be very focused and ambitious, plus my parents taught me to work, and growing up on a farm offered more than its share of opportunities to engage in it, with plenty of purpose to it. We didn't have to go to the gym to get exercise; there was plenty for everyone, just trying to make a living. There was no need for senseless running back and forth between lines on a basketball court.

What I failed to grasp as a teen was the importance of "senseless" activity like wind sprints, if one were actually going to be capable of athletic success. It wasn't like farm work, where you don't clean the barn for exercise—you clean it because it needs it, which happens to require exercise. Wind sprints weren't about getting to the other end of the court, they were about getting players into shape. The purpose was conditioning, obedience and discipline. The floor didn't need wind sprints, but the players did.

Goal-oriented people like me need to remember that a lot of the time, God is having us do wind sprints. It's not about accomplishing things for God; it's about us getting in shape and learning patience and perseverance and discipline. This isn't about accomplishing the "goal." It's about *us!* It's about us growing and changing and becoming more rugged in our faith, more disciplined in our lives, more confident in our God, *"that we may share his holiness."*

So God has us run wind sprints. About the time we start to gripe about "meaningless activity," we find out the whole thing is really about us getting to share in His holiness. Not bad.

All God's Children

I entreat Euodia and I entreat Syntyche to agree in the Lord. Yes, I ask you also, loyal Syzgus, help these women, who have labored side by side with me in the gospel together with Clement and the rest of my fellow workers, whose names are in the book of life. Philippians 4:2-3

Would all God's children please stop fighting in the back seat?

I'm thinking the Lord must get tired of it, sometimes; I'm sure that pastors get tired of it—breaking up little fights between well-meaning believers who are beating one another over the head with Bible verses, doctrines, pet peeves, hymns and choruses. Sigh.

I don't know what the deal was with Euodia and Syntyche, but they both knew they were right. Both felt justified in their position. Each one could not believe the immaturity being demonstrated by the other. What a shock it must have been to receive a letter from Paul to the whole church, calling attention to their argument, publicly pleading with them to agree with one another, calling on an onsite moderator to referee their issue.

It must have been embarrassing to see their own names in print, along with the admonition to "Please shape up and get along with each other." Some sorts of fame we can do without! It's one thing to act up in class at school and get your name on the board as a troublemaker, but getting your name in the Bible?! And not in a good way, either. All we know about these two is that they were believers, they had done good things for the Kingdom, and they had a disagreement with each other so sharp that word of it traveled from Philippi to Rome, where Paul felt the need to address it from his prison cell! The man had enough troubles already, without adding to it a spat between "saints"! How does it feel to realize your strongly held opinions are causing heartburn for everyone who knows you, up to the throne of God?

"Hmm. Yeah, but I'm right!" Is that why the SWAT team is outside?

Would all God's children please stop fighting in the back seat?

"But they started it."

"Yes, they probably did. So, whoever really is mature back there, put your hands in your lap, quit whining and look straight ahead. Do you hear me? If I have to stop this car, you'll wish you had done what I told you!"

All God's children need to learn how to behave in the back seat. And I think God's car sports a bumper sticker that says, "Stop global whining."

Invisible

No one has ever seen God; the only God, who is at the Father's side, he has made him known. John 1:18

One day, as a prayer meeting exercise, I asked people in the group to tell God something they liked about Him. One lady prayed, "I like it that you're invisible."

I've heard people *complain* about God being invisible—including me—but I don't think I'd ever heard anyone *thank* Him for being that way. I think that prayer blessed God. It blessed me, too, and made me think.

After all, it's hard to worship a God we can't see. It's harder to believe God is real when we can't see Him or prove His existence. It can be embarrassing to talk to Him, at times when our friends make fun of our prayers, the same as they would if we were talking to an imaginary friend.

I worship a God I can't see.

But "invisible" doesn't mean He's not real. There are so many other evidences of His existence. All of Creation points directly toward the Creator.

If I stumbled across a completely furnished house out in the middle of a forest, I would immediately surmise, "Somebody lives here!" The fact that I don't see the occupants of the dwelling at the moment doesn't mean they don't exist. I would also assume there had been a builder, whether the current occupants of the house or someone else. Just because I didn't see the builder of this house wouldn't mean there never had been one. I've never yet seen a house that built itself—even if you neatly stacked all the raw materials in one place and granted it permission! My guess is that you could wait quite a few billion years and you'd still have no house, until you got a builder. (I know folks who feel they've waited close to this, just trying to get a permit)! If there's a house, there's a builder: *(For every house is built by someone, but the builder of all things is God.)* (Heb 3:4)

The Builder, my Creator, Redeemer and Friend, is invisible to my eyes, not because He's imaginary, but because He transcends the matter He created. I worship a God who is invisible—*now*. He will not always be invisible to me. One day I will see Him face to face (1 Jn 3:2). Meanwhile, though I can't see Him, I can see His handiwork, I can experience His love. He is willing to call me His child; I am willing to call Him God and Father.

I can't see Him, but He's real, and He's there. I love you, invisible God.

When God Asks the Questions

Then the LORD answered Job out of the whirlwind and said:
"Who is this that darkens counsel by words without knowledge?
Dress for action like a man; I will question you, and you make it known to
me. Where were you when I laid the foundation of the earth?
Tell me, if you have understanding." Job 38:1-4

On the ash heap of loss, amidst miserable comfort, Job is addressed by
God, whose questions snap Job out of total despondency, and render his
theologically challenged friends squirming. For four chapters (Job 38-41)
God peppers the little crew with unanswerable questions, to Job's delight.

We think we're so smart. We're not. God is.

Since so many intelligent people would say that life as we know it
"came to be" through nothing more than copious measures of time and really exceptional luck, it stands to reason that we should be able to replicate
at least some of what chance has accomplished by simply adding a bit of
our intelligence.

Let's make a tree.

This should be easy, right? Just one little Douglas fir. Simple.

Before trees or any other plants can grow, we'll need quite a lot of
stuff: Soil. Sunlight. Water, and a way to get it to our tree. We'd better
design a system of evaporation that forms clouds (assuming we've already
made water), we need to make wind to blow the clouds over our tree, and
we need gravity so our tree won't fly away. We also need to spin the earth.
Otherwise, there will be no night and day, and our tree will get too hot or
too cold. We need for the earth to orbit around the sun too, in such a way
that we'll have seasons of spring, summer, fall and winter, or this kind of
tree won't grow. In fact, all of our systems need to be pretty much perfect
and simultaneous or this isn't going to work, but we're smart. We can do
this! Spin the earth. It's easy—we've been to college. Just give it a spin.

We're getting it! Earth is spinning just right—we have seasons and
sunlight, we're working on photosynthesis. I didn't think making one little
tree was going to be this hard! It's not like you can just make the thing and
be done with it; we're needing to design entire systems—perfect ones at
that—just to keep it going, assuming we ever get it to live in the first place!
I'm ready for a Sabbath, and I don't even have one tree made, yet.

The One Who Can

*For his invisible attributes, namely, his eternal power and divine nature,
have been clearly perceived, ever since the creation of the world, in the
things that have been made. So they are without excuse.* Romans 1:20

We're still working on making our own tree.

It's turned out to be pretty complicated, and we're not even close, yet.
We would need to create entire systems, just to get one little part of the thing
to work right! Let's forget about the other stuff like making sunlight, wind,
rain, etc., and just focus on the tree itself for the moment.

We need this tree to produce seeds so it can reproduce itself. I'm thinking we'll need a lot of seeds to do the job, with each tiny seed containing
a whole mapping system of instructions on it, so it will know to become a
Douglas fir very much like its parent. If we can design the seed right, we
could have all the trees we want, as long as we've got the basic planet, the
sun, the rotation, the seasons, the soil, the water, the photosynthesis, the
wind to flex the trees and make the sap flow in them—oops, forgot about
the sap—Oh, never mind—and we'll need wind or birds or animals or
something to get the seeds spread around, so there will be new trees from
the seeds we've made.

Have we talked yet about the cells knowing whether they're supposed
to become bark or needles?

This is not that complicated. All we're making is one little Douglas
fir!

The game's up. We can try to make ourselves believe that all we see
around us just designed itself and then, when it got done, somehow got itself
all organized into a perfect, self-perpetuating system, so precise we can set
our watches by it, and so predictable that we *need* a watch. We can try to
believe that mankind is just part of this amazing, self-made, lucky system,
that we're a product of Mother Nature, that the only difference between
us and the animals is that for some reason we enjoy building freeways and
sitting in traffic so we can go watch a baseball game in a stadium where
35,000 people can watch a guy step out of the batter's box and spit.

Creation all just "came to be," right? Yeah, right. Believing there was
nobody behind all this would take a lot more faith than I'll ever have!

The faith I do have is in the One, the *invisible God,* maker of heaven
and Earth, my Creator, my Redeemer, my Friend. And since I can't even
make a tree, I think I'll put my trust in the One who can.

Nicknames from God

One of the two who heard John speak and followed Jesus was Andrew, Simon Peter's brother. He first found his own brother Simon and said to him, "We have found the Messiah (which means Christ). He brought him to Jesus. Jesus looked at him and said, "So you are Simon the son of John? You shall be called Cephas" (which means Peter). John 1:40-42

My Bible notes remind me that both "Cephas" and "Peter" are from the word for rock in Aramaic and Greek, respectively.

Why was it important for Jesus to give Simon a nickname?

Considering that Simon's whole identity would be changing if he chose to follow Jesus, it seemed appropriate to give him a new name to go with his new identity. It was an ever-present reminder of how the Lord saw him—as a rock, strong and dependable. The name helped to shape the character.

Post-resurrection, when Jesus came to the beach and Peter threw himself into the water to get to Jesus before the other disciples, how did Jesus address him? "Simon, son of John." (Jn 21:15) One of the questions Simon was being asked that day was, "Do you want to be Simon, or do you want to be Peter? Do you want to slip back into who you used to be, or resume the walk with me?" Simon son of John once again chose to be Peter. Peter's reinstatement as an apostle was an epic event. For the rest of his life, he was always Peter, servant of Jesus Christ. The nickname helped him go forward as a new person in Christ.

That wasn't the only time when God confirmed His call by providing a new name for someone, or leading them to take on a new name to coincide with their new identity. Abram, whose name meant "exalted father," one day became Abraham—"father of a multitude"—just because God said: *"No longer shall your name be called Abram, but your name shall be Abraham, for I have made you the father of a multitude of nations."* (Gen 17:5) How's that for direct? I like the "I have made you" part. As far as God was concerned, it had already happened. Every time Abraham used his new name, he was agreeing with God, although bystanders may have still snickered. Abraham got the last laugh, at age 100, when the promised son by Sarah came along and they named him "laughter" (Isaac). Isaac's son Jacob ("He cheats") was renamed Israel ("He strives with God"). Saul of Tarsus, the enemy of the Church, became Paul the apostle and the Church's first missionary.

A new life is what God offers to all. Sometimes a new name helps, too.

Just Write the Bible

I want you to know, brothers, that what has happened to me has really served to advance the gospel, so that it has become known throughout the whole imperial guard and to all the rest that my imprisonment is for Christ.
Philippians 1:12-13

I'm not really a Type A personality, but I'm definitely goal-oriented. There are fewer things more frustrating to me than spinning my wheels for a day or a week, and having little to show for my efforts except fatigue!

I'm trying to get inside the mind of the apostle Paul, a man so consumed with his mission that lesser souls must have found it nearly impossible to live with him, much less keep up with him. He is so driven, so passionate—he lets nothing stand in the way of accomplishing his task: to spread the Gospel of Jesus Christ throughout the whole world.

Once again, he's parked in prison, here for who knows how long—and maybe this is it. What's on Paul's mind? The Church. He lives for the Church, the same one he formerly tried to destroy, but which has become the focal point of all his energy and passion. He can easily imagine the wolves rending sheep bought with the blood of the Lamb—not animals, but people. He hears of the distress they're in. He can do nothing. Paul's mind races as he recalls all the many things he "should" be doing for God right now. He should be preaching to lost people, he should be rebuking troublemakers in the Church, he should be training new pastors, he should be checking up on persecuted believers in churches he started, he should be going to new places with the Gospel. A lesser man would pine and whine about his circumstances, especially when he doesn't feel well. Paul had probably forgotten what it *was* to feel well! He's a man of action, not complaining. He resorts to what for him has become a familiar plan: He writes. Since he can't be there in person to encourage the Philippians, he will write to them—even if it has to be dictated to a scribe sitting nearby—even if the letter may never get to its intended destination, he has to try.

He still wishes so very much that he could be *doing* something!... accomplishing things, important things that would make a lasting difference.. And all he can do is helplessly dictate a few pages to send off to those he desperately wants to encourage in person. He doesn't realize he just encouraged billions, including me. Paul didn't whine, but if he had, God might have gently chided His faithful servant, chafing to be free so he could "do" stuff: "Paul, you *are* doing stuff. Just write the Bible!"

Filtered Glory

"I do not receive glory from people. But I know that you do not have the love of God within you. I have come in my Father's name, and you do not receive me. If another comes in his own name, you will receive him. How can you believe, when you receive glory from one another and do not seek the glory that comes from the only God?" John 5:41-44

The reason Jesus could be free from the clutches of men was because He did not allow Himself to be captivated by their praise or approval, nor did He allow their disapproval to change His direction. By being independent of the approval of men, He was free to please one Person and one Person only: His Father.

I am not there, yet. What my wife says or thinks matters immensely, to me. Ditto for all other family members, and for a whole cadre of friends. I even let my enemies jerk me around by their little comments, usually supplied through numerous channels until they find their way to my ears and heart. Why? Who am I trying to please? Basically, everybody. (Sigh). It's no wonder that my life has rarely been marked by anything that riled many feathers; feather-ruffling has been one of the big no-no's of my existence since Day One.

Jesus didn't carry that burden. It wasn't because it wasn't available to Him; He stayed clear of that trap because He didn't accept the praise or disapproval of men as a valid indicator of how He was doing. He managed to listen for one voice. As nearly as I can tell, there is only One He didn't disappoint at some time in His earthly life: God the Father. Everyone else, even His mother and brothers, misunderstood Him or were offended by Him at some time or another. The hometown crowd in Nazareth was so impressed they were willing to push Him off a cliff! Mom and His brothers showed up at the back of a huge crowd, in order to take Him off somewhere, since He seemed to be off His rocker. Fortunately, they couldn't even get to the front of the crowd! It was a lonely existence, living without the praise of people, but Jesus lived in the consistent praise of His Father, the only One He always pleased.

I'm not there, yet. But that's the direction I need to head.

Second-Place Servants

While they were worshiping the Lord and fasting, the Holy Spirit said, "Set apart for me Barnabas and Saul for the work to which I have called them." Then after fasting and praying they laid their hands on them and sent them off. Acts 13:2-3

And after the meeting of the synagogue broke up, many Jews and devout converts to Judaism followed Paul and Barnabas, who, as they spoke with them, urged them to continue in the grace of God. Acts 13:43

What happened? How did "Barnabas and Saul" get to be "Paul and Barnabas"—the way it would stay through the rest of the Bible? It's part of the grace of God of which the two apostles were speaking on their missionary journey, how you can slide from first place "pretty big man on campus" to being a second place sidekick to someone you rescued, and not only live with it, but be comfortable in it. Not just anyone can withstand that kind of fall and not grow sullen, but God's grace worked in Joseph, nicknamed "Barnabas" (which means "son of encouragement"), and we don't even see a change in attitude. I think God was pretty proud of him, too.

The apostle Andrew experienced something similar when his brother Simon Peter got included in the "inner circle" and he didn't, even though Andrew is the one who brought Simon to Jesus in the first place. The other two fishermen, James and John, also made it into the top three, but not Andrew. What was his reaction? He kept bringing people to Jesus, just like before. Good job, Andrew.

Then there's John the Baptist. Talk about a career dive! Had they been plagued with such things as magazines in John's Palestine, his hairy face would have graced every cover. Along came Jesus, and John was a sudden has-been. His disciples (including Andrew) flocked to Jesus, and John's pointed messages earned him a prison berth, followed by an early grave. Prior to John's death, Jesus said there was no one on earth like him.

The grace of God is at work in the lives of those willing to drop from first to second place without complaint or bitterness, in order to please their Master. The blessing of God is upon those willing to accept a role which places them in the shadow of those they once directed. Being a second-place servant is not easy, especially when it's a step down. However, there's a God who fondly commends those willing to be second-place servants.

What If?

Then all the congregation raised a loud cry, and the people wept that night. And all the people of Israel grumbled against Moses and Aaron. The whole congregation said to them, "Would that we had died in the land of Egypt! Or would that we had died in this wilderness! Why is the LORD bringing us into this land, to fall by the sword? Our wives and our little ones will become a prey. Would it not be better for us to go back to Egypt? And they said to one another, "Let us choose a leader and go back to Egypt."
Numbers 14:1-4

What if?

What if, when the 12 spies came back from Canaan and gave their reports, instead of whining and crying, the Israelites had broken into a chorus of praise to God? What if they'd had a praise-fest instead of a whine-a-thon? They would have been in the Promised Land within a week!

Sigh.

The Israelites passed up the perfect chance to express their faith in God. After all, this same God had led them out of slavery in Egypt under the hand of the most powerful man on Earth. This same God had parted the waters of the Red Sea, then dumped them in on Israel's pursuing enemies. This was the God of the Ten Commandments, the cloud by day and pillar of fire by night, water from rocks, manna from heaven. This God could do anything! They had seen it with their own eyes. They had survived on nothing but His daily miraculous provision. This would have been such a good time to proclaim aloud their faith.

Instead, they expressed their doubts, fears and complaints, then cried about it. God, of course, was not at all pleased! The people were so close to the Land of Promise, but they blew their chance by crying in despair when they should have been rejoicing in faith.

Ironically, nothing had changed, in terms of circumstances. The people of Israel decided to be disheartened, but there wasn't one more giant than there had been the previous day, nor one more walled city. The only change had been in their attitude, and their attitude cost them the Promised Land.

What if every report we received we used as an excuse to praise our God and express our faith in Him? And the whining and complaining and moaning ceased among us! We'd be in the Promised Land within a week! Hmm.

We Belong To Him

She was deeply distressed and prayed to the LORD and wept bitterly. And she vowed a vow and said, 'O LORD of hosts, if you will indeed look on the affliction of your servant and remember me and not forget your servant, but will give to your servant a son, then I will give him to the LORD all the days of his life, and no razor shall touch his head."

1 Samuel 1:10-11

"And in due time Hannah conceived and bore a son, and she called his name Samuel, for she said, 'I have asked for him from the LORD.'"
1 Samuel 1:20

Hannah knew what answered prayer was all about!

Being a noble woman, she makes good on her promise. Hannah starts out by naming the child "Samuel—"heard of God", because she asked the Lord for him. After Samuel is weaned, he is brought to the house of the Lord and presented to Eli the priest. Surprise! I'm trying to see Eli's face... It's not every day that someone for whom you prayed drops off their little boy for you to raise!

If you're going to be a special servant of God, this is a pretty good start, I'd say! Miracle baby, direct answer to prayer, given to God to be raised in the tabernacle by the priest.... I don't think Samuel probably ever saw himself as anything *but* God's servant. His whole identity was wrapped up in that. Mine, too.

Samuel grew up believing that he belonged to God, and acting accordingly. Would that millions more could know that pleasure and that identity!

"Servants"
Or "Great Christian Leaders"?

...And when he was in the house, he asked them, "What were you discussing on the way?" But they kept silent, for on the way they had argued with one another about who was the greatest. And he sat down and called the twelve. And he said to them, "If anyone would be first, he must be last of all and servant of all." Mark 9:33-35

Simeon Peter, a servant and apostle of Jesus Christ,... 2 Peter 1:1

Things have certainly changed. The disciples used to have arguments over which of them was the greatest; now they want to be called "servant." No longer are they scrambling for position. Now, they're lunging for the title of "slave"! In Greek, the word *doulos* means either "slave" or "bondservant"; they didn't make much distinction between the two because there wasn't all that much difference between the two! After the resurrection, people in the Early Church wanted to be known as a *doulos*— a slave/bondservant of Jesus Christ. That's funny. Now, people want to be known as "a great Christian leader," which being interpreted, often means, "I'm an important person who tells a lot of other people what to do." Could it be that we're once again charging in the wrong direction?

A Destiny-Defining Dream

"And now, O LORD my God, you have made your servant king in place of David my father, although I am but a little child. I do not know how to go out or come in. And your servant is in the midst of your people whom you have chosen, a great people, too many to be numbered or counted for multitude. Give your servant therefore an understanding mind to govern your people, that I may discern between good and evil, for who is able to govern this your great people?" 1 Kings 3:7-9

Even though according to 1 Kings 3, it was a dream, what Solomon received formed his self-identity for the rest of his life. (I can relate to that—my self-identity as God's servant came from my mom's dream)!

Solomon referred to himself as "your servant" when addressing God, just like his father, David, had.

He also, in his own mind, is incapable of being king without God's help. *"I am but a little child. I do not know how to go out or come in."* (1 Ki 3:7b)

It pleased God that instead of some form of success, Solomon asked for discernment and an understanding mind. God granted him "all of the above"! Solomon gets riches, honor, (provisional) long life, plus that for which he had asked: *"Behold, I now do according to your word. Behold, I give you a wise and discerning mind, so that none like you has been before you and none like you shall arise after you."* (1 Ki 3:12)

"And Solomon awoke, and behold, it was a dream..." (1 Kings 3:15)

It was a dream, but it was a dream which defined Solomon's destiny. When God speaks into our lives, regardless of how He does it, we know who we are.

Servant Mentality

"God, having raised up his servant, sent him to you first, to bless you by turning every one of you from your wickedness." Acts 3:26

The Early Christians had a servant mentality. They referred to themselves as servants, they referred to their ancestors as servants, they repeatedly referred to Jesus as a servant. This was definitely not a term of derision, for them; it was a word signifying high honor and purpose, used lovingly.

In the prayer of the believers in Acts 4, they use it four times:

"Our father David, your servant" (v. 25)

"Your holy servant Jesus, whom you anointed" (v. 27)

"Grant to your servants to continue to speak your word with all boldness" (v. 29)

"Your holy servant Jesus" (v. 30)

There is a difference in the Greek words used, though. When referring to themselves, they use the word "doulois", which means "bondservants." When referring to their ancestor, David, and to Christ, the word used is, "paidos," of which the first meaning is "male child" and the second meaning is "servant." "Servant" is such an exalted concept for them, that they don't mind applying it to the King of Kings and Lord of Lords! "Your holy servant Jesus."

Which is He—Son or Servant? To them, He is both, with no need to distance the two identities from one another. He is no less a servant for being a son; He is no less a son for being a servant. He is both, and He is absolutely splendid!

It was Christ's pattern they were trying to follow, as they asked God for the courage and boldness needed to serve Him faithfully, in a time of persecution. Rather than whining at God, they praised Him. They asked for boldness, rather than deliverance. God was pleased with His servants, and answered their prayers in a mighty fashion.

The servant has a mentality that doesn't chafe at being a servant. Instead, he sees it as a high privilege, and even a term worthy of his ultimate hero, Jesus Christ.

Servant–
Our Preferred Identity

"James, a servant of God and of the Lord Jesus Christ"... James 1:1

Remember Jesus' unbelieving brothers? It wasn't until after the resurrection that they finally swung over to His side. Now that they were believers, and even in leadership, it's hard to imagine skipping over the chance to make reference to the fact that they were Jesus' siblings, especially in correspondence as important as this.

James, who used to completely deny the authenticity of his brother's claim to messiah-ship, now identifies his own station in life as "a servant" of said brother, whom he also refers to as "Lord" and "Christ"! Things certainly changed, from years ago!

"Jude, a servant of Jesus Christ and brother of James"... Jude :1

Here's another brother of Jesus who doesn't even grab that name for himself, but instead calls himself a "servant" of Jesus Christ, and a "brother of James"!

These men had grown up with Jesus, as His brothers. Talk about some credentials to flash! Why wouldn't you use them? Because serving out of love is a different, and better relationship than happening to share the same mother. Blessed as it was to be physically related to Him, they had come to realize that it was far better to be a servant of the Lord Jesus Christ than it was even to be His brother!

They were no longer unbelieving brothers. Their brother was the Son of God, and they knew it. Their service was not out of family obligation or a desire to ride their brother's coattails. Their service was out of love—the same as ours.

Can we believe that "servant of Jesus Christ" is such a good identity that it would be preferred even over "brother of Jesus Christ," by those who could have laid claim to the title?

"Servant of Jesus Christ"—now there's a good term, and a good identity!

Humility Marks a True Servant

And they came to John and said to him, "Rabbi, he who was with you across the Jordan, to whom you bore witness—look, he is baptizing, and all are going to him." John answered, "A person cannot receive even one thing unless it is given him from heaven. You yourselves bear me witness, that I said, 'I am not the Christ, but I have been sent before him.' The one who has the bride is the bridegroom. The friend of the bridegroom, who stands and hears him, rejoices greatly at the bridegroom's voice. Therefore this joy of mine is now complete. He must increase, but I must decrease."
John 3:26-30

Humility marks a true servant.

His Master is proud of him, but he is not proud of himself—he's proud of his Master.

He isn't seeking the approval of others—just the approval of his Master. What's the difference? The Pharisees and John the Baptist. Think of the difference between the two. The Pharisees were very proud of their own righteousness, and sought one another's approval, along with the approval of the crowds. They were proud of themselves, but despised Jesus.

Now think of John the Baptist. The pride just isn't there. Instead, here is a servant who so loves Jesus that he encourages his own disciples to transfer their allegiance to Him, and rejoices that his own ministry is decreasing, while that of Jesus is increasing! He's proud of his Master, not himself. And one of the most popular figures of the day won't accept the praise of men, but only that of his Master.

Servanthood is much different from apprenticeship. Apprentices say, "Get me started, teach me what I need to know, and someday, I will be the master!" Servanthood says, "My plan is to serve you, not to take over."

Anybody can "increase" for Jesus; it takes a true servant to be willing to decrease for Him.

The Servant King

Then King David went in and sat before the LORD and said, "Who am I, O Lord God, and what is my house, that you have brought me thus far?"...

And now, O Lord God, you are God, and your words are true, and you have promised this good thing to your servant. Now therefore may it please you to bless the house of your servant, so that it may continue forever before you. For you, O Lord God, have spoken, and with your blessing shall the house of your servant be blessed forever. 2 Samuel 7:18,28-29

David goes into the tent and sits before the LORD. David just talks to Him, thanks Him, worships Him. He refers to himself again and again as a "servant." Even though God has made him king, he's still first and foremost God's servant. That's why He *is* king!

There are several things about this prayer that must have been pleasing to God. First of all, David believed Him. On nothing more than the word of Nathan the prophet, who says to him, "This is what God says concerning you," David is willing to believe the outrageous promises he's hearing from God, through Nathan. It always blesses God when His servants believe Him, and don't take a "wait and see" attitude!

Another thing that is pleasing to God is the humility shown by someone who, at that time, must have ranked among the most powerful men on earth. David isn't coming before the Lord as "King David;" he's coming as "your servant," in an attitude of complete submission. It's not the king of Israel who is sitting there, worshiping his God; it's the shepherd boy who knows that every single blessing he has ever received, or ever will receive, came from the hand of a loving Father.

A third thing that must have pleased that Father was the gratitude shown by His child. A fourth thing, the relationship. This is not some sort of business transaction taking place, where a head of state goes through some ritual, in order to satisfy protocol. This is a servant who wants to be in the presence of his Master and his Father. It's a beautiful thing. Passages like this are what it means when God calls someone "a man after my heart." May I be that kind of man.

January 23
Acting as a Servant, Rewarded as a Son

Then Jesus came from Galilee to the Jordan to John, to be baptized by him. John would have prevented him, saying, "I need to be baptized by you, and do you come to me?" But Jesus answered him, "Let it be so now, for thus it is fitting for us to fulfill all righteousness." Then he consented. And when Jesus was baptized, immediately he went up from the water, and behold, the heavens were opened to him, and he saw the Spirit of God descending like a dove and coming to rest on him; and behold, a voice from heaven said, "This is my beloved Son, with whom I am well pleased."
Matthew 3:13-17

The Son doesn't need to be baptized, but is, anyway, acting like a servant. He is rewarded as the Son. That was the pattern of Jesus' ministry—acting as a servant, rewarded as a Son.

Some of the best employees I've ever seen were the children of the owners. They have a certain grace about them. They pay attention to what they're doing, they pay attention to the customer, they obviously pay attention to the values of their parents, even when the parent is not present. It's a beautiful thing to see! Here is a child of the owner, acting like a servant.

At other times, I've witnessed a child of the owner, acting like a spoiled brat. They were behaving in a self-centered manner, oblivious to the needs of others or the responsibilities on their shoulders, mindful only of the fact that they, being the owner's child, could not be dismissed from this position, no matter how poorly they might be carrying out their assigned duties. It was always a sad spectacle, and one that often resulted in a vow to never return to that establishment! This is what it's like when a child of the owner focuses only on his privileges, to the disregard of his responsibilities.

Then there is the hired employee who has absolutely no interest in the good of the business. Woe to anyone desiring their help or attention if they happen to be on "break," which seems to be much of the time. Their concern is only for themselves, or possibly fellow employees. They seem to be bothered by the mere presence of customers, as if people who might put money into the business represent an imposition! This is the "servant" who sees himself as nothing more than a hired hand, and has no connection or feeling of personal responsibility to either the boss or the company.

It seems to me that God desires us to see ourselves as His dearly loved children, who act in the capacity of a trusted servant, rather than a spoiled heir. This seems to be a balancing act, but when it's done, it is indeed a beautiful thing to see!

The Son Who Is the Servant

And a voice came from heaven, "You are my beloved Son; with you I am well pleased."

The Spirit immediately drove him out into the wilderness. And he was in the wilderness forty days, being tempted by Satan. And he was with the wild animals, and the angels were ministering to him. Mark 1:11-13

So much for getting to bask in the glories of "Son-ship"! The moment Jesus is publicly identified as the Son of God, the attacks begin in a concentrated fashion. Unable to physically eliminate Jesus in His early years, Satan now tries the temptations of compromise, which, if effective, could rob Jesus of His authority by getting Him to misuse His power.

Mark doesn't mention the individual temptations in the wilderness, but they have to do with grabbing the rights of the Son, don't they? "You deserve to eat–even a servant does!" "If you're the Son of God, jump off the temple, and make the angels catch you. That will show people who you really are! Then they'll believe in you!" "If you worship me, I'll get out of your way and you can have what you want." Jesus rejects the temptations and continues His life of servanthood.

Aren't many of Satan's temptations to us along that same track? "You *deserve* this!" "Claim this verse, and make God prove Himself." "If you just acknowledge me and compromise a little, I'll give you the authority to accomplish all the great things you want to do. Think of all the good that you could do." "After all, you're a child of God—claim your rights!"

Our example was the bonafide Son of God—voice from heaven, dove and all—who lived not as the Son of God, able to turn stones to bread, but as the servant of all. Serving God is not about showing off our son-ship powers and privileges; it's following the example of the Son who is the servant.

You Are Greatly Loved

Now therefore, O our God, listen to the prayer of your servant and to his pleas for mercy, and for your own sake, O Lord, make your face to shine upon your sanctuary, which is desolate. Daniel 9:17

Part of being a servant of God is identifying yourself as such. This is not, "Hey, I'm Daniel, one of your best guys—better listen to me!" Instead, it's a sincere prayer of confession on behalf of his nation, followed by a submissive and respectful request to "listen to the prayer of your *servant.*" Daniel insists on thinking of himself as "your servant," even though in the previous chapter, he was addressed by the angel Gabriel as "son of man." Regardless of our honors, it's a good idea to continue to think of ourselves as "your servant."

Daniel has such a love for his people, that he is praying and fasting on their behalf, in sackcloth and ashes. His heartfelt confession, on behalf of the Israelites, bears not a trace of bitterness, only sadness. Daniel accepts total responsibility, on behalf of his nation, for all that has happened. He confesses their corporate sin, begs forgiveness for it, proclaims God's righteousness, and pleads for His mercy.

Daniel's prayer so touches the heart of God that, once again, He sends out the angel Gabriel, with a message for Daniel:

"He made me understand, speaking with me and saying, 'O Daniel, I have now come out to give you insight and understanding. At the beginning of your pleas for mercy a word went out, and I have come to tell it to you, for you are greatly loved. Therefore consider the word and understand the vision." Daniel 9:22-23

What must it be like to have one of the archangels hand you a note from God that says, "You are greatly loved. Here are the answers you wanted." So this is how God treats His "servants"! When you are God's servant, you're not some nameless slave; you are *greatly loved!* You are cherished as a member of the family. Why would anyone not want to serve God?!

January 26

More than Slaves

And behold, a hand touched me and set me trembling on my hands and knees. And he said to me, "O Daniel, man greatly loved, understand the words that I speak to you, and stand upright, for now I have been sent to you." And when he had spoken this word to me, I stood up trembling. Then he said to me, "Fear not, Daniel, for from the first day that you set your heart to understand and humbled yourself before your God, your words have been heard, and I have come because of your words. Daniel 10:10-12

What does God's servant do? In this particular instance, Daniel has been "mourning" for three weeks—self-denial and partial fasting, praying and studying. Daniel had chosen to humble himself before God in this way, apparently on his own volition. In the midst of this time of seeking God, Daniel once again receives a special messenger, and an incredible message from God, that pinpoints events of the future as if one were reading a newspaper account. Prior to the vision, though, is the affirmation: *"O Daniel, man greatly loved."* For me, God could have just stopped there! If God is calling my name, telling me that He "greatly loves me," that's enough for me—I don't even need the vision!

Not once, but three times, Daniel is addressed as a "man greatly loved" (Da 9:23, 10:11, 10:19). This is not some worthless slave, to God! God *loves* him—"greatly"—and tells him so!

It's not the only time. A young man being baptized in the Jordan River hears a voice from heaven, saying, *"You are my beloved Son; with you I am well pleased."* (Mark 1:11b)

To get a direct message from God, expressing His love for you—what could be better?! That affirmation, that pronouncement of blessing, is available for every one of God's servants. We're a lot more than slaves! We are "greatly loved."

Servanthood with Purpose

While walking by the Sea of Galilee, he saw two brothers, Simon (who is called Peter) and Andrew his brother, casting a net into the sea, for they were fishermen. And he said to them, "Follow me, and I will make you fishers of men." Immediately they left their nets and followed him.
Matthew 4:18-20

The people Jesus calls, He calls to a life of servanthood, but with purpose: It's not, "Follow me and you get to be my slaves;" it's "Follow me, and I will make you fishers of men." There's a challenge and a purpose, here. It's also crucial that this is seen not as a hobby or a part-time commitment; it's 100%, and it's forever.

There is an aspect of partnership in the call of Jesus, which is very, very different from the call one might expect to come from one with this kind of power. Contrast the call of Jesus with the call of a dictator, who demands unflinching allegiance and total submission, in exchange for nothing more than the right to live! The subjects of dictators and evil rulers are treated with contempt. They are nothing more than mere pawns, tools to be used in maintaining preeminent authority. Particularly faithful and loyal subjects may one day be rewarded with a greater degree of power, but every privilege is tentative; both authority and life itself might be eliminated at any moment, according to the whims of the ruler.

Jesus calls His followers not just to serve Him, but to serve alongside Him, even as He serves others. There is a noble purpose in the commission of Jesus. To follow Him is to know—absolutely know—that your life counts for something. Whatever He asks us to do, we can know that we matter. We are not just subjects in a kingdom; we are co-laborers in the most magnificent, exciting cause in the universe, serving alongside the Lord of Glory.

The Frustration of Manna

And he humbled you and let you hunger and fed you with manna, which you did not know, nor did your fathers know, that he might make you know that man does not live by bread alone, but man lives by every word that comes from the mouth of the LORD. Deuteronomy 8:3

I'm beginning to relate to the Israelites. Two years into a new calling definitely from God, but also definitely weird to practically everyone else, I get the shakes toward the end of the month, contemplating a growing pile of bills and a dwindling checkbook. In this new deal, I don't have a job—just a calling, and a non-profit ministry solely dependent on what God prompts folks to send me in the mail. It's a scary business.

There's a yearning to be "normal," and in control—especially the latter. The manna system was neither, which is what made it so frustrating for the Israelites. Think of it. Your only source of food is what appears on the ground in the morning, gone by noon. You can gather it, but not produce it. It won't even keep overnight, except when God says it will, another glaring example that this is under His control, not yours.

What's this do to a guy's ego? How does one show off entrepreneurial skills with manna? How do you get rich off manna? How do you show you are a hardworking, "Type A" guy with manna? The answer to these and other pertinent manly questions is always, "You don't." Manna is the place where man is humbled before God, totally dependent on His routine miracle grace.

How frustrating is it when you can't work your way to wealth, when there's no way to get ahead, when you're utterly dependent upon God's grace to provide one day's worth of food for your family, and since there's no way to get a week's worth at once, you'll have to depend on God tomorrow, too? It's the frustration of being helpless before the Almighty, unable to do anything but yield to His system, His timing. The choices are gratitude or complaining, and that's it. No wonder they suffered from manna depression.

And so, three days from month's end, irritable because I don't yet have tomorrow's provisions and helpless to do much about it, I have two choices: Complain, or be thankful for the privilege of depending on the provision of a God who is always faithful and gracious, who humbles us and allows us to be helpless and needy, but only so we can learn how good He really is.

Sons Who Live Like Hirelings

But he was angry and refused to go in. His father came out and entreated him, but he answered his father, 'Look, these many years I have served you, and I never disobeyed your command, yet you never gave me a young goat, that I might celebrate with my friends. But when this son of yours came, who has devoured your property with prostitutes, you killed the fattened calf for him! And he said to him, 'Son, you are always with me, and all that is mine is yours. It was fitting to celebrate and be glad, for this your brother was dead, and is alive; he was lost, and is found.'"
Luke 15:28-32

Jesus is concerned for the lost. He wants His servants to be concerned for the lost, too! I think He'd like for us to help Him look! Instead, our all-too-common habit is to sit around griping, like the older brother—not enjoying what we have, and resenting the fact that some prodigal brother of ours is getting better than he deserves!

The older brother was a son, but lived like a hireling.

"And he said to him, 'Son, you are always with me, and all that is mine is yours."

This is one of the principles of servant son-ship. Everything we have is required of us, but in this relationship with the Father, "all that is mine is yours," so we have total access to all of God's resources! I'm sure that I'm not living in that realm, mentally. I need to be moving in that direction; otherwise, I'm like the older brother, who lives as if he's broke, but resents his Father's generosity toward others.

Also in this parable of the prodigal son is the theme that God truly wants us to live as His children, rather than as a bunch of slaves/servants, who have no rights and no joy in the relationship. We are more than just servants, yet our goal needs to be to serve, and not just lie around like a bunch of lazy, rich kids.

A Letter of Grace

So if you consider me your partner, receive him as you would receive me. If he has wronged you at all, or owes you anything, charge that to my account. Philemon :17-18

Onesimus, fugitive slave, carries in his trembling hands the letter from Paul which he trusts will spare his life. The slave has been sent back to his owner by Paul. Onesimus, once a runaway slave, had become a believer in Christ. He was being sent back to make it right with his master, Philemon. The only thing standing between Onesimus and punishment, or possibly death, is a brief epistle penned by an old man in prison. But it's not just any old man; Philemon owes his very life to Paul. Onesimus is not able to come before his master on his own authority; Paul loans him his. This letter of grace is the difference between slavery and freedom for Onesimus, life and death.

We are that runaway slave. Each of us who knows Jesus Christ as Savior bears in our hands a letter of grace and pardon, from Him. We only need present it to the Father, and on Jesus' account, our sins and debts are forgiven, and we are accepted into the family, not as slaves, but as sons! Slaves are basically property, which can be sold or traded. But Jesus has promoted us from bondservants to brothers! Nevertheless, we still fulfill a servant's role—even the Son did that! Consequently, wherever we are placed, that's where we serve. Whomever God sends us to, that's whom we serve, because we're doing this at His orders, not our own. That means that I'm not to go looking for where I'd *like* to serve, and for whom it's *fun* to be around; I go where God sent me, and do what God wants me to do!

I am a bondservant of Christ, because He bought me with His own blood. His will for me is that I would be an adopted brother of His, and a co-heir in His kingdom. Although Christ has made me a brother, I am still a servant, because Christ has called me to serve as He did, and love as He did. It's really pretty simple where I fit in!

Jesus' Real Family

And his mother and his brothers came, and standing outside they sent to him and called him. And a crowd was sitting around him, and they said to him, "Your mother and your brothers are outside, seeking you." And he answered them, "Who are my mother and my brothers?" And looking about at those who sat around him, he said, "Here are my mother and my brothers! Whoever does the will of God, he is my brother and sister and mother." Mark 3:31-35

When Jesus' family members come to take charge of Him, they can't even get to Him, due to the size of the crowd. At this time, His physical brothers don't even believe in Him as the Son of God, so they're attempting to act in the capacity of responsible brothers, coming to take their neurotic sibling home.

Jesus makes a statement which shows how it is that any of us can grow in a true relationship with Him: *"Whoever does the will of God, he is my brother and sister and mother."* Blood ties are irrelevant in this case, particularly when it comes to claiming any authority over Jesus; what counts is obedience. Any of us is able to have a relationship with Jesus Christ that is closer than that of a mother, sister or brother—all we need to do is to follow the will of God, and that relationship is ours! Jesus *wants* us to be in this sort of relationship with Him!

February 1

The Temple Of God

Do you not know that you are God's temple and that God's Spirit dwells in you? If anyone destroys God's temple, God will destroy him. For God's temple is holy, and you are that temple.

Let no one deceive himself. If anyone among you thinks that he is wise in this age, let him become a fool that he may become wise. For the wisdom of this world is folly with God. For it is written, "He catches the wise in their craftiness," and again, "The Lord knows the thoughts of the wise, that they are futile." So let no one boast in men. For all things are yours, whether Paul or Apollos or Cephas or the world or life or death or the present or the future—all are yours, and you are Christ's, and Christ is God's. 1 Corinthians 3:16-23

I've read and heard this scripture since childhood, usually associating it with our responsibility to care for our own body, since it is "God's temple." While it is true that we should respect our body as the temple of God (rather than building on some "fat rooms" to it, etc!), I'm seeing the promise aspect of the passage. We don't just *have* a temple, which we are to care for; we get to *be* a temple—a holy place where God's Spirit dwells.

This also places a different slant on some other aspects of our humanity—worldly wisdom, for instance. It's nothing, to God! We could pile all of human intelligence together and not make it to the first rung of God's wisdom. Pretentiousness and pride in our own knowledge only keeps us dumb. Humility of the mind before the Creator of the universe opens up a holy place which He is willing to fill with His wisdom.

Then there's this aspect which eliminates the need for competition or rivalry: "All things are yours," he says, again and again. No need to boast about our association with spiritual great's—they belong to everyone. We are not in competition with fellow servants because *all* of us have *all* of Him—and along with Him, *all things!*

All things are ours: Paul is ours, Apollos, Cephas, are ours. The world is ours. Life is ours. Death is ours. The present is ours. The future is ours. It's all ours, and we are Christ's, and Christ is God's. Worldly wisdom? It's nothing compared to what God has for us. Competition? No need to prove anything—it's all ours, anyway. We are God's temple, with nothing to prove.

Go and Tell My Brothers

But the angel said to the women, "Do not be afraid, for I know that you seek Jesus who was crucified. He is not here, for he has risen, as he said. Come, see the place where he lay. Then go quickly and tell his disciples that he has risen from the dead, and behold, he is going before you to Galilee; there you will see him. See, I have told you." So they departed quickly from the tomb with fear and great joy, and ran to tell his disciples.
Matthew 28:5-8

It's always amused me how many Christians treat Easter much like Groundhog's Day—Once a year Jesus comes out of the grave, and "He is risen!"—the rest of the year He goes back in the tomb, I guess! Anyway, some Christians make a big deal out of Easter, but act as if Jesus were dead, the rest of the year! The Resurrection isn't Groundhog's Day, it's forever!

I love the accounts of God's resurrection power! The angels, the Risen Lord, the earthquake and the resurrection of the saints... I love it! What a God!

And behold, Jesus met them and said, "Greetings!" And they came up and took hold of his feet and worshiped him. Then Jesus said to them, "Do not be afraid; go and tell my brothers to go to Galilee, and there they will see me." (Matt 28:9-10)

Go and tell my *whom*? The angel calls them "his disciples;" Jesus calls them "my *brothers*." The men who ran off into the night, three days ago?! That would be them. "My brothers." God's servants aren't a bunch of peons who have no say in anything. They aren't worker bees who are expendable nothing's when it comes to His Kingdom. Jesus' disciples are, to Him, His *brothers*. Totally amazing!

Thou My Great Father, I Thy True Son

I mean that the heir, as long as he is a child, is no different from a slave, though he is the owner of everything, but he is under guardians and managers until the date set by his father. In the same way we also, when we were children, were enslaved to the elemental spirits of the world. But when the fullness of time had come, God sent forth his Son, born of woman, born under the law, to redeem those who were under the law, so that we might receive adoption as sons. And because you are sons, God has sent the Spirit of his Son into your hearts, crying, 'Abba! Father!' So you are no longer a slave, but a son, and if a son, then an heir through God.
Galatians 4:1-7

God didn't want us to miss it, so here it is, again—the promise of son-ship. And because of the nature of adoption, we are "all the way in"! We're not foster-children, in the keeping of the Lord until we're grown up; we're not orphans for which He is caring; we're true sons, like it says in the great, ancient hymn, "Be Thou My Vision": "Thou my great Father, I Thy true son, Thou in me dwelling and I with Thee one."

We are true heirs. Money is no longer a problem. Neither is lack of anything else! Why? We are sons! This is not just the Creator of the universe we're addressing, this is "Abba"—Daddy!

To live like a son of God who is serving his Father—I think that's where all of this is going. Like Jesus, we are to be a son who serves, because there is no one we would rather please than our loving Father.

Born into God's Family

But to all who did receive him, who believed in his name, he gave the right to become children of God who were born, not of blood nor of the will of the flesh nor of the will of man, but of God. John 1:12-13

I think it's important to realize how we get into God's family. We don't work our way in. We don't just become smart enough that we get in. It's not a matter of trying hard enough, or persevering in our efforts, and then we make it. No, this is how we get in to God's family: We're *born* into God's family! Luck of the draw? No, it's *whoever receives Him, whoever believes in His name.* That's all it takes, and you're in, forever! What a deal!

Why is it, then, that we linger on the fringe of the family, sometimes resenting those who seem to be closer to the Father, envying the gifts and talents of others? Why do we persist in acting like people with something to prove? As if, in our pursuit of worthy service to God, we would finally achieve enough significance through our contributions to His Kingdom that we would at last deserve the recognition befitting a true family member! We're already in! We've been invited in, we've been adopted. We're not foster children, and we're not boarders, working to earn our keep. We are *family members*, the same as anyone else born into a family. We've been *born of God*—that makes us *God's children.*

We might be lazy children, or we might be obedient, industrious children, but our performance isn't what determines our family status. How did we become members of God's family? We were *born* of God. We're as "in" as we're ever going to be! We might as well live like it. Rather than working to try to deserve this position (which we already possess and which is impossible to earn, anyway), how about if we work because it pleases our Father? Interestingly enough, our greatest sense of purpose and fulfillment comes when we do the things we know will please Him, for simply that reason: To please Him.

Imitators of God

Therefore be imitators of God, as beloved children. Ephesians 5:1

It's a little weird in our house. Our seven-year-old is singing the Cocoa Wheats commercial by heart, although he has never seen the commercial, nor a Cocoa Wheat. Where did he get it? Dad. That's the same place he got many of the other silly songs, stories and jokes that he loves so much. Someone told us the other day that he has my mannerisms. They've always told us that he looks like me. We receive both as great compliments, since he's adopted! It's not uncommon at all to hear him recite something verbatim that I might have just said in passing. What's the line? "Imitation is the sincerest form of flattery"? He even imitates the not-so-good stuff, which can be embarrassing, since I know where he got that, too. But what a wonderful thing it is to have a family, especially one where there are people who *want* to be like you!

And so it is with God. We are beloved children, and I don't know if there is anything which pleases that Father's heart more than when His children imitate Him. The world really, really needs to see people who are singing the songs they learned from the Father, quoting lines they heard from Him, picking up His habits and His heart. When the world sees us imitate God, how are they going to stay away from the Father any longer? They aren't. They will want what they see, because it's real, and it represents the most wonderful relationship possible—an intimate relationship with our Heavenly Father.

We're not just a bunch of servants, sitting around waiting for orders. We are God's children, who mimic Him just because we want to be like Him.

What trait of God would He have me to imitate?

Children of Light

...Walk as children of light... Ephesians 5:8

I'm glad that it says "children of light," instead of "servants of light." It just sounds so much better, so much more exciting and attractive. It's much more personal. That's not how *we* said it was supposed to be; that's how *God* said it's supposed to be! Children of light.

What is it to walk as "children of light"? Ephesians 5 gives a number of practical instructions regarding how to disassociate ourselves from the darkness, and to identify with the light: We are not only to abstain from sexual immorality, impurity and covetousness; we are not to even talk about it! Our conversation is to focus on thanksgiving, and on giving praise to God through music, rather than on coarse language or crude joking.

One of the best indicators of our heart's condition will always be in our speech. This is why the Bible says it is shameful even to speak of the various works of darkness. When we focus on the darkness, it is going to bring spiritual harm to us. We are to concentrate on the light.

"For the fruit of the light is found in all that is good and right and true." (Eph 5:9) This is where our focus should be, on what is clearly light, rather than what is questionable.

God wants us to be thinking of how we can please Him, and how we can represent Him. He has given us His name, He has made us His own—now He expects us to act like His children!

When a wise parent is nagged by their children regarding one of those many issues where "everybody else is doing it," the proper response is usually, "You're not 'everybody else.' They're not part of our family, but you are, and this is how we act." I think God is telling His children, "You're not part of the darkness. You are my child, which makes you a child of light. Act like it."

Bona fide Family Members

For all who are led by the Spirit of God are sons of God. For you did not receive the spirit of slavery to fall back into fear, but you have received the Spirit of adoption as sons, by whom we cry, 'Abba! Father!' The Spirit himself bears witness with our spirit that we are children of God, and if children, then heirs—heirs of God and fellow heirs with Christ, provided we suffer with him in order that we may also be glorified with him.

For I consider that the sufferings of this present time are not worth comparing with the glory that is to be revealed to us. For the creation waits with eager longing for the revealing of the sons of God.

For the creation was subjected to futility; not willingly, but because of him who subjected it, in hope that the creation itself will be set free from its bondage to decay and obtain the freedom of the glory of the children of God. For we know that the whole creation has been groaning together in the pains of childbirth until now. And not only the creation, but we ourselves, who have the firstfruits of the Spirit, groan inwardly as we wait eagerly for adoption as sons, the redemption of our bodies.
Romans 8:14-23

As an adoptive parent, I am no longer a stranger to the concepts and feelings which accompany adoption. One of the startling realizations is how an adopted child becomes your own, in every sense of the word. They are not "*like* your own child;" they *are* your own child! They are all the way in! This is one of many reasons why it's so exciting to become a part of God's family—we get to actually, truly become a part of it, rather than being a guest, or a servant on probation. We're all the way in!

Part of being a bonafide member in a family is that the sufferings and blessings and work are all shared. Real family members are included, when it comes to both pain and pleasure; meanwhile, guests are politely excluded from the hardships, expectations and the inheritance (*particularly* the inheritance). When we belong to a family, we get it all! When we belong to God's family, we are genuinely *included*. What a privilege!

Inescapable Love

Likewise the Spirit helps us in our weakness. For we do not know what to pray for as we ought, but the Spirit himself intercedes for us with groanings too deep for words. And he who searches hearts knows what is the mind of the Spirit, because the Spirit intercedes for the saints according to the will of God. And we know that for those who love God all things work together for good, for those who are called according to his purpose. For those whom he foreknew he also predestined to be conformed to the image of his Son, in order that he might be the firstborn among many brothers. And those whom he predestined he also called, and those whom he called he also justified, and those whom he justified he also glorified.

What then shall we say to these things? If God is for us, who can be against us? He who did not spare his own Son but gave him up for us all, how will he not also with him graciously give us all things? Who shall bring any charge against God's elect? It is God who justifies. Who is to condemn? Christ Jesus is the one who died—more than that, who was raised——who is at the right hand of God, who indeed is interceding for us. Who shall separate us from the love of Christ? Shall tribulation, or distress, or persecution, or famine, or nakedness, or danger, or sword? As it is written, 'For your sake we are being killed all the day long; we are regarded as sheep to be slaughtered.'

No, in all these things we are more than conquerors through him who loved us. For I am sure that neither death nor life, nor angels nor rulers, nor things present nor things to come, nor powers, nor height nor depth, nor anything else in all creation, will be able to separate us from the love of God in Christ Jesus our Lord. Romans 8:26-39

It's hard to add anything to Romans 8 without feeling that I'm wrecking it! Here are reminders of everything we need: protection, security, destiny, the reminder that there is nothing which can separate us from God's love; the reminder that everything works together for good for those who love Him; the picture of Jesus, *"firstborn among many <u>brothers</u>"* (another reminder of our standing with God), personally interceding for us in heaven's throne room. What else could we want?! Then there is the reminder that if we *did* need anything beyond what we already have, the God who gave His only Son for us would certainly not withhold it. We have it *all*! *Absolutely everything we need* is provided for us, through God's grace!

God's Fellow Worker

What then is Apollos? What is Paul? Servants through whom you believed, as the Lord assigned to each. I planted, Apollos watered, but God gave the growth. So neither he who plants nor he who waters is anything, but only God who gives the growth. He who plants and he who waters are one, and each will receive his wages according to his labor. For we are God's fellow workers. You are God's field, God's building.

According to the grace of God given to me, like a skilled master builder I laid a foundation, and someone else is building upon it. Let each one take care how he builds upon it. For no one can lay a foundation other than that which is laid, which is Jesus Christ. Now if anyone builds on the foundation with gold, silver, precious stones, wood, hay, straw—each one's work will become manifest, for the Day will disclose it, because it will be revealed by fire, and the fire will test what sort of work each one has done. If the work that anyone has built on the foundation survives, he will receive a reward. If anyone's work is burned up, he will suffer loss, though he himself will be saved, but only as through fire. 1 Corinthians 3:5-15

As a kid, one of my regularly assigned tasks on our farm was to scoop into an open trailer a load of ear corn, to provide feed for our cattle. It was a tedious, sometimes discouraging process, and I recall wasting a great deal of time examining my progress, to see if I could consider the job done, yet. On several occasions, I squandered even more time, spreading the corn around in the trailer in a vain attempt to make it look like more than was actually there. It neither fooled nor pleased my Dad, when he arrived on the scene! The last time I tried that stunt, he came and found me at the house, marched me out to the corn crib, and we proceeded together to fill that trailer to overflowing! Thanks, Dad. That was the day I learned to work.

This passage in Corinthians makes me think of that story. My Heavenly Father desires that I would learn to work, just as my earthly father did. I am God's "fellow worker," just as I was my father's fellow worker, side by side in the corn crib, scooping grain into a trailer. Trying to fluff my accomplishments is a waste of time! One glance from the Father reveals everything. Meanwhile, He's teaching me to work, much as my Dad did: "Match me. Do what I do." Whatever I do with the Father will last, and will need no embellishment to show its true worth.

Ambassadors for Christ

Therefore, if anyone is in Christ, he is a new creation. The old has passed away; behold, the new has come. All this is from God, who through Christ reconciled us to himself and gave us the ministry of reconciliation; that is, in Christ God was reconciling the world to himself, not counting their trespasses against them, and entrusting to us the message of reconciliation. Therefore, we are ambassadors for Christ, God making his appeal through us. We implore you on behalf of Christ, be reconciled to God. For our sake he made him to be sin who knew no sin, so that in him we might become the righteousness of God.

Working together with him, then, we appeal to you not to receive the grace of God in vain. 2 Corinthians 5:17-6:1

"Working together with him"—doing what? Our mission is one of reconciliation, imploring people to be reconciled to God, just as we have been. As a new creation, reconciled to God through the sacrifice of Jesus for our sins, we are commissioned as *"ambassadors for Christ."*

What does an ambassador do? He represents the good will of the one who sent him. He speaks not on his own, but with official authority representing a sovereign nation or leader. He is not responsible for formulating policies or taking positions; only communicating them. An ambassador's mission is to be the next best thing to having the president or leader there in person. Whatever he says or does is a reflection upon the one he represents.

So, too, with *"ambassadors for Christ."* We are commissioned as representatives of His favor toward those who have been distanced from Him. We are to love people as Christ loves them. We are to attempt to reconcile people to God by letting them know and see that God loves them, through our actions on His behalf. We are responsible to communicate the Gospel, without altering it to fit our personal whims. We are to so accurately reflect our Master that people are drawn toward the One who sent us. Christ's ambassadors should always make people think better of Christ.

Our Heritage Clearly Defined

So then, the law was our guardian until Christ came, in order that we might be justified by faith. But now that faith has come, we are no longer under a guardian, for in Christ Jesus you are all sons of God, through faith. For as many of you as were baptized into Christ have put on Christ. There is neither Jew nor Greek, there is neither slave nor free, there is neither male nor female, for you are all one in Christ Jesus. And if you are Christ's then you are Abraham's offspring, heirs according to promise.
Galatians 3:24-29

Once again, our heritage is clearly defined. We are sons and daughters of God, through faith. We are *"heirs according to promise."* We are *"one in Christ Jesus."* How did we get into this kind of standing and relationship? By faith, when we trusted in Christ. When we were baptized, we were *"baptized into Christ."* We became a part of Him. We became one with Him. *"For as many of you as were baptized into Christ have put on Christ."* In putting on Christ, we receive His heritage as our own, and become heirs along with Him, and sons and daughters of God along with Him.

Sons and daughters of God, heirs along with Jesus—this is so much different than being mere servants, hanging around the Kingdom! Yes, we are to be faithful servants, but we are servants who belong to the family of God. We are genuine children of God, adopted all the way into His family. No one has a better heritage than the person, Jew or Gentile, male or female, slave or free, who has been baptized into Christ. We have been grafted into the greatest family of all! In putting on Christ Jesus, not only does His righteousness become ours; so does His heritage.

Hard to accept? Yes. But that's what it says! *"For in Christ Jesus you are all sons of God, through faith."* We might as well enjoy it!

How Do I Get Into This Family?

And you were dead in the trespasses and sins in which you once walked, following the course of this world, following the prince of the power of the air, the spirit that is now at work in the sons of disobedience—among whom we all once lived in the passions of our flesh, carrying out the desires of the flesh and the mind, and were by nature children of wrath, like the rest of mankind. But God, being rich in mercy, because of the great love with which he loved us, even when we were dead in our trespasses, made us alive together with Christ—by grace you have been saved—and raised us up with him and seated us with him in the heavenly places in Christ Jesus, so that in the coming ages he might show the immeasurable riches of his grace in kindness toward us in Christ Jesus. For by grace you have been saved through faith. And this is not your own doing; it is the gift of God, not a result of works, so that no one may boast. For we are his workmanship, created in Christ Jesus for good works, which God prepared beforehand, that we should walk in them. Ephesians 2:1-10

How do I get into this family?

By grace. Period.

We don't get into God's family by our hard work, our dedication to the cause, our intelligence, our ability, our perseverance, our attractiveness; we get in by grace, just pure grace.

We're offered a seat in glory not because we earned it, but because God desired to give it to us! Our God is rich in mercy. He deigned to show that mercy to us through Christ Jesus, in kindness beyond measure. We are not "byproducts of conception," with value assigned to us according to the whims of society; we are God's workmanship, *"created in Christ Jesus for good works, which God prepared beforehand, that we should walk in them."*

"If I work hard enough, maybe I'll become valuable...." No. We already possess a value God has placed upon us which has nothing to do with our works, and which could never be attained through them, anyway. Our God and Creator invites us to take a seat in the family, where every member got in the same way we did—by grace. The works? That's not the entrance fee; that's part of the reward! Good works, individually prepared, perfectly suited to us, by a Father infinitely rich in grace. Yes!

February 13

Willing To Accept Reinstatement

And he arose and came to his father. But while he was still a long way off, his father saw him and felt compassion, and ran and embraced him and kissed him. And the son said to him, 'Father, I have sinned against heaven and before you. I am no longer worthy to be called your son.' But the father said to his servants, 'Bring quickly the best robe, and put it on him, and put a ring on his hand, and shoes on his feet. And bring the fattened calf and kill it, and let us eat and celebrate. For this my son was dead, and is alive again; he was lost, and is found.' And they began to celebrate. Luke 15:20-24

How much of my trouble is caused by refusing to accept son-ship? The prodigal son felt unworthy of being reinstated into the family, and came back with the intention of just trying to establish a working relationship with his father. The father insisted on reinstating him as a son—no probation period, no groveling—get the robe and the ring, prepare the feast!

What if the son had listened to his jeering older brother, and rejected his son-ship, refusing to live as a son of his father? He could have spent his days in misery, remembering his pitiful past, longing for the way it used to be, unable to enjoy any of the privileges of his restored heritage because of the undying guilt of his sin. And what good would it have done anyone?! That kind of attitude would have pleased only the enemy of his soul, who lured him away from home in the first place, and fed the judgmental carnality of his older brother, a problem in its own right.

What does God wish us to do? First of all, like the prodigal son, come to our senses and head home. But when we've come before our Father, He wants us to *accept* the forgiveness and the restored relationship He offers, and *live as sons!* Obviously, not perfect sons, but not groveling or morose ones, either.

How much of my trouble is caused by refusing to accept son-ship? How much envy, regret, worry and discouragement residing in my life is absolutely needless? The answer is: "All of it." I am a son of God. I can either accept that, or choose to live otherwise, but it's a fact.

Nothing Else Counts

If I speak in the tongues of men and of angels, but have not love, I am a noisy gong or a clanging cymbal. And if I have prophetic powers, and understand all mysteries and all knowledge, and if I have all faith, so as to remove mountains, but have not love, I am nothing. If I give away all I have, and if I deliver up my body to be burned, but have not love, I gain nothing.

Love is patient and kind; love does not envy or boast; it is not arrogant or rude. It does not insist on its own way; it is not irritable or resentful; it does not rejoice at wrongdoing, but rejoices with the truth. Love bears all things, believes all things, hopes all things, endures all things.

Love never ends. As for prophecies, they will pass away; as for tongues, they will cease; as for knowledge, it will pass away. For we know in part and we prophesy in part, but when the perfect comes, the partial will pass away. When I was a child, I spoke like a child, I thought like a child, I reasoned like a child. When I became a man, I gave up childish ways. For now we see in a mirror dimly, but then face to face. Now I know in part; then I shall know fully, even as I have been fully known.

So now faith, hope, and love abide, these three; but the greatest of these is love. 1 Corinthians 13

It's easy to forget that service without love is not really service. Without love, our service doesn't even count! Nor does our great knowledge, our faith or our sacrifice. The component of love is so crucial that its absence negates all our good deeds, and we gain nothing. The other stuff is all going to vanish: prophecies, tongues, knowledge; love will last.

What this is saying to me is that if love isn't at the forefront, nothing else counts—not my sacrifice, my learning, my hard work—if love isn't the motivating force, none of it counts for anything. It's also a reminder that when I have love, it doesn't stay as some sort of gushy emotion, but will be evidenced in these different ways. Love will produce sacrifice; love will spawn heroic deeds as well as thoughtful everyday service; it's love which causes me to stretch my faith to the breaking point out of compassion for others, when it would be easier to let go. It's love that causes me to remain in the relationship and seek patience rather than escape, and to desire to grow in patience, rather than being comfortable in my habitual irritability.

When love is at the center, all kinds of good things spring from it. If it's missing, nothing else counts.

A Son Who Serves—Joyfully!

Blessed be the God and Father of our Lord Jesus Christ, who has blessed us in Christ with every spiritual blessing in the heavenly places, even as he chose us in him before the foundation of the world, that we should be holy and blameless before him. In love he predestined us for adoption through Jesus Christ, according to the purpose of his will, to the praise of his glorious grace, with which he has blessed us in the Beloved. Ephesians 1:3-6

Son, servant or brother? It's clear. You don't adopt servants, you adopt sons and daughters. The inheritance doesn't go to servants, it goes to sons and daughters. God calls us His children; Jesus calls us His brothers (and sisters). We're in! We are *all the way in!* By virtue of the blood of Jesus, we belong to the family of God.

"For I consider that the sufferings of this present time are not worth comparing with the glory that is to be revealed to us. For the creation waits with eager longing for the revealing of the sons of God." (Ro 8:18-19)

And who would those sons be? I am one of them!

Who am I?

I'm a SON OF THE FATHER.

I'm a BROTHER OF JESUS.

Am I a SERVANT OF GOD? Yes, but I am serving, not to try to gain a place in the Kingdom, but because I love my Father, and I want to please Him. That is also why I serve others—He told me that the best way I can demonstrate my love for Him is by serving other people in His name. I'm "helping Dad." It's not because He really needs my help, or couldn't do these things without me; it's because He wants me to grow up and be just like Him.

That's why I am:

A SON WHO SERVES—JOYFULLY!

February 16

The First Job of a Servant—Pay Attention

Now the Lord said to Abram, "Go from your country and your kindred and your father's house to the land that I will show you. And I will make of you a great nation, and I will bless you and make your name great, so that you will be a blessing. I will bless those who bless you, and him who dishonors you I will curse, and in you all the families of the earth shall be blessed. Genesis 12:1-3

From this point on, whenever I talk about a "servant of God," what I'm really talking about is a "son (or daughter) of God," who is serving Him. Since "servant" is such a good title, one preferred by apostles and even Jesus' brothers, we'll continue to use it, in the satisfying knowledge that we are much more than slaves or hired help; we are bonafide members of God's family, who serve Him out of love.

Back to the principle question of this study: How do we best serve God? We'll spend the next several weeks focusing on three "jobs" of a servant, which come through in scripture, often.

Abram's call (which I believe was an extension of the call to Abram's father, Terah) mostly consisted of, "Are you willing to leave behind your old life and follow me?" He did. The rest is history. Whether it's Noah, Abram, or whomever, God first of all just looks for those who will listen to Him and who are willing to follow and obey.

Maybe the first job of a servant is to be paying attention.

There are few things more frustrating than a servant who is not paying attention, or one you have to go and find, before you can get them to do anything. Ask my Dad.

Other frustrations include having to repeat things because the servant wasn't paying attention the first time you told them, or worse yet, having them tell you they understand when they really still don't have a clue. And if they have their own agenda all planned out and pay no heed to yours, they may have pretty good ideas, but they shouldn't refer to themselves as "servants"—"entrepreneurs for God," maybe?

I think I'm close to the mark when I say that the first job of a servant is to pay attention.

The First Job of a Servant—Pay Attention

In Order To Help, You Must Be Available

"If anyone serves me, he must follow me; and where I am, there will my servant be also. If anyone serves me, the Father will honor him."
John 12:26

I remember "helping Dad," on the farm. Sometimes there wasn't that much a young kid could do, to help. But if I wasn't around, and he had to go look for me in order to get me to do some small thing, I wasn't helping him much! It was easier and faster for him to just do it, himself, than it was to hunt down his "helper." Being available was actually the most valuable part of my service. I wasn't very proficient at most things, yet, but if I was *there*, I could at least be of some assistance. In other words, I was better than no help at all. Usually.

Jesus always used the same phrase when calling disciples. He didn't give them a grandiose strategy for magnificent deeds to be done in His name—at least not at first. They didn't even get a specific assignment, to start out with. All they got was, "Follow me." Not even the destination was included in the admonition. "Follow you *where?*" He didn't tell them. He's still not telling. It's just "Follow me."

That's always the first order, for a would-be disciple.

"If anyone serves me, he must follow me; and where I am, there will my servant be also. If anyone serves me, the Father will honor him."

It's nice to know that it comes with a promise of honor and reward, but it comes back to this: Serving the Father starts with just following Him, hanging around, staying close, being available. The first job of a servant is to pay attention. You can't pay attention if you're not there. "Follow me."

The First Job of a Servant—Pay Attention

Abide In Me

"Abide in me, and I in you. As the branch cannot bear fruit by itself, unless it abides in the vine, neither can you, unless you abide in me. I am the vine; you are the branches. Whoever abides in me and I in him, he it is that bears much fruit, for apart from me you can do nothing. If anyone does not abide in me he is thrown away like a branch and withers; and the branches are gathered, thrown into the fire, and burned. If you abide in me, and my words abide in you, ask whatever you wish, and it will be done for you. By this my Father is glorified, that you bear much fruit and so prove to be my disciples." John 15:4-8

Regardless of how good the branch might look, apart from the vine it produces nothing. In order to be productive, we must abide in the Vine.

When I think of "abiding," I think of my old bird-dog, Brownie, who used to roam the fields with me in pursuit of game birds. The first few times out, I didn't get any pheasants, because I couldn't get close to any! Brownie, aspiring hunting dog that she was, could be seen off on the horizon, barking madly and flushing out whatever birds were in the country, then coming back to receive praise from her master for doing her job.

I had a hard time convincing Brownie that unless she would "abide" with me—stay close to me without running off on her own—neither one of us was going to get anything! No abide? No pheasants! When she finally got the idea, our hunting success improved dramatically! The key was "abiding."

That's the key when it comes to being a fruitful disciple, too. Jesus makes it clear: No abide? No fruit! *"Apart from me, you can do nothing."* Meanwhile, if we do abide, we can't help but be fruitful. The only thing that results in spiritual fruit is abiding in Christ.

Like a disconnected branch, an unplugged electrical tool, or a bird dog in the next county, so is the disciple who doesn't abide in the Master. There is no positive result unless there is a positive, continuing connection. Jesus calls it "abiding." Without it, we can forget about fruit. Or pheasants.

The First Job of a Servant—Pay Attention

You Never Know What He Might Tell You

For the Lord GOD does nothing without revealing his secret to his servants the prophets. Amos 3:7

Amos, reluctant prophet, is also apparently the first of the writing prophets. The message he is given to deliver is not only difficult, but comes during a time of prosperity, which must have made it even less palatable. Who wants to be a voice of doom during boom times?

But for Amos, like all true prophets, prophecy has little to do with choice. It's clear that he neither aspired to be a prophet in the first place, nor made up his own agenda. This was only about faithfully communicating God's word to people, regardless of its popularity. True prophets say what God tells them, without distorting the message in any way. That's why they are called "servants"—they do what their Master tells them to do, even when it's hard, which it usually is.

God counts the prophets as His servants because they're paying attention to Him and He can count on them to deliver His message. God has chosen His faithful prophets to be His "early warning system" for Earth's inhabitants. God doesn't have to tell anyone anything, but because of His mercy and love, He tells His secret to His servants the prophets. It's up to us to either receive their words as coming from God, or reject them, but we can't say we haven't been told! And, like Amos, when it's our turn to give others instructions or an admonition we received from God, we may be a reluctant prophet, but we need to be a faithful one.

February 20

The First Job of a Servant—Pay Attention
Speak, Lord, For Your Servant Hears

And the LORD called Samuel again the third time. And he arose and went to Eli and said, "Here I am, for you called me." Then Eli perceived that the LORD was calling the young man. Therefore Eli said to Samuel, "Go, lie down, and if he calls you, you shall say, 'Speak, LORD, for your servant hears.'" So Samuel went and lay down in his place.

And the LORD came and stood, calling as at other times, "Samuel! Samuel!" And Samuel said, "Speak, for your servant hears."
1 Samuel 3:8-10

Eli does at least know what to tell Samuel, when God calls him the third time: *"Go, lie down, and if he calls you, you shall say, 'Speak, LORD, for your servant hears."*

Such an appropriate response for a servant.

Sure enough, for the fourth time that night, the young man hears God calling his name. His response indicates he is paying attention. The message Samuel receives, though, is an unnerving one, especially for a first-timer! It's all about Eli's wicked sons and God's judgment on the house of Eli, *"because his sons were blaspheming God, and he did not restrain them."*

No wonder Samuel wanted to not tell Eli!

Though the first time was difficult, this is not the last time Samuel hears from God, but the first of many. He will soon become the established prophet of Israel, although in a junior capacity. Never again when he hears the voice of God will Samuel mistake it for another. He knows God's voice.

It starts with paying attention, and hearing from God. When you've heard from God, you're qualified! Even if you're just a kid.

The First Job of a Servant—Pay Attention

SADD Saul

He waited seven days, the time appointed by Samuel. But Samuel did not come to Gilgal, and the people were scattering from him. So Saul said, "Bring the burnt offering here to me, and the peace offerings." And he offered the burnt offering.. As soon as he had finished offering the burnt offering, behold, Samuel came. And Saul went out to meet him and to greet him. Samuel said, "What have you done?" And Saul said, "When I saw that the people were scattering from me, and that you did not come within the days appointed, and that the Philistines had mustered at Michmash, I said, 'Now the Philistines will come down against me at Gilgal, and I have not sought the favor of the LORD.' So I forced myself, and offered the burnt offering." And Samuel said to Saul, "You have done foolishly. You have not kept the command of the LORD your God, with which he commanded you. For then the LORD would have established your kingdom over Israel forever. But now your kingdom shall not continue. The LORD has sought out a man after his own heart, and the LORD has commanded him to be prince over his people, because you have not kept what the LORD commanded you." 1 Samuel 13:8-14

King Saul was ADD. At least when it came to staying focused on spiritual things or obeying God, Saul seemed to have a bad case of Attention Deficit Disorder. When you attach "spiritual" to the front of that acronym, you get SADD, which pretty well describes Israel's first king. What a waste! It isn't like Saul didn't have anything going for him! A head taller than everybody else, good-looking, off to a good start—he's the kind of king people would have chosen out of a monarch catalog. And now this.

This is what you get when you try to do it the world's way: A king who won't listen to anybody, who *still* can't win the battles! Saul does it all by the flesh. He even panics by the flesh! He's going to make this thing spiritual by offering the sacrifice, scoring God's blessing, and maybe that will help him, since most of his little army already left. All it does is get him into more trouble with God than he already is! God has already passed over Saul and gone on to someone "after his own heart." A servant who won't listen to anyone, not even his own master, is one worthless servant!

The First Job of a Servant—Pay Attention

Ask God, And Listen!

Now they told David, "Behold, the Philistines are fighting against Keilah and are robbing the threshing floors." Therefore David inquired of the LORD, "Shall I go and attack these Philistines?" And the LORD said to David, "Go and attack the Philistines and save Keilah." But David's men said to him, "Behold, we are afraid here in Judah; how much more then if we go to Keilah against the armies of the Philistines?" Then David inquired of the LORD again. And the LORD answered him, "Arise, go down to Keilah, for I will give the Philistines into your hand." And David and his men went to Keilah and fought with the Philistines and brought away their livestock and struck them with a great blow. So David saved the inhabitants of Keilah.

...Then said David, "O LORD, the God of Israel, your servant has surely heard that Saul seeks to come to Keilah, to destroy the city on my account. Will the men of Keilah surrender me into his hand? Will Saul come down, as your servant has heard? O LORD, the God of Israel, please tell your servant." And the LORD said, "He will come down." Then David said, "Will the men of Keilah surrender me and my men into the hand of Saul?" And the LORD said, "They will surrender you." Then David and his men, who were about six hundred, arose and departed from Keilah, and they went wherever they could go. When Saul was told that David had escaped from Keilah, he gave up the expedition. 1 Samuel 23:1-5,10-13

Because David is listening to God and obeying, he goes against an enemy army to rescue an Israelite city, defeats the Philistines, then escapes before they can betray him into Saul's hands. Every part of that scenario was difficult, fraught with danger and didn't make sense, but it all worked out perfectly because he was listening to God, and God was giving directions. Checking with God, heeding His direction even over the advice given by friends or associates, is the difference between being God's servant and being some free-lance maverick who is always getting himself into trouble!

Ask God, and listen! He is always willing to help and guide His servants, if we will only ask.

February 23

The First Job of a Servant—Pay Attention

When That Isn't God's Voice

Then Saul took three thousand chosen men out of all Israel and went to seek David and his men in front of the Wildgoats' Rocks. And he came to the sheepfolds by the way, where there was a cave, and Saul went in to relieve himself. Now David and his men were sitting in the innermost parts of the cave. And the men of David said to him, "Here is the day of which the LORD said to you, 'Behold, I will give your enemy into your hand, and you shall do to him as it shall seem good to you.'" Then David arose and stealthily cut off a corner of Saul's robe. And afterward David's heart struck him, because he had cut off a corner of Saul's robe. He said to his men, "The LORD forbid that I should do this thing to my lord, the LORD'S anointed, to put out my hand against him, seeing he is the LORD'S anointed." So David persuaded his men with these words and did not permit them to attack Saul. And Saul rose up and left the cave and went on his way. 1 Samuel 24:2-7

David's men tell him, "This is it–this is the big chance God has given you," and even make it sound spiritual. The servant is close enough to God that he doesn't fall for it when others—even his friends—put words in God's mouth. David's trust is in the Lord. By refusing to try to fulfill God's promise himself by ungodly means, David stays in the center of God's will and avoids the trap into which so many others have fallen, that of presumptuous sin which says, "This is God's will and I'm just helping Him." Good move, David! Talk about courage!

How do we know the difference between God's will and man's presumption? Stay close enough to God that even the message of a friend or brother doesn't get through the filter of what we know to be God's will. When we've heard from God, confirmation from others is nice, but not crucial. We have to be willing to sort through the advice of those who are theologically creative, who work hard at making their agenda God's. It pays to be able to recognize the difference, and the best way to recognize a falsehood or a distortion is to be extremely familiar with the truth.

Sometimes discernment is a gift, and sometimes it's simply a result of having spent so much time with God that we easily recognize when something attributed to Him doesn't fit with His character or His Word.

The First Job of a Servant—Pay Attention

How to Get More "Discernment"

He said to them, "But who do you say that I am?" Simon Peter replied, "You are the Christ, the Son of the living God." And Jesus answered him, "Blessed are you Simon Bar-Jonah! For flesh and blood has not revealed this to you, but my Father who is in heaven. And I tell you, you are Peter, and on this rock I will build my church, and the gates of hell shall not prevail against it. I will give you the keys of the kingdom of heaven, and whatever you bind on earth shall be bound in heaven, and whatever you loose on earth shall be loosed in heaven." Then he strictly charged the disciples to tell no one that he was the Christ.

From that time Jesus began to show his disciples that he must go to Jerusalem and suffer many things from the elders and chief priests and scribes, and be killed, and on the third day be raised. And Peter took him aside and began to rebuke him, saying, "Far be it from you, Lord! This shall never happen to you." But he turned and said to Peter, "Get behind me, Satan! You are a hindrance to me. For you are not setting your mind on the things of God, but on the things of man." Matthew 16:15-23

Poor Peter. First you're a divinely inspired "rock," next you're Satan! All he was trying to do was help. Peter was unaware of Satan's tactic of utilizing the mouths of people like our best friends to gain an audience for his message. It didn't work with Jesus, who discerned the genesis of that thought, even though Simon Peter thought it was original with him, and that he might even be due a little praise for his support. He must have been shocked to receive such a stern rebuke, just for saying he didn't want his Master to die!

Jesus was on the wavelength of the Father, rather than the world. What others considered well-wishing Jesus counted a threat, because the suggestion was to veer from His mission, and accept security at the cost of obedience.

Is much of "discernment" really just paying attention? When we walk close to God, we have a keener ability to recognize those suggestions that don't match God's character, and label them for what they are—Satan's lies.

February 25

The First Job of a Servant—Pay Attention

God's Obedience
Training Camp in the Desert

At the command of the LORD the people of Israel set out, and at the command of the LORD they camped. As long as the cloud rested over the tabernacle, they remained in camp. Even when the cloud continued over the tabernacle many days, the people of Israel kept the charge of the LORD and did not set out. Sometimes the cloud was a few days over the tabernacle, and according to the command of the LORD they remained in camp; then according to the command of the LORD they set out. And sometimes the cloud remained from evening until morning. And when the cloud lifted in the morning, they set out, or if it continued for a day and a night, when the cloud lifted they set out. Whether it was two days, or a month, or a longer time, that the cloud continued over the tabernacle, abiding there, the people of Israel remained in camp and did not set out, but when it lifted they set out. At the command of the LORD they camped, and at the command of the LORD they set out. They kept the charge of the LORD, at the command of the LORD by Moses. Numbers 9:18-23

What God did with the cloud was good practice for the Israelites. They got used to not being able to plan anything other than following God. "When are we leaving?" "We don't know. All we know is that we have to stay with God."

The Israelites *had* to pay attention to God, in the desert. They basically had no other choice. Consequently, an entire generation of Israelites grew up thinking it was natural to follow a cloud representing the invisible presence of God. This was an obedient generation, willing to do seemingly absurd things like march around an enemy city for seven days in silence, simply because these were God's instructions.

When we get to the point where it's natural for us to follow wherever our invisible God leads us, when we get to the point where we refuse to make plans without His direction, when we get to where we'll sit still for a year or two if need be, simply because God has not yet given the signal to march, we will have gotten to the point of usefulness which seems always to precipitate God's miraculous engagement and blessing. God is raising up people of obedience. May I be one of them. It starts with just paying attention to Him.

The Second Job of a Servant—
Believe the Master

After these things the word of the LORD came to Abram in a vision: "Fear not, Abram, I am your shield; your reward shall be very great." But Abram said, "O Lord God, what will you give me, for I continue childless, and the heir of my house is Eliezer of Damascus?" And Abram said, "Behold, you have given me no offspring, and a member of my household will be my heir." And behold, the word of the LORD came to him: "This man shall not be your heir; your very own son shall be your heir." And he brought him outside and said, "Look toward heaven, and number the stars, if you are able to number them." Then he said to him, "So shall your offspring be." And he believed the LORD, and he counted it to him as righteousness. Genesis 15:1-6

God wasn't asking Abram to do anything except believe the promise. He did, and that was good enough for God. *"And he counted it to him as righteousness."* Later on, at his wife's urging, Abram would try to fulfill the promise himself, resulting in the painful episode surrounding Hagar and Ishmael, but even then, Abram believed the promise God had given him; he was just trying to creatively help God accomplish it. Abram was not only paying attention to God; when God spoke, Abram believed Him.

I've had the personal experience of having God promise me a son, and believing Him. I still have the toy fire truck I bought for our son, a year and a half before he was born. I remember going home and telling my wife what the Lord had told me in the Prayer Room. "You're going to have a son. This year." It had taken me by surprise, but I believed it was true, because it came out of the blue, yet was from God. It *was* true (Although, like Abram, I had to wait longer than I thought)! Our son was a child of that promise. It was as perfect as an adoption could be. When it happened, I *knew* it was the fulfillment of God's promise to me.

What God wants of us is not our resources (as if He needs anything, or that we can really "help" Him); it's that we would *believe* Him and trust Him.

Righteousness begins with believing what God says. It's the second job of being a servant, right after "paying attention."

The Second Job of a Servant—Believe the Master

Pleading Incompetence Is an Insult to God

But Moses said to the LORD, "Oh, my Lord, I am not eloquent, either in the past or since you have spoken to your servant, but I am slow of speech and of tongue." Then the LORD said to him, "Who has made man's mouth? Who makes him mute, or deaf, or seeing, or blind? Is it not I, the LORD? Now therefore go, and I will be with your mouth and teach you what you shall speak." But he said, "Oh, my Lord, please send someone else." Then the anger of the LORD was kindled against Moses and he said, "Is there not Aaron, your brother, the Levite? I know that he can speak well. Behold, he is coming out to meet you, and when he sees you, he will be glad in his heart. You shall speak to him and put the words in his mouth, and I will be with your mouth and with his mouth and will teach you both what to do. He shall speak for you to the people, and he shall be your mouth, and you shall be as God to him. And take in your hand this staff, with which you shall do the signs." Exodus 4:10-17

The priesthood sort of started here, didn't it? Moses will "be as God" to Aaron; Aaron will take what Moses says, and tell it to the people.

God was not at all pleased with Moses' reluctance or his excuses! I guess God doesn't appreciate it when His creation tells Him they think He messed up! That might be a good thing to remember! When I tell God I "can't" do what He asks, I'm really telling Him that He made a mistake— that the God who can speak worlds into existence would be unable to accomplish His purposes were He to utilize me as His tool. The incompetence excuse reflects more on my faith in God than it does in my self-confidence.

Moses' classic argument, "But I'm not good at this!" is one I've tried myself, with similar result. When God decides to use someone, He's persistent! And He is pleased with faith on the part of His servants, and displeased when they question either His judgment or His ability. I need to remember this—especially the part about, "But I can't do this, because I'm not good at it..."

Who made my mouth? Who made my mind? Who gave me this memory? I'd better just go do what God said, instead of providing Him with excuses for my disobedience!

The Second Job of a Servant—Believe the Master

Five Stones—and God

And David said to Saul, "Let no man's heart fail because of him. Your servant will go and fight with this Philistine." And Saul said to David, 'You are not able to go against this Philistine to fight with him, for you are but a youth, and he has been a man of war from his youth." But David said to Saul, "Your servant used to keep sheep for his father. And when there came a lion, or a bear, and took a lamb from the flock, I went after him and struck him and delivered it out of his mouth. And if he arose against me, I caught him by his beard and struck him, and killed him. Your servant has struck down both lions and bears, and this uncircumcised Philistine shall be like one of them, for he has defied the armies of the living God." And David said, "The LORD who delivered me from the paw of the lion and from the paw of the bear will deliver me from the hand of this Philistine." And Saul said to David, "Go, and the LORD be with you!" 1 Samuel 17:32-37

David didn't start out by volunteering to fight Goliath; he merely declared his faith that somebody *should* fight him, since Goliath had defied God. When Saul sent for him, David put his faith into practice and offered to take on the giant.

Saul, typically, declares his lack of faith, but David is able to change his mind with his "lion and bear" rationale. Saul's big contribution is his "permission" and his armor! David wisely foregoes the armor and resorts to what's familiar to him: A shepherd's sling, five smooth stones—and God.

And so it goes. Today the shepherd musician will become a warrior. He explains his theology to a giant who has not long to live: ... *"For the battle is the LORD'S, and he will give you into our hand."* (1 Sa 17:47)

One day the shepherd musician become warrior will become king will become ancestor of the Messiah. For all of David's life, God would keep expanding the horizons of a man who believed that *all* the battles were the LORD'S. Wouldn't He do the same for me, if I believed that all the battles were His?

February 29
The Second Job of a Servant—Believe the Master
He Hears Us

For everyone who has been born of God overcomes the world. And this is the victory that has overcome the world—our faith. Who is it that overcomes the world except the one who believes that Jesus is the Son of God?...

Whoever does not believe God has made him a liar, because he has not believed in the testimony that God has borne concerning his Son. And this is the testimony, that God gave us eternal life, and this life is in his Son. Whoever has the Son has life; whoever does not have the Son of God does not have life.

I write these things to you who believe in the name of the Son of God that you may know that you have eternal life. And this is the confidence that we have toward him, that if we ask anything according to his will he hears us. And if we know that he hears us in whatever we ask, we know that we have the requests that we have asked of him.   1 John 5:4-5,10-15

Not only is belief in Jesus as the Son of God the only way to eternal life; if we refuse to believe in Jesus despite the testimony God has given us concerning Him, we are making God out to be a liar!

Then there is the aspect of God hearing our prayers. Do we really believe that God has heard us when we pray? *Really?* Wouldn't our prayers be considerably different, if we absolutely knew that every word was being heard by the God who made the universe?

I know from experience that if I really, truly believed that I was speaking to someone of great importance, I wouldn't ramble! My prayers would be more like the centurion's, who sent someone to Jesus to tell Him, "Lord, my servant needs healing. You don't need to come, though. Besides that, I don't deserve to have you come under my roof. Please just say the word, and he'll be healed." He knew he would be heard, and he got right to the point. Not only do we need to believe that Jesus is the Son of God, we need to believe that our prayers are truly heard by God—every word— rather than incautiously blathering on as if no one was heeding us and our words didn't count. A prayer I need to pray more often is, "Lord, what do you want me to ask you?" A prayer that has God's will on both sides of it is a prayer sure to be answered!

Promises to Servants

Irreverent Babble

But avoid irreverent babble, for it will lead people into more and more ungodliness, and their talk will spread like gangrene. Among them are Hymenaeus and Philetus, who have swerved from the truth, saying that the resurrection has already happened. They are upsetting the faith of some. But God's firm foundation stands, bearing this seal: "The Lord knows those who are his," and, "Let everyone who names the name of the Lord depart from iniquity." 2 Timothy 2:16-19

The Lord knows those who are his. What a comforting scripture, in light of the many and silly controversies which swirl around us constantly! If we trace back to the root of some of these latest legends, we'll probably find something which could be described as *"irreverent babble."* Apparently, it's not new.

Irreverent babble occurs when we take our mind out of gear and let our mouth run free. We pretty much always wind up in a ditch, especially when we're pontificating on the things of God without employing a proper respect for God. That's where the "irreverence" comes in. The babble part is when we basically don't know what we're talking about, but we don't let that stop us. Either way, the end is that ungodliness and more irreverent babble both spread like a bad disease, and God is far from honored. Advice? *"Let everyone who names the name of the Lord depart from iniquity."* God's advice, not mine. It just makes sense to head *away* from iniquity instead of toward it, once our Savior has freed us from its grip.

It *doesn't* make sense to waste a lot of time trying to determine who is in and who is out of His kingdom, though. I love this little promise, which reminds us that it is not our assignment to try to figure out who is living in God's grace and who is not: *"The Lord knows those who are his."* This is a foundational truth! That tells me that God doesn't need me to let Him know my opinion regarding who should be allowed into heaven, and He doesn't need me "squealing" on a fellow servant, as if He were unaware of their sin—or mine. He already knows! And His Word reminds me to stay away from the conversations, attitudes, accusations and theories which would unnerve people whose faith might already be shaky. *"The Lord knows those who are his."* I'm really glad it's not my job to tell Him!

The Second Job of a Servant—Believe the Master

Faith Is Not Optional

Now faith is the assurance of things hoped for, the conviction of things not seen. For by it the people of old received their commendation. By faith we understand that the universe was created by the word of God, so that what is seen was not made out of things that are visible.

By faith Abel offered to God a more acceptable sacrifice than Caan, through which he was commended as righteous, God commending him by accepting his gifts. And through his faith, though he died, he still speaks. By faith Enoch was taken up so that he should not see death, and he was not found, because God had taken him. Now before he was taken he was commended as having pleased God. And without faith it is impossible to please him, for whoever would draw near to God must believe that he exists and that he rewards those who seek him. Hebrews 11:1-6

The thing that seems to get God's attention most quickly in one of His servants is faith. He wants His servants to believe Him! In this legendary chapter, God is just getting started in a roll call of faith heroes. He desires to be able to add our names to the growing list.

Faith isn't just commended; it is required, if we want to please God. A faithless servant is basically a worthless servant! Faith starts out as basic: I believe there is a God, and that He is good enough to reward those who believe in Him and seek Him. Faith acts in obedience upon the promise of God, without having to wait for the fulfillment before we make the first step.

If we desire to draw closer to God, here's the formula: *"Whoever would draw near to God must believe that he exists and that he rewards those who seek him."* The first part has never been a problem for me; sometimes the second part has. It's good to remember there's a reward in this! Faith is living with the sure knowledge that the reward is there, when we haven't actually seen it, yet. Faith is the way God wants His children to live.

The Second Job of a Servant—Believe the Master

Believing Enough to Obey

By faith Noah, being warned by God concerning events as yet unseen, in reverent fear constructed an ark for the saving of his household. By this he condemned the world and became an heir of the righteousness that comes by faith. Hebrews 11:7

God's servant Noah condemned the world by simply *believing God, and acting accordingly.* To God, that is righteousness! It's the righteousness that comes by faith. (Is there another kind)?

There are some similarities between Noah's mission and ours. Noah's first job was to pay attention to God, when literally no one else was; his second job was to believe the truth God was revealing to him. This belief was not some sort of intellectual assent, but a belief strong enough to motivate him to many years of action, based on absolutely nothing other than God's instruction to him.

We are called to pay attention to God, even though it seems few others are listening, or making much effort to please Him. Noah is the perfect example of the truism "If you were the only person on Earth, God would have done this for you." The extremes to which God will go to save those who look to Him are beyond comprehension!

We are called to believe God's Word, with or without support of natural evidence. Noah didn't have any, and didn't wait for it, prior to applying himself to the task at hand. A flood which would cover the earth, when mankind had never witnessed rain? Fortunately for Noah (and his descendants), he took God at His word. The return of Jesus Christ? Here again, just try to "prove" the validity of that promise, to skeptics. If we wait for proof, it will be too late. So, like Noah, we toil, year after year, in the sure hope that the God we serve does not lie, and one day the reality of that promise will be self-evident to all the world. When it comes-and it will-God will consider those righteous who believed His Word, and acted accordingly.

The Second Job of a Servant—Believe the Master

Out of Nothing

By faith Abraham obeyed when he was called to go out to a place that he was to receive as an inheritance. And he went out, not knowing where he was going. By faith he went to live in the land of promise, as in a foreign land, living in tents with Isaac and Jacob, heirs with him of the same promise. For he was looking forward to the city that has foundations, whose designer and builder is God. By faith Sarah herself received power to conceive, even when she was past the age, since she considered him faithful who had promised. Therefore from one man, and him as good as dead, were born descendants as many as the stars of heaven and as many as the innumerable grains of sand by the seashore. Hebrews 11:9-12

If one were to begin a new nation, wouldn't it be prudent to at least start with people able to bear children?! Not God. He creates a universe using precisely nothing except His Word, and when it comes to bringing into that world a special people who will belong to Him and be His own, God begins by searching out an elderly, *infertile* couple, then letting them wait even longer before giving them the promised son. When Isaac arrives, everyone knows this is a miracle baby.

The Jewish nation was a nation created by faith. It was fitting that this would be their foundation, since the rest of their story would also be one of faith. When the Messiah would come in fulfillment of the promises, how fitting that He would come through an absolutely miraculous and impossible virgin birth. Miracle babies were already part of their national heritage!

When it comes to God's promises, He's not looking for help in fulfilling them; He's looking for people who will take Him at His Word and believe Him. God delights in His children when they simply trust Him, especially when there is no way in the world that the promise could come true—without Him.

March 5

The Second Job of a Servant—Believe the Master

Citizen of Heaven, With an Earthly Address

These all died in faith, not having received the things promised, but having seen them and greeted them from afar, and having acknowledged that they were strangers and exiles on the earth. For people who speak thus make it clear that they are seeking a homeland. If they had been thinking of that land from which they had gone out, they would have had opportunity to return. But as it is, they desire a better country, that is, a heavenly one. Therefore God is not ashamed to be called their God, for he has prepared for them a city. Hebrews 11:13-16

Delayed gratification is not exactly our national motto, in America. If we can't have it now, then why couldn't we have had it, yesterday! This corporate cultural impatience definitely doesn't fall off when people go through church doors. Not only are we generally less than patient, but few of us seem to even seek after or desire what Galatians 5:21-22 lists as a fruit of the Spirit: Patience ("the fruit of the Spirit nobody wants")!

Why do so many who term themselves Christians have so little desire to be in heaven? I've heard it said that if we spent as much energy in praying sinners out of hell as we do in praying Christians out of heaven, we'd get somewhere! Our prayer times are often what one has termed "organ recitals"—"bless Aunt Maude's kidneys, and Artie's heart, and Fred's lungs, and...."

Like the patriarchs, we need to let go of this world, and get used to the idea that this is not to be our permanent address! This world is not our home! God's people continue in this present world, but our primary interest is to be in the one to come. It makes me think of how urgently Abraham told his servant, when looking for a wife for Isaac, "Don't take my son back there!" Abraham knew that if Isaac ever went back to the tribe, it would be that much harder for him to ever come back to the Promised Land. We're to live as "strangers and exiles on the earth." We shouldn't get too comfortable with "how it is"! We're looking forward to "how it's *going* to be"! Do we really want what God has for us, or would we prefer to hang on to this fallen world?

The Second Job of a Servant—Believe the Master

Trading Today for Tomorrow

By faith Moses, when he was born, was hidden for three months by his parents, because they saw that the child was beautiful, and they were not afraid of the king's edict. By faith Moses, when he was grown up, refused to be called the son of Pharaoh's daughter, choosing rather to be mistreated with the people of God than to enjoy the fleeting pleasures of sin. He considered the reproach of Christ greater wealth than the treasures of Egypt, not being afraid of the anger of the king, for he endured as seeing him who is invisible. By faith he kept the Passover and sprinkled the blood, so that the Destroyer of the firstborn might not touch them. Hebrews 11:23-28

Here's a servant who is ready to trade this world's stuff off for what he can gain from following God. The Passover was by faith; all they had to go on was God's instruction. There was no evidence any of this would take place, until after the fact. Once again, the servant of faith is the one who simply believes God, and acts accordingly.

Moses and the others were faith heroes who understood that in order to attain the promises of tomorrow, they would have to let go of today. The trade was made. There was a release of "what is," in order to gain "what will be." Meanwhile, they had no other proof of "what will be," other than God's word to them. They still made the trade. They exchanged safety and "reality" for a future based on promises, filled with temporary suffering.

Jesus asks each of us to do the same. Are we willing to release "what is," in order to pursue "what will be"? Are we willing to endure suffering for His name's sake? Are we immature enough to demand that in order to follow Christ, we must experience nothing but pleasure both now and in eternity, or will we follow in the footsteps of the people of faith who were willing to forfeit today in order to gain God's tomorrow?

The Second Job of a Servant—Believe the Master

Living on Promises

And what more shall I say? For time would fail me to tell of Gideon, Barak, Samson, Jephthah, of David and Samuel and the prophets—who through faith conquered kingdoms, enforced justice, obtained promises, stopped the mouths of lions, quenched the power of fire, escaped the edge of the sword, were made strong out of weakness, became mighty in war, put foreign armies to flight. Women received back their dead by resurrection. Some were tortured, refusing to accept release, so that they might rise again to a better life. Others suffered mocking and flogging, and even chains and imprisonment. They were stoned, they were sawn in two, they were killed with the sword. They went about in skins of sheep and goats, destitute, afflicted, mistreated—of whom the world was not worthy—wandering about in deserts and mountains, and dens and caves of the earth. And all these, though commended through their faith, did not receive what was promised, since God had provided something better for us, that apart from us they should not be made perfect. Hebrews 11:32-40

God is looking for people who are willing to live on promises. The heroes of Hebrews 11 were people who at best had a down payment on what God had promised. All some of them had to go on was God's word to them. They lived on promises. This is in direct contrast to the skeptic who has to have proof before step one is ever taken; God's servants follow His leading when they have absolutely nothing except a word from Him.

I've been a commercial fisherman, working night and day with a crew to catch and deliver hundreds of thousands of pounds of salmon to a buyer. A month into the season, with only a down payment and the verbal promise that we would eventually receive what was owed us for our catch, we continued to deliver to the buyer. We lived on promises. We were ultimately paid in full.

This is the way God wants His people to live—working for Him, in the firm assurance that one day we'll receive a reward. All we need is His promise, because His promise is the same thing as "reality." The featured saints in Hebrews 11 knew this, and lived accordingly. God is still looking for people willing to live on promises.

The Second Job of a Servant—Believe the Master

Angels Packing Lunches

Ahab told Jezebel all that Elijah had done, and how he had killed all the prophets with the sword. Then Jezebel sent a messenger to Elijah, saying, "So may the gods do to me and more also, if I do not make your life as the life of one of them by this time tomorrow." Then he was afraid, and he arose and ran for his life and came to Beersheba, which belongs to Judah, and left his servant there.

But he himself went a day's journey into the wilderness and came and sat down under a broom tree. And he asked that he might die, saying, "It is enough; now, O LORD, take away my life, for I am no better than my fathers." And he lay down and slept under a broom tree. And behold, an angel touched him and said to him, "Arise and eat." And he looked, and behold, there was at his head a cake baked on hot stones and a jar of water. And he ate and drank and lay down again. And the angel of the LORD came again a second time and touched him and said, "Arise and eat, for the journey is too great for you." And he arose and ate and drank, and went in the strength of that food forty days and nights to Horeb, the mount of God. 1 Kings 19:1-8

So, what kind of cake *was* that?! I guess it must have been angel food cake. (Smile).

It's good to know that even super-servants like Elijah are sometimes intimidated and they sometimes have very low days. It's even better to know that in times like this, rather than sending a rebuke, God sends an angel, and occasionally, even angel food cake!

God wants us to have faith, but in the times when our faith is running low, He sends whatever we need to continue. There are times when what God wants of His servant is nothing more than to eat, drink and sleep!

The Second Job of a Servant—Believe the Master

Because He Believed God

And when Elijah heard it, he wrapped his face in his cloak and went out and stood at the entrance of the cave. And behold, there came a voice to him and said, "What are you doing here, Elijah?" He said, "I have been very jealous for the LORD, the God of hosts. For the people of Israel have forsaken your covenant, thrown down your altars, and killed your prophets with the sword, and I, even I only, am left, and they seek my life, to take it away." And the LORD said to him, "Go, return on your way to the wilderness of Damascus. And when you arrive, you shall anoint Hazael to be king over Syria. And Jehu the son of Nimshi you shall anoint to be king over Israel, and Elisha the son of Shaphat of Abel-meholah you shall anoint to be prophet in your place. And the one who escapes from the sword of Hazael shall Jehu put to death, and the one who escapes from the sword of Jehu shall Elisha put to death. Yet I will leave seven thousand in Israel, all the knees that have not bowed to Baal, and every mouth that has not kissed him. I Kings 19:13-18

In just a few moments' time, Elijah receives not only comfort and encouragement from God, but also the blueprint for the next several decades of Israelite history! God reveals to Elijah the replacements for two kings, the identity of Elijah's own successor, and the assurance that the remnant situation is about 7,000 times better than he had thought.

Just as Elijah was able to continue for 40 days in the strength of the food God had provided, so he was able to continue for the rest of his earthly days in the encouragement and strength of a few sentences whispered to him by God on a mountaintop. This seems to have been the end of Elijah's fear and self-pity and discouragement! Why? *Because he believed God.* Had he not believed what God told him, Elijah would have received no comfort at all from the experience, since none of the things God told him could be proven at the time. It was his faith that what God was saying to him was true which energized him for the rest of his life. What comfort and encouragement is available to every one of us through nothing more than believing God's Word to us?

The Second Job of a Servant—Believe the Master

When the Bad Report Implies a Bad God

But Caleb quieted the people before Moses and said, "Let us go up at once and occupy it, for we are well able to overcome it." Then the men who had gone up with him said, "We are not able to go up against the people, for they are stronger than we are." So they brought to the people of Israel a bad report of the land that they had spied out, saying, "The land, through which we have gone to spy it out, is a land that devours its inhabitants, and all the people that we saw in it are of great height. And there we saw the Nephilim (the sons of Anak, who come from the Nephilim), and we seemed to ourselves like grasshoppers, and so we seemed to them."

Then all the congregation raised a loud cry, and the people wept that night. And all the people of Israel grumbled against Moses and Aaron. The whole congregation said to them, "Would that we had died in the land of Egypt! Or would that we had died in this wilderness! Why is the LORD bringing us into this land to fall by the sword? Our wives and our little ones will become a prey. Would it not be better for us to go back to Egypt? And they said to one another, "Let us choose a leader and go back to Egypt."
Numbers 13:30-33, 14:1-4

I can't help but sigh every time I read this sad passage. I identify with Caleb, who sees the promise but can't get the others to believe it, and I also identify with the ten spies who think they are just being "realistic," when in fact what they are doing is making the God of miracles appear to be a liar. That's what happens every time we trust our own perceptions (or statistics) more than we trust in His promises or His goodness. With the bad report, the 10 spies were in effect saying, "God lied to us. We can't do this, this was a bad plan from the beginning, we should find a leader we can trust and go back to Egypt." Slavery in Egypt was preferable to trying to follow this dismal plan of God's! In a round-about way, what they were saying was that God is bad, He can't be trusted.

God was not pleased. The ten "realistic" spies were all soon dead, and their dire predictions came true—on their loved ones who should have spent their lives in the Promised Land instead of wandering in the desert. Had they only trusted God enough to believe His promises, an entire generation could have enjoyed their fulfillment. Their loss should be our lesson.

The Second Job of a Servant—Believe the Master

Faith That Will Face the Wind

If any of you lacks wisdom, let him ask God, who gives generously to all without reproach, and it will be given him. But let him ask in faith, with no doubting, for the one who doubts is like a wave of the sea that is driven and tossed by the wind. For that person must not suppose that he will receive anything from the Lord; he is a double-minded man, unstable in all his ways. James 1:5-8

If any of you lacks wisdom, let him ask God, who gives generously to all without reproach, and it will be given him. (James 1:5)

I have very often used James 1:5 as a promise, and been rewarded with exactly the direction I needed. There have been times, however, when I neglected the subsequent verses. The result was confusion. It's what happens when, instead of seeking God's wisdom and direction, we seek His "advice." If we are not committed to following whatever path He shows us in answer to our prayers, we shouldn't expect clear direction, and shouldn't ask in the first place. God doesn't do "second opinions."

The point is, if we're going to believe God, we need to believe Him! It doesn't work to ask Him for information which we're only planning to throw in the hopper with everything else, so we can then arrive at our own "wise" decision. He has promised to give us wisdom if we ask for it, but we have to believe Him when He gives it to us. Seeking wisdom from God means that we accept whatever it is that He gives us, in faith that it's the right way to go. No second guessing! The comparison to wind and waves is the perfect picture of the double-minded individual whose path is directed by whoever last spoke to him.

God offers His children stability—the utter confidence that He is directing our path, just as He promised. We can afford to believe Him. If we have carefully prayed through a decision, asking for His wisdom and believing we have received it, we can apply it without hesitation and without doubt. That's a faith which will withstand the wind, and a servant who can be guided.

The Second Job of a Servant—Believe the Master

Gideon, God, and 300 Water-Lappers

And the LORD said to Gideon, "The people are still too many. Take them down to the water, and I will test them for you there, and anyone of whom I say to you, 'This one shall go with you,' shall go with you, and anyone of whom I say to you, 'This one shall not go with you,' shall not go." So he brought the people down to the water. And the LORD said to Gideon, "Every one who laps the water with his tongue, as a dog laps, you shall set by himself. Likewise, every one who kneels down to drink." And the number of those who lapped, putting their hands to their mouths, was 300 men, but all the rest of the people knelt down to drink water. And the LORD said to Gideon, "With the 300 men who lapped I will save you and give the Midianites into your hand, and let all the others go every man to his home." So the people took provisions in their hands, and their trumpets. And he sent all the rest of Israel every man to his tent, but retained the 300 men. And the camp of Midian was below him in the valley.
Judges 7: 4-8

I can only hear the military advisors and well-meaning supporters of Gideon, as a respectable army of 32,000 Israelites is pared down to 300 water-lappers: "God wouldn't want us to do something that doesn't even make sense!" "What would it hurt to at least keep them around, just in case?" "This can't be God—this is stupid!" "Why can't God's army be more like a business?"

Then there are the discarded volunteers, themselves: "Why did you send me home?" "You drink like a human."

None of this makes sense at all from the mortal perspective, and the courage Gideon demonstrates from start to finish is breathtaking. He is operating solely on the basis of God's instructions. Gideon so firmly believes it is God's messenger who has spoken to him that he is willing to disconnect from all rational plans to exclusively follow God's directions. There is no hedging of his bets, even though everything is at stake. This is a plan which is pure faith from start to finish. God makes sure it works perfectly.

Gideon's courage sprang from his intense belief that he was only following God's orders. God only needed one person with that combination of faith and obedience to change an entire nation.

The Second Job of a Servant—Believe the Master

One Man's Nightmare Is another Man's Faith

That same night the LORD said to him, "Arise, go down against the camp, for I have given it into your hand. But if you are afraid to go down, go down to the camp with Purah your servant. And you shall hear what they say, and afterward your hands shall be strengthened to go down against the camp." Then he went down with Purah his servant to the outposts of the armed men who were in the camp... When Gideon came, behold, a man was telling a dream to his comrade. And he said, "Behold, I dreamed a dream, and behold, a cake of barley bread tumbled into the camp of Midian and came to the tent and struck it so that it fell and turned it upside down, so that the tent lay flat." And his comrade answered, "This is no other than the sword of Gideon the son of Joash, a man of Israel; God has given into his hand Midian and all the camp."

As soon as Gideon heard the telling of the dream and its interpretation, he worshiped. And he returned to the camp of Israel and said, "Arise, for the LORD has given the host of Midian into your hand."

Judges 7:9-11,13-15

The famous fleece test which Gideon originated and God answered had given Gideon sufficient faith to follow God's instructions precisely; God now graciously offers Gideon even more assurance that His plan will work. It's interesting that in this case, God doesn't just command Gideon to "be not afraid," but instead invites him to go down into the camp "if you are afraid," knowing that what Gideon hears will encourage him. What a compassionate God.

I like the way God speaks in the past tense about future events: *"Arise, go down against the camp, for I have given it into your hand."* I like the way Gideon echoes Him, in faith, when addressing his men: *"Arise, for the LORD has given the host of Midian into your hand."*

When we've heard from the Lord, when we recall the bowl of water wrung from the fleece, when God's enemies are telling each other nightmares of their impending doom, it's not as hard as we might think to round up our 300 water-lappers, pass out torches and empty pitchers, and go engage an immense army in the dark. This is already a done deal. God said.

March 14

The Second Job of a Servant—Believe the Master

From Fear to Faith

Then the three companies blew the trumpets and broke the jars. They held in their left hands the torches, and in their right hands the trumpets to blow. And they cried out, "A sword for the LORD and for Gideon!" Every man stood in his place around the camp, and all the army ran. They cried out and fled. When they blew the 300 trumpets, the LORD set every man's sword against his comrade and against all the army. And the army fled...
Judges 7:20-22

God knows how to start a human stampede! What must it be like to be fast asleep, only to have 300 trumpets blasted at you simultaneously in surround-sound! How about waking in a camp surrounded by blazing torches while 300 men scream "a sword for the LORD and for Gideon" as your disoriented neighbors come at you in the dark, swinging their swords! No wonder they didn't stop running until they got back to Midian!

When it's all over, the Israelites come to Gideon and ask him to rule over them. He graciously declines: *"I will not rule over you and my son will not rule over you; the LORD will rule over you."* (Judges 8:23) Gideon's faith and obedience are used of God to usher in four decades of rest for Israel.

This all began with an obscure, fearful man, hiding from his enemies, of no account in his own estimation when God sent His angel to commission him. Gideon's statements changed from his original response to the angel, *"Please, Lord, how can I save Israel?.."* (Judges 6:15) to the confident address given to his troops *"Arise, for the LORD has given the host of Midian into your hand"* (Judges 7:15), and the only thing that transpired between those two pronouncements is that Gideon has repeatedly been reassured by God (fleeces, signs, dreams) and he has come to *believe God.* The enemy intimidating the Israelites in Judges 7:15 is precisely the same one sprawled across the valley in Judges 6:15. What has changed in the course of one chapter is that God's servant has been transformed from fear to faith. It's a transformation God is always willing to perform, and always ready to reward!

The Second Job of a Servant—Believe the Master

Believe In Him Whom He Has Sent

Then they said to him, "What must we do, to be doing the works of God?" Jesus answered them, "This is the work of God, that you believe in him whom he has sent." John 6:28-29

So often, our question is, "What do you want me to do, God, in order to please you?" "What is your will for me?" *"What must we do, to be doing the works of God?"* Jesus' stunning answer is easily missed: *"This is the work of God, that you believe in him whom he has sent."*

Yes, there are specific missions on which God sends us. There is a Great Commission which applies to every disciple. There is a Great Commandment that focuses our attention on love, first for God, then for one another. But preceding all of it is the most basic thing in Christianity—*"that you believe in him whom he has sent."* It either all starts with believing in Jesus, or it doesn't start! Nothing we can do will please the Father if we refuse to believe in the Son. Doing "the work of God" begins with believing His testimony concerning Jesus. It doesn't stop there, but without a sincere belief in Christ, there is no beginning. Faith in Christ can't be skipped, nor can it be replaced by lots of good deeds. God is able to do anything He wants, so it's not like He needs human flesh in order to get something done. Our "help" is never critical to God's being able to accomplish a task; though He often grants us the favor of getting to participate in meaningful ways, it's to our benefit rather than His necessity.

What does He want us to *do?!* He wants us to believe. That's the work which pleases Him most—that we would exercise our faith, and simply believe that what He is saying is true, trust in the One He has sent, and live accordingly. Plenty of tasks will accompany that belief, but until we realize that the first thing God requires of His followers is that they *believe in Him whom He has sent*, we're missing everything else. The first job of a servant is to just pay attention, to be listening for the Master's voice. The second job of a servant is to believe that voice when we hear it, and to totally trust in the One sent from above.

The Third Job of a Servant— Obey, Regardless

"What do you think? A man had two sons. And he went to the first and said, 'Son, go and work in the vineyard today.' And he answered, 'I will not,' but afterward he changed his mind and went. And he went to the other son and said the same. And he answered, 'I go, sir,' but did not go. Which of the two did the will of his father?" They said, "The first."
Matthew 21:28-31

Jesus' parable was aimed at the religious hierarchy who had first refused to believe John the Baptist and now were refusing to believe Him, but the story also applies to each of us. It's the action that counts, rather than the intention or the promise of action.

Our first child was compliant in disposition, but it didn't stop her from being disobedient at times. The times were rare when she would openly defy us, but a pattern emerged of "agreeable disobedience," as requests she found not to her liking would simply be ignored or purposely forgotten. As parents, we had to learn that disobedience without an argument was nevertheless still disobedience, and needed to be corrected, just as defiant disobedience did.

I've not been one to shake my fist at God. I'm trying to think of a time when I told God "No!" and openly defied Him. (There have probably been times, but I've managed to forget them). On the other hand, there have been many, many times when I have known God's will and not gotten around to doing it, when I've purposely forgotten about what it was He had commissioned me to do. I've stretched my imagination to come up with excuses to justify my disobedience. I've allowed any and every distraction to take me "off task." Worse yet, many of these transgressions have been on the heels of a promise of obedience from me! "Yes, Lord!" I've said, then stayed put, hoping He would forget He'd called me (He never does).

Obedience keys on our actions, not our promises or intentions. The first job of a servant is to pay attention, so we know what the Master is saying to us. The second job is to believe the Master. The third job of a servant is to obey, regardless—regardless of the cost, regardless of the excuses, regardless...! If the end result of the Master's instructions to us is not obedience, we need another name for ourselves, because "servant" doesn't fit. A servant obeys.

The Third Job of a Servant—Obey, Regardless

God Has the Blueprints

Now the day before Saul came, the LORD had revealed to Samuel: "Tomorrow about this time I will send to you a man from the land of Benjamin, and you shall anoint him to be prince over my people Israel....

When Samuel saw Saul, the LORD told him, "Here is the man of whom I spoke to you! He it is who shall restrain my people." Then Saul approached Samuel in the gate and said, "Tell me where is the house of the seer?" Samuel answered Saul, "I am the seer. Go up before me to the high place, for today you shall eat with me, and in the morning I will let you go and will tell you all that is on your mind. As for the donkeys that were lost three days ago, do not set your mind on them, for they have been found. And for whom is all that is desirable in Israel? Is it not for you and for all your father's house?" Saul answered, "Am I not a Benjamite, from the least of the tribes of Israel? And is not my clan the humblest of all the clans of the tribe of Benjamin? Why then have you spoken to me in this way?"

Then Samuel took Saul and his young man and brought them into the hall and gave them a place at the head of those who had been invited, who were about thirty persons. And Samuel said to the cook, "Bring the portion I gave you, of which I said to you, 'Put it aside.'" So the cook took up the leg and what was on it and set them before Saul. And Samuel said, "See what was kept is set before you. Eat, because it was kept for you until the hour appointed, that you might eat with the guests."
1 Samuel 9:15-16a,17-24

There are still a chapter's worth of signs to follow, all confirming what God's servants understand: God knows everything! With His foreknowledge, God at times gives His servants intimate details of future events completely beyond their control, in order that people might have faith in Him. Acting on these instructions from God is not presumption—it is nothing more than obedience, if we know God has spoken to us and revealed His plan to us. It isn't difficult at all for God to show one of His servants what will happen, to the extent they are able to relate details of things which have not yet happened and over which they have no control—*at God's direction.* It is very important that prophecy be initiated by God, not the prophet. If we know it is God who spoke to us, we can go ahead and plan the banquet for the new king God will send us, tomorrow.

The Third Job of a Servant—Obey, Regardless

Listening, Believing, Obedience

"Has the LORD as great delight in burnt offerings and sacrifices, as in obeying the voice of the LORD?

Behold, to obey is better than sacrifice, and to listen than the fat of rams.

For rebellion is as the sin of divination, and presumption is as iniquity and idolatry.

Because you have rejected the word of the LORD, he has also rejected you from being king." 1 Samuel 15:22-23

Poor Samuel. First he has to "king" Saul; now his job is to "un-king" him! It's not always fun to be a prophet.

Disobedience is what brought down Israel's first king and made him unuseable. Saul's great potential is totally wasted as he stubbornly persists in doing things his own way without regard for God's commands. He lives by excuses and rationalizations; the monuments he builds are to himself, never to the God who made him king. When confronted by Samuel regarding his disobedience, Saul's response is once again to justify himself and pass blame. God's orders had been very specific; Saul had obeyed where convenient, and disobeyed where it fit his purposes, or where obedience required backbone. He now attempts to twist disobedience into a form of worship! What was to have been destroyed will supposedly be presented to the LORD as sacrifice. The response he gets from God's servant is timely for every generation: *"Has the LORD as great delight in burnt offerings and sacrifices, as in obeying the voice of the LORD?*

Behold, to <u>obey</u> is better than sacrifice, and to <u>listen</u> than the fat of rams."

Listening comes first for a servant, believing comes next, and there's no substitute for obedience—none. Either we are an obedient servant who can be trusted with God's instructions, or we are disobedient. Partial disobedience does not become obedience by re-labeling it sacrifice. God always looks at the heart first—and if the heart is not totally committed to Him and to obeying Him, offerings don't change a thing. Human frailties and failure aren't what disqualify servants; rebellion is—the stubborn refusal to obey, acknowledge guilt, accept correction. There is no substitute for genuine obedience.

The Third Job of a Servant—Obey, Regardless

The Cornerstone of Obedience

"Why do you call me 'Lord, Lord,' and not do what I tell you? Everyone who comes to me and hears my words and does them, I will show you what he is like: he is like a man building a house, who dug deep and laid the foundation on the rock. And when a flood arose, the stream broke against that house and could not shake it, because it had been well built. But the one who hears and does not do them is like a man who built a house on the ground without a foundation. When the stream broke against it, immediately it fell, and the ruin of that house was great." Luke 6:46-49

"Why do you call me 'Lord, Lord,' and not do what I tell you?" Hmmm. Good question. *Very* good question. Maybe we ought to drop the "Lord" thing until we're ready to obey!

"Everyone who comes to me and hears my words and does them"... This verse pretty much prescribes the formula we've been working on for the past few weeks:

(1) *Everyone who comes to me* (First job of a servant—Pay attention)

(2) *and hears my words* (Second job of a servant—Believe the Master)

(3) *and does them* (Third job of a servant—Obey, regardless)

We live in a world in which foundations matter, because the storms are inevitable. Jesus illustrates that the only house which will withstand the flood is a house built on a secure foundation. *"Everyone who comes to me and hears my words and does them"* represents a spiritual foundation, with obedience being the necessary cornerstone.

It comes back to the "Lord, Lord" question. If we are not willing to pay attention, believe the Master, then obey what we hear from Him, there is no reason to call Jesus "Lord." On the other hand, if we have built on a foundation of belief and obedience, we have something so solid that no storm will be able to shake us. We can't stop at just hearing God's Word, or even with saying we believe it. Acting on what we have heard—obedience, is the difference between an unshakeable life based on Christ, and just another sad disaster story, filled with waste and regret. Without the foundation of obedience, it doesn't really matter what we build on top—eventually, it will topple. We must build on Christ. They don't call Him the "Cornerstone" for nothing.

The Third Job of a Servant—Obey, Regardless

Faith without Training Wheels

After this the Lord appointed seventy-two others and sent them on ahead of him, two by two, into every town and place where he himself was about to go. And he said to them, "The harvest is plentiful, but the laborers are few. Therefore pray earnestly to the Lord of the harvest to send out laborers into his harvest. Go your way; behold, I am sending you out as lambs in the midst of wolves. Carry no moneybag, no knapsack, no sandals, and greet no one on the road. Whatever house you enter, first say, 'Peace be to this house!' And if a son of peace is there, your peace will rest upon him. But if not, it will return to you. And remain in the same house, eating and drinking what they provide, for the laborer deserves his wages. Do not go from house to house. Whenever you enter a town and they receive you, eat what is set before you. Heal the sick in it and say to them, 'The kingdom of God has come near to you.' Luke 10:1-9

These people were not just sent out with a vague commission—it was very specific. They didn't have to figure out a plan; Jesus gave them one. He expected them to follow His instructions. This was not freelance discipleship, it was obedience.

Jesus purposely disarms His disciples of all the things on which they tend to rely—money, friends, back-up plans, etc.—in order to send them out on a faith field trip which will prove the Father's faithfulness to them in a way they've never before experienced.

It's one thing to sit on a hillside listening to Jesus talk about God providing in the Sermon on the Mount; it's quite another thing to arrive in a village as a complete stranger, with no money or food or spare clothes, no connections, no place to stay, and your job is to heal the sick there!

The result is anything but disappointment, though! For dozens of disciples, this was the time when their existing faith grew by leaps and bounds, and their theoretical faith became real faith. They no longer just "wanted to believe" God would come through for them; now they *knew* He could and would. They now understood that when God is teaching us to live by faith, we don't need training wheels.

The Third Job of a Servant—Obey, Regardless

Smiling Jesus

The seventy-two returned with joy, saying, "Lord, even the demons are subject to us in your name!" And he said to them, "I saw Satan fall like lightning from heaven. Behold, I have given you authority to tread on serpents and scorpions, and over all the power of the enemy, and nothing shall hurt you. Nevertheless, do not rejoice in this, that the spirits are subject to you, but rejoice that your names are written in heaven."

In that same hour he rejoiced in the Holy Spirit and said, "I thank you, Father, Lord of heaven and earth, that you have hidden these things from the wise and understanding and revealed them to little children; yes, Father, for such was your gracious will. All things have been handed over to me by my Father, and no one knows who the Son is except the Father, or who the Father is except the Son and anyone to whom the Son chooses to reveal him." Then turning to the disciples he said privately, "Blessed are the eyes that see what you see! For I tell you that many prophets and kings desired to see what you see, and did not see it, and to hear what you hear, and did not hear it." Luke 10:17-24

There aren't a lot of times in scripture when we know Jesus is smiling, but here's one. Why is this such a special occasion? Because His followers are getting it! They've just come back from a faith field trip, so fired up they can't wait to go, again. The fulfillment of prophecies hundreds of years old are taking place, and His mission is being successfully accomplished. The plan is coming together. The enemy is being driven back, by raw tax collectors and fishermen! This is one of the times when Jesus *feels* that it's worth it.

If we want to make the Master smile, all we have to do is live by faith. If we pay attention, trust Him at His word, and are willing to obey, regardless, if we're willing to charge into enemy territory armed only with our faith in Him, with no back-up plan, we're on our way to a joyous experience and a Savior who rejoices with us.

The Third Job of a Servant—Obey, Regardless

Deep-Water Disciples

And when he had finished speaking, he said to Simon, "Put out into the deep and let down your nets for a catch." Luke 5:4

Jesus' instruction to Simon reminds me of something I've learned about myself: I swim better in deep water.

Here's what I mean by that: Being a true conservative, my tendency is to not go out any deeper than I absolutely have to. And since I'm in the shallows, why not just stand up and quit swimming whenever I get a little tired?

I swim better in deep water.

Once I know I can't touch bottom, I quit thinking about it and focus on swimming, since there are no other options. I'll probably never be a very good swimmer, but I swim better in deep water, because in shallow, safe water, I hardly swim at all; I just stand around in the pool.

Here's the spiritual application: When I'm in deep water, I pay attention to God; when it's shallow, or I'm close to shore, it's harder to focus on Him, because all I have to do is stand up, or head for "safety."

What is "deep water"? For one thing, it's when we don't get to know what the plan is. We plead with God to show us what's ahead, and He replies, "What would you do, if I told you what was next? You would immediately begin to make your own plans, and you'd not be focusing on me at all—you'd be focusing on your plan. So, for the time being, you don't get a plan—all you get is *Me. I AM the 'plan.'*

"If you keep your focus on Me, and pay attention, and obey, you'll get to wherever you need to be, in plenty of time. But if you insist on making your own plans and going your own way, it doesn't matter what the plan might be, you won't be following Me, because you're not watching Me.

"It's not 'watch me so you can get "the plan;" watching me *is* the plan!

"Do you want my plan? Here it is. *Watch me!"*

March 23

The Third Job of a Servant—Obey, Regardless
Deep-Water Disciples, II

... "Follow me." Luke 5:27

How many times has "Follow me" been the only plan offered by God to would-be disciples? God has often been skimpy on the details, when it comes to what's next for His servants. It often just comes down to "Watch me! Follow me!" A great example is when over a million Israelites traversed the wilderness, guided only by the cloud God provided. I'm sure most of them would have preferred a plan, a schedule or almost anything to a cloud, but God was training a nation to pay attention to Him. When they paid attention, they also obeyed. He didn't need a million entrepreneurs, making up their own plans and rules as they went along. He didn't need a million shallow-water, play-it-safe disciples, who would never venture beyond their comfort zone.

What God was looking for was a nation of people who would pay attention to Him, listen to Him and *obey*, regardless. God needed people willing to take their little kids out into the middle of a river, while He held the water back. He needed people who had the faith and the self-discipline to march around a city for a week without saying a word—not because this made sense but because "God said"—then shout and watch the walls fall down on the seventh day. God was looking for deep-water disciples, people willing to launch out into the deep, having neither their own plan nor a back-up plan, people who fully expected God to come through.

God has always been looking for deep-water disciples, those willing to get out of the shallows in obedience to His command. There are plenty of wading pool Christians, ready to serve Jesus so long as they can touch bottom, so long as it's not too scary, too hot, too cold, too poor, too far from home... Then there are the deep-water variety. They remind me of a quote I love: "A ship is safe in a harbor, but that is not what ships are for." Neither are disciples made for the shallows. We are called by Christ to follow Him into the deep, knowing He can and will guide us, provide for us, and protect us. We need not fear, but we *must* follow.

The Third Job of a Servant—Obey, Regardless

The Rewarding Life of a Faithful, Wise Manager

And the Lord said, "Who then is the faithful and wise manager, whom his master will set over his household, to give them their portion of food at the proper time? Blessed is that servant whom his master will find so doing when he comes. Truly, I say to you, he will set him over all his possessions. But if that servant says to himself, 'My master is delayed in coming,' and begins to beat the male and female servants, and to eat and drink and get drunk, the master of that servant will come on a day when he does not expect him and at an hour he does not know, and will cut him in pieces and put him with the unfaithful. And that servant who knew his master's will but did not get ready or act according to his will, will receive a severe beating. But the one who did not know, and did what deserved a beating, will receive a light beating. Everyone to whom much was given, of him much will be required, and from him to whom they entrusted much, they will demand the more." Luke 12:42-48

Do we think that somehow God is not going to remember what it is that He entrusted to us? Is He not going to notice if we did absolutely nothing with it?! This parable is a sobering reminder of how deadly serious the Master is about the responsibilities He has entrusted to us. For one thing, the responsibility is real—it's for real people with genuine needs. This is not some game without serious consequences; when a manager is unfaithful, some of God's children actually do go hungry or suffer abuse. This, in turn, activates the wrath of the Master! Since God is taking all of this seriously, and the results are real, perhaps we had better take it seriously as well, and keep to the tasks at hand.

It pleases me to see the word "manager" in a good light: *"Who then is the faithful and wise manager,..."* In recent years, few have aspired to be a "manager," when the focus is on the importance and the glories of "leadership," but here the Master is not asking for someone to come up with a big vision of their own, but instead to conscientiously and faithfully fulfill *His* own. There's something very beautiful about a servant who can be entrusted with the well-being of many people, whose Master may return to find him on task, his charges well cared-for. No wonder there's a reward for faithful and wise managers.

The Third Job of a Servant—Obey, Regardless

Obedience is the Natural Result

This is the message we have heard from him and proclaim to you, that God is light, and in him is no darkness at all. If we say we have fellowship with him while we walk in darkness, we lie and do not practice the truth. But if we walk in the light, as he is in the light, we have fellowship with one another, and the blood of Jesus his Son cleanses us from all sin...

My little children, I am writing these things to you so that you may not sin. But if anyone does sin, we have an advocate with the Father, Jesus Christ the righteous. He is the propitiation for our sins, and not for ours only but also for the sins of the whole world. And by this we know that we have come to know him, if we keep his commandments. Whoever says "I know him" but does not keep his commandments is a liar, and the truth is not in him, but whoever keeps his word, in him truly the love of God is perfected. By this we may be sure that we are in him: whoever says he abides in him ought to walk in the same way in which he walked.
1 John 1:5-7, 2:1-6

While obedience has and always will be God's standard for His children, there is forgiveness and grace available for each of us when we fail to meet that standard. We are able to access His "propitiation"— the atoning sacrifice Jesus made for us which regains for us God's favor—by merely "walking in the light."

What does it mean to "walk in the light"? It is complete honesty and transparency before God. No hiding. No pretending. Instead of lingering in the shadows, hoping our sins will go unnoticed, we walk out into His light, allowing all our failures to be exposed, forgiven and healed. It is at this point of openness that we find what it is to be in fellowship with Him. Every spiritual issue in our lives is dealt with in the light of His love, and we are clean. There is nothing left to hide. We can relax in God's presence! In the process, we also can relax with one another. Walking in the light gives us fellowship with both God and man. Could spiritual peace be this simple?

No longer do we think of obedience to God's commands as the way to gain God's favor. Instead, obedience is simply the natural result of walking each day in fellowship with Him. Sin? Mistake? If we're walking in the light with our Lord, everything that might harm our relationship with the Lord is dealt with as we go along, and we remain in perfect fellowship with Him.

The Third Job of a Servant—Obey, Regardless

I Have Come To Do Your Will, O God

For it is impossible for the blood of bulls and goats to take away sins. Consequently, when Christ came into the world, he said, "Sacrifices and offerings you have not desired, but a body have you prepared for me; in burnt offerings and sin offerings you have taken no pleasure. Then I said, 'Behold, I have come to do your will, O God, as it is written of me in the scroll of the book.'" Hebrews 10:4-7

The theme Jesus recites from Psalm 40 is the theme of His earthly ministry. *"'Behold, I have come to do your will, O God, as it is written of me in the scroll of the book.'"*

Jesus repeatedly made it clear that His purpose for being on earth was to do the will of His Father, and nothing else. The fulfillment of the scriptures—all the prophecies and promises regarding the Messiah—was an established part of His mission before ever He was born, and He knew it. Much of Jesus' life was scripted, recorded by various prophets hundreds of years prior to His arrival. He not only followed the script meticulously, careful to fulfill every prophecy; He *rejoiced* in following the path already established for Him. He *exulted* in performing the will of His Father. There was no rebellion, no competing agenda. His only ambition was to accomplish the task set before Him by the Father.

What would happen in my life if my sole ambition was to do the will of God, and every other desire fell away? Many times I have *said* that was the case, but the reality finds all kinds of competing desires and ambitions. I need to remind myself on a regular basis that the reason I have been given this body and this life is to do the will of my Father in heaven. That is my purpose in life. The more I focus on that purpose, the more I become like Jesus. What brings pleasure to God is a heart devoted to Him, fixated on Him, living in obedience to His direction and seeking only His approval. *"I have come to do your will, O God."* There is a freedom in that kind of surrender.

The Third Job of a Servant—Obey, Regardless

Blind Faith

By faith Abraham obeyed when he was called to go out to a place that he was to receive as an inheritance. And he went out, not knowing where he was going. Hebrews 11:8

One of the things God appreciated about Abraham was his willingness to exercise *blind* faith. It's one thing to obey when we have the details, understand the situation and can readily see the outcome; it's another to simply obey, when there are no reference points and we are completely unaware of the master plan. Some servants get to know where they're going; others are called upon to pack and leave, without so much as a forwarding address.

A servant especially useful to God is one who doesn't require an explanation for everything. A simple order is all it takes to get him moving. I want to be that kind of servant.

When Abraham left Haran, he didn't even know his destination, much less the blessings which would accompany obedience. The first step in becoming a legendary "man of faith" was just to obey God, in blind faith and trust. God would use this first bold act of obedience to begin to build within Abraham a faith that would astound the world—and set the stage for an even greater faith and obedience which would save it.

The Third Job of a Servant—Obey, Regardless

Echoes of Obedience

By faith Abraham, when he was tested, offered up Isaac, and he who had received the promises was in the act of offering up his only son, of whom it was said, 'Through Isaac shall your offspring be named.' He considered that God was able even to raise him from the dead, from which, figuratively speaking, he did receive him back. Hebrews 11:17-19

The echoes of Abraham's obedience still reverberate throughout history. This is the kind of faith and unwavering obedience that get God's attention. Not only is it faith; it's faith that doesn't make any sense! Why would God want Abraham to be willing to sacrifice the promised child? Because God was going to allow that same thing to happen to His own Son, in order to save the world—but Abraham didn't know that. All Abraham knew was God's voice, and blind obedience.

Abraham's incredible faith is rewarded incredibly. God had been looking for someone to whom He could make the promises which would ultimately result in the salvation of the world. In Abraham, He found His man. Here was someone who loved Him and trusted Him enough to *obey, regardless.* This was the sort of man out of whom God could raise up a holy people.

And the angel of the LORD called to Abraham a second time from heaven and said, "By myself I have sworn, declares the LORD, because you have done this and have not withheld your son, your only son, I will surely bless you, and I will surely multiply your offspring as the stars of heaven and as the sand that is on the seashore. And your offspring shall possess the gate of his enemies, and in your offspring shall all the nations of the earth be blessed, because you have obeyed my voice." (Gen 22:15-18)

God always honors those who obey Him, and great obedience always brings great honor. If I desire great honor from God, it's simple how that may be obtained: Obedience to His voice, regardless.

The Third Job of a Servant—Obey, Regardless

Turning Terror to Triumph

The LORD said to Joshua, "Get up! Why have you fallen on your face? Israel has sinned; they have transgressed my covenant that I commanded them; they have taken some of the devoted things; they have stolen and lied and put them among their own belongings. Therefore the people of Israel cannot stand before their enemies. They turn their backs before their enemies, because they have become devoted for destruction. I will be with you no more, unless you destroy the devoted things from among you. Get up! Consecrate the people and say, 'Consecrate yourselves for tomorrow; for thus says the LORD, God of Israel, "There are devoted things in your midst, O Israel. You cannot stand before your enemies until you take away the devoted things from among you. Joshua 7:10-13

The sin of one man (Achan) has resulted in a humiliating defeat for the Israelites, and terror has settled down on the camp. Joshua, confused, resorts to whining at God. God reprimands Joshua, and gives specific instructions which must be carried out, in order that the situation may be rectified. Joshua's role is not to come up with a solution for Israel's dilemma; all he has to do is obey. The whole nation's fate is wrapped up in the question of whether or not their leader will fully obey God. Joshua's complete compliance with God's commands results in a miraculous turn-around, and Israel is once again victorious, once sin has been dealt with.

The problem for the servant is that sometimes God's commands are the furthest thing from our own desires. A true servant is willing to do the dirty work and keep focused on the mission, even when he dislikes the mission. Obedience is not just for when it coincides with our wishes! A servant doesn't just do the things he feels like doing, or the things he completely understands. A servant obeys God, regardless. That's the only solution, when it comes to turning terror to triumph. Sin begets fear; obedience begets the calm assurance of victory.

March 30

Uneven Playing Field

And behold, a man of God came out of Judah by the word of the LORD to Bethel. Jeroboam was standing by the altar to make offerings. And the man cried against the altar by the word of the LORD and said, "O altar, altar, thus says the LORD: 'Behold, a son shall be born to the house of David, Josiah by name, and he shall sacrifice on you the priests of the high places who make offerings on you, and human bones shall be burned on you.' 1 Kings 13:1-2*

1 Kings 13 relates the unusual story of a prophet sent by God to King Jeroboam, in order to pronounce judgment against an idolatrous altar the king had made purely for his own political protection. God's message is so specific that He names the person who will unknowingly fulfill it, hundreds of years later (2 Kings 23:15-20 gives the exact fulfillment)!

Along with this one-sentence message to deliver, the prophet has also received a strict command from God not to eat bread or drink water in Israel, nor to return back the way he had come.

After he delivers the prophecy, escapes with his life through a miraculous sign, and successfully declines the king's invitation to eat and drink, the man of God is on his way home, still true to his mission. This is where it gets really weird.

An old prophet tracks him down, lies to him about having an angel of God tell him something different and convinces him to come home and eat with him, then gets a real message from God about the prophet getting killed because he disobeyed! Sure enough. A lion gets him on the way home. The prophet who lied him to death in the first place is the one who goes and buries him in his own tomb, and wants to be buried next to him!

It's an uneven playing field. Servants of God are held to God's standards, regardless of what anybody else is doing or saying. We can get tricked into disobeying and still get punished?! Yes. Ask Eve. The point is *obedience, regardless.* If there is anything the enemy of our souls knows will convince us to disobey God's direct orders, he will be sure to provide it. Satan has never played fair, nor have those under his control. It's up to us to get our signals from God, believe what He says and not secondguess Him, and *obey, regardless.*

March 31

The Third Job of a Servant—Obey, Regardless

Uneven Playing Field, II

And he said to him, "I also am a prophet as you are, and an angel spoke to me by the word of the LORD, saying, 'Bring him back with you into your house that he may eat bread and drink water.'" But he lied to him. So he went back with him and ate bread in his house and drank water.
1 Kings 13:18-19

What's so bad about getting a drink of water, especially when a nice guy is saying, "God said it was O.K."? Because it directly contradicted what the prophet knew God had already said, and what the prophet had already testified to the king that God had said. Just a little disobedience cost the prophet in 1 Kings 13 his life.

In the Garden of Eden, Eve was quite familiar with God's command, until the serpent's theology lesson convinced her that disobedience couldn't possibly be that big of a deal. It was.

Moses didn't think a technicality in how he would perform a miracle would cost him the Promised Land, but it did. Little acts of disobedience turn out to be disproportionately expensive.

Lessons?

Remember that God doesn't change His mind, so don't believe everything that someone says was told them by an angel! If it contradicts God's Word, His nature, or makes Him out to be fickle, it's a lie.

Although the message was strange, and dangerous to deliver, the man of God had all the power and protection he needed, until he was tricked into disobeying God's direct commandment. Stay in His will! There is always a lion (Satan) waiting for those who walk in disobedience to God, even if they were tricked into it!

The power belongs to the Master, not the servant. The veracity of the message is due to God's faithfulness, not the messenger's. The prophecy ultimately came true because God said, not because the prophet behaved flawlessly. There is no power given to God's servants apart from the power and protection that accompany obedience. Even a little disobedience leaves us wide open to the lions. Even if we were tricked. It's an uneven playing field, but complete obedience puts us on the side where we can't lose!

Promises to Servants

Ask, Please!

"Truly, truly, I say to you, whoever believes in me will also do the works that I do; and greater works than these will he do, because I am going to the Father. Whatever you ask in my name, this I will do, that the Father may be glorified in the Son. If you ask me anything in my name, I will do it." John 14:12-14

"If you abide in me, and my words abide in you, ask whatever you wish, and it will be done for you. By this my Father is glorified, that you bear much fruit and so prove to be my disciples." John 15:7-8

"You did not choose me, but I chose you and appointed you that you should go and bear fruit and that your fruit should abide, so that whatever you ask the Father in my name, he may give it to you." John 15:16

"Truly, truly, I say to you, whatever you ask of the Father in my name, he will give it to you. Until now you have asked nothing in my name. Ask, and you will receive, that your joy may be full." John 16:23b-24

Jesus wants His disciples to *ask!* Six times in the same night He promises answers for those who ask in His name. The only qualifier I notice in these passages? "Abiding" in Him, like a branch connected to a vine. (Jn 15) Asking and abiding are tied together, a point which seems to have escaped many of us, resulting in a lot of disappointment:

"I thought we were supposed to get whatever we asked for in Jesus' name. I used it and came up empty-handed. What's the deal?"

The "deal" is, "Can I ask for this in His name? Does it fit with His purposes? Does it contribute to the harvest? Or is it basically a selfish grab for power or pleasure?" Bottom line: Since I'm using His name, this ought to be something Jesus would be asking for, or I probably shouldn't be asking, or using His name.

But He wants us to ask! On the night before the crucifixion, He is almost pleading with His disciples to, *"Ask!"* If we are abiding in Him, connected, working for the same purpose, and asking for what He Himself would request, He is eager to answer, and pleased when we ask.

The Third Job of a Servant—Obey, Regardless

We Don't Have To Come Back

"So you shall speak all these words to them, but they will not listen to you. You shall call to them, but they will not answer you." Jeremiah 7:27

In America, pragmatism has become a religion, and in much of the Church, it's become a religion within a religion. "If it doesn't work, why do it?" "God wants His Church to be successful, doesn't He? If it's not working, it can't be God's will." "God loves us. He would never want us to suffer, and for me, failure is suffering, so this can't be God's will!"

It's not hard to accept success as God's plan for our lives; failure is a different story. How could God ask us to do something He knows will fail?!

First of all, because He's God, and it's not up to us to decide whether He continues in that position (Thank God)!

Second, because in some cases, the important thing is not the response of the people, but the fact that they were told. Jeremiah's entire ministry was like that: "They won't listen to you, but they must be told, anyway."

Third, it is the job of the servant to *obey, regardless.* Obedience does not bring with it a guarantee of "success," either in this world or the world to come. But obedience to God always brings blessing, the blessing of knowing we have faithfully obeyed our orders, regardless of the outcome.

One of my favorite stories is of a young Coast Guard recruit, discussing with his commanding officer the bleak outlook as they prepared to launch a helicopter into a ferocious storm, in order to attempt a rescue at sea. The recruit yelled above the wind, "Sir, if we go out in this, we may never come back!" The officer gravely answered, "Son, we don't have to come back. But we have to go out."

The attitude of the Coast Guard needs to be the attitude of the Christian. Success is not mandatory, but faithful obedience is. The servant of Christ may look ahead and see failure or disaster, we may even be assured of it by God Himself, but our business is to obey, regardless. This is what it means to be a servant of God. This is some of what Jesus was talking about when He said, *"Whoever does not bear his own cross and come after me cannot be my disciple."* (Lk 14:27) Crucifixion was always a one-way trip. No one ever came back down the hill, dragging their cross. We are called to go out in His name, even when we know we're not coming back.

The Third Job of a Servant—Obey, Regardless

The Ministry of Whining

Now the rabble that was among them had a strong craving. And the people of Israel also wept again and said, "Oh that we had meat to eat!..."

Moses heard the people weeping throughout their clans, everyone at the door of his tent. And the anger of the LORD blazed hotly, and Moses was displeased. Moses said to the LORD,... "Where am I to get meat to give to all this people? For they weep before me and say, 'Give us meat, that we may eat.' I am not able to carry all this people alone; the burden is too heavy for me. If you will treat me like this, kill me at once, if I find favor in your sight, that I may not see my wretchedness."
Numbers 11:4,10-11,13-15

The ministry of whining is a ministry that is not. It's contagious, it bugs God, it discourages leaders to the point of begging God to kill them rather than continue being responsible for this crowd!...

Moses' complaint is met with God's mercy. First, there is a plan to lighten the load: Appoint 70 elders. Difficult as it is for leaders to relinquish control, Moses was sufficiently burned out that it must have come as a relief. He did it.

Part two of God's response is to promise the whining Israelites that on the following day, they will be provided all the meat they can eat for a month! Moses, faced with getting to deliver this promise without benefit of a single detail, helps God do the math on this one. God's response: *"Is the LORD'S hand shortened?"* (Nu 11:23)

The decision Moses faces is one of obedience. Will he or will he not follow through on God's instructions? His job is to tell the people, not to figure out how it might happen. I'm trying to imagine telling all of these people that they will have meat, tomorrow, when I don't know where I would get *any* meat. Faith. "Can You at least give me a hint of how you're going to do this? Do I have to just tell them, when I don't even know? Can I see the meat, first? How about if I just tell them there will be a 'surprise,' tomorrow—or 'soon,' and leave it vague so we're not locked in?"

The promise is made, without one shred of evidence to back it up. Once again, it's pure obedience. When the first of the quail started to blow in from the sea, everyone understood again that God keeps His promises.

The Third Job of a Servant—Obey, Regardless

Is Obedience That Important?

"And if you faithfully obey the voice of the LORD your God, being careful to do all his commandments that I command you, today, the LORD your God will set you high above all the nations of the earth. And all these blessings shall come upon you and overtake you, if you obey the voice of the LORD your God.... But if you will not obey the voice of the LORD your God or be careful to do all his commandments and his statutes that I command you today, then all these curses shall come upon you and overtake you...." Deuteronomy 28:1-2,15

Obedience has never ceased to be God's expectation of His people. In the Garden of Eden, the first humans received clear instructions as to the necessity of obedience, and the inevitable consequences of disobedience. In Deuteronomy 28, an entire chapter outlines the promises of God toward the Israelites regarding the subject. Fourteen verses of promised blessing are followed by 54 verses of horrible curses, all hinging on obedience. The Israelites will choose the consequences for their entire nation, based upon their actions. Obedience will see the fulfillment of promised blessing; disobedience to God's commands will ultimately bring God's promised curses.

Does this have anything to do with 21st century Christians, bought by the blood of the Lamb? Obedience and disobedience both still bring consequences, for individuals and for nations. The grace that saves us does not come with a license to sin. While it is not our obedience that grants us access to eternal life—rather, it is the free gift of God's grace—obedience is still part of the picture. It's not how we get in to God's Kingdom, but it is expected of all God's children, in much the same way as we do not enter a human family by way of obedience, yet it is expected of each maturing child.

The principles still apply, both for nations and for individuals. Obedience to God triggers blessing; disobedience triggers heartache. The fact that these effects are not often instantaneous does not negate the promises, bad or good. We choose our consequences by our choice of action, and grace never releases us from the responsibility to obey God. Grace covers our failures, but God still expects His children to obey Him.

The Third Job Of A Servant—Obey, Regardless
We Must Obey God Rather Than Men

And when they had brought them, they set them before the council. And the high priest questioned them, saying, "We strictly charged you not to teach in this name, yet here you have filled Jerusalem with your teaching, and you intend to bring this man's blood upon us." But Peter and the apostles answered, "We must obey God rather than men." Acts 5:27-29

This was not the apostles' first trip before the Sanhedrin, nor the last time they would face persecution for their faith, but their response capsulizes the attitude of discipleship: *"We must obey God rather than men."*

This critical decision is one that must be made by every disciple of Jesus Christ, on a regular basis. "Are we going to obey God, or men?" The consequences can include persecution, misunderstanding, alienation, even death. Obeying God sometimes gains us favor with people; at other times, it can be the death knell for a career. It is not ours to decide on the prudence of obeying God, based on the projected consequences; it is ours to obey, regardless.

As the concepts of obedience and submission seem to become increasingly foreign to our society, God continues to look for servants who can be counted on to follow His instructions without wavering. These are the people He will use to transform nations.

The great saints of the past have always been people willing to obey God. Some, like Jonah, were reluctant and moody in their eventual obedience, and lost out on the majority of their blessings. Some, like King Saul, persisted in compromising God's plans with their own ambitions and disqualified themselves for service. The heroes and heroines of the faith have always been those willing to follow God's leading, believe His promise and, when everything was on the line, obey, regardless.

"Should we obey God, or men?" For disciples God uses in mighty ways, the answer has always been obvious.

Tellers On The Take

"Hear another parable. There was a master of a house who planted a vineyard and put a fence around it and dug a winepress in it and built a tower and leased it to tenants, and went into another country. When the season for fruit drew near, he sent his servants to the tenants to get his fruit. And the tenants took his servants and beat one, killed another, and stoned another. Again he sent other servants, more than the first. And they did the same to them. Finally he sent his son to them, saying, 'They will respect my son.' But when the tenants saw the son, they said to themselves, 'This is the heir. Come, let us kill him and have his inheritance.' And they took him and threw him out of the vineyard and killed him. When therefore the owner of the vineyard comes, what will he do to those tenants?" They said to him, "He will put those wretches to a miserable death and let out the vineyard to other tenants who will give him the fruits in their seasons."
Matthew 21:33-41

Whose vineyard was it? Whose tower? Whose winepress? Whose fruit? The tenants knew the answer to all of those questions was, "The master's," yet they had somehow transformed themselves in their minds from tenant to owner. It had become their vineyard. The rightful owner was rejected at every turn, as the tenants desperately clung to possessions not theirs.

One of the key points for me in this parable is that it all belongs to the Master. It's not just a tithe of my income which belongs to Him, and the rest of it is mine; the whole planet belongs to Him! It's His vineyard. I'm just taking care of what belongs to Someone else. I am a tenant.

When God directs what is to be done with the resources or the fruit under my control, He's not being unreasonable or domineering. He's not taking my stuff; it's already His! Somehow, I have to keep that in mind! In a society where many people are owned by their possessions, it's hard to keep in mind my "tenant" status. On a daily basis, I need to be going before the Father and reminding myself of His complete ownership. The only way I will be a good and faithful tenant is if I don't imagine myself to be the owner. As a faithful bank teller must keep in mind that the millions of dollars going through her fingers are other people's money, not hers, so I must keep in mind that none of this belongs to me; it's all His. My job is to be a faithful tenant of the Father's possessions, ready to do whatever He asks.

Reasonable Terms

And as he was setting out on his journey, a man ran up and knelt before him and asked him, "Good Teacher, what must I do to inherit eternal life?" And Jesus said to him, "Why do you call me good? No one is good except God alone. You know the commandments: 'Do not murder, Do not commit adultery, Do not steal, Do not bear false witness, Do not defraud, Honor your father and mother.'" And he said to him, "Teacher, all these I have kept from my youth." And Jesus, looking at him, loved him, and said to him, "You lack one thing: go, sell all that you have, and give to the poor, and you will have treasure in heaven; and come, follow me." Disheartened by the saying, he went away sorrowful, for he had great possessions.
Mark 10:17-22

The rich young man wants to be a disciple, but on "reasonable terms." Jesus requires that he cash out. It's unreasonable—unless it all belongs to the Master. Then, it's like a shareholder telling his stockbroker, "Please sell all of my stock and do such and such with it." The stockbroker can't say "No" to the request, because it's not his money. It belongs to the investor, not the manager.

It's one thing to agree to the *theory* that God owns absolutely all of our possessions; it's quite another to act like it.

In the film "Ghost," Whoopi Goldberg's character, suddenly in possession of a check for four million dollars, is told to give it to the nuns running a homeless shelter. Though the money is not really hers, anyway, and having the check is jeopardizing her life, when it comes time to actually hand it over, she can't seem to do it. It's comical to watch her try to let go of something that doesn't even belong to her.

The reason it's funny is because it's fiction, not reality, and it's someone else, not me. Truth be told, it's hard to part with things in our possession, even if we have known all along that they didn't really belong to us, and the more we have, the harder it is to let go. The Master is not being unreasonable, though, even if He requires us to turn every penny over to whomever He might designate. It's *His money, all of it.* Living in that mindset just may save us from being strangled by our own possessions. Instead, we could be trustworthy, relaxed, joyful stewards of God. Impossible? In our own strength, yes. But Jesus' response to His astonished disciples is His response to me, too: *"With man it is impossible, but not with God. For all things are possible with God."* (Mark 10:27)

The Hungry 90%

And a scribe came up and said to him, "Teacher, I will follow you wherever you go." And Jesus said to him, "Foxes have holes, and birds of the air have nests, but the Son of Man has nowhere to lay his head."
Matthew 8:19-20

I heard about a new simplified tax code the Internal Revenue Service is working on, composed of only two lines. The first line asks, "How much money did you make?" The second line says, "Send it in."

That joke is much like Jesus' actual requirement of His disciples. On more than one occasion, He warns that discipleship costs *everything*.

What was Jesus' address, during His ministry years? He didn't have one. No house to maintain. No lawn to mow. No cattle to feed. He was here on a mission, and didn't own so much as a donkey.

Is Christ against home ownership? No. But He is against our possessions owning us.

I know my tendency to hang onto things, to try to expand what I have, to want more. If I convince myself that a 10% tithe takes care of God and the other 90% is totally mine, I am easily consumed with the care and maintenance of what the 90% buys. Even a little pile of material possessions gobbles up the lion's share of my emotional, physical and financial energy.

Jesus knew that if the rich young ruler had retained even a little bit of his property, it would have occupied enough of his energy to keep him from ever being effective as a disciple.

The lesson for me is not to spend my life in the accumulation of things, unless I want my life to be basically wasted. I'm supposed to be God's servant. If I keep anything back as "my own," it will prevent me from being as effective a disciple as I could be. Either the possessions I hold in my hands are God's, and I am a steward, or they are mine, keeping me from the life that could be.

Lord, please help me to take my hands off, relinquish my grip on stuff, and live as a useful steward of yours, managing things not my own, wisely and cheerfully, and ready at an instant's notice to do whatever you would tell me to do with them. Help me not to spend the rest of my life trying to hang on to things I can't keep, anyway. Help me not to waste the precious time allotted to me, in the pursuit of possessions, when I could be living as a servant of yours!

Can I Afford To Let Go?

Peter began to say to him, "See, we have left everything and followed you." Jesus said, "Truly, I say to you, there is no one who has left house or brothers or sisters or mother or father or children or lands, for my sake and for the gospel, who will not receive a hundredfold now in this time, houses and brothers and sisters and mothers and children and lands, with persecutions, and in the age to come eternal life. But many who are first will be last, and the last first." Mark 10:28-31

Immediately following the episode of the rich young man, and Jesus' subsequent comments about the difficulty of a rich man entering the kingdom of God, Peter becomes concerned that his own sacrifices may have been for nought. Jesus reassures Peter that the Father is indeed keeping track, and everything given up for the sake of the gospel will be replaced many times over.

Once again, God's kindness shines through. He is appreciative of the sacrifices made by each of His servants, even though the Master has the right to everything in our possession, anyway. Jesus understands how difficult it is to let go, even of things which never really belonged to us. He gives us His word that each sacrifice we make for His sake is noted and will be rewarded.

Is that enough? On occasion, I have had to give up something important to me, in order to obey Christ. I've found God's promise to be true, in every instance I can recall! The rewards have far outweighed the sacrifices, already, and I have yet to even glimpse what is to come in the next life!

The question in mind is, "Can I afford to let go of the things and ties of this world, in order to pursue Jesus Christ?" The answer is a resounding "Yes!" In fact, I can't afford *not* to let go, when I consider what's in store for me as a committed follower of the Lord Jesus.

When Winning Is Losing

Someone in the crowd said to him, "Teacher, tell my brother to divide the inheritance with me." But he said to him, "Man, who made me a judge or arbitrator over you?" And he said to them, "Take care, and be on your guard against all covetousness, for one's life does not consist in the abundance of his possessions." And he told them a parable, saying, "The land of a rich man produced plentifully, and he thought to himself, 'What shall I do, for I have nowhere to store my crops?' And he said, 'I will do this; I will tear down my barns and build larger ones, and there I will store all my grain and my goods. And I will say to my soul, Soul, you have ample goods laid up for many years; relax, eat, drink, be merry.' But God said to him, 'Fool! This night your soul is required of you, and the things you have prepared, whose will they be?' So is the one who lays up treasure for himself and is not rich toward God." Luke 12:13-21

We're not here to accumulate stuff. We're just not.

That's a hard philosophy to embrace when we feel we've just been shortchanged, cheated, or neglected. It's difficult not to seek our "rights," particularly when it comes to finances, and especially when dealing with people who believe that taking advantage is just part of the game. *"Teacher, tell my brother to divide the inheritance with me."* What's greedy about that? The poor guy has a jerk for a brother, and all he wants is what's coming to him. Doesn't the Lord care about everyone getting their fair share?

Apparently, "Yes and no." The Lord definitely cares for us (tracking our hair count is a pretty good indicator that His concern extends to the smallest detail of our lives! [Lk 12:7]), but His primary interest will always be in our *soul*, our spiritual character. Our soul is easily damaged by a love of possessions, and that includes whether we *have* them or just *want* them.

If our heart becomes set on material things, it doesn't even matter whether we attain them or not, we still lose out on the joy which comes when our hearts are set on God. Getting into a slugfest with someone over money is a battle from which our soul will not emerge unscathed, not to mention the inevitable resulting break in human relationships. There are times when winning is actually losing, when to even participate in the fight is to cripple our own character, when "getting ahead" only means there is more to leave behind.

Faith or Famine

And the LORD said to Aaron, "You shall have no inheritance in their land, neither shall you have any portion among them. I am your portion and your inheritance among the people of Israel." Numbers 18:20

While the other eleven tribes were assured of their inheritance in the Promised Land, God's promise to the tribe of Levi was that *He* would be their inheritance. The tribe of the priests would be a tribe supported by the worshipers of the one true God, not supported by their own skill in farming or other forms of business. For those of us who have been bombarded for years with "Why can't the church be more like a business?" the short answer is, "Because it's not a business." The Church is designed to run on faith, not a spreadsheet. In the forerunner of the Church, the nation of Israel, the people are commanded to support their priests and the tribe of priests by their tithes, as an act of obedience and worship, and the tribe God has set aside (the Levites) is commanded to live off the faithfulness and generosity of the worshipers rather than their own independent industry.

This is a tenuous system! If the Israelites give up worshiping God, there is no income for an entire tribe of people, who have no land inheritance of their own. If the people are faithless or stingy, the Levites will go hungry. Their whole identity is that they are to be at the mercy of the spiritual climate of their nation! This is not *their* plan, it is *God's.*

The Levites were to be a living example that *faith works,* that it is a legitimate lifestyle as long as it is directed by God and not simply used as a cover-up for laziness. I think God wants us to live with the same attitude as the Levites were supposed to—our inheritance is *the Lord,* not the things we have, here. The faith mindset seems to be more important than the actual dependency on God, but when push comes to shove, we just can't beat the real thing—either God comes through, or we don't eat! When there is no back-up plan and we are still able to survive and even prosper, faith is not only a great way to live; it's an excellent advertisement for the God who has promised to be our inheritance and called us to be His own, entirely dependent upon Him.

April 12

It's Not about Me

"When the Spirit of truth comes, he will guide you into all the truth..."
John 16:13

Prayer Journal: Lord, tell me about me.

It's not about you. You're too introspective. All of life gets translated into how it affects you—even ministry—whether or not you are "successful" or "fulfilled." If your focus was more on Me and less on you, you would be both more successful and more fulfilled, and considerably less frustrated! The same thing for others: If you focused more on others, and less on yourself, you would find more fulfillment and success, and less frustration.

Even your life's goals need to be adjusted a little: Instead of "to be a good husband, ... a good Dad,.... good pastor,.... servant of God," try being more of a servant to all, in the sense of removing the issue of pride from it. For example, "good husband" carries some ego with it that makes it harder to change or admit your faults because that would be admitting that right now, you're not the best husband. "Serving your wife" gets it off of your performance and puts the emphasis on meeting her needs, which results in you being a better husband without you knowing it or gloating in it! Same thing for fathering or pastoring. If it's not about how "good" you are, it frees you to serve them, and it minimizes the pride which makes it hard to serve others, because pride is always self-serving.

One last thing: If you will focus more on Me and less on you, it will greatly help you in serving Me. There's nothing like a "servant" who insists on being the center of attention and "serving" in his own way, and with his own agenda!

Have you really learned, yet, that my agenda is better than yours? (You'll even like it better)! I'm also more successful.

Ah, Lord, what a treat the past few minutes have been! You have this way of just opening my heart and shoving the truth in! And, with you, it doesn't even hurt! It's more like this "Aha!" experience of suddenly seeing something you want me to understand, and being very glad to see it. In just a few minutes, you illuminated something major, which is, I'll bet, the root cause of many frustrations in my life, these days. Thank you!! Now, please help me out. I am from the "Me" generation, you know. It's about all we know! Show me how to serve you, and others, without it being about me, and without it being my own agenda. Please?

Servant of All

And they came to Capernaum. And when he was in the house he asked them, "What were you discussing on the way?" But they kept silent, for on the way they had argued with one another about who was the greatest. And he sat down and called the twelve. And he said to them, "If anyone would be first, he must be last of all and servant of all." And he took a child and put him in the midst of them, and taking him in his arms, he said to them, "Whoever receives one such child in my name receives me, and whoever receives me, receives not me but him who sent me." Mark 9:33-37

"*If anyone would be first, he must be last of all and servant of all.*" You'd think that a couple thousand years would take the bite out of that statement, and that somewhere along the line it would have begun to sound reasonable and normal. You'd think that it would have become more the credo of the Christian faith, something you'd see printed on coffee cups for sale in Christian bookstores. Jesus' statement is still waiting for its popularity to kick in—any day, now! "*If anyone would be first, he must be last of all and servant of all.*" It isn't something He only mentioned a time or two in passing, either; He made it a point to make this point, again and again! Plus, He not only taught it; He lived it.

Why is it so hard for us to live it? Why do I go to Christian conferences and get the distinct impression that on the way there, half the attendees had been arguing about who was the greatest? Why do I see "Christian" books that focus so much on the greatness of the author, and so little on the greatness of God? Why the media ministries where evangelists and "Christian performers" preen and parade like rock star wannabee's?

Wouldn't Jesus want us to be aggressive? "You snooze, you lose." "If you want something, you have to go after it." The philosophy of our age is not hard to find within church walls—it just gets spiritualized, that's all. "God wants me to be happy." Is that in the Bible somewhere?* (*Answer: No) If all else fails, go to that famous, well-loved verse: "God helps those who help themselves." What a proverb to live by! It's the foundation stone of the Protestant work ethic. People struggle with the reference on that one, they just know it's in the Bible somewhere. Would you believe *Poor Richard's Almanac* ? Ben Franklin.

The line to greatness forms at the rear. *Servant of all.* Don't expect to see it on many coffee cups. But at least it *is* in the Bible.

Servant of All

Thinking Ahead

And James and John, the sons of Zebedee, came up to him and said to him, "Teacher, we want you to do for us whatever we ask of you." And he said to them, "What do you want me to do for you?" And they said to him, "Grant us to sit, one at your right hand and one at your left, in your glory." Jesus said to them, "You do not know what you are asking. Are you able to drink the cup that I drink, or to be baptized with the baptism with which I am baptized?" And they said to him, "We are able." And Jesus said to them, "The cup that I drink you will drink, and with the baptism with which I am baptized, you will be baptized, but to sit at my right hand or at my left is not mine to grant, but it is for those for whom it has been prepared." And when the ten heard it, they began to be indignant at James and John. And Jesus called them to him and said to them, "You know that those who are considered rulers of the Gentiles lord it over them, and their great ones exercise authority over them. But it shall not be so among you. But whoever would be great among you must be your servant, and whoever would be first among you must be slave of all. For even the Son of Man came not to be served but to serve, and to give his life as a ransom for many."
Mark 10:35-45

James and John were thinking ahead. They got to counting seats, realized that the "inner circle" of disciples was composed of one too many for a two seat arrangement in glory, and decided they would get there first. They probably even convinced themselves they were being humble—after all, they weren't asking for the throne itself, just the spots on the right and left!

"Thinking ahead" is so often just trying to plot out things to our own advantage. "Thinking ahead" seems mostly to consist in thinking of ourselves—how to get the best seats, how to be first in line. What a beautiful thing it is when "thinking ahead" becomes thinking of others, and how to best serve them. How am I *ever* going to get there? How do I disengage from the world's system of status and status-seeking, and plug into Jesus' simple plan: *Doulos* (servant/slave) of all? I guess all I need to do is follow the Leader, who didn't come to grab the glory, but who left all the glory to be a servant of all.

Servant of All

Vicarious Glory-Seeking

Then the mother of the sons of Zebedee came up to him with her sons, and kneeling before him she asked him for something. And he said to her, "What do you want?" She said to him, "Say that these two sons of mine are to sit, one at your right hand and one at your left, in your kingdom."...

But Jesus called them to him and said, "You know that the rulers of the Gentiles lord it over them, and their great ones exercise authority over them. It shall not be so among you. But whoever would be great among you must be your servant, and whoever would be first among you must be your slave, even as the Son of Man came not to be served but to serve, and to give his life as a ransom for many." Matthew 20:20-21, 25-28

There are lots of ways to be selfish. It is clear that the rush for best seats in the kingdom was not exclusive to James and John, but appears to have been spearheaded by their mother turned lobbyist. As a relative of Jesus, and mother of two of the three disciples who formed Jesus' inner circle (Simon Peter being the third), the favor asked must not have seemed to her nearly as audacious as it came across to others.

It is possible to be self-seeking even under the guise of serving others. The petition wasn't for honor for herself; it was for honor for her sons. Or was it? Isn't the search for glory for our family often just a search for vicarious glory for ourselves? The scholar-who-never-was finally is realized as brilliant through his son, the frustrated athlete at last can enjoy glory through his offspring.

The Son of Man did not come to be recognized and honored and served, but to serve. As followers of Christ, our mission is likewise to seek service, not glory. That includes when we are tempted to seek glory for our own family, that we might share in a little of it. Serving is not about grabbing places of privilege, even if it's for people we love. Once again, the line to greatness forms at the rear.

Servant of All

An Argument to Lose

A dispute also arose among them, as to which of them was to be regarded as the greatest. And he said to them, "The kings of the Gentiles exercise lordship over them, and those in authority over them are called benefactors. But not so with you. Rather, let the greatest among you become as the youngest, and the leader as one who serves. For who is the greater, one who reclines at table or one who serves? Is it not the one who reclines at table? But I am among you as the one who serves.

You are those who have stayed with me in my trials, and I assign to you, as my Father assigned to me, a kingdom, that you may eat and drink at my table in my kingdom and sit on thrones judging the twelve tribes of Israel." Luke 22:24-30

Here, once again, is the enduring argument among the disciples: "Which of us is the greatest?" The fact that this has been a running dispute for a long time, and that it resumes on the heels of Jesus' solemn prediction that one of them will betray Him, only makes it the more odious. This is taking place during the Last Supper! By tomorrow night, their Lord will have been taken from them and crucified, just as He said. Given the context, the discussion seems particularly revolting.

This is an argument that should be laid to rest! Time and again, Jesus has told them, He has shown them, that Kingdom greatness is all about service to others, not about vaunted authority. In one more demonstration of that selfless kind of love, Jesus refrains from chewing out His disciples and instead blesses them with the promise of authority beyond their wildest imagination, then proceeds to literally lay down His life for them—and us.

The well-worn discussion as to which of us is the greatest is still a smelly one, reeking of the old life and all the old attitudes which preceded our encounter with Christ. I've spent far too many hours jockeying for position in the Kingdom, in an endless game of comparison, where mere participation in the discussion guarantees defeat for all involved.

A dispute also arose among them, as to which of them was to be regarded as the greatest. It's time to lose the argument. For good.

Servant of All

God's Insistent Blessing

Then Abram said to Lot, "Let there be no strife between you and me, and between your herdsmen and my herdsmen, for we are kinsmen. Is not the whole land before you? Separate yourself from me. If you take the left hand, then I will go to the right, or if you take the right hand, then I will go to the left." And Lot lifted up his eyes and saw that the Jordan Valley was well watered everywhere like the garden of the LORD, like the land of Egypt, in the direction of Zoar. (This was before the LORD destroyed Sodom and Gomorrah.) So Lot chose for himself all the Jordan Valley, and Lot journeyed east. Thus they separated from each other. Abram settled in the land of Canaan, while Lot settled among the cities of the valley and moved his tent as far as Sodom....

The LORD said to Abram, after Lot had separated from him, "Lift up your eyes and look from the place where you are, northward and southward and eastward and westward, for all the land that you see I will give to you and to your offspring forever.... Arise, walk through the length and the breadth of the land, for I will give it to you." Genesis 13:8-12,14-15,17

Abram shows generosity when he lets Lot choose which way to go. Whose trip is this?! And who is older? And who is following God's promises? On all accounts, the answer is "Abram."

Lot, rather than deferring to his uncle, immediately chooses the good stuff. As soon as he's out of sight, God tells Abram, "Guess what? It's *all* yours, in every direction. Go check it out and walk through it. It belongs to you."

What happens to a servant who isn't possessive? He gets more possessions! What happens to a servant who honors others above himself, and is taken advantage of for his efforts? God Himself makes sure His servant receives honor and blessing! This is not a bad deal, to serve the Most High God! As a matter of fact, we can't lose!

Servant of All

The Prayers of a Friend

Then the LORD said, "Because the outcry against Sodom and Gomor-rah is great and their sin is very grave, I will go down to see whether they have done altogether according to the outcry that has come to me. And if not, I will know."

So the men turned from there and went toward Sodom, but Abraham still stood before the LORD. Then Abraham drew near and said, "Will you indeed sweep away the righteous with the wicked? Suppose there are fifty righteous within the city. Will you then sweep away the place and not spare it for the fifty righteous who are in it?...

So it was that, when God destroyed the cities of the valley, God re-membered Abraham and sent Lot out of the midst of the overthrow when he overthrew the cities in which Lot had lived. Genesis 18:20-24; 19:29

If God had really wanted to destroy Lot, He wouldn't have told Abra-ham about His plans; He just would have gone ahead and done it. What He wanted was for Abraham to intercede for his nephew. The reason He told the person of faith what He was going to do was so the person of faith would pray. Abraham did exactly that. He respectfully bargains with God on behalf of his nephew—and God likes it!

Judgment is coming upon this world, as a consequence of sin, but God's response to sin is to provide a Savior, and to tell the people of faith about what's coming, so they can pray. When faced with Sodom-like issues, our role as believers is not to condemn nor to compromise, but to *pray*. The reason we know about impending judgment and disaster is not to discour-age us, but to cause us to pray for our relatives and friends so they can be saved. God is not willing that any of His children should perish.

Everyone knows someone living in Sodom. The question is, "What are we going to do about it?" God wants to save people, not condemn them. Some refuse to be saved, and are lost, but others find that they've been saved through nothing but God's grace—and the *prayers of a friend*. Our prayers may make the eternal difference for someone—if we care. That's what we can do, and that's why we know. God has told us so we can pray.

Servant of All

The Basin and Towel Habit

Then he poured water into a basin and began to wash the disciples' feet and to wipe them with the towel that was wrapped around him....

When he had washed their feet and put on his outer garments and resumed his place, he said to them, "Do you understand what I have done to you? You call me Teacher and Lord, and you are right, for so I am. If I then, your Lord and Teacher, have washed your feet, you also ought to wash one another's feet. For I have given you an example, that you also should do just as I have done to you. Truly, truly, I say to you, a servant is not greater than his master, nor is a messenger greater than the one who sent him. If you know these things, blessed are you if you do them....

A new commandment I give to you, that you love one another; just as I have loved you, you also are to love one another. By this all people will know that you are my disciples, if you have love for one another."
John 13:5,12-17,34-35

The footwashing was the example which Jesus wanted to have linger in the minds of His disciples. This serving business is not about pecking order, nor is it about reciprocity. Both times in this passage, Jesus misses the chance to say, "Since I've done this for you, do this for *me*." The sign of discipleship is not going to be in how much we love Jesus, but in how much we love one another! In the light of some of the classic church conflicts of all time, this information is not particularly comforting!

The message is clear—again. We are here to serve one another, to wash one another's feet, to love one another. That is our mission. We can talk all we want about how much we love Jesus, but it's the person with the basin and towel, serving in the jobs nobody else wanted, who is a convincing witness to the watching world.

Albert Gray has said, "The successful person has formed the habit of doing things that failures don't like to do." He notes that successful people don't like to do these things, either, but they do them, anyway. It seems to me that this observation especially applies to Christians, who are called to love one another as the very starting point of our identity, and to serve one another as a lifestyle, specializing in the least desirable tasks. The basin and towel habit points straight to Jesus.

Servant of All

A Close-Up Mission Field

Wives, submit to your own husbands, as to the Lord. For the husband is the head of the wife even as Christ is the head of the church, his body, and is himself its Savior. Now as the church submits to Christ, so also wives should submit in everything to their husbands.

Husbands, love your wives, as Christ loved the church and gave himself up for her, that he might sanctify her, having cleansed her by the washing of water with the word, so that he might present the church to himself in splendor, without spot or wrinkle or any such thing, that she might be holy and without blemish. In the same way husbands should love their wives as their own bodies. He who loves his wife loves himself. For no one ever hated his own flesh, but nourishes and cherishes it, just as Christ does the church, because we are members of his body. "Therefore a man shall leave his father and mother and hold fast to his wife, and the two shall become one flesh." This mystery is profound, and I am saying that it refers to Christ and the church. However, let each one of you love his wife as himself, and let the wife see that she respects her husband. Ephesians 5:22-33

Sometimes our mission field is as close as the other side of the bed. Scripture reminds us that marriage very much resembles our relationship with the Lord. Just as He has loved us and cared for us, and it is our duty to submit to Him, one of the best ways a wife can serve Christ is by respecting her husband. One of the best ways a husband can serve Christ is by loving his wife, with the same kind of tenderness Christ shows for the Church.

Jesus has commissioned us to be missionaries of mercy wherever we go, but it starts at home. If we are not willing to submit to those Christ has placed in authority over us, we are not truly willing to submit to Christ, either. We are ignoring His chain of command, as surely as if we were in the army, and would only take orders from a general, but never a sergeant.

If we claim to love Christ, but treat our wives harshly, we are not only dishonoring Jesus, but according to scripture, we are hurting ourselves, as surely as if we were beating on our own body!

..Let each one of you love his wife as himself, and let the wife see that she respects her husband.

Talk about a close-up mission field! But this is where it starts.

Servant of All

Won Without a Word

Likewise, wives, be subject to your own husbands, so that even if some do not obey the word, they may be won without a word by the conduct of their wives—when they see your respectful and pure conduct. Do not let your adorning be external—the braiding of hair, the wearing of gold, or the putting on of clothing—but let your adorning be the hidden person of the heart with the imperishable beauty of a gentle and quiet spirit, which in God's sight is very precious. For this is how the holy women who hoped in God used to adorn themselves, by submitting to their husbands, as Sarah obeyed Abraham, calling him lord. And you are her children, if you do good and do not fear anything that is frightening.

Likewise, husbands, live with your wives in an understanding way, showing honor to the woman as the weaker vessel, since they are heirs with you of the grace of life, so that your prayers may not be hindered.
1 Peter 3:1-7

In an age when this entire passage sounds so antiquated, and feminists would be quick to pounce on it as an example of the "offensive," "patriarchal" nature of the Bible, if we would really listen to what God is saying to us, we just might find the answer we so desperately seek, particularly regarding ongoing tensions between husbands and wives.

The all-too-common situation endured by church-going wives is having an apathetic husband. Well-intended nagging about spiritual things ("Why won't you be the spiritual leader of our home?" "Please come to church with me!") seems to have little effect. This problem is not new, and the Bible gives the answer: The wife's *respectful and pure conduct.* Respect will win him over without a word; nagging only drives him away. A *"gentle and quiet spirit"* is not only very precious in God's sight, but in the sight of a husband who longs to receive respect, even if it might be undeserved. Once again, "serving the Lord" starts with serving our spouse.

As for the Christian husband, serving God begins with living with our wife in an understanding way, showing honor to her as an equal. Unresolved issues in that area will definitely hinder our prayers! It's because our first God-given mission is to love our wife as Christ loved the Church, and gave Himself for it. This "service" thing definitely begins at home.

Servant of All

A Tender Heart, And a Humble Mind

Finally, all of you, have unity of mind, sympathy, brotherly love, a tender heart, and a humble mind.

Do not repay evil for evil or reviling for reviling, but on the contrary, bless, for to this you were called, that you may obtain a blessing. For "Whoever desires to love life and see good days, let him keep his tongue from evil and his lips from speaking deceit; let him turn away from evil and do good; let him seek peace and pursue it. For the eyes of the Lord are on the righteous, and his ears are open to their prayer. But the face of the Lord is against those who do evil." 1 Peter 3:8-12

This wonderful little passage of practical advice could, all by itself, dramatically change a person's life. Want to "love life and see good days"? It's simple: Keep your tongue from evil and your lips from deceitful speech. Seek peace and pursue it. When evil comes against you, return blessing, because this is your calling.

I particularly like the admonition to have *a tender heart, and a humble mind*. Neither is easy to come by. It's hard to keep a tender heart when going through painful circumstances, or when being overlooked, criticized or abused in some way. Likewise, it's a challenge to have a "humble mind," particularly in the wake of an advanced education, plus the wisdom gained by experience and study. Humility of mind seems to decrease as the degrees and accolades begin to pile up, at least in the natural realm.

But we're talking a supernatural realm here, one where a person can still have *a tender heart, and a humble mind*, even after years of adversity and years of schooling. It is that tenderness of heart and humility of mind which will enable a person to be led into areas of wisdom and even greatness that would be denied those who became bitter or hardened along the way, or whose accumulated learning caused them to stop learning, because they stopped seeking to learn.

Lord, I don't know all the answers, and never will, here on earth. Please help me to have *a tender heart, and a humble mind*, no matter what.

Servant of All

Captain of the Mis-Fits

David departed from there and escaped to the cave of Adullam. And when his brothers and all his father's house heard it, they went down there to him. And everyone who was in distress, and everyone who was in debt, and everyone who was bitter in soul, gathered to him. And he became captain over them. And there were with him about four hundred men.
1 Samuel 22:1-2

As Chuck Swindoll has said, "The cave of Adullam was no Holiday Inn." David must have wondered, "Can't I even hide by myself?!" Four hundred mis-fits who are in debt or bitter come and find him, and this is what he has to work with. I can only imagine the kind of folks he has with him! He gets to be captain of them. So this is what an anointing gets you?!

Lord, I'm reminded that we often don't get to pick our own team, in your service. You send us ornery, bitter people with nothing but needs, then require that we help them! It's because we *are* in your service, and you have sufficient resources for every need, both ours and theirs, that You entrust these people to our care. You allowed that motley bunch to end up under David's leadership, not because he needed *them*, but because they needed *him*, rather than Saul. You apparently gave him all the resources required, and he survived. Before David was ready to be king of Israel, he needed to learn how to be captain of the mis-fits.

You are good, and Your plans are good! That's a concept onto which David had to cling, even for years, and most of us who have attempted to follow You have found ourselves dangling by that same hope. "This is not what I had in mind, and these are not the people I was hoping would be on my team, but I'm committed to serving You, which means serving them."

When the anointing finally kicked in, and David eventually found himself king over all Israel, there emerged a special bodyguard, "The Thirty," David's most trusted men. I wonder how many of "The Thirty" had once been with David in the cave of Adullam.

Lord, help me not to be picky about whom it is I will serve, or whom I am willing to serve alongside. "Servant of *all*" is the phrase. Help me to love whomever You put in my cave.

Servant of All

Called To a Different Standard

"But I say to you who hear, Love your enemies, do good to those who hate you, bless those who curse you, pray for those who abuse you. To one who strikes you on the cheek, offer the other also, and from one who takes away your cloak do not withhold your tunic either. Give to everyone who begs from you, and from one who takes away your goods do not demand them back. And as you wish that others would do to you, do so to them.

If you love those who love you, what benefit is that to you? For even sinners love those who love them. And if you do good to those who do good to you, what benefit is that to you? For even sinners do the same. And if you lend to those from whom you expect to receive, what credit is that to you? Even sinners lend to sinners, to get back the same amount. But love your enemies, and do good, and lend, expecting nothing in return, and your reward will be great, and you will be sons of the Most High, for he is kind to the ungrateful and the evil. Be merciful, even as your Father is merciful.

"Judge not, and you will not be judged; condemn not, and you will not be condemned; forgive, and you will be forgiven; give, and it will be given to you. Good measure, pressed down, shaken together, running over, will be put into your lap. For with the measure you use it will be measured back to you." Luke 6:27-38

We get to choose our standard. We may either live by the standard of this world or the standard of our Lord. The world's standard does not demand much which is unexpected; the Father's standard requires us to be kind to even the ungrateful and evil. It is precisely in this way that we show ourselves to be His children, because when we are merciful, generous and loving, we are revealing ourselves to be people after His own character.

The same scenario applies to judging and condemning others: We get to choose the measuring stick which will be held up against our own lives—it's the exact same standard we applied to others.

In giving, forgiving, judging, lending, showing mercy and responding to insult, we have the opportunity to choose whose standard we will live by—the Father's or the world's. In those day-to-day choices, we bear witness to our true Master. If I were a child of the world, I wouldn't have to bother with it. But I want to live as a son of the Most High.

Servant of All
The Servanthood Seminar

An argument arose among them as to which of them was the greatest. But Jesus, knowing the reasoning of their hearts, took a child and put him by his side and said to them, "Whoever receives this child in my name receives me, and whoever receives me receives him who sent me. For he who is least among you all is the one who is great."

John answered, "Master, we saw someone casting out demons in your name, and we tried to stop him, because he does not follow with us." But Jesus said to him, "Do not stop him, for the one who is not against you is for you." Luke 9:46-50

Not only is there a tendency among us to constantly compare our status; there is also a tendency to mistrust anyone who does not march to the same drumbeat to which we're accustomed. What is it that makes us want to climb over people to reach the top, or shut the door on those who are different or who color outside the lines?

There is usually a line forming when it comes to leadership—particularly if there's any significant amount of power or prestige attached to the position; I don't notice the same phenomenon taking place when it comes to serving. There are leadership seminars, leadership books galore—today I even saw a "leadership" Bible—but when I read the Bible, I see passage after passage about aspiring to be a servant, and few if any about trying to be a leader. I think we're missing something!

For years I have gotten slick mail advertisements touting the latest seminar or conference guaranteed to turn me into a world-class leader; I'm trying to recall if I've ever been invited to a conference about being a servant. I don't think I ever have. If we pay our money and take the time, we ought to have a reasonable expectation of this thing helping us to get further *up* the ladder, not down, right?

And here's Jesus, one more time, emphasizing that the great person is not the well-accredited "leader," with amazing charisma and a forceful yet winsome personality. Rather, *"he who is least among you all is the one who is great."* That message probably won't fill many auditoriums, especially at $300 a pop. But at least that message is in the Bible. Lots.

Servant of All

Unplanned Mercy

But he, desiring to justify himself, said to Jesus, "And who is my neighbor?" Jesus replied, "A man was going down from Jerusalem to Jericho, and he fell among robbers, who stripped him and beat him and departed, leaving him half dead. Now by chance a priest was going down that road, and when he saw him he passed by on the other side. So likewise a Levite, when he came to the place and saw him, passed by on the other side. But a Samaritan, as he journeyed, came to where he was, and when he saw him, he had compassion. He went to him and bound up his wounds, pouring on oil and wine. Then he set him on his own animal and brought him to an inn and took care of him. And the next day he took out two denarii and gave them to the innkeeper, saying, 'Take care of him, and whatever more you spend, I will repay you when I come back.' Which of these three, do you think, proved to be a neighbor to the man who fell among the robbers?" He said, "The one who showed him mercy." And Jesus said to him, "You go, and do likewise." Luke 10:29-37

What strikes me the most today about this story is the unplanned nature of the Samaritan's response. He didn't set out looking for someone to help; he wasn't doing this as part of a program to help poor, wounded Jews everywhere—he was responding to the need he saw in front of him, to the best of his ability, then going on about his business. There is such a lesson in here for people like me, who tend to think in terms of comprehensive, incremental solutions, and who then give up before starting because the problem is too vast and my resources too small.

It seems that I need help, in order to get it right. I need the Holy Spirit to tip me off that there is a test coming, and that I need to respond in love to the situation before me. Otherwise, my tendency is to notice the problem and go home to work on some sort of big plan for dealing with it, soon to get discouraged or distracted, and eventually to forget the whole thing. I like to plan out my mercy. Unfortunately, that's the stage in which it often remains—the planning, good intention stage. I usually don't do very well with unplanned opportunities. So how do I pass the unplanned mercy test, especially when I don't know it's coming?

Unplanned mercy happens when mercy is *always* the plan.

Servant of All

Fighting For the Cheap Seats

Now he told a parable to those who were invited, when he noticed how they chose the places of honor, saying to them, "When you are invited by someone to a wedding feast, do not sit down in a place of honor, lest someone more distinguished than you be invited by him, and he who invited you both will come and say to you, 'Give your place to this person,' and then you will begin with shame to take the lowest place. But when you are invited, go and sit in the lowest place, so that when your host comes he may say to you, 'Friend, move up higher.' Then you will be honored in the presence of all who sit at table with you. For everyone who exalts himself will be humbled, and he who humbles himself will be exalted."
Luke 14:7-11

Aggression is so much a part of our culture that those who don't exhibit it, rather than being praised, will more likely be criticized for it, even by members of their own family. It's painful for parents to watch their non-aggressive children play soccer, when they politely let their opponents get to the ball before they do. "Be aggressive! Get in there and fight for the ball!" Back in the van after the game, they are then yelled at because they're hogging the treats. Aggression: "Turn it on!" "Now turn it off!" "You snooze, you lose." "Nice guys finish last." "Nice guys are lucky if they even finish!"

There's never much of a fight for the cheap seats. We are geared to grab the best, and feel it's our birthright. (Remember James and John?) And along comes Jesus, once again, to tell us to seek out the cheap seats, to not just settle for the lowest places but to pursue them, to remind us that "... *everyone who exalts himself will be humbled, and he who humbles himself will be exalted."*

Learning from Jesus Christ instead of learning from the world is a daily mind-washing experience! There's a lot to get rid of, a lot that needs to be cleared away in our way of thinking. To follow Christ is humbling, but I guess that's the idea. Humility isn't learned at the head of the line, nor the places of honor. You get humility in the cheap seats. Then comes honor.

Servant of All

A Channel of God's Kindness

When she rose to glean, Boaz instructed his young men, saying, "Let her glean even among the sheaves, and do not reproach her. And also pull out some from the bundles for her and leave it for her to glean, and do not rebuke her."

So she gleaned in the field until evening. Then she beat out what she had gleaned, and it was about an ephah (3/5 bushel) of barley. And she took it up and went into the city. Her mother-in-law saw what she had gleaned. She also brought out and gave her what food she had left over after being satisfied. And her mother-in-law said to her, "Where did you glean today? And where have you worked? Blessed be the man who took notice of you." So she told her mother-in-law with whom she had worked and said, "The man's name with whom I worked today is Boaz." And Naomi said to her daughter-in-law, "May he be blessed by the LORD, whose kindness has not forsaken the living or the dead!" Ruth 2:15-20

Ruth is a book about kindness: God's, Boaz's, Ruth's. It is such a sweet and wonderful story, one that began so badly and turned out so well. Kind of like the story of mankind! There is a Redeemer for all of us!

Boaz is kind to Ruth, but he seems to be kind to everybody! One of the best ways we can serve God is by serving others, noticing them, appreciating their kindnesses and faithfulness. Boaz does all of that and more for Ruth. He's thinking about Ruth's dignity, about her needs, about her devotion, about her emotions in leaving her own country, about her safety....he commends her for her character... Here is a man who really is concerned for the needs of others. Help me to be that kind of man, Lord, especially around the wife and the children you have given me, but also around others. Help me to be a reflection of your love.

Boaz is a channel of God's kindness. That kindness begins to turn around the bitterness Naomi has felt for so long. Her reaction to Ruth's return shows she's getting it: "Where have you been?! Who took notice of you?!" *And Naomi said to her daughter-in-law, "May he be blessed by the LORD, whose kindness has not forsaken the living or the dead!"*

Not only does God's kindness lead us toward repentance—it's God's kindness that rekindles hope.

Servant of All

Selfish Salvation

We who are strong have an obligation to bear with the failings of the weak, and not to please ourselves. Let each of us please his neighbor for his good, to build him up.

For Christ did not please himself, but as it is written, "The reproaches of those who reproached you fell on me." For whatever was written in former days was written for our instruction, that through endurance and through the encouragement of the Scriptures we might have hope. May the God of endurance and encouragement grant you to live in such harmony with one another, in accord with Christ Jesus, that together you may with one voice glorify the God and Father of our Lord Jesus Christ. Therefore welcome one another as Christ has welcomed you, for the glory of God. Romans 15:1-7

I'm uncomfortable with the individual nature of Christianity in America, the philosophy that says, "As long as I have my own personal relationship with the Lord, everything's O.K." Again and again, the Bible reminds us of a great deal of responsibility for one another, from the first chapters of Genesis ("Am I my brother's keeper?") to Revelation, where we are referred to as a kingdom of priests. Priests have a responsibility for others, as well as themselves. We are saved, not so we can smugly look down on other people, but so we can help them into the lifeboat, too.

It doesn't stop with getting them into the lifeboat. If we really are as strong as we think we are, we are called upon to use that strength to help people besides ourselves to continue in the Christian walk. As Christ bears with our failings and shortcomings, we are to bear with one another. We are to look for ways to build up, rather than criticize.

The Christian life is not a solo pursuit. We can't just say "I'm serving God," and have nothing to do with fellow servants. Part of our service to God is treating our fellow servants with love and respect. God's glory is not found in a bunch of individuals each doing their own thing, independently, but when they encourage one another and live in harmony. If we serve each other like Christ serves us and we learn to join together in praising God, if we discard the attitude that lets us be selfish with our salvation, the world will see us glorifying God with one voice, and many will praise Him, too.

April 30

Servant of All

The Name to Proclaim

For what we proclaim is not ourselves, but Jesus Christ as Lord, with ourselves as your servants for Jesus' sake. 2 Corinthians 4:5

Really? *Really?* Is what we proclaim *not ourselves, but Jesus Christ as Lord, with ourselves as your servants for Jesus' sake?*

I think I may be on to part of our problem.

Just last night, I saw a television show advertised featuring the latest, greatest superstar pastor. I don't want to criticize someone I've never even met—obviously God has granted him a huge degree of success—but time after time in these scenarios, with precious few exceptions, what I'm seeing is the "name" being proclaimed—and the name is not Jesus; it's the name of the rising superstar. An empire sprouts seemingly overnight, the name and face are everywhere, and all too often, what happens next is that someone sees that face in a place it's not supposed to be, doing something no Christian should be doing, the empire implodes, and when it's all a big mess, suddenly then the name of Jesus appears, to be stuck to this embarrassment.

If we *started* with proclaiming the name of Jesus, we'd do a lot better! If we refused to get on the Christian celebrity bandwagon, and focused on *serving* a non-Christian world instead of trying to razzle-dazzle them, we'd be more on track. Sadly, we have a hard time resisting the temptation to proclaim ourselves, even though "ourselves" are absolutely nothing without the grace of God. "Ourselves" are not supposed to be jostling each other up the ladder of fame, in order to lead the biggest churches in America, or have our face plastered on the sides of busses. "Ourselves" are not what we're supposed to be proclaiming; Jesus Christ is what we are supposed to be proclaiming.

Once again, serving is the answer. The unsaved world simply doesn't need more people offering to "lead" them, but they desperately need more people who are willing to serve them in the name of Jesus. We have a name to proclaim, and a job to do. Let's get started.

Promises to Servants

An Assigned Kingdom

A dispute also arose among them, as to which of them was to be regarded as the greatest. And he said to them, "The kings of the Gentiles exercise lordship over them, and those in authority over them are called benefactors. But not so with you. Rather, let the greatest among you become as the youngest, and the leader as one who serves. For who is the greater, one who reclines at table or one who serves? Is it not the one who reclines at table? But I am among you as the one who serves.

"You are those who have stayed with me in my trials, and I assign to you, as my Father assigned to me, a kingdom, that you may eat and drink at my table in my kingdom and sit on thrones judging the twelve tribes of Israel." Luke 22:24-30

The frequent theme of Jesus' teaching cuts through the frequent argument of the disciples: They kept wondering who was the greatest; Jesus kept telling them that leadership is all about serving. He once again corrects their perspective, but doesn't stop there. He goes beyond mild correction and adds an unfathomable promise: An assigned kingdom and authority beyond their wildest dreams.

Why so much? It is the purpose of the Lord to give us responsibility that excites us, and relationship that satisfies. He doesn't want us to play the world's frustrating game of "King of the Mountain" where every individual is either trying to gain the top spot or hold on to it and keep from losing it to another. God's "game" is fulfilling, builds a beautiful, winsome, peaceful character within people, and results in eternal reward and eternal relationship with God, Himself.

We get to choose our approach. We can either fight to be "King of the Mountain," worldly style, or we can serve, Jesus-style, and be *assigned* a kingdom by the Lord, Himself. We can claw our way toward the top, friendless and alone, seeking only power and fleeting authority, or we could endure trials at the feet of Jesus, not give up, and be granted not just unbelievable authority but eternal access to the heart of God, in unbroken fellowship and *friendship* with Him, forever. Is this supposed to be a hard choice?! Once we get the first taste of what it is to sit at God's table, only an idiot would ever leave to return to the dog-eat-dog games of the world.

Servant of All

None of Us Is Alone

Brothers, if anyone is caught in any transgression, you who are spiritual should restore him in a spirit of gentleness. Keep watch on yourself, lest you too be tempted. Bear one another's burdens, and so fulfill the law of Christ. For if anyone thinks he is something, when he is nothing, he deceives himself. But let each one test his own work, and then his reason to boast will be in himself alone and not in his neighbor. For each will have to bear his own load. One who is taught the word must share all good things with the one who teaches. Do not be deceived: God is not mocked, for whatever one sows, that will he also reap. For the one who sows to his own flesh will from the flesh reap corruption, but the one who sows to the Spirit will from the Spirit reap eternal life. And let us not grow weary of doing good, for in due season we will reap, if we do not give up. So then, as we have opportunity, let us do good to everyone, and especially to those who are of the household of faith. Galatians 6:1-10

The Christian life is not a matter of walking alone with Christ. He has tied us together in such a way that everywhere we look, there is responsibility to our fellow man, particularly to those who also are followers of Christ. We are responsible for the gentle restoration of transgressors. We are responsible to bear one another's burdens; it's not just "everyone for themselves." We are responsible to keep a handle on pride, and not make ourselves worthless by supercharging our own egos. We are responsible to be generous with what we've been given, particularly in sharing with our teachers. We are responsible to sow to the Spirit, not the flesh, knowing that whatever we plant is what will return to us, many fold. We are responsible to keep doing good, even when we get tired and our efforts seem in vain. We are responsible to do good to everyone, but particularly those who are fellow Christians.

We're talking a lot of responsibility! We're also talking a lot of reward! Every single thing done in Jesus' name will return to us—there's a harvest and a reward. Saved by works? No, that's not how we get into the Kingdom. But there's work to do for everyone in God's Kingdom, and we are not to walk alone, or satisfy ourselves in merely looking out for our own needs. The wonderful responsibility we've been granted means none of us is on our own.

Servant of All

Servant of Whom? Servant of All

And he sat down and called the twelve. And he said to them, "If anyone would be first, he must be last of all and servant of all." Mark 9:35

"But whoever would be great among you must be your servant, and whoever would be first among you must be slave of all. For even the Son of Man came not to be served but to serve, and to give his life as a ransom for many." Mark 10:43-45

To serve Jesus Christ is to receive the commission to be a "servant of all." This is not "selective service," where we get to choose the objects of our service, the people on our team or the types of jobs we will do; this is Christlike service, where the leader is the servant, and the most mature disciple is the one who habitually heads for the least desirable place. The line to greatness forms at the rear.

The story of the Good Samaritan reminds me that unplanned mercy happens when mercy is *always* the plan. The story of Ruth and Boaz paints a picture of how one person can be a channel of God's kindness, especially when blessing others is made a life habit, and it's practiced indiscriminately.

Serving is the answer, and in our world, "leadership" is overrated. What is often called "leadership" is in reality only pride elbowing its way to the top. Jesus directs His followers *away* from the best seats, the prestige and authority, and *toward* the tasks no one else dared or cared to do. The unsaved world simply doesn't need more people offering to "lead" them, but they desperately need more people who are willing to serve them in the name of Jesus. That's where we come in: "Servant of all"—it's in there again and again. We can try to ignore it, or relegate the philosophy to ancient times, but every time the real Jesus shows up, real service shows up along with Him. We might as well accept the fact that when we sign up to serve Christ, we are signing up to be "servant of all." That's a *good* thing.

Signs of Servanthood

Our Times Belong To Him

Remember the Sabbath day, to keep it holy. Exodus 20:8

I gave them my statutes and made known to them my rules, by which, if a person does them, he shall live. Moreover, I gave them my Sabbaths, as a sign between me and them, that they might know that I am the LORD who sanctifies them. Ezekiel 20:11-12

If a service truck pulls up in our driveway, it's not too difficult to tell whose truck it is—there's almost always a company logo emblazoned all over the truck, or at least on the doors. The man who comes to the door will be wearing a uniform representing his company. Even the receipt he leaves with us bears the organization's identifying marks. The desire of the company is that everyone would know whose truck this is, whose employee this is, and who should get the credit for what was hopefully a job well done.

The servant of Christ Jesus likewise bears identifying marks. The world shouldn't have to guess at whose servant we are! They should be able to tell almost right away that we are servants of the Lord. He's the One who should be getting the credit for the good we do in His name.

There are signs of servanthood. The main sign is that we are carrying out our Father's commands—we are obeying His instructions. It's obvious that we aren't writing our own script, but are approaching life from the perspective of one who serves another.

A sign so key that it was given in the context of the Ten Commandments is the sign of the Sabbath. The observance of the seventh day set the Israelites apart from all other nations. When they kept the Sabbath, their entire culture was giving witness as to whose Law they were keeping. Many Christians these days have come to totally disregard the fourth commandment (sometimes along with the other nine!). While the Pharisees of Jesus' time had wrongly turned Sabbath-keeping into a ridiculous burden, it seems that American Christians have made it into a meaningless option, to be taken or left according to our whims, when God intended the Sabbath to be one of the signs of His Lordship over our lives. Somehow, people need to see that we belong to Him. Observing the Sabbath is still a good way to show His Lordship.

Signs of Servanthood

A Sign That I Belong To Him

*I am the LORD your God; walk in my statutes, and be careful to obey
my rules, and keep my Sabbaths holy that they may be a sign between me
and you, that you may know that I am the LORD your God. But the children rebelled against me. They did not walk in my statutes and were not
careful to obey my rules, by which, if a person does them, he shall live; they
profaned my Sabbaths.*

*Then I said I would pour out my wrath upon them and spend my anger
against them in the wilderness.* Ezekiel 20:19-21

The Sabbaths were a sign of God's ownership over the Israelites. It
was a silent national witness. Although it was silent, it was powerful! It
was the kind of witness America used to have, too. When the nation used
to pretty much shut down on Sunday, for religious reasons, rather than just
people wanting a day off, there was a witness even as a nation.

How far away from that are we, now? Even within the Church, do we
have a witness of God's ownership over us? How many things in a given
week do we do just because "God says," with no other reason?

I realize that the Pharisees turned Sabbath-keeping into a religion all
by itself, and made the "witness" of pretty much no effect, but Christians
have come to so neglect even the concept of a Sabbath that we also have
very little witness in the matter.

When we ignore this historic symbol of God's ownership, one so important that it's one of the Ten Commandments, we are at the very least
missing an opportunity to witness to God's importance in our lives. And
at worst, we are rebelling against Him. We are using our "freedom" from
rules and regulations as license to abandon one of the most effective ways
of showing our allegiance to God.

Maybe the Sabbath is a little like a wedding ring. It's not a legal requirement—one doesn't have to wear a ring in order to be married. But
the wearing of a wedding ring is a sign to the world that I am married, and
I gladly wear that symbol so everyone will know that I belong to someone.

God made *all* the days—the days *all* belong to Him. But when I regularly take the Sabbath day to worship Him, honor Him, and rest in Him, it
becomes obvious to others that *I* belong to Him, too—willingly. It's a sign.

Signs of Servanthood

The Witness of Parked Tractors

Thus the heavens and the earth were finished, and all the host of them. And on the seventh day God finished his work that he had done, and he rested on the seventh day from all his work that he had done. So God blessed the seventh day and made it holy, because on it God rested from all his work that he had done in creation. Genesis 2:1-3

The Sabbath is the rhythm of God. I don't think God was the least bit tired, after creating the heavens and the earth, but He chose to rest. Many a Sunday, growing up, I moaned to my napping parents, "But I'm not tired!" They didn't require me to sleep, but they did require me to attend church, and to refrain from unnecessary labor. (The last part didn't require much persuasion). We took care of the livestock, as always, but even during planting or harvest, the farming equipment lay idle on Sunday, even as we could hear the roar of a neighbor's tractor in the distance.

It wasn't hard for other farmers to know we were Christians. All they had to do was drive by on Sunday, and they knew. It was the witness of the parked tractors, and the absent car. We were at church, worshiping the One who had determined the rhythm of our lives. Staying on His rhythm was more important to us than the very harvest that would provide an income for our family. The harvest belonged to Him, too. The land, the money, the days—all His. We are His. It pleases Him when we watch for His signals, wait for His instructions, attempt to imitate Him, like I used to try to imitate my Dad, walking behind him, trying to match his gait, stride for stride. My Heavenly Father is pleased when I try to imitate His rhythm, when I start and stop at His direction, when, rather than rebelling against His authority over my life, I relish it, to the point of being willing to do or not do things for no other reason than that "God said."

When the rain is coming and the crops aren't in yet, it's not too hard to tell that it's a God-loving farmer whose tractors are parked neatly in a row on a sunny Sabbath, while he's in the house taking an after-church nap. It isn't just the neighbors who notice, either. The Creator of heaven and earth sees, too, and smiles.

Signs of Servanthood

When Push Comes To Shove

And when they had brought them, they set them before the council. And the high priest questioned them, saying, "We strictly charged you not to teach in this name, yet here you have filled Jerusalem with your teaching, and you intend to bring this man's blood upon us." But Peter and the apostles answered, "We must obey God rather than men."...

And when they had called in the apostles, they beat them and charged them not to speak in the name of Jesus, and let them go. Then they left the presence of the council, rejoicing that they were counted worthy to suffer dishonor for the name. And every day, in the temple and from house to house, they did not cease teaching and preaching Jesus as the Christ.
Acts 5:27-29,40-42

Whom are we serving, God or men? Sometimes, especially in a nation with a strong Christian heritage, we get to please both. We do something great for God, and the culture thinks it's great, too. An example is the relief trip I was on to help victims of Hurricane Katrina. When 103 people from 18 different denominations or churches in a town 3,000 miles away get together to fly to Mississippi and help perfect strangers, even the world thinks that's pretty cool. A lot of the time, we get to serve God *by* serving men, in the name of Jesus.

Then there are the other times. There are the times when push has come to shove, and we look at the situation, knowing this isn't a hypothetical deal—we have to choose between serving God or serving men—and either way, it's going to be expensive. Either we whimp out on God, and cave in to the demands of the world, or we stand for God, and bear the consequences. We show whom we're really serving in those times when we have to make a difficult choice and we consistently choose God.

The disciples didn't want to offend people any more than we do, today. The sign of their servanthood comes when they quickly choose to obey God, even when they fully understand that this is going to be very costly for them. Not only do they take their beating, but they rejoice in it afterward! How do you defeat people like this?! You don't. If we are going to get anywhere in America, we'd better toughen up, and *expect* some suffering, if we're going to obey God rather than men.

Signs of Servanthood

The Joy of Obedience

And the word of the Lord was spreading throughout the whole region. But the Jews incited the devout women of high standing and the leading men of the city, stirred up persecution against Paul and Barnabas, and drove them out of their district. But they shook off the dust from their feet against them and went to Iconium. And the disciples were filled with joy and the Holy Spirit. Acts 13:49-52

Paul and Barnabas have had mixed success in Pisidian Antioch. Some believe, some get mad. The missionaries do what they can, and move on.

So, how can a person be filled with joy and the Holy Spirit, when the results don't seem to be cause for joy? How can you be joyful when people actually hate you?! How can there be joy without success?

It's the joy of obedience. The joy of God's servant does not depend on the "success" enjoyed by that servant. It is apart from success. The joy has to do with obedience. There is a joy which comes when we have done what the Holy Spirit instructed us to do, even if our actions resulted in rejection or seeming failure.

It's the joy of asking forgiveness from someone you didn't even wrong, when your apology only brings a grunt in return, and walking away free, because you did what God told you to do.

It's the joy that comes when you preach or teach the Word of God, even when there was only stiff-necked opposition to the message, and no visible positive response. It wasn't about the results; it was about faithfully delivering the message from God.

There is a joy which accompanies obedience to God which is not connected with the outward results of that obedience. In fact, joy *is* the result! The consequence of obeying God is inward joy, irregardless of outward consequences. That's the kind of thing that gets us through days when we've been offered the left foot of fellowship, just because we said or did as God instructed us.

And the disciples were filled with joy and the Holy Spirit. That can be me! Any time.

Signs of Servanthood
It Shows In the Planning

And they went through the region of Phrygia and Galatia, having been forbidden by the Holy Spirit to speak the word in Asia. And when they had come up to Mysia, they attempted to go into Bithynia, but the Spirit of Jesus did not allow them. So, passing by Mysia, they went down to Troas. And a vision appeared to Paul in the night: a man of Macedonia was standing there, urging him and saying, "Come over to Macedonia and help us." And when Paul had seen the vision, immediately we sought to go on into Macedonia, concluding that God had called us to preach the gospel to them. Acts 16:6-10

What kind of strategic planning is this?! Obviously not man's planning. What seems to be confusion and indecision is in reality the perfect guidance of the Holy Spirit.

They skip Asia because the Holy Spirit "forbid them," and the same thing for Bithynia. They end up crossing the sea to arrive in Macedonia. They had a plan, but it was subject to God's guidance, and when the Holy Spirit indicated otherwise, they *did* otherwise! They're not really under a system, here, of man's making; they are under the guidance of the Holy Spirit. Knowing that really helps, when encountering difficulties!

Once in Macedonia, they cast out a demon, get beaten with rods and are thrown in jail. They are fastened in the stocks, and spend their time praying and singing hymns to God, with the other prisoners listening. After the earthquake God sends, the jailer is converted, due to Paul and Silas' kindness. The girl with the demon was right: *"These men are servants of the Most High God, who proclaim to you the way of salvation."* (Ac 16:17)

One of the distinguishing characteristics of these early missionaries was that their mission was obviously being orchestrated by God. It's one more of those signs of servanthood: It shows up in the planning. They don't even make plans without praying through, and seeking God's direction. They're willing to change course at a moment's notice, if they know it's the Holy Spirit. They're willing to face what seems to be disaster, and praise God through it, knowing it's His will for them to be there.

When we let God make the plans for our lives, it becomes quite obvious to everyone who our real Leader is. I want to be a "servant of the Most High God."

May 10

Instructions from The Right Voice

And many of the Corinthians hearing Paul believed and were baptized. And the Lord said to Paul one night in a vision, "Do not be afraid, but go on speaking and do not be silent, for I am with you, and no one will attack you to harm you, for I have many in this city who are my people." And he stayed a year and six months, teaching the word of God among them. Acts 18:8-11

After about so many times getting beaten up, persecuted, jailed, etc., one would start to get a little gun-shy! Paul has been through it all—he is desperately in need of a place where he can minister in peace—and God gives him one. There is probably not any way to overestimate the significance to a weary apostle of this vision from God. At last, he knows what is in store for him, at least for a time. He knows what he is supposed to do, he has a promise of personal safety from God—it's all he needs!

Sometimes what a servant needs is just the voice of his Master, reminding him that the Master is near. That single sentence of encouragement was enough to fuel Paul for 18 months! What a great Master we have!

Another blessing for Paul was that God provided not only an encouraging promise of protection, but He also provided a plan: Keep speaking, stay here a while.

How many of my efforts have been wasted through the years because I spent all kinds of time concocting grandiose plans for God to bless, when all He wanted of me at the time was to be attentive so that He could give me *His* plan! He wasn't asking strategy of me at the time, just obedience! There have been times when I didn't even ask God for the general direction He wanted me to go, much less the specifics. Let's see: My plan, my idea, my goals, my strategy... and I'll call this "serving God." Something's wrong with this picture! If He's really the Master, I'll bet that means He makes the plans and gives the commands, and the only authority anyone else has is whatever authority He may have delegated.

Paul understood who should be making the plans. I don't think his entire missionary team could have persuaded Paul to remain in Corinth for a year and a half, with a world to still be won for Christ, but God did it with one sentence, in a vision! If we listen to the right voice, we'll never go wrong.

Serving God   137

Signs of Servanthood

Looking For Whose Approval?

For am I now seeking the approval of man, or of God? Or am I trying to please man? If I were still trying to please man, I would not be a servant (bondservant) of Christ. Galatians 1:10

This is important. I need to let this sink in.

If I were still trying to please man, I would not be a servant (bondservant) of Christ.

If I'm trying to please man, I'm not really a bondservant of Christ. Really? Really. The master of my life will be shown clearly by whom I am trying to please consistently, by whose approval I seek first. If I'm seeking the approval of God, it will show in my life, and I may call myself a servant of Christ. On the other hand, if what most concerns me most is the approval of man, I need to realize that my allegiance is going to determine my usefulness to God—the only times when He can expect a response of obedience from me is if His orders happen to coincide with the wishes of mortals I am trying to impress. In effect, if my priority is man over God, I am deceiving myself to say that God is my Master.

Jesus Himself said it: *"No one can serve two masters."* (Mt 6:24) Either I strive to please Christ and serve Him, or I go ahead and try to please man; I can't do both.

I choose Christ. I will consistently obey His commands and His guidance, regardless of consequences. That doesn't mean that I'll always make man unhappy with me (fortunately), but if my motive is in trying to gain the favor of people, I'm not truly a servant of Christ; I'm a servant of man, hoping that Christ will be pleased. I choose to be a servant of Jesus Christ, glad for the times when man is also pleased, but willing to obey Christ, my Master, with or without the approval of man.

Signs of Servanthood

You Are Serving the Lord Christ

Wives, submit to your husbands, as is fitting in the Lord. Husbands, love your wives, and do not be harsh with them. Children, obey your parents in everything, for this pleases the Lord. Fathers, do not provoke your children, lest they become discouraged. Slaves, obey in everything those who are your earthly masters, not by way of eye-service, as people-pleasers, but with sincerity of heart, fearing the Lord. Whatever you do, work heartily, as for the Lord and not for men, knowing that from the Lord you will receive the inheritance as your reward. You are serving the Lord Christ. For the wrongdoer will be paid back for the wrong he has done, and there is no partiality.

Masters, treat your slaves justly and fairly, knowing that you also have a Master in heaven. Colossians 3:18-4:1

Nowhere does servanthood for Jesus Christ show up more plainly than in the home, or the day-to-day, routine things of life. This passage could be titled "How to Serve God on the Home Front." It's in the practical things that it becomes most obvious whom we are serving.

It's the wife who submits to her husband's authority, even though his idea seems foolish to her; she's not going along with it because she thinks it's a good idea—she's going along with it because she is a servant of Christ, and she believes that when she supports her husband, she is in actuality supporting the Lord—and she's right.

It's the husband who loves his wife and treats her with honor and tenderness when he feels like yelling at her, and is convinced that he has good cause to do just that. He shows that he is serving Christ because he is showing love to his wife.

It's the child who learns early to please God by obeying his parents.

It's the father who shows respect for his Heavenly Father by being consistently tender with his earthly children; the slave or employee who continues to work hard because he's really serving Jesus; the boss who acts like he has a master in heaven—because he does.

You are serving the Lord Christ. What a good, *daily* reminder. When it shows up in every relationship, and it motivates everything we do, the people who know us best see whom it is we serve—and are glad!

Signs of Servanthood

Proud Servant

He also told this parable to some who trusted in themselves that they were righteous, and treated others with contempt: "Two men went up into the temple to pray, one a Pharisee and the other a tax collector. The Pharisee, standing by himself, prayed thus: 'God, I thank you that I am not like other men, extortioners, unjust, adulterers, or even like this tax collector. I fast twice a week; I give tithes of all that I get.' But the tax collector, standing far off, would not even lift up his eyes to heaven, but beat his breast, saying, 'God, be merciful to me, a sinner!' I tell you, this man went down to his house justified, rather than the other. For everyone who exalts himself will be humbled, but the one who humbles himself will be exalted." Luke 18:9-14

"Proud servant"? It seems to be an oxymoron, yet there have been times when I've been one! God's servant, and proud of it! He should be honored to have me around, considering how valuable I am to Him!

Pride is a stumbling-block, which, of course, leads to a fall. Pride is a slippery sin, hard to pin down; it's a moving target. I conquer my pride in sinfulness, only to have it re-emerge as pride in righteousness! It's like trying to hold basketballs underwater. Pride fights its way to the top, one way or another.

Pride and true servanthood don't go together. But how do I rid myself of it? The only thing I've found that helps is when the focus is no longer on me. When I go down the road marked humility, and humble myself before God, at some point, it stops being about "me" at all; now it's about Him. If I don't do that, then I'm stuck with pride either way—either pride in my accomplishments or pride in my humility!

I never seem to get rid of pride until the focus is off of me and on to God. As long as I'm thinking about myself, pride is unavoidable, because self is in the middle of the picture, and I can't help but notice how well I'm doing. Pride in my achievements, or pride in my great humility! Either way, it's "me," and it's pride.

Humility is when I'm not even thinking about "me"—just Jesus, and I'm no longer even looking at the "pride meter." I stop being a "proud servant" when I no longer even know what my score is, and I no longer look.

Signs of Servanthood

Screening for God

Now they were bringing even infants to him that he might touch them. And when the disciples saw it, they rebuked them. But Jesus called them to him, saying, "Let the children come to me, and do not hinder them, for to such belongs the kingdom of God. Truly, I say to you, whoever does not receive the kingdom of God like a child shall not enter it." Luke 18:15-17

The disciples thought they were doing Jesus a favor. They were only screening for Him, running interference for Him so He would have time for the truly important things and the truly important people. They didn't get it, and I'm not sure I do, either. I guess maybe it goes back to the pride questions: Who's the greatest?" "Who's really important, and who is less important?" "What is too insignificant for God to be bothered with?"

I already know the answer to the first question. The greatest in the kingdom is the least, the servant. As to the second question, the pecking order question, when it comes to God's love for people, like a good parent, He refuses to prioritize us; He loves each of us with a love which defies description, and which is undiminished by His love for others.

Love makes a mess out of mathematics! In mathematics, if you have ten apples and you give one away, you only have nine apples left. In the world of love, if you could measure love quantitatively and you had ten measures of love, you could give away one measure and still have ten left. More likely, you could start out with ten, give away one and end up with 100!

Maybe that's why love can't be measured, especially God's love. His love is not reserved for the strong, the deserving, the important, those who can pay Him back. His love is unreserved, unrestrained, limitless and measureless! Not only does our God have time for babies who can't even talk back; He has time to keep track of the hairs on our head—and wants to! *("But even the hairs of your head are all numbered."* Mt. 10:30)

What is too insignificant for our God to care about? The answer is "Nothing." There's no sense in holding anything back, from a God like that. There's also no sense in trying to hold anyone else back, who's trying to get to Him! We needn't screen for God; He has time for each of us, and *all* of us. He lavishes His love and attention upon us in focused, measureless fashion—and there is never less love to go around; there's more. Let 'em in.

Signs of Servanthood

A Cut of God's Glory

Then he returned to the man of God, he and all his company, and he came and stood before him. And he said, "Behold, I know that there is no God in all the earth but in Israel; so accept now a present from your servant." But he said, "As the LORD lives, before whom I stand, I will receive none." And he urged him to take it, but he refused....

But when Naaman had gone from him a short distance, Gehazi, the servant of Elisha the man of God, said, "See, my master has spared this Naaman the Syrian, in not accepting from his hand what he brought. As the LORD lives, I will run after him and get something from him."...

He went in and stood before his master, and Elisha said to him, "Where have you been, Gehazi?" And he said, "Your servant went nowhere." But he said to him, "Did not my heart go when the man turned from his chariot to meet you? Was it a time to accept money and garments, olive orchards and vineyards, sheep and oxen, male servants and female servants? Therefore the leprosy of Naaman shall cling to you and to your descendants forever." So he went out from his presence a leper, like snow.
2 Kings 5:15-16,19-20,25-27

This is a wonderful story, with a sad epilogue. All the glory is going to God, until Gehazi grabs some for himself. The miracle started with the testimony of a servant girl, and continued with the careful obedience of Elisha. Elisha is about to let $70,000 worth of gifts go back to Syria, and God will get all the credit for His miracle, but Gehazi can't stand it anymore. He runs after Naaman and lies to him in order to get something, lies to Elisha upon his return, and in the process is making God out to be a liar. Gehazi thought this would be a win-win situation for everybody. In fact, it's just sin, which is always lose-lose for everybody. The servant who should have succeeded Elisha instead ends his days in leprosy, after marring the focus of a miracle of God, and changing it into a human transaction. Why is this passage making me feel uncomfortable?!

God's servants are worthy of honor and support, but that doesn't entitle us to a cut of God's glory, nor buy us the right to take advantage of people. When we're privileged to be part of a miracle of God, we dare not embezzle any of the credit due Him. Better leave the tip jar at home.

Signs of Servanthood

Down The Career Ladder

John answered, "A person cannot receive even one thing unless it is given him from heaven. You yourselves bear me witness, that I said, 'I am not the Christ, but I have been sent before him.' The one who has the bride is the bridegroom. The friend of the bridegroom, who stands and hears him, rejoices greatly at the bridegroom's voice. Therefore this joy of mine is now complete. He must increase, but I must decrease." John 3:27-30

John the Baptist has such a great attitude, when the crowds switch over from him to Jesus: *"He must increase, but I must decrease."* That's the reply of a true servant. It's one thing to allow God to lead you *up* the career ladder; it's quite another when He leads you *down*. "Decreasing for Jesus"—there's a concept that won't sell too many books! Why is it that we "followers" of Christ find it so difficult to follow Christ, if He's not leading to greener pastures, more recognition or better benefits? There's a kind of "ratchet" mentality among us: We'll follow Jesus *up*, but not *down*.

John the Baptist is willing to head *down* the career ladder, in order that Jesus might go up. He hits the nail on the head, when it comes to serving Jesus. He realizes that this is *not* about him; it's entirely about Jesus. Consequently, his "ministry" is not allowed to have any significance in John's mind. He won't go to any lengths to protect it, or to keep himself in the limelight. John allows his own disciples to drift over to Jesus, he watches his own "star" sink, never to return, he continues to speak boldly against sin and winds up in prison and even losing his head over it. He does have a time of doubt, during which he sends disciples to Jesus to double-check that Jesus is the Messiah, but John simply is a sterling example of what God would call a servant—and what an impact the life of one servant can be.

Lord, help me to be willing to decrease, if that's part of your plan! Decrease in salary, decrease in attendance, decrease in popularity,.... I'm not asking for trouble, but help me to be willing to accept decrease as readily as increase, for myself, so long as *you* increase! Whether I go up or down the career ladder, or even if you want me to get off the ladder entirely, I want *you* to increase. May people see how great You are.

Signs of Servanthood

Serving Is Part of The Reward

They have washed their robes and made them white in the blood of the
Lamb.
  "Therefore they are before the throne of God,
  and serve him day and night in his temple;
  and he who sits on the throne will shelter them with his presence."
Revelation 7:14-15

Though the passage is specifically referring to saints coming out of the great tribulation, the implication is clear for all of us: Not only is serving God our earthly mission; it's our eternal one. We'll go from serving Him day and night on earth to serving Him continually in heaven.

If serving God were the same thing as serving an earthly master, this would not be thrilling news! In many earthly situations, the reward for good service is more work and the resentment of fellow employees. Serving some earthly masters forever is an idea closer to "hell" than "heaven." But we're not talking about serving an earthly master, here; we're talking about serving Almighty God. Serving Him is so good that getting to do it forever is actually part of our reward! Serving God is not like "eternal slavery"—demeaning, thankless, endless tasks with no hope of escape. Serving God is more like getting to help Someone who is infinitely creative, who allows us to do more than hand Him things, who allows us to actively participate in astounding things He is doing. Serving God is getting to help Someone who can do anything and who never fails! If we are helping God, we cannot help but grow. We cannot help but succeed. We never have to stop!

What we are experiencing now on earth is something like the first year of school. That wasn't the end—that was preparation for learning for all the rest of life. Our lives here of serving God are like that first year of school, like learning to read. For all of eternity we will be putting to use the skills and faith we are learning right now! We're not being trained to walk by faith and obey God so we can spend forever glad that we learned something we barely ever put to use. Instead, this whole adventure is preparation for joyful and meaningful service beyond belief. Serving God is part of the reward!

May 18

Most of All, It Shows Up In Obedience

Moreover, he said to me, "Son of man, all my words that I shall speak to you receive in your heart, and hear with your ears. And go to the exiles, to your people, and speak to them and say to them, 'Thus says the LORD GOD,' whether they hear or refuse to hear." Ezekiel 3:10-11

For a while now, Ezekiel has been my least favorite book in the Bible. Ezekiel's task is so difficult, so thankless; his wife dies! He has to prophesy further destruction for his people, knowing in advance that they won't listen to him, regardless; he is required to do exceedingly difficult things as God's sign to people, knowing they won't be persuaded, anyway.

I guess the reason I've sometimes avoided the book is the same reason employees often make themselves scarce whenever undesirable jobs are needing "volunteers"—"Maybe the boss will forget I'm around, and pick somebody else!" Translated into Bible-reading philosophy: "Maybe if I don't read this book, God won't ask me to do hard things like He did Ezekiel. How about some Psalms, instead?"

I've found that neither bosses nor God forget about me if I lay low. They find me, anyway. In both situations, I do better if I just show up in the first place, accept whatever task I'm assigned, and *trust* them to do what is best. This especially works well with a God who can be totally trusted.

Prayer Journal:

Are you really willing to serve Me, no matter what? Or is your service limited to what you want to do, or what is convenient? Are you like a child who wants to "help," but only when it's fun or when it's easy, and you're not interested in things which are difficult or tedious or boring? The kind of servant I can truly use is the kind who will follow orders, no matter what. Do you want to be that kind of servant?

Yes.

Good.

If a servant is not living in obedience to the Master, he's not really a servant, no matter what he says he is.

May 19

Signs of Servanthood
Wicked, Lazy Servants

He also who had received the one talent came forward, saying, 'Master, I knew you to be a hard man, reaping where you did not sow, and gathering where you scattered no seed, so I was afraid, and I went and hid your talent in the ground. Here you have what is yours.' But his master answered him, 'You wicked and slothful servant! You knew that I reap where I have not sowed and gather where I scattered no seed? Then you ought to have invested my money with the bankers, and at my coming I should have received what was my own with interest. So take the talent from him and give it to him who has the ten talents. For to everyone who has will more be given, and he will have an abundance. But from the one who has not, even what he has will be taken away. And cast the worthless servant into the outer darkness. In that place there will be weeping and gnashing of teeth.' Matthew 25:24-30

I don't even want my Dad calling me lazy, much less the Lord! This parable Jesus told of three servants shoots holes in all of the excuses I have heard (and made) for slothfulness.

God seems to be quite serious regarding the resources He has entrusted to us, be they time, abilities, opportunities or money. He is expecting us to do something with it! Excuses don't cut it. Failure is acceptable, but indolence is not.

"But I didn't know what to do" doesn't get a servant off the hook, especially when there on the coffee table is an entire Book of instructions! A good servant will first of all refer to the commands already given in the Bible, then check with the Master for further directions. If I don't know what to do, it's my responsibility to *ask*. When the Master returns, pleading ignorance is not going to work. Ignorance is no excuse for disobedience.

If a good servant runs out of work, or doesn't know what to do next, he'll still find a way to make himself useful while awaiting further instructions. He uses his creativity in finding ways to please his Master and spends his energies in serving, rather than in creating excuses.

It is the true servant who is rewarded. *His master said to him, 'Well done, good and faithful servant. You have been faithful over a little; I will set you over much. Enter into the joy of your master.* (Mt. 25:23)

Signs of Servanthood

Whom We Will Honor

Thus, the sin of the young men was very great in the sight of the LORD, for the men treated the offering of the LORD with contempt.

And there came a man of God to Eli and said to him, "Thus the LORD has said... 'Why then do you scorn my sacrifices and my offerings that I commanded, and honor your sons above me by fattening yourselves on the choicest parts of every offering of my people Israel? Therefore the LORD the God of Israel declares: 'I promised that your house and the house of your father should go in and out before me forever,' but now the LORD declares: 'Far be it from me, for those who honor me I will honor, and those who despise me shall be lightly esteemed....' "

"...And I declare to him that I am about to punish his house forever, for the iniquity that he knew, because his sons were blaspheming God, and he did not restrain them...." 1 Samuel 2:17,27,29-30; 3:13

Eli the priest is in very hot water with God because he refuses to do anything about his reprobate sons, other than occasionally whine at them. Meanwhile, they have persistently defiled the office of the priesthood and the sacrifice of the people, with no sign of repentance. When God has had enough, messages of warning and judgment are sent to Eli, first through a prophet, then through the boy Samuel.

When it comes to serving God, we are responsible for our own actions, but we also share in the responsibility for the actions of those under our authority. Nowhere is this more evident than in the parent/child relationship. A parent who refuses to restrain a child is contributing to the child's delinquency and to their own disgrace. Those who coddle and cover the sinful behavior of their offspring will find themselves bearing a degree of the punishment, too. Much as we might love a family member, our first responsibility is always going to be to God. We're not doing anyone any favors to juggle that order.

Since Eli neglected to take charge of his sons when he could do so, he and his family lost the privilege of representing God. *'And I will raise up for myself a faithful priest, who shall do according to what is in my heart and in my mind...'* (1 Sa 2:35) That's what a servant does: What's according to his *master's* heart and mind, not his own. Our true master? The one we honor.

Signs of Servanthood

Sent Home to Be a Missionary

And they came to Jesus and saw the demon-possessed man, the one who had had the legion, sitting there, clothed and in his right mind, and they were afraid. And those who had seen it described to them what had happened to the demon-possessed man and to the pigs. And they began to beg Jesus to depart from their region. As he was getting into the boat, the man who had been possessed with demons begged him that he might be with him. And he did not permit him but said to him, "Go home to your friends and tell them how much the Lord has done for you, and how he has had mercy on you." And he went away and began to proclaim in the Decapolis how much Jesus had done for him, and everyone marveled.
Mark 5:15-20

The formerly demon-possessed man called "Legion" was so grateful to Jesus for delivering him from the demons that he begged to go with Him. Jesus had a better idea. Legion was to be a missionary to his own people. Jesus sent him home.

A sign of servanthood is that we are stationed according to the desires of our Master, rather than according to our own wishes. Serving is doing what the Lord wants, even if it's different from what we want.

Legion's idea of service was to go with Jesus; Jesus' idea of service for Legion was to go home. The fact that Legion obeyed indicated he was truly interested in service.

Are we willing to do what we'd rather not do, just because the Lord told us to? Am I willing to toss my great plans in the trash, in order to do something as inglorious as testifying to my relatives, when I'd rather be a high-profile disciple, sharing a little of the limelight with Jesus? My answer to that question is a key indicator of my real allegiance. If I'm a bonafide servant of Jesus Christ, I'm willing to step out of the spotlight and the comfort zone, and do whatever He asks wherever He sends me—even if it's home.

Legion went from being totally controlled by demons to being totally controlled by Jesus. Total control. Being under the total control of Jesus is another sign of servanthood.

Signs of Servanthood

Vacation from God

In the spring of the year, the time when kings go out to battle, David sent Joab, and his servants with him, and all Israel. And they ravaged the Ammonites and beseiged Rabbah. But David remained at Jerusalem.

It happened, late one afternoon, when David arose from his couch and was walking on the roof of the kings's house, that he saw from the roof a woman bathing; and the woman was very beautiful. And David sent and inquired about the woman. And one said, "Is not this Bathsheba, the daughter of Eliam, the wife of Uriah the Hittite?" 2 Samuel 11:1-3

No one can afford a vacation from God, not even the "man after God's own heart." This one short chapter in David's life would haunt him for the rest of his days.

While in work relationships, a vacation is a welcome and desirable thing, bringing refreshment, in love relationships a vacation from wedding vows is simply termed "adultery." In relationships based on mutual commitment, even a brief break in that commitment only brings pain.

Such is our relationship with God. We're not in the situation where we can put in a certain number of hours or days in a week in service to Him, and then we're "off." Our allegiance is to be constant, or it's not really allegiance—more like "part-time marriage." There are not times when obedience to Jesus becomes optional, because we're "on vacation." We're either committed to Christ, or not. Jesus has never yet called part-time disciples.

Christianity is not a matter of hours of service, church attendance or jobs completed; this is a matter of a love relationship between ourselves and God. Any break in that relationship will bring us painful consequences. Taking a vacation from God is not a good thing! In fact, it could turn out to be the worst choice we ever made. Faithfulness is what is rewarded. God never takes a vacation from His faithfulness. We don't need a vacation from Him.

Signs of Servanthood

Serving God by Serving Others

"...And the King will answer them, 'Truly I say to you, as you did it to one of the least of these my brothers, you did it to me.'...

...Then they also will answer, saying, 'Lord, when did we see you hungry or thirsty or a stranger or naked or sick or in prison, and did not minister to you?' Then he will answer them, saying, 'Truly, I say to you, as you did not do it to one of the least of these, you did not do it to me.' And these will go away into eternal punishment, but the righteous into eternal life."
Matthew 25:40,44-46

I can't think of a more distinct representation of how serious Jesus is about what is sometimes termed the "social gospel" than Matthew 25. The allegory of the sheep and the goats is a haunting pronouncement of judgment against any who think they can love Jesus without demonstrating compassion to others, and an affirmation to those who realize that serving others is precisely how they best show their love for Christ.

As God's servants, we are here to minister to others as unto Him, in His name. If we don't, we're missing a major purpose for even being here. Every time we see a need around us, we have the opportunity to show we are representatives of Christ.

The fact that this allegory immediately follows the parable of the talents may be significant. I've always considered the parable of the talents to be about using the resources given to us for the benefit of the *Master;* maybe it's even more about using our resources to benefit *others* in His name. Maybe *that's* the investment we are to make to which He was referring, or at least part of it. In fact, the lazy servant who hides his Master's money instead of investing it, and the servant who ignores the needs all around him may basically represent the same servant! Their punishment is the same, anyway!

This is a passage and a concept we dare not skip. The fact that the "goats" will receive punishment, regardless of "bleating" ignorance, is a reminder to me that the "social gospel" is part of the real gospel, and that excuses won't get me a sheep's reward, if I've spent my life acting like a goat.

Signs of Servanthood

False Credentials

Thus says the LORD of hosts: "Do not listen to the words of the prophets who prophesy to you, filling you with vain hopes. They speak visions of their own minds, not from the mouth of the LORD. They say continually to those who despise the word of the LORD, 'It shall be well with you'; and to everyone who stubbornly follows his own heart, they say, 'No disaster shall come upon you.'"...

"I did not send the prophets, yet they ran; I did not speak to them, yet they prophesied. But if they had stood in my council, then they would have proclaimed my words to my people, and they would have turned them from their evil way, and from the evil of their deeds."...

"Let the prophet who has a dream tell the dream, but let him who has my word speak my word faithfully." Jeremiah 23:16-17,21-22,28

The prophets had been appointed by God to be gatekeepers for the whole nation. Instead of waiting upon God for words to say, they had gotten into the pattern of making it up as they went along, or stealing each other's words, then proclaiming it as the word of the LORD. God was not pleased! Through Jeremiah, He lets the prophets know of His displeasure.

It will always be tempting to proclaim to people the message, "It shall be well with you," or "No disaster shall come upon you," even if it didn't come from God. Those prophecies always play well to an audience.

The point is, prophecy is not about those receiving the message; it's about the One sending the message. True prophecy is God-centered, not audience-centered. This is why it's so odious for a prophet to make up his own stuff, then attach God's name to it—even if it sounds good!

"Let him who has my word speak my word faithfully." And let him who thinks he is a prophet not speak until he has heard from God, and then speak only what goes along with the faithful delivery of that message. A faithful prophet concentrates on relating the word he received from the LORD, rather than on pleasing his hearers.

Signs of Servanthood

Prayer in the Plural

Now Jesus was praying in a certain place, and when he finished, one of his disciples said to him, "Lord, teach us to pray, as John taught his disciples." And he said to them,

"When you pray, say:

"Father, hallowed be your name.

Your kingdom come.

Give us each day our daily bread,

and forgive us our sins,

for we ourselves forgive everyone who is indebted to us.

And lead us not into temptation." Luke 11:1-4

Within the Lord's Prayer is a glaring absence of "I." It's not there! Also missing is "me," "my," or any of its first-person singular friends. It's all plural—it's supposed to be.

So how did so much of modern-day prayer become so personalized? So selfish? I've heard an awful lot of "me" and "my" and "I" prayers, many of them coming from me!

Jesus was showing that prayer is not supposed to be self-centered; it's to be God-centered, and when we come before Him, we don't come alone, even when we are. As has been pointed out by some, there is not a single mention of the word "me" or "I" in the Lord's Prayer. It's either plural— "we" or "us," or it's focused on God: "your," "you." The life of the servant is supposed to be like that. There just isn't an emphasis on "me" in the life of a servant. It's not about the servant; it's about the Master.

Hallowed be *your* name,

Your kingdom come.

Give *us* what we need: Daily bread, forgiveness, deliverance from temptation.

Lord, help me to live this day focused not on myself or even on *my* ministry, but focused on you and on others besides myself. Amen.

May 26

Thankless Chores and Eternal Rewards

"So you also, when you have done all that you were commanded, say, 'We are unworthy servants; we have only done what was our duty.'"
Luke 17:10

On the farm on which I grew up, each family member old enough to do anything had chores to do—everything from gathering eggs to feeding cattle. My allowance as a kid was never tied to completion of my chores; completed chores were an expectation, not an option or a way to earn money. Expressions of gratitude toward me for doing my chores were rare, just like expressions of gratitude toward my mother for preparing meals or toward my father for changing the oil in a vehicle.

Had someone *not* a member of our family done our duties for us at our family's request, they would have received gracious thanks, and money as well. The difference in the level of expressed appreciation had to do with who was performing the service: We did it because we *were* family members and it was expected of us; a non-family member received the praise, honor and remuneration afforded a guest because he *was* a guest. The occasional temporary hired help would take their pay and go home and we were square; the farmer's children would do their chores before and after school without acknowledgement, then later receive a college education funded by savings the parents had been setting aside for them since birth. The hired guest gets $20; the son goes to college!

I want to know where we ever got the idea that we were supposed to receive special rewards for doing the things God told us. After all, we're members of His family! We have chores to do, and we do them not because of the pay or the praise, but *because* we are part of God's family. Work is not how we got *into* this family, nor is it how we *stay* in this family; work is *part* of being in God's family.

Where did we come up with the idea that attending church or putting some money in the offering plate was something for which we deserved praise? If we weren't members of God's family, our little deeds of service or sacrifice might be noted and promptly repaid; since we *are* family members, we are only doing what is rightfully expected of us. The reward is not what we are paid, now, or what comes to us, now. The reward is belonging to the family, and receiving what only family members receive.

Signs of Servanthood
The Only Approval That Counts

Not that we dare to classify or compare ourselves with some of those who are commending themselves. But when they measure themselves by one another and compare themselves with one another, they are without understanding. ...

"Let the one who boasts, boast in the Lord." For it is not the one who commends himself who is approved, but the one whom the Lord commends.
2 Corinthians 10:12,17-18

Paul feels the need to write a chapter defending his ministry. In the process, he points out that the comparison game is a game for those without understanding. It doesn't really matter how well we compare with one another; it matters if we're pleasing to God. It's not man's approval that counts; only God's.

A sign of servanthood is where our boasting is focused. If our boasting is in ourselves, our own credentials and accomplishments, or in how well we compare with others, we're demonstrating a lack of understanding. When we boast in the Lord, we're honoring the One worthy of praise, and it's obvious to others whom we are serving. When we boast of ourselves, it's clear that we are basically self-serving. When we engage in comparisons, it shows that we are more interested in the approval and esteem of our peers than our God. Ouch. The comparison game is for those without understanding. I'd like to get out of this game and stay out! I don't need man's approval, in order to function, but I really need God's. And all I have to do to get it is to seek it. If I accept what God says about me, and obey what He tells me, I will be commended by Him! For a servant of the Most High God, it's the only approval that counts.

Signs of Servanthood

Disciples Who Resemble Christ

"A disciple is not above his teacher, but everyone when he is fully trained will be like his teacher." Luke 6:40

One of the signs of servanthood is whom we are starting to resemble. It pains me to see people who have for years termed themselves "Christians," yet who seem to be becoming *less* Christlike instead of more, as the years go by. It's an embarrassment to me to examine my own life and attitudes and discover some of the same trends.

The longer a disciple serves his master, the more he ought to resemble him, right? Then how can it be possible for a Christian to be less godly now than he was twenty years ago?

I think the key is in the word "disciple." "Disciple" implies discipline. It assumes a Master/servant relationship. Disciples are not equal to their teachers. Subservience is required of a disciple.

All of these things are lacking, in what passes for Christianity, in America. The title "Christian" is claimed by anyone who wants it, with all kinds of definitions assigned to the term. Most churches require very little of their members, in terms of Christlikeness, either in outward lifestyle or in evidence of inward grace. Discipline is often minimized, and sometimes non-existent. The new believer is often not at all convinced that he now has a Master—Jesus; based on what he is being taught, he may well come away with the perception that obedience to God is optional, and that "grace" has freed him from the obligation to ever grow up in his faith—or even try. I could go on about this, but I think I'd rather not, because it's depressing!

What is needed in this nation are disciples of Jesus Christ, men and women, boys and girls who are determined to become more like their Master, people who would do *anything* for Jesus, people who are willing to accept His discipline of their lives, people who are willing to submit to His will, learn from Him and serve Him, for all eternity. These are the disciples in whom the world will see the resemblance to Christ. When they are fully trained, they will look like their Teacher. I've seen disciples like this, and they are beautiful to behold. I want to be one! Am I willing to be "fully trained"? Yes. Then I have God's promise that *"everyone when he is fully trained will be like his teacher."* I choose to be a disciple of Jesus.

Signs of Servanthood

The Greatest Commandment

You shall love the LORD your God with all your heart and with all your soul and with all your might. Deuteronomy 6:5

This is what Jesus called the greatest commandment of all—the commandment to love God. Many religions require submission to a god, usually coupled with dread; some religions maintain a god as some sort of personal consciousness or a vague, nondescript presence; which other religion commands that we *love* our God? Not only are we to serve and obey Him; we are to *love* Him—with all our heart, soul and might!

For the Israelites fresh out of Egypt, this must have been an amazing concept. After generations of slavery to cruel taskmasters, many of them must have assumed that their relationship with the powerful God who had delivered them out of Egypt would also be based on a slave/master model; they had escaped slavery to Pharaoh in order to serve as slaves of an unseen and even bigger Master. It appears that many of them never made the stretch from resentfully obeying a master they feared and hated to loving a God who had rescued them and called them to be His own. They often seemed to merely transfer the stubborn resistance they had used to survive in Egypt to their new Master. Most never got as far as love.

When Jesus reiterated the significance of this commandment, centuries later, He was repeating it to those who knew the words by heart, but who had themselves never taken it to heart. The Pharisees were caught up in a legalistic observance of the Law which was, for them, devoid of the love which should have driven their obedience. Like their ancient ancestors under Pharaoh, they obeyed grudgingly, quick to let their resentment spill out upon others who didn't follow the rules according to their standards. There was a great deal of "service," if religious observances and works counted as service, but very little love. So great was their resentment that one of the prime reasons for killing Jesus was that He claimed to be what He told them they had a right to be: Sons of God.

It is our God's intention that His children treat Him like a Father, love Him like a Father, and serve Him not out of resentment or fear, but out of love. If we will do just that one thing, everything else will fall into place.

Signs of Servanthood

Careful With the Yoke

Do not be unequally yoked with unbelievers. For what partnership has righteousness with lawlessness? Or what fellowship has light with darkness? What accord has Christ with Belial? Or what portion does a believer share with an unbeliever? What agreement has the temple of God with idols? For we are the temple of the living God; as God said,

"I will make my dwelling among them and walk among them, and I will be their God, and they shall be my people. Therefore go out from their midst, and be separate from them, says the Lord, and touch no unclean thing; then I will welcome you, and I will be a father to you, and you shall be sons and daughters to me, says the Lord Almighty."

Since we have these promises, beloved, let us cleanse ourselves from every defilement of body and spirit, bringing holiness to completion in the fear of God. 2 Corinthians 6:14-7:1

This is not saying that we are not to associate with unbelievers; it's being "yoked" with them which compromises our faith. It's the "yoke" which prevents us from truly being able to follow Christ, because we can't drag our yokefellow with us, unless they choose to go that direction, too. We can't be a bondservant of Christ in the areas of life where we're tied with someone who doesn't even love Christ. We need to be quite careful about "yokes."

As servants and sons of God, we must be willing to be separate. We *must* be willing to go against the flow, if that's what it takes to honor God. At the same time, the command to love one another and to evangelize the world for Christ demands that we engage our culture and not retreat into a monastery, permanently. It's hard to know what we are to do at a particular time! I guess it goes back to being "among them," without being one of them. That's what Jesus did. He was among the tax collectors and sinners, but He was definitely not one of them. His holiness set Him apart, even in the crowd, but He didn't withdraw into the wilderness and spend His whole life there in order to live in purity and isolation. *With* them, but not one of them. We need to be careful of the "yoke," because compromising connections with ungodly individuals taint the name of Christ. At the same time, Christ's command to love our neighbor will cause us to continue to love and be with unbelievers, without allowing ourselves to be yoked with them.

Signs of Servanthood
Not Here To Live For Me

We ourselves are Jews by birth and not Gentile sinners; yet we know that a person is not justified by works of the law but through faith in Jesus Christ, so we also have believed in Christ Jesus, in order to be justified by faith in Christ and not by works of the law, because by works of the law no one will be justified.

But if, in our endeavor to be justified in Christ, we too were found to be sinners, is Christ then a servant of sin? Certainly not! For if I rebuild what I tore down, I prove myself to be a transgressor. For through the law I died to the law, so that I might live to God. I have been crucified with Christ. It is no longer I who live, but Christ who lives in me. And the life I now live in the flesh I live by faith in the Son of God, who loved me and gave himself for me. I do not nullify the grace of God, for if justification (or righteousness) were through the law, then Christ died for no purpose.
Galatians 2:15-21

Passages like this hammer away at the old self-identity, which says that I'm here on this earth to live for myself, to make some kind of career, to raise a family, to write a book..... I'm here to serve God. The old "me" died when I came to Christ. That included all the ambitions and the career path, as well as the sins. A new person came into being, one devoted to serving Christ, not as an "important" thing, but as the *only* thing.

A slave has no "time off" to call his own. He doesn't "clock out" at the end of a day to go do whatever he likes; he's a slave all the time, and there's no vacation from it, just as married people don't have times of the week or day when they're not married.

As a son of God who is serving God, there are no "down times" when my relationship with God and the accompanying responsibilities go away.

It is no longer I who live, but Christ who lives in me. And the life I now live in the flesh I live by faith in the Son of God, who loved me and gave himself for me.

I am *not here to live for me!* I am here to live for Christ, who lives in me. It's not even me in this body, anymore; it's my Savior living in a reclaimed life.

June 1

Promises to Servants

Lip Protection, Hair Protection, Life

Then he said to them, "Nation will rise against nation, and kingdom against kingdom. There will be great earthquakes, and in various places famines and pestilences. And there will be terrors and great signs from heaven. But before all this they will lay their hands on you and persecute you, delivering you up to the synagogues and prisons, and you will be brought before kings and governors for my name's sake. This will be your opportunity to bear witness. Settle it therefore in your minds not to meditate beforehand how to answer, for I will give you a mouth and wisdom, which none of your adversaries will be able to withstand or contradict. You will be delivered up even by parents and brothers and relatives and friends, and some of you they will put to death. You will be hated by all for my name's sake. But not a hair of your head will perish. By your endurance you will gain your lives." Luke 21:13-19

At first glance this entire chapter is frightening: Earthquakes, famines, pestilences, wars, terrors...etc., etc.! Add to this the prediction that Christ-followers will be dragged before kings and governors, and will incur persecution, imprisonment and death, betrayal from their own families, and general hatred from all sides for no other reason than bearing the name of Jesus, and we begin to wonder why the Lord would even tell us in advance!

Looking below the surface, though, He is once again doing us a kindness, by giving advance warning of trials to come, and the promises to accompany each test. In the same paragraph where Jesus says that some will be killed, He says, *"But not a hair of your head will perish"!* How do *"be killed"* and *"not a hair of your head will perish"* end up in the same paragraph? He must be referring to a protection which transcends death—where even in physical death we are preserved in absolute safety into His presence. I don't know how it works, but I trust the One who made the promise!

How about the other promises in here? There's one about persecution being nothing more than a chance to "bear witness" in front of powerful people. There's the promise that when that time comes, the Spirit will protect our mouth and fill it with His irrefutable wisdom. There's the promise that our endurance will end in life which is indestructible. Endure.

Signs of Servanthood

A Servant of Christ?

Now when they saw the boldness of Peter and John, and perceived that they were uneducated, common men, they were astonished. And they recognized that they had been with Jesus. Acts 4:13

Even the skeptics could tell the apostles were servants of Jesus. What are some of the signs which tip off people to the fact that we are followers of Christ?

—Boldness is one. When we readily identify with our Savior, and are willing to stand for Him, regardless of the consequences, it's pretty clear whom our Lord is.

—Submission is another. It's clear that we are following God's orders rather than trying to get God to follow ours.

—Generosity. When everything in our possession is considered to be something which really belongs to the Lord, we maintain a very light hold on things. Unselfish generosity is the result.

—Direction. The servant of Christ is driven not by personal ambition, but by divine direction. Instead of a career path, it's God's path.

—Our approach to the Sabbath. Is our attitude reverent or nonchalant? Observing the Sabbath is a powerful witness of God's ownership over our lives.

—Day-to-day dealings with people. Kindness and honesty are a couple of character traits which point toward Christ's growing influence in our lives.

—Attitude. Humility and cheerfulness, particularly in the face of conflict or adversity, are indicators of Christ's power and our commitment to Him.

—Service to others, as a way of serving God. It's easy to see that for some, serving God is not just the "main thing;" it's the *only* thing.

—Most of all, the sign of a servant is simply obedience. God's servants do what He says. They obey.

As I contemplate this partial list of the signs of servanthood, I have to ask myself if people recognize at least some of these signs in me. If they don't, why should they think me a servant of Christ?

Three Jobs of a Servant

...Noah was a righteous man, blameless in his generation. Noah walked with God....

And God said to Noah, "I have determined to make an end of all flesh, for the earth is filled with violence through them. Behold, I will destroy them with the earth. Make yourself an ark of gopher wood..."

...Noah did this; he did all that God commanded him.

Then the LORD said to Noah, "Go into the ark, you and all your household, for I have seen that you are righteous before me in this generation...."
Genesis 6:9,13-14,22; 7:1

It's good to review what the jobs of a servant are: Pay attention; believe the Master; obey, regardless. Noah was an example of a servant who did these three jobs successfully. He was paying attention to God's voice, in a day and age when no one else was! He had faith that what God was telling him was true, even though it's hard to imagine how far-fetched it must have seemed, in a world which had up to that point never experienced rain, much less a global flood. His faith led to his obedience. Years of hard work were required in order to obey—work which would have been completely unrewarded until the day God shut the door of the ark and sealed Noah, his family and the animals inside, where they alone would ride out the devastation coming upon the earth. It all happened just as God had said, but Noah was the only one who had been paying attention to God, the only one who had believed Him, and the only one who had obeyed. Noah's obedience saved mankind from extinction.

Many have been the examples since, of faithful servants, descended from Noah, who have simply paid attention, believed the Master, and obeyed, regardless. These are requirements of those who will walk with God and serve Him.

Three Jobs of a Servant

So when they had come together, they asked him, "Lord, will you at this time restore the kingdom to Israel?" He said to them, "It is not for you to know times or seasons that the Father has fixed by his own authority. But you will receive power when the Holy Spirit has come upon you, and you will be my witnesses in Jerusalem and in all Judea and Samaria, and to the end of the earth." Acts 1:6-8

Like most of us, the disciples wanted to know what was going to happen next. Jesus' answer to their question was, "You don't need to know." What Jesus did choose to tell them, moments before His ascension into heaven, was their mission. First they were to receive the Holy Spirit's power, then they were to be witnesses throughout the whole world, and all of it was to be by God's timing, not theirs.

That is still true. Like the disciples, we still want to ask the questions about what will happen, and when, and we usually get the same reply they did: "That's not for you to know." What we get instead is the reminder that our mission is identical to theirs: Receive the power of the Holy Spirit, and be witnesses to the end of the earth.

The Early Christians in the Upper Room didn't even get to determine when the Holy Spirit would come upon them. They were told to wait in the city until they were clothed with God's power (Lk 24:49), and Jesus didn't tell them how long it would be. Everything was by God's timing.

The disciples didn't need to know God's timing in advance; they only needed to know their assignment. Even more importantly, they didn't need to hunt around and try to figure out where to get the power. God was going to supply all the power they would ever need, in His time and in His way.

Have I learned these two lessons, yet—that it's not my job to figure out the times and seasons under the Father's authority, that it's not my responsibility to come up with the power for the mission? It's not the servant's job to supply the timing or the power. The servant's job is to wait for God's signal, then obey what he has been commanded to do, in the full knowledge that through the Holy Spirit there will always be sufficient power for the mission at hand.

Two Jobs We Can Do Without

This is how one should regard us, as servants of Christ and stewards of the mysteries of God. Moreover, it is required of stewards that they be found trustworthy. But with me it is a very small thing that I should be judged by you or by any human court. In fact, I do not even judge myself. I am not aware of anything against myself, but I am not thereby acquitted. It is the Lord who judges me. Therefore do not pronounce judgment before the time, before the Lord comes, who will bring to light the things now hidden in darkness and will disclose the purposes of the heart. Then each one will receive his commendation from God.

I have applied all these things to myself and Apollos for your benefit, brothers, that you may learn by us not to go beyond what is written, that none of you may be puffed up in favor of one against another. For who sees anything different in you? What do you have that you did not receive? If then you received it, why do you boast as if you did not receive it?
1 Corinthians 4:1-7

It is not the servant's job to judge. I know this concept is constantly thrown in our faces, these days, particularly by those who know it's in the Bible and who want to be able to continue in their various "alternative lifestyles" of sin without hearing from those who know sin when they see it. But it's still true that it isn't our job to judge other people. It's our job to love.

An even harder principle to grasp is that it's not even our job to judge ourselves! Satan is always anxious to help us in that regard. He quickly reminds us of what miserable examples of Christianity we are, and suggests that since we aren't very good at being Christians, anyway, we might as well at least enjoy the benefits of living "reasonably" (i.e., for ourselves), rather than trying to attain some impossible standard of perfection.

It's very clear in the Bible that "not judging" in no way implies that "everything anybody does is O.K.;" it only means that it's not our job to figure out the spiritual status of others, seeing as we have incomplete information, anyway. And the business of exalting certain people (or ourselves) over others is also pointless and harmful, since everything anyone has was issued from heaven in the first place.

The Christian life can be complicated, but not nearly as complicated as we tend to make it. Judging and comparison are not our jobs.

When God's Not Fooling, but He's Faithful

...Those who honor me, I will honor,... 1 Samuel 2:30

I still remember staring down that long aisle, knowing what I had to do. The question God had posed to me through the speaker of the evening was simple: "Are you willing to follow Jesus alone?" I instinctively knew this was not a hypothetical question. The girl in the pew beside me knew it, too. Though it felt like going to my own funeral, I made my way down the aisle to an altar of prayer, alone, to say "Yes." There was no sense of release, relief, of anything,... except obedience. It was June 6.

That night I volunteered to plant a church in the remote Alaskan town of Cordova. The next four years as a single church planter were proof that God had been serious about the commitment to follow Jesus alone. By the time I got to Cordova, I'd said goodbye to everyone I knew in the world, including the girl in the pew, who married a work partner of mine.

Four years later, in the same church, at the same altar, I announced my engagement to a young lady whom God had miraculously brought into my life. We've been married 22 years, now. June 6 is still a special day, to me. It's the day I made a commitment to serve Jesus alone. Rather than keep it that way, He sent me the best earthly friend I've ever had.

Those who honor me, I will honor.
It's true.

Accepting God's Provision

Now Elijah the Tishbite, of Tishbe in Gilead, said to Ahab, "As the LORD the God of Israel lives, before whom I stand, there shall be neither dew nor rain these years, except by my word." And the word of the LORD came to him, "Depart from here and turn eastward and hide yourself by the brook Cherith, which is east of the Jordan. You shall drink from the brook, and I have commanded the ravens to feed you there." So he went and did according to the word of the LORD. He went and lived by the brook Cherith that is east of the Jordan. And the ravens brought him bread and meat in the evening, and he drank from the brook. And after a while the brook dried up, because there was no rain in the land. 1 Kings 17:1-7

"You shall drink from the brook, and I have commanded the ravens to feed you there."

No wonder most of the prophets were single!

"What does your husband do?"
"Oh, he's a prophet."
"Does that pay well?"
"Actually, it doesn't pay anything."
"How do you live, then? Do you even have a house? Where do you get money for food?"
"We live by the brook, and the ravens bring us food."
"I'd been wondering why you'd never invited me over."

So, you sign up to be a prophet, you have so much authority that you can cause a three-year drought through nothing more than prayer, and the provision you get for your personal needs are... *ravens?!*

I can see Elijah trying to qualify for a loan at the bank, and showing up with two ravens for co-signers!

Here's the beauty of this whole deal. Elijah *accepted* God's provision! God didn't have to coddle this guy. He was willing to accept *whatever* God provided, *however* God provided. And on this day when I myself have no guaranteed source of income except for God's promise of provision, this is a good example to follow.

God-Sent Widows

So he went and did according to the word of the LORD. He went and lived by the brook Cherith that is east of the Jordan. And the ravens brought him bread and meat in the evening, and he drank from the brook. And after a while the brook dried up, because there was no rain in the land.

Then the word of the LORD came to him, "Arise, go to Zarephath, which belongs to Sidon, and dwell there. Behold, I have commanded a widow there to feed you." 1 Kings 17:8-9

Great! We've gone from ravens to widows! It would be like telling us that we are supposed to go to some foreign country, and when we get there, "I've commanded this homeless guy to take care of you"!

Instead of laughing, Elijah immediately obeys and goes. God's men are like that.

He gets there. This is great—not only is she a widow; she's a *starving* widow!! She's gathering sticks to make a fire, so she can make something with all she has—a handful of flour and a tiny amount of oil—and then she and her son can die! Is there something wrong with this picture?!

Nope. This is God, in action. What He is doing is showing His servant, Elijah, step by step, that it's not about what resources we have; it's about Him. *He* is our resource!

When God wants to make a world, He starts with nothing!

When God wants to start a nation, He looks for an infertile couple.

When God's Son is born into the world, He is born of a virgin.

I used to think that my *Dad* did everything the hard way!—God not only does it the hard way; He does it when there's *no* way!

God is *wonder-ful*, in every sense of the word. He does *wonders*. To us, it's impossible. To Him, that's just the way He does things. With God, *nothing* is impossible.

Elijah is learning, step by step. You don't need to know where the food is coming from, or even the water. You only need to know God. You don't need a good "source" before you'll have what you need. God can do it through ravens, or starving widows in foreign countries; if you're going to call fire down from heaven to burn up the sacrifice, you might as well add water!

When we have God, we don't need "resources;" God *is* our resource!

Two-Sentence Prayers

And at the time of the offering of the oblation, Elijah the prophet came near and said, "O LORD, God of Abraham, Isaac, and Israel, let it be known this day that you are God in Israel, and that I am your servant, and that I have done all these things at your word. Answer me, O LORD, answer me, that this people may know that you, O LORD, are God, and that you have turned their hearts back." Then the fire of the LORD fell and consumed the burnt offering and the wood and the stones and the dust, and licked up the water that was in the trench. And when all the people saw it, they fell on their faces and said, "The LORD ,he is God; the LORD; he is God." 1 Kings 18:36-39

This is not a "faith healer" who is telling God what to do, and putting on a performance. This is a prophet of God who is merely taking orders from the Almighty. Two sentences, and there is a major cultural shift in the whole nation! It's God who makes all the difference. This is not Elijah's master plan; it's God's, and Elijah gets to play a major part.

In the first part of Elijah's short prayer, he gives the theology of divine miracles: *"Let it be known this day that you are God in Israel, and that I am your servant, and that I have done all these things at your word."* The miracles are not for the prophet's glory, but for God's; this miracle is not a matter of personal ambition but of pure obedience. Elijah is nothing more than a servant carrying out orders.

Where are the people willing to be used of God in this way, in these days? At least in this country, they seem few and far between. There is interest in miracles, particularly those of healing, but so many who purport to have some kind of gift in this area seem intent on magnifying themselves more than glorifying God. It always makes me wince when I hear someone giving God orders as if God were the servant and the one "praying" was the master!

I think we'll start to see a lot more actual miracles in America when there are more people who can honestly say, "This wasn't my idea or my plan; I'm only doing what God told me to do. And if anything good happens, it's God who deserves the credit, not me!" With that kind of humble obedience, like the Israelites, we might also witness national revival sparked by two-sentence prayers.

God-Powered

After many days the word of the LORD came to Elijah, in the third year, saying, "Go, show yourself to Ahab, and I will send rain upon the earth."
1 Kings 18:1

It wasn't up to Elijah to decide to proclaim the drought in the first place, nor was it left to him to determine when it should be over. Elijah is God's prophet—His messenger, not His advisor.

What *is* Elijah's job is to show himself to King Ahab, who has been relentlessly searching for him for years, seeking to take his life! Not only that, but Elijah gets to tell this same king that it's going to rain, when it hasn't for three years, and there's not a cloud in the sky.

Oh, and prior to this, Elijah gets to take on hundreds of Baal's prophets singlehandedly in a contest of calling down fire from heaven! Yahweh's victory on Mount Carmel, as Elijah calls on His name, results in the destruction of the prophets of Baal, and the declaration of bitter vengeance against Elijah by Ahab's wife, Jezebel.

Immediately following the showdown on Mt. Carmel is the rain episode, in which Elijah's servant spots a cloud the size of a man's hand, Elijah sends word to Ahab to get going before the rain stops him, and Elijah outruns the chariot to Jezreel (Something like 20 miles)! Is this man amazing or what?!

Yes, Elijah is pretty incredible, but it's obviously God who is the amazing one. It's God who withholds the rain or sends it, according to His own wishes. God sends the fire on Mount Carmel. When Elijah races a horse-drawn chariot and wins, it's because he's God-powered. When Elijah goes for 40 days and nights on the strength of food brought to him by an angel, once again, he's God-powered.

It's all God. The timing, ideas, the strength—all God. Elijah is nothing more than a willing vessel through whom God's power flows. Is that the way it's supposed to be with me? Yes, I'm pretty sure it is. It's not my job to determine what great things God will do, or when. It's my job to obey Him, immediately and completely, courageously, to make sure the glory goes to Him when it's all over. There is no limit to what God can do. He uses willing servants to accomplish the impossible. These servants understand that this power is not their own; they are merely a conduit through which it flows.

If God wants to use me for a channel of His power and love, may I be available and useful for all of His purposes.

The "He" Generation

"The whole commandment that I command you today you shall be careful to do, that you may live and multiply, and go in and possess the land that the LORD swore to give to your fathers. And you shall remember the whole way that the LORD your God has led you these forty years in the wilderness, that he might humble you, testing you to know what was in your heart, whether you would keep his commandments or not. And he humbled you and let you hunger and fed you with manna, which you did not know, nor did your fathers know, that he might make you know that man does not live by bread alone, but man lives by every word (Hebrew 'by all') that comes from the mouth of the LORD. Your clothing did not wear out on you and your foot did not swell these forty years. Know then in your heart that, as a man disciplines his son, the LORD your God disciplines you. So you shall keep the commandments of the LORD your God by walking in his ways and by fearing him..." Deuteronomy 8:1-6

It's the word of God which keeps us alive, which sustains us. His provision for His children is miraculous when it needs to be, practical and routine when He wants it to be. Either way, He is the Source, not us. Later on in this chapter is a warning to not let ourselves think that somehow *we* attained this wealth by our own strength. It all comes from God's hand—even the ability to produce wealth.

I wonder if we really believe that. As I look around at a nation awash in riches, I'm not seeing much acknowledgment of God's provision, even among Christians. Most Americans have seldom been in a situation where dependence on God was the only option, when it came to food or basic necessities. There is a generation which survived the Great Depression, who have memories of what it was like to do without, and who knew the meaning of gratitude for simple things, but they've transferred the reins of leadership to generations who have known little of that kind of want, and who have come to view a pretty high standard of living as an entitlement, and extraordinary riches as a symbol of superior intelligence and diligence. Like I said, not much of the credit for any of it is floating up toward God.

Do I really believe it is God's Word which sustains me? I like to think I do, but the dependence on myself runs deep. The "me" generation has a hard time living as the "He" generation. God knows how to fix that.

Highway of Blessing

"The Levitical priests, all the tribe of Levi, shall have no portion or inheritance with Israel. They shall eat the LORD's food offerings as their inheritance. They shall have no inheritance among their brothers; the LORD is their inheritance, as he promised them. Deuteronomy 18:1-2

Going back to the concept of Deuteronomy 8—*"man does not live by bread alone, but man lives by every word that comes from the mouth of the LORD"*—God wanted some of His people to be living proof of that, on a continuing and daily basis. He picked the Levites.

God is firm in His instruction to the Israelites that the Levites are to have no other portion or inheritance in Israel except Him. Every other tribe gets a major tract of land as an inheritance; the Levites only get cities in which to live. They are not to become dependent upon farming for their livelihood. They are to depend on God, as they are supported through the gifts of the people.

The Levites are to be God's special servants, and the ownership of farms or lands or another good way to make a living, would only have been a major distraction to them. God removes this distraction, promises to provide for them, and commissions them to spend their lives, generation after generation, in serving Him. The edict given by God through Moses sets apart an entire tribe to perpetually live by faith. They are to be the continuing example which reminds people that life on earth is not about accumulating lands and worldly wealth—life on earth is about serving God—and here are people who not only survive but thrive, doing nothing else.

We're all called to live by faith, but I think God still calls some people to live it in a more literal sense. Not everyone, mind you—until we're in our heavenly digs, somebody has to tend the farms and do the other necessary work for human survival. But I believe that there will always be some to whom God says, "Trust me. I can provide for you. I have a special mission for you, and it requires you to let go of everything but Me, in order to see it accomplished. Are you willing to let go of your back-up system, in order to follow Me into a place where I am your only provision?"

To those with the courage to trust God, when the distractions of lands and businesses to maintain are in the rear-view mirror, who have been *called* to this by God Himself, what may appear to others to be a road to ruin will in fact turn out to be a highway of blessing.

June 13

Holy Ignorance

"When you come into the land that the LORD your God is giving you, you shall not learn to follow the abominable practices of those nations. There shall not be found among you anyone who burns his son or his daughter as an offering, anyone who practices divination or tells fortunes or interprets omens, or a sorcerer or a charmer or a medium or a wizard or a necromancer, for whoever does these things is an abomination to the LORD. And because of these abominations the LORD your God is driving them out before you. You shall be blameless before the LORD your God, for these nations, which you are about to dispossess, listen to fortunetellers and to diviners. But as for you, the LORD your God has not allowed you to do this." Deuteronomy 18:9-14

Why is God so down on fortune-tellers? Do they pose a threat to Him? Aren't these harmless pursuits?

If there were absolutely nothing to these practices, I don't think God would have made a big deal of it; instead, He lists this as one of the key reasons why He is overthrowing the Canaanite nations! What does this say about our American practices of horoscopes, astrology, fortune-telling, and so forth? Will America face the same judgment as Canaan did, for some of the exact same reasons?

I'm afraid we qualify: Sacrificing our children to the god of "choice" through abortion; idolatry so rampant that it defies description; sexual immorality which is being enshrined as morality; not to mention the things which are in comparison hardly noticeable, such as sorcery and witchcraft! God, help us and forgive us!

For many in our society there is little distinction made regarding the source of spirituality. It's a "One size fits all" attitude, which lumps the Creator in with palm readers as being just different manifestations of the same spiritual "source." This attitude is so reprehensible to God that He is willing to dispossess entire countries over it! What some would call "cute" or "harmless fun," God calls an abomination. This is one place where naivety is good, much like in the Garden of Eden before Adam and Eve discovered the knowledge of good and evil. There's a lot about the spirit world that I'm blessed *not* to know about. All these pseudo-spiritual practices only take away from my dependence upon Him, and place it instead on wizardry or divination or fortune-telling—all pitiful substitutes for the real thing.

It's pretty simple, really. God wants His people to depend on *Him.*

God-Confidence

Not by might, nor by power, but by my Spirit, says the LORD of hosts.
Zechariah 4:6

This is not by the servant's own power or resources. What a relief! We don't have to try to come up with the power, ourselves. God has promised that He will take full responsibility to provide through the Holy Spirit everything that is needed. We supply the obedience. It's not our job to come up with the power.

The Early Church in the Upper Room didn't finally get their act together, then launch out on an offensive; they were filled with God's Holy Spirit, and the plan and the power were directly from God.

Paul asks the Corinthians what they have that they didn't receive from God. The answer, of course, is "nothing." Every good gift comes from above.

Elijah gets multiple lessons in God's provision. With each test, his faith grows.

The Israelites in the wilderness learn that even their bread and water come from God, and without Him, they can't so much as survive.

The Levites are to depend upon God, and God is to be their inheritance, rather than having their own land.

God *is* our resource!

When God looks for servants, He doesn't look for rich people or smart people who can share their resources with Him; He looks for people who are poor in spirit, who are willing to be totally dependent upon Him. Then He gives them everything they need to get the job done. It's not the strong or smart person who has the most power; the one with the most power is the person who is depending upon God for everything. That person's resources are unlimited!

There's an old Ethiopian proverb which states: "The man who has only God to look to can do all things and never fail."

The apostle Paul put it this way: *I can do all things through him who strengthens me.* (Philippians 4:13) There's a world of difference between self-confidence and God-confidence. One gets you whatever man's strength and wisdom can get you, then it's done. The other connects you to unlimited power and resources. Self-confidence gets a person farther than self-doubt; God-confidence is reliance upon Someone who cannot fail.

Wet Feet for God

The LORD said to Joshua, "Today I will begin to exalt you in the sight of all Israel, that they may know that, as I was with Moses, so I will be with you. And as for you, command the priests who bear the ark of the covenant, 'When you come to the brink of the waters of the Jordan, you shall stand still in the Jordan.' " And Joshua said to the people of Israel, "Come here and listen to the words of the LORD your God." Joshua 3:7-9

It must have been such a relief to Joshua that it wasn't his responsibility to come up with the plan, when it came to invading the Promised Land. All he has to do is follow orders! God is personally coaching him through the whole process, while giving continual encouragement at the same time. In the way God does things, even the appointed leaders don't have to make all their own plans. They just execute God's orders and pass them down to others.

It does take a great deal of faith to follow His orders, though! Some of them seem so *dangerous!* Take for instance the command to circumcise the men, once they're on the dangerous side of the Jordan. What are they supposed to do if they're attacked, now?! If God had told them to be circumcised a few months before they crossed the Jordan, that would have made a little more sense, or if they'd been circumcised in shifts.... Instead, the whole army renders themselves helpless, right after they've gone into enemy territory! And God blesses their obedience. *"Today I have rolled away the reproach of Egypt from you."* (Josh 5:9)

They celebrate the Passover, and begin to eat the fruit of the land of Canaan. The next day, the manna ceases. The miracle food is no longer needed.

When we follow God's direction, we sometimes do some pretty unconventional things, but His provision is there for His children, *as long as we need it.* When it is no longer needed, it is often no longer there.

And it is not our planning and strategizing ability which makes us effective in God's army; it is our willingness to pay attention, to take Him at His word, to carefully obey His orders in faith, which make us useful to His purposes. If God wants us to plan the attack, He'll let us know. Usually, what He's looking for are not would-be generals, but servants willing to risk getting their feet wet for Him. And the plan? Obedience. Just obedience.

When God Sends a General

When Joshua was by Jericho, he lifted up his eyes and looked, and behold, a man was standing before him with his drawn sword in his hand. And Joshua went to him and said to him, "Are you for us, or for our adversaries?" And he said, "No; but I am the commander of the army of the LORD. Now I have come." And Joshua fell on his face to the earth and worshiped and said to him, "What does my lord say to his servant?" And the commander of the LORD's army said to Joshua, "Take off your sandals from your feet, for the place where you are standing is holy." And Joshua did so. Joshua 5:13-15

I like the way one pastor put it. When Joshua asked the angel, "Whose side are you on, ours or theirs?" the angel answered, "I didn't come to take sides; I came to take over!"

It's not every day that God sends you a general to take over your army for you! But then, it's not every day that you receive orders like, "March around this city for six days in silence, then on the seventh day shout like crazy and the walls will fall down." And it works!

Joshua is so glad to receive divine help and direction that his response to finding out the "general" was sent from God is to fall on his face and worship God in gratitude. Interestingly, the first order Joshua hears from the commander of the LORD's army is not one having to do with battle tactics, but one having to do with worship: *Take off your sandals from your feet, for the place where you are standing is holy." And Joshua did so.*

If we want help from God, doesn't it always start there? Even when God sends a general, it doesn't begin with "Do this and this, and you'll win the battle;" it starts with worship—recognizing and honoring God's holiness. I think we're mostly wasting our time if all we want from God is the latest tip on what will happen next, so we can proceed with our own plans, helped by inside information from above. God rarely responds to our selfish curiosity or our desire to better our station in life at His expense. But I've found that He *always* responds when I come before Him in recognition of His holiness and in submission to Him, ready to obey wherever He might direct. It's not our job to come up with the plan! It's our responsibility to worship God, to seek His direction with the full intention of obeying whatever He tells us, then to do exactly that. His Holy Spirit gives all the direction we need. In these days of the Spirit's leadership in the Church, God always sends a "General." He doesn't come to take sides, He comes to take over. Hallelujah!

Faithfulness Is Success

"For twenty-three years, from the thirteenth year of Josiah the son of Amon, king of Judah, to this day, the word of the LORD has come to me, and I have spoken persistently to you, but you have not listened. You have neither listened nor inclined your ears to hear, although the LORD persistently sent to you all his servants the prophets, saying, 'Turn now, every one of you, from his evil way and evil deeds, and dwell upon the land that the LORD has given to you and your fathers from of old and forever. Do not go after other gods to serve and worship them or provoke me to anger with the work of your hands. Then I will do you no harm.' Yet you have not listened to me, declares the LORD, that you might provoke me to anger with the work of your hands to your own harm." Jeremiah 25:3-7

Twenty-three years! From a very good king on down through a succession of terrible ones, Jeremiah said what God told him to say, but had gotten no response. Success is not always what it's about! Had Jeremiah simply adapted his message to the times, he could have joined the tribe of prophets who were doing pretty well, prophesying lies that the people wanted to hear! Instead, he was God's lonely man. Good job, Jeremiah.

I think it's interesting that Jeremiah is told at least twice by the Lord, "Don't pray for this people." (Jer 11:14 ; 14:11) In fact, in Jeremiah 15:1, God simply tells Jeremiah "Let them go!" He is to continue speaking the message of impending judgment, but Jeremiah is informed in advance that the nation will not listen to him. In this case, the servant's responsibility is to proclaim a message to which no one will respond! Not only that, but the message of doom earns Jeremiah the hatred of the people who don't want to hear it.

God's commission to His servant: "They won't listen to you, but you still have to tell them."

Can I be content with a mindset that values faithfulness alone, regardless of "success"? In God's eyes, faithfulness *is* success.

It's not the job of the servant to be successful, in terms of acceptance from people. It's not the job of the servant to make the message palatable, if doing that would distort the message. It's not the job of the servant to come up with a message people will like. He dare not change what God has spoken, even though the servant knows it may fall on deaf ears, or offend people. The prophet's responsibility is to speak faithfully and accurately the word of the Lord, regardless of the reaction it produces.

Hope through Obedience

The word that came to Jeremiah from the LORD in the tenth year of Zedekiah king of Judah, which was the eighteenth year of Nebuchadnezzar. At that time the army of the king of Babylon was besieging Jerusalem, and Jeremiah the prophet was shut up in the court of the guard that was in the palace of the king of Judah....

Jeremiah said, "The word of the LORD came to me: Behold, Hanamel the son of Shallum your uncle will come to you and say, 'Buy my field that is at Anathoth, for the right of redemption by purchase is yours.' Then Hanamel my cousin came to me in the court of the guard, in accordance with the word of the LORD, and said to me, 'Buy my field that is at Anathoth in the land of Benjamin, for the right of possession and redemption is yours; buy it for yourself.' Then I knew that this was the word of the LORD.

And I bought the field at Anathoth from Hanamel my cousin, and weighed out the money to him, seventeen shekels of silver. Jeremiah 32:1-2,6-9

Not all of God's orders make sense to us. Jeremiah is told to buy a field while he is imprisoned in the palace courts, and the city of Jerusalem is under siege. (I suspect realtor's were having a tough time)!

Jeremiah's cousin must have been pretty surprised to have Jeremiah actually accept his offer! Jeremiah is the one who had predicted the demise of Judah in the first place, and now when it's about to take place, he's speculating on land?!

Probably no one was more surprised than Jeremiah. His question and answer session with God over this deal occupies the rest of the chapter. But God is using His servant to infuse hope into the Israelites, reminding them that although calamity is at hand, there will come a time when, once again, lands and houses will be bought and sold. There is a future for His people.

Jeremiah is the kind of servant willing to obey his God even when obedience doesn't make sense (although, in God's perspective, this *does* make sense). Jeremiah's example is a reminder that in serving God, the idea is not "what makes sense;" the idea is always "obedience." Jeremiah came through.

How often among American Christians does obedience trump pragmatism or logic? Not often enough, I'm sure! It's not the servant's task to make sense of God's orders, or to prove they are workable. It's the servant's job to obey. And God uses our obedience to bring hope to others.

Trust What It Says On the Fridge

"For I know the plans I have for you, declares the LORD, plans for wholeness and not for evil, to give you a future and a hope." Jeremiah 29:11

This verse is on a lot of refrigerator magnets, but not so many hearts. It's a great promise (my daughter's favorite); it's also a reminder that God is the One with the plans, and it doesn't need to be us.

That's a hard one. Who among us doesn't have a few ambitions we want to see fulfilled, sooner or later? And even when we are confident that the goal for which we're aiming is indeed God's goal for us, we'd just as soon make our own plans on how to arrive there. It's a mixture of relief and disappointment to realize it's not our job to come up with a plan—relief, in that the risk of coming up with a bad plan and wrecking everything is no longer in the picture—disappointment, in that our creativity must take a back seat to obedience.

Once in a while, someone gets the nod to come up with their own strategy—Nehemiah, for example. The burden on his heart for Jerusalem is strong, God-given and God-blessed. He prays and asks favor, from both God and the king, in order to see the walls of Jerusalem rebuilt. Although he is praying each step of the way, God seems to leave it to Nehemiah to arrive at the actual plan for how to get this thing done. Being a very skillful administrator and leader, Nehemiah does a wonderful job of it, all of the time giving honor to God.

Nehemiah is the exception, though. Most of the time, all we're supposed to do is seek God, then follow orders. It's not the servant's job to come up with a plan. It wasn't Joshua's job; it wasn't Jeremiah's job; it wasn't Moses' job; it wasn't Elijah's job; in each of these instances and many more, the job of the servant was simply to obey the orders that God supplied through whatever means.

Most of the time, God doesn't seem to ask His servants to supply plans for Him to bless; He asks His servants to very carefully follow *His* specific plans (building the tabernacle and the temple, various battle plans, all of the sacrifices and rituals, the dietary laws, ...on and on...). It's just not the servant's job to make the plans. What *is* the servant's role is to seek God's plans, trust that if they're really from God, then they really must be good—and follow His plans carefully and courageously. If we do, the promise is ours: wholeness, a future, hope. Trust what it says on the fridge.

Ready For Honorable Use

Now in a great house there are not only vessels of gold and silver but also of wood and clay, some for honorable use, some for dishonorable. Therefore, if anyone cleanses himself from what is dishonorable, he will be a vessel for honorable use, set apart as holy, useful to the master of the house, ready for every good work. 2 Timothy 2:20-21

Cleanliness. Availability. Exclusivity.

If it's clean, it can be used for anything. If it's not clean, the only uses for which the object qualifies are those where cleanliness is optional.

Availability is important. If the object is already committed to another use, it's too much trouble to disengage it in order to use it elsewhere. The object which will be used is the available one.

Exclusivity. This is the "reserved" sign which says the object is clean and available, not just for any purpose, but for a special purpose, and that purpose alone.

This is the idea of holiness: Clean, and available for God's exclusive use. I think it's interesting that in this passage, the responsibility is more on the servant than on the Lord: *"Therefore, if anyone cleanses himself from what is dishonorable,...."* Heart cleansing is a job only the Holy Spirit can handle; this is more like "hand cleansing." This passage is about being willing to disengage from what we know to be dishonorable, in order to be qualified to pursue holiness. Only God can perform the inner cleansing, but it looks like we're responsible for staying out of the sewer, at least if we want to be working with food and not plumbing.

Years ago, I hosted an early morning weekly teen Bible study, after which the teens would cook their own breakfast, prior to leaving for school. One morning, I came into the kitchen to discover one of the teens had grabbed my dog's water dish, and had been mixing scrambled eggs in it. I just turned around and walked out! It wasn't going to help anything at this venture to let her know that vessel wasn't ready for "honorable" use!

Am I ready for honorable use? Unless I'm "set apart as holy," I'm not. If I wonder why I don't seem to get picked for the "important," "honorable" jobs, this may be the reason. Until I'm willing to cleanse myself from what is dishonorable, and allow myself to be reserved for God's special purposes, clean and available for His exclusive use, I'm not ready for "honorable."

Scrubbing In

Therefore, if anyone cleanses himself from what is dishonorable, he will be a vessel for honorable use, set apart as holy, useful to the master of the house, ready for every good work.
So flee youthful passions and pursue righteousness, faith, love, and peace, along with those who call on the Lord from a pure heart.
2 Timothy 2:21-22

If I ever have surgery, I hope everyone scrubs in. They might be well-meaning, and just there to help, but if they're not clean, I'd prefer they "help" somewhere else. It's just really important to me that if my body is lying there exposed to anything and everything, we have as few homeless bacteria as possible floating around looking for a landing pad.

In a surgical procedure, the presence of just one person who is not scrubbed in contaminates the whole room. A surgeon is not "ready for every good work" unless he or she is scrubbed in.

Neither is a Christian. We must allow the Holy Spirit to scrub us clean before we are prepared for the kinds of works which require a pure heart. Nor does it count that we "did that once," back in 1973, regardless of how great the experience was at the time; surgeons need to scrub in before *every* surgery, not just the first one. And Christians who want God to use them need to submit to the cleansing power of the Holy Spirit *every* day, not just one great day.

Continual cleansing. The same reason we keep washing those dishes, again and again, and washing the same clothes, over and over. They keep getting dirty, and if we're going to use them, they need to be cleaned regularly, and kept clean until they are used, then cleaned again afterward, in preparation for the next use.

I'm talking about allowing the Holy Spirit to cleanse my life, so that I'm ready for anything God wants me to do, and allowing Him to maintain my life in a state of "readiness." Only God can cleanse my soul, but it's up to me to choose to stay out of the things which contaminate my life—those things which always leave me feeling dirty and dull—things like pornography, gossip or slander. If God has an "honorable" duty He wants to give me, I want to be scrubbed in and ready. The only way I'm ready is if I habitually choose to cleanse myself from what is dishonorable.

Holiness Is Attainable

Therefore, if anyone cleanses himself from what is dishonorable, he will be a vessel for honorable use, set apart as holy, useful to the master of the house, ready for every good work.

So flee youthful passions and pursue righteousness, faith, love, and peace, along with those who call on the Lord from a pure heart.
2 Timothy 2:21-22

Yeah, I now—this is the third day on the same passage! But this is important. I really think God wants us to get this.

If I'm to be a useful, trusted servant of Christ Jesus, I need to be clean, available, and devoted to Him? That's right. Otherwise, I am disqualified from all the good works God might have in mind for me which require a holy vessel. For honorable use, holiness is a requirement.

The sad thing is that so many Christians think holiness is unattainable, so they don't even bother to pursue it: "If I can't be perfectly clean, why try? Might as well dive into sin, and ask forgiveness, later!" This foolhardy attitude contaminates so many believers, who might otherwise be productive, but instead are relegated to the equivalent of spiritual "welfare"—constant consumers of God's grace, but refusing to participate in the life it has freed them to pursue, like prisoners who squat on the floor of their prison, facing an open door but never walking out into freedom.

Holiness is attainable! When we choose to pursue the world, we never catch the fulfillment we seek. It's always elusive, always just out of reach, like the mechanical rabbit used in greyhound races. The pursuit of money, fame, power or beauty is a pursuit which inevitably ends in disappointment. Even if we attain our goal, there's always someone ahead of us with more; if we ever do get to the top, we find ourselves quickly displaced.

But holiness is attainable! When we pursue righteousness, faith, love, and peace, God makes sure we get it! Not only do we get it, but we get to keep it! Once we choose to cleanse ourselves from what is "dishonorable" (and if we have to ask, that's probably what it is), we are candidates for holiness, and thus, holy uses. Holiness is a continuing way of life, not a momentary achievement. It's not nearly as much about "perfection" as it is about being available for God's exclusive use, and a willingness to be clean and live clean, whether that cleansing comes from God or whether it's our own responsibility to get out and stay out of the mud.

June 23

The Conduct of a Servant

Remind them to be submissive to rulers and authorities, to be obedient, to be ready for every good work, to speak evil of no one, to avoid quarreling, to be gentle, and to show perfect courtesy toward all people. For we ourselves were once foolish, disobedient, led astray, slaves to various passions and pleasures, passing our days in malice and envy, hated by others and hating one another. But when the goodness and loving kindness of God our Savior appeared, he saved us, not because of works done by us in righteousness, but according to his own mercy, by the washing of regeneration and renewal of the Holy Spirit, whom he poured out on us richly through Jesus Christ our Savior, so that being justified by his grace we might become heirs according to the hope of eternal life. The saying is trustworthy, and I want you to insist on these things, so that those who have believed in God may be careful to devote themselves to good works. These things are excellent and profitable for people. Titus 3:1-8

The conduct of a servant is to reflect well on the Master. One of the ways in which we do this is by our attitude to those placed in authority over us, whether they are believers or not. Of even more importance is the way in which we respond to other Christians. Quarreling, harshness, gossip and generally rude behavior toward one another is an indicator that Christianity hasn't really made much of a change in our lives. When Christians act like the world, we lose whatever positive witness we might otherwise have had.

Jesus cares about how we act! We need to care, too—everything we do reflects on Him.

This passage reminds us of the contrast which should exist between the conduct of believers and non-believers, the fact that we are saved through nothing but grace, and the importance of focusing on what helps to build people up, rather than tear them down. The idea of "good works" sometimes gets a bad rap in Christian circles, lost in the flood of "salvation by grace." Here is a firm reminder that those who believe in God are to *"devote themselves to good works."* The true and accurate concept of salvation by grace doesn't grant us a license for laziness! God has things for us to do—it's why we're so often called "servants." One of the things expected of us is that we will conduct ourselves in such a way that those who don't know our Savior will see Him in us, and that it will be a good reflection. Good works, and refusing to speak evil of others, is a great place to start.

What to Do With Stinkers

Remind them to be submissive to rulers and authorities, to be obedient, to be ready for every good work, to speak evil of no one, to avoid quarreling, to be gentle, and to show perfect courtesy toward all people. ...

But avoid foolish controversies, genealogies, dissensions, and quarrels about the law, for they are unprofitable and worthless. As for a person who stirs up division, after warning him once and then twice, have nothing more to do with him, knowing that such a person is warped and sinful; he is self-condemned. Titus 3:1-2,9-11

What do we do with stinkers—those people who make sure the quarrel never dies down, whose hobby is stirring up division and keeping it stirred up?

First of all, don't be one! We need to make sure it's not us stirring the pot, refusing to let go of our pet peeve or our treasured bit of controversial theology or worship style preference. It's our sincerity which makes people listen to us; it's our persistence which makes it hard to coexist in peaceful disagreement. It's about time to let it drop—for *good (*as in, *everybody's).*

Second, don't let the stinkers set the agenda. God has called us to live in peace, not quarreling. The one who insists on arguing as the centerpiece of activities is not helping himself or anyone else. This is the place where a kind, but firm, private rebuke is called for. Rinse and repeat the process, if necessary, and call for back-up. If nothing works, get the thing back on track, spiritually, *without* the divisive individual, rather than allowing him to sulk his way back into control of the situation by manipulative tactics. If his desire is not for unity, seek it without him. Do it without guilt.

Third, avoid the controversies in the first place. Some questions don't need to be answered! Bringing them up in the first place is hazardous and a waste of time. *"Unprofitable and worthless"*—that's an accurate description of many discussions. If the fire never gets started, we don't have to put it out.

The part about speaking evil of no one gets to me! This is right after a passage telling us to rebuke and encourage! When I set my mind to it, I do O.K. at encouraging; I stink at rebuking, and I sometimes find myself speaking evil of someone, to a person who can do nothing about it. I need to reverse those last two. I need to be willing to rebuke, when necessary, and forget how to gossip and slander. I need to not be a stinker, and not let stinkers control my life.

Youthful Authority

Now the word of the LORD came to me, saying, "Before I formed you in the womb I knew you, and before you were born I consecrated you; I appointed you a prophet to the nations."

Then I said, "Ah, Lord God! Behold, I do not know how to speak, for I am only a youth." But the LORD said to me, "Do not say, 'I am only a youth'; for to all to whom I send you, you shall go, and whatever I command you, you shall speak. Do not be afraid of them, for I am with you to deliver you, declares the LORD."

Then the LORD put out his hand and touched my mouth. And the LORD said to me, "Behold, I have put my words in your mouth. See, I have set you this day over nations and kingdoms, to pluck up and to break down, to destroy and to overthrow, to build and to plant." Jeremiah 1:4-10

The concept that God would ordain a servant even before birth is well reinforced in scripture. It's not the idea that God would do this which hits us as strange—it's the idea that it would be *us!* The kind of person God chooses to use nearly always feels the same way about their commission: Incompetent and scared. God's reaction to their response is also nearly always the same: Reassurance, clarification, detailed instructions—and best of all—*authority!* Here's a servant who sees himself as "only a youth"—an incompetent one at that—and look at the authority God has just given him! *"Behold, I have put my words in your mouth. See, I have set you this day over nations and kingdoms, to pluck up and to break down, to destroy and to overthrow, to build and to plant."*

Authority over nations? Good grief! Jeremiah has a pre-ordained role, a commission, all the provision and authority he could possibly need, and God's reassuring touch. The wonderful news is that it's not just Jeremiah whom God would treat like this! Every one of His servants gets all of the equipment we need, in order to fulfill His commission on our lives. Nor is it just a big job and some gear handed over to us—it all comes with the personal touch of the God who ordained us for this role before we were even born.

June 26

Fruit of the Flesh, Fruit of the Spirit

But I say, walk by the Spirit, and you will not gratify the desires of the flesh. For the desires of the flesh are against the Spirit, and the desires of the Spirit are against the flesh, for these are opposed to each other, to keep you from doing the things you want to do. But if you are led by the Spirit, you are not under the law. Now the works of the flesh are evident: sexual immorality, impurity, sensuality, idolatry, sorcery, enmity, strife, jealousy, fits of anger, rivalries, dissensions, divisions, envy, drunkenness, orgies, and things like these. I warn you, as I warned you before, that those who do such things will not inherit the kingdom of God. But the fruit of the Spirit is love, joy, peace, patience, kindness, goodness, faithfulness, gentleness, self-control; against such things there is no law. And those who belong to Christ Jesus have crucified the flesh with its passions and desires.

If we live by the Spirit, let us also walk by the Spirit. Let us not become conceited, provoking one another, envying one another. Galatians 5:16-26

Our character is shaped by what we allow to grow. As followers of the Lord Jesus, the Holy Spirit's presence in us will be evidenced by the "fruit of the Spirit," if we allow Him to cultivate those attributes in our lives, and we welcome the fruit (and the accompanying change).

Meanwhile, the "fruit of the flesh" remains available to us, too, in the form of temptations, bad habits, etc., much like the best of gardens still sports an occasional weed. Like weeds, the "flesh" needs to be dealt with decisively, or it will soon take over and cause ruin. The long list of fleshly "fruits" is a reminder that these things are not to be considered inevitable or normal for a Christ-follower; rather, they are to be "crucified"!

Instead of tolerating in ourselves the fleshly habits of jealousy, fits of anger and the like, we are to do whatever it takes to remove them, and be led by the Spirit instead of by the old nature of the flesh. Yank out the weeds, nurture the fruit. It's not as easy as it sounds, but this direction of our life is so very important. We are accepted by God "as is," but it is never His intent to leave us like He found us. He immediately begins to transform us into the image of His Son. The longer we serve Him, the more we should resemble Christ, and the more the fruit of our lives should be obviously fruit of the Spirit and not fruit of the flesh.

What will grow? Whatever we water.

Not Ashamed To Worship

So David and the elders of Israel and the commanders of thousands went to bring up the ark of the covenant of the LORD from the house of Obed-edom with rejoicing....
And as the ark of the covenant of the LORD came to the city of David, Michal the daughter of Saul looked out of the window and saw King David dancing and rejoicing, and she despised him in her heart.
1 Chronicles 15:25,29

God's servant David celebrates with all his might, not caring what anyone else thinks of him, as the ark is triumphantly brought into Jerusalem. His wife cares, and she *"despised him in her heart."* I think it's not because he embarrassed himself—which he didn't—but because he embarrassed *her*, for a couple of reasons. One was that the noble king was her husband, and everything he did reflected on her. His indignity really galled her, and she felt it made her look bad.

Another reason, much more important, is that Michal didn't love God. I don't personally think she ever did. She didn't even understand what worship was about, and episodes like this only highlighted the enormous difference, spiritually, between her husband and herself. I think it's why it bothered her so very much, and why it still bothers people who aren't in love with God, to see what they consider excesses in worship, when deep down they realize that they themselves have no true love at all for God. Consequently, the love others show only makes them look and feel bad.

Michal's heart seems to be like her Dad's. Both seemed to be pretty well self-centered, and never fully committed to what God wanted. A "servant" like Saul—or his daughter, Michal, is never going to be much of a blessing to the Master. Sad.

A servant who is so in love with the Master that he doesn't care what anyone else thinks, who is in constant, adoring communication with Him, cannot *help* but be a blessing to the Master.

A servant is not embarrassed by acts of service or worship, because it's not about the servant; it's about the Master.

Not Ashamed
School Bus Religion

And he began to teach them that the Son of Man must suffer many things and be rejected by the elders and the chief priests and the scribes and be killed, and after three days rise again. And he said this plainly. And Peter took him aside, and began to rebuke him. But turning and seeing his disciples, he rebuked Peter and said, "Get behind me, Satan! For you are not setting your mind on the things of God, but on the things of man."

And he called to him the crowd with his disciples and said to them, "If anyone would come after me, let him deny himself and take up his cross and follow me. For whoever would save his life will lose it, but whoever loses his life for my sake and the gospel's will save it. For what does it profit a man to gain the whole world and forfeit his life? For what can a man give in return for his life? For whoever is ashamed of me and of my words in this adulterous and sinful generation, of him will the Son of Man also be ashamed when he comes in the glory of his Father with the holy angels."
Mark 8:31-38

It is ironic that in a world crammed full of hideous sin, we should find ourselves bashful about being aligned with Jesus Christ, and we would shy away from identifying with His words. After all the Lord has done for us, not only dying that we might live, but also enduring the humiliation and shame surrounding that death, to think we would be ashamed of Him!

But I have been, on numerous occasions. I vividly recall tucking the book of Acts inside Newsweek magazine for the bus ride to high school. I knew I needed to study for Bible quizzing, but I didn't care to take the heat that reading the Bible on the school bus would be sure to generate. I slyly thought I was getting the best of both worlds, as I studied the Bible in an open magazine, undisturbed. I wanted to be a Christian, but was ashamed to be labeled one. Why? It wasn't like I had any "cool" to protect! Looking back, if I was going to be a geek, anyway, I wish I would have gone ahead and been a geek for Jesus! I could have had a ministry on the school bus. Instead, all I had was a headache.

If we're ashamed of Jesus in a sinful world, He would be ashamed of us in a spotless heaven. If the world is so great, we ought to go ahead and just forget Jesus. But it's the other way around. Jesus is great. We ought to just forget the world.

Not Ashamed

Secret Saints

And he said to all, "If anyone would come after me, let him deny him-self and take up his cross daily and follow me. For whoever would save his life will lose it, but whoever loses his life for my sake will save it. For what does it profit a man if he gains the whole world and loses or forfeits himself? For whoever is ashamed of me and of my words, of him will the Son of Man be ashamed when he comes in his glory and the glory of the Father and of the holy angels. But I tell you truly, there are some standing here who will not taste death until they see the kingdom of God." Luke 9:23-27

"And he said to all" (not just the Twelve). The standard is set. If I'm not willing to lose my life for Christ, I'm not a follower of Christ. This requirement is not just for those "called into full-time Christian service," but for every follower of Christ Jesus. In that respect, we're *all* "called into full-time Christian service."

Nor is there a "middle ground," where we can choose to be neutral, neither fully supporting nor opposing Jesus. His own words, from Luke 11:23 close the door on that one: *"Whoever is not with me is against me, and whoever does not gather with me scatters."*

Then there is the "secret disciple" route which has been chosen by many—myself included, far too many times—which reasons that being an undercover disciple is better than being no disciple at all. That plan bears very unpleasant rewards: *"And I tell you, everyone who acknowledges me before men, the Son of Man also will acknowledge before the angels of God, but the one who denies me before men will be denied before the angels of God."* (Lk 12:8-9)

"Secret saints," seeking to keep the favor of the world while simultane-ously trying to be an incognito Christian, instead of garnering the best of both worlds, find themselves faced with the worst—a Savior who grants them their wish of not being identified with Him, and the disdain of a world that never cared about them in the first place. Far better to "lose" our lives—including reputation, friends and whatever—and gain Christ, than to try to hang onto it all, and end up eternally empty-handed.

Not Ashamed

The Wonderful Place of Disgrace

We have an altar from which those who serve the tent have no right to eat. For the bodies of those animals whose blood is brought into the holy places by the high priest as a sacrifice for sin are burned outside the camp. So Jesus also suffered outside the gate in order to sanctify the people through his own blood. Therefore let us go to him outside the camp and bear the reproach he endured. For here we have no lasting city, but we seek the city that is to come. Hebrews 13:10-14

This passage is referring to the sacrifice Christ made, "outside the gate," and how he suffered there. We are to go to Him, bearing the reproach He bore.... because Jesus is our Sacrifice, not the food offered on the temple altars, where only the priests can go. Just as the common person doesn't have the right to eat that sacrifice (only the priests), we have a sacrifice in Christ which is only for those willing to go outside the camp.

Being a servant is not something which commands respect from the rest of the world. Jesus was despised by many; His followers will be, too. He was willing to endure disgrace, in order to purchase our redemption. His followers need to be ready to suffer disgrace, as well.

Therefore let us go to him outside the camp and bear the reproach he endured. (Hebrews 13:13)

Why?

For here we have no lasting city, but we seek the city that is to come. (Hebrews 13:14)

We're like workers, stationed in a foreign land. We're in their culture, but we're not like them. We're there on a temporary assignment, and then we're going home. We Christians are here on this earth on temporary assignment, and then we're going home! So what if, for now, not all the privileges of earth are accessible to us? We have access to a table from which others have no right to eat. It's O.K. that the table is outside the camp, in the place associated with disgrace. That's where our Savior is. Wherever He is, it's home.

Promises for Servants

Bullet-Proof Disciples

"...no weapon that is fashioned against you shall succeed, and you shall confute every tongue that rises against you in judgment. This is the heritage of the servants of the LORD and their vindication from me, declares the LORD." Isaiah 54:17

This verse ends a chapter on God's protection; the next verse begins a chapter on God's compassion and provision. The bases are covered for God's servants.

The Lord wants His children to know that we are under His protection. This does not eliminate the fact that we will from time to time endure suffering of one form or another, but it is a reminder that a loving Father watches over our *every* move, and is never caught off-guard by the enemy.

Notice the nuances in this verse. It doesn't promise us a conflict-free existence where weapons are never formed against us; He says *"no weapon that is fashioned against you shall succeed."* We aren't promised freedom from attack, but servants of the Lord are propped up by the promises of a God who says our enemy won't win over us as long as we're serving and trusting in Him. Hey, that's pretty good!

We even get the promise that we will be victorious against the verbal attacks waged by judgmental tongues lashing out at us: *"and you shall confute every tongue that rises against you in judgment."* I don't think that means we win all arguments, especially ones we started; I think it means God makes sure we are vindicated when we are reproached for His name's sake while we are trying to honor Him with our lives.

Why does the Lord make His servants bullet-proof? *"This is the heritage of the servants of the LORD and their vindication from me, declares the LORD."* With service to God comes God's promised protection. It's part of the heritage He offers. He promises vindication as well, so we don't have to worry about retaliating against those who try out their weapons on us, or use their tongue as one. He is a really big God, and He has promised all the protection His servants need. He hasn't told us we'll never encounter hostility aimed in our direction, but He has given us the assurance that if we will stand with God, He will make sure that when the onslaught is over, we're still standing. No weapon, no word. *Nothing* prevails against God's servant.

July 2

Not Ashamed
Fearless Suffering

For God gave us a spirit not of fear but of power and love and self-control.

Therefore do not be ashamed of the testimony about our Lord, nor of me his prisoner, but share in suffering for the gospel by the power of God, who saved us and called us to a holy calling, not because of our works but because of his own purpose and grace, which he gave us in Christ Jesus before the ages began, and which now has been manifested through the appearing of our Savior Christ Jesus, who abolished death and brought life and immortality to light through the gospel, for which I was appointed a preacher and apostle and teacher, which is why I suffer as I do. But I am not ashamed, for I know whom I have believed, and I am convinced that he is able to guard until that Day what has been entrusted to me.
2 Timothy 1:7-12

When our lives are plagued by fear, we can rest assured it didn't come from God! The spirit God gives is one of power and love and self-control, not one of fear. There is a peace which is our birthright, even in the midst of our worst trials and scariest circumstances.

Another part of our birthright is suffering, despite what some modern-day health-and-wealth-gospel proponents fervently promise. On more than one occasion, we are given the heads-up that when suffering arrives, it should not come as a big surprise to us.

Paul knew suffering was just part of the bargain of being a disciple of Jesus. He also was very aware that what he had been given was a trust from the Lord.

A faithful servant is willing to suffer. He also learns to see everything as a trust from God, including trials and suffering. Because he understands this process and the nature of the Spirit within him, the servant does not give way to fear, but instead allows the Spirit to build in his life a power, love and self-control which points like a compass back to God. It's like a trademark. The Spirit of God is not one of fear. The powerful, loving life of self-discipline is the life which bears the mark of the Spirit's control. That's the life every believer gets to have, if we simply live surrendered to His Spirit.

Not Afraid

The Key to God's Faithfulness

Remember Jesus Christ, risen from the dead, the offspring of David, as preached in my gospel, for which I am suffering, bound with chains as a criminal. But the word of God is not bound! Therefore I endure everything for the sake of the elect, that they also may obtain the salvation that is in Christ Jesus with eternal glory. The saying is trustworthy, for:
If we have died with him, we will also live with him;
if we endure, we will also reign with him;
if we deny him, he also will deny us;
if we are faithless, he remains faithful—
for he cannot deny himself.
Remind them of these things, and charge them before God not to quarrel about words, which does no good, but only ruins the hearers. Do your best to present yourself to God as one approved, a worker who has no need to be ashamed, rightly handling the word of truth. 2 Timothy 2:8-15

Mis-handling God's truth is a serious thing. Evidently, so is "quarreling about words." It seems to ruin both participants and spectators. I've been in some theology classes where that seemed to be the theme—and outcome.

On the other hand, there are "trustworthy sayings" we are to hold on to, and pass along to other believers, for their benefit. This four-line proverb packed with promises is apparently one of them. There's a lot of theology crowded into four simple couplets which would fit on a coffee cup.

The first two couplets are beautiful, solid promises: *"If we have died with him, we will also live with him; if we endure, we will also reign with him"*; the third couplet is a warning: *"If we deny him, he also will deny us"*; and then there's the fourth one, the one I love the most: *"If we are faithless, he remains faithful"*—

Wait. Shouldn't that be like the others? Shouldn't it say, *"If we are faithless, he will break faith with us, too"?*

No! Because this is our glorious Heavenly Father, who is faithful, *always,* regardless of what we do! We're not the key to His faithfulness. No one is. Our God is *always* faithful, and there's no "key" to it. Pass it on!

Not Afraid

Blood-Stained Handprints

And now, behold, I know that none of you among whom I have gone about proclaiming the kingdom will see my face again. Therefore I testify to you this day that I am innocent of the blood of all of you, for I did not shrink from declaring to you the whole counsel of God. Pay careful attention to yourselves and to all the flock, in which the Holy Spirit has made you overseers, to care for the church of God, which he obtained with his own blood. I know that after my departure fierce wolves will come in among you, not sparing the flock; and from among your own selves will arise men speaking twisted things, to draw away the disciples after them. Therefore be alert, remembering that for three years I did not cease night or day to admonish everyone with tears. And now I commend you to God and to the word of his grace, which is able to build you up and to give you the inheritance among all those who are sanctified. I coveted no one's silver or gold or apparel. You yourselves know that these hands ministered to my necessities and to those who were with me. In all things I have shown you that by working hard in this way we must help the weak and remember the words of the Lord Jesus, how he himself said, 'It is more blessed to give than to receive.' "

"And when he had said these things, he knelt down and prayed with them all. And there was much weeping on the part of all; they embraced Paul and kissed him, being sorrowful most of all because of the word he had spoken, that they would not see his face again. And they accompanied him to the ship. Acts 20:25-38

It's been twenty centuries, but the pathos of that moment still lingers. The dedication, the determination shown by those early believers! Those were our spiritual parents—people who were willing to lay down *everything*, in order to follow Christ.

The Ephesian elders were informed they would never see Paul's face again—now it was up to them. Would they watch over the flock, follow the example, work hard, finish the course? The torch had been passed.

And what of us? Are we willing to accept what has been passed down to us? Our spiritual ancestors are gone. Now, it's up to us. Will we mirror their determination, and go forward with Christ? As we look at the blood-stained handprints on that torch, we know there's really no choice. We must go on.

Not Ashamed

Signs and Sins

"And I tell you, everyone who acknowledges me before men, the Son of Man also will acknowledge before the angels of God, but the one who denies me before men will be denied before the angels of God." Luke 12:8-9

This is not just a minor point in serving God. If we are not willing to be fully identified with Christ, we cannot be true disciples of His. If we are not willing to suffer or to pick up our cross in order to follow Him, we cannot be His servants. He's not looking for "sympathizers;" He's looking for disciples. In these days of rampant, belligerent and public sin, it's very important that we not be ashamed to align ourselves with Jesus Christ, or His Word, and it is very important that we are willing to take the heat that comes with that alignment. The days for being an incognito disciple in America are about over.

A servant is not ashamed of his Master. He's not ashamed of his Master's words; he's not ashamed to suffer for the sake of the Master, or even to die for Him; he's not ashamed to be identified with the Master; he's not embarrassed or ashamed to worship the Master with utter abandon.

Does this mean we're to be obnoxious in our faith? I'm thinking of people who have gained media attention by tormenting those with unpopular sins, carrying their signs about hell's judgment and seeming to exult in the prospect, as long as it's somebody else and not them. The way I read it, Jesus said that without Him, we're *all* lost, not just the ones whose sins look the worst on a cardboard sign. I could fill a sign or two with my own sins, but they're under the blood. And that's the point, for me. My Savior is Jesus—no one else! My self-righteousness isn't going to get me very far! My only hope of avoiding the penalty of my sins is the forgiveness offered me by the Son of God, who paid the price in full, for me. But if I think I'm going to just live my life however I please, refuse to be identified with the Christ who died for me, then be welcomed into heaven by a Savior whom I treated as an embarrassment to my dying breath, I'm as mistaken as I can be!

Salvation is serious business. We can't have it both ways: We belong to Jesus, or we do not. I want the world to know I belong to Jesus, and they can, too. Everyone who wants to can avoid hell, no matter what our sign used to say.

Not Afraid

A Plague for Jesus

"For we have found this man a plague, one who stirs up riots among all the Jews throughout the world and is a ringleader of the sect of the Nazarenes. He even tried to profane the temple, but we seized him."
Acts 24:5-6

Serving God doesn't mean that everyone likes you!

When you have done everything Paul did, and endured the kind of hardships and persecutions he endured, what must it feel like to have your service presented before the governor like this?!

Paul's enemies told numerous lies against him, but to little effect. The governor, Felix, had enough sense to realize who was telling the truth and who was not, even though the Jewish leaders did their best to butter him up. In fact, Paul's message so penetrated Felix's heart that he summoned Paul often to converse with him, though he never made the step of becoming a believer, himself.

Back to the name-calling. *"For we have found this man a plague,..."* What does it feel like to have repeatedly risked your life for no other reason than to try to save strangers from eternal ruin, only to be publicly labeled a "plague"? "Plague"—a disease, something to get rid of, something inhuman, worse than no value.

Am I willing to so associate myself with Christ that I would let people lie about me before governors and kings, for His sake, then calmly make my defense, all the while honoring the name of Jesus? Am I willing to be a "plague" for Jesus?

And which one is it, anyway—"plague" or "missionary"? It all depends on whose side we're on. To one, it's the sweet smell of eternal life; to others, it's an obnoxious plague which won't go away to leave them in their sin.

May my life be so marked by His Spirit that wherever I am, the Gospel spreads like a plague!

Not Afraid

Dumped By the World

"If the world hates you, know that it has hated me before it hated you. If you were of the world, the world would love you as its own; but because you are not of the world, but I chose you out of the world, therefore the world hates you. Remember the words that I said to you: 'A servant is not greater than his master.' If they persecuted me, they will also persecute you. If they kept my word, they will also keep yours. But all these things they will do to you on account of my name, because they do not know him who sent me. If I had not come and spoken to them, they would not have been guilty of sin, but now they have no excuse for their sin. Whoever hates me hates my Father also. If I had not done among them the works that no one else did, they would not be guilty of sin, but now they have seen and hated both me and my Father. But the word that is written in their Law must be fulfilled: 'They hated me without a cause.'

But when the Helper comes, whom I will send to you from the Father, the Spirit of truth, who proceeds from the Father, he will bear witness about me. And you also will bear witness, because you have been with me from the beginning." John 15:18-27

The mark of Jesus upon our lives separates us from a world which chose to hate and persecute Him. When we join up with Jesus, we are no longer part of the "world," and the popularity we may formerly have enjoyed as one of its residents will often be jerked away.

What's the difference? It's the scandal of the cross. An unresponsive world rejected the Savior who came to earth to save them. Ignorance turned to rebellion, as the sacrifice was delivered up before their very eyes. Ever since, it only takes the slightest reminder—the symbol of the cross, a fish sign, a head bowed in prayer—and the rebellion is reactivated.

We remind people of Jesus! If that reminder exposes sin rather than salvation, we catch the consequences of a wrath directed toward God, but which lands on whomever bears His name. It's all part of being a witness. And it's all part of having to choose a side. When we pick Jesus, we may as well get used to the idea that the world won't love us like it used to. So what?

Not Afraid

Free From Fear

"And they have conquered him by the blood of the Lamb and by the word of their testimony, for they loved not their lives even unto death." Revelation 12:11

The weapons which are effective against Satan are clear: The blood of the Lamb, the word of our testimony, a willingness to die serving the One who died for us.

The blood of Jesus, the Lamb of God, is most important of all—without His shed blood there is no salvation, and the accuser of the brethren prevails against us. When our sins are covered by the blood of our Savior, the accusations of the enemy must fall silent; the devil has no choice. It is the blood of Jesus which saves us, and we are His.

The word of our testimony completes the circle of power represented by His blood. Salvation is available to all who will receive it, but those who ignore or reject it are yet liable to the accusations of the enemy. When we receive the gift of salvation, and we testify to what Christ has done for us and in us, the circle is completed, and Satan is shut out. Any claim he may have had to us is canceled. We move from death to life.

Then there's the last piece: *"for they loved not their lives even unto death."* Satan's tactics have always centered on lies and intimidation. When we proclaim the truth of Jesus' lordship and we trust in His promises, the power of the lies is broken. But there is still intimidation. Satan can threaten to harm us or kill us, if we don't succumb to his plans.

This is where the last hold is severed. If we have determined in our soul that we are willing to give *anything* in order to follow Jesus, including our very life, we are set free from the intimidation Satan attempts to use on us linked to our instincts of self-preservation. He's out of bullets! If he can no longer lie us into submission, because we believe only God's truth, and it no longer works to scare us with threats of death or injury, because we're no longer afraid of death, what does he have left?! There's no more foothold on our life. We overcome him by the blood of the Lamb, by our testimony about that Savior, by the fact that we're no longer afraid to die, since it only puts us even closer into His presence. When we love Jesus more than we love life, the enemy loses his grip, and we get to live free from fear.

Not Afraid

The Anointing Is Worth It

Saul was afraid of David because the LORD was with him but had departed from Saul. So Saul removed him from his presence and made him a commander of a thousand. And he went out and came in before the people. And David had success in all his undertakings, for the LORD was with him. And when Saul saw that he had great success, he stood in fearful awe of him. But all Israel and Judah loved David, for he went out and came in before them. 1 Samuel 18:12-16

Just because you're God's servant doesn't mean that everyone will like you! On the contrary, sometimes that's precisely the reason they don't! In this situation, the praise of the people only made the king increase in his jealousy of David, the champion who had saved the day for the Israelites. It didn't help that everyone seemed to recognize God's Spirit on David's life, and though they probably didn't mention it, publicly, His absence in Saul's.

At one time, the anointing had obviously been upon Saul's life. He had repeatedly been given opportunities to trust God and gain favor through obedience. He had repeatedly failed those tests. Now the anointing was gone, and he knew it. The presence of this youth who defeated giants and handily succeeded in every task, with God's help, was such a threat to the errant king that he chose to devote the rest of his life to eliminating him. The focus in Saul's life, from here on, is going to be getting rid of David, rather than challenging Israel's enemies, the Philistines. Yet another waste, in a life characterized by waste.

Why did Saul hate David? Saul saw that God's Spirit was upon David, and had left Saul, and Saul was threatened by what he saw in David. Hence, he was David's enemy for the rest of his life. Had David not been under the anointing of God, Saul wouldn't have even known who he was, much less hated him. But the anointing is worth it! Having God's favor is worth everything—even if it seems that the whole rest of the world is mad at you!

Not Afraid

The Gift of a Rebuke

And the LORD sent Nathan to David. 2 Samuel 12:1

On the tails of David's scandalous actions regarding Bathsheba, the wife of Uriah the Hittite, including Uriah's planned demise at David's orders, God sends a prophet to the king of Israel. This was not a mission without peril! In fact, had Nathan gone on his own, without God's direction, he would have never returned, and he knew it.

Bringing bad news or correction to the sovereign of a nation is never going to be a welcome task, under any circumstances; it didn't help that in David's case, in times past, he had been known to kill the messenger, if he deemed it appropriate! David had already killed several men in this cover-up; what was one more?

Not all jobs that a servant gets are easy ones. This had to rank as one of the hardest ever! God's servant, Nathan, seems unafraid.

I'm pretty sure that the "lamb" story Nathan tells David was divinely inspired. The result of the story is that David is unknowingly trapped into condemning himself, so Nathan isn't the one doing it. Nathan tells the story, David reacts by angrily stating, *"The man who has done this deserves to die,"* (2 Sa 12:5) and all Nathan has to do is close the trap with four words: *"You are the man!"* (2 Sa 12:7) David had already pronounced judgment on himself, by that time; all Nathan was doing was pointing that out.

One of the best things Nathan ever did was to bravely and graciously deliver a difficult message from God, not knowing if he would survive the day. When finished with his mission, he wisely made a quick retreat! He'll live to be used of God another day.

Interesting to me is David's reaction, when rebuked. Instead of defending himself, or killing the messenger, he immediately owns up to it: *"I have sinned against the LORD."* (2 Sa 12:13) Rather than another murder, or yet another attempted cover-up, David responds by writing Psalm 51. The man is overcome with repentance. Forgiveness and grace restore to him a clean heart. His relationship with God is renewed.

As difficult as it was for all concerned, one of the best things God ever did for David was to send His messenger to David's door with the gift of a rebuke.

Not Afraid

Cowards to Volunteers

In the year that King Uzziah died I saw the Lord sitting upon a throne, high and lifted up; and the train of his robe filled the temple. Above him stood the seraphim. Each had six wings: with two he covered his face, and with two he covered his feet, and with two he flew. And one called to another and said:

"Holy, holy, holy is the LORD of hosts;
the whole earth is full of his glory!"

And the foundations of the thresholds shook at the voice of him who called, and the house was filled with smoke. And I said: "Woe is me! For I am lost; for I am a man of unclean lips, and I dwell in the midst of a people of unclean lips; for my eyes have seen the King, the LORD of hosts!"

Then one of the seraphim flew to me, having in his hand a burning coal that he had taken with tongs from the altar. And he touched my mouth and said: "Behold, this has touched your lips; your guilt is taken away, and your sin atoned for.

And I heard the voice of the Lord saying, "Whom shall I send, and who will go for us?" Then I said, "Here am I! Send me." Isaiah 6:1-8

When Isaiah sees the Lord, and the seraphim touches his lips, he suddenly wants to be a volunteer. Does he understand for what he's volunteering? The cost? The consequences? Probably not, but Isaiah had already stopped caring about anything else. Close encounters with the Almighty do that to people.

When God manifests Himself, there's always a reason. He never does it just to show off; if we want to see God's power and handiwork, all we need to do is look around at the constant witness of nature. But those rare and intimate times, when God chooses to display a glimpse of His glory to an individual always seem to precipitate something: A miracle, a promise, a commission. The initial human response is always pretty much the same: Fear, humility, feelings of inadequacy. Then comes the promise, the rebuke or the mission.

The second response of the human who encounters God is also nearly always the same: "I can't do this, but I also can't ever forget this moment, and I have to obey you. O.K., I'll go!" God turns cowards to volunteers.

Not Afraid

Fearful King, Fearless Prophet

In the days of Ahaz the son of Jotham, son of Uzziah, king of Judah, Rezin the king of Syria and Pekah the son of Remaliah the king of Israel came up to Jerusalem to wage war against it, but could not yet mount an attack against it. When the house of David was told, "Syria is in league with Ephraim," the heart of Ahaz and the heart of his people shook as the trees of the forest shake before the wind.

And the LORD said to Isaiah, "Go out to meet Ahaz, you and Shear-jashub your son, at the end of the conduit of the upper pool on the highway to the Washer's Field. And say to him, 'Be careful, be quiet, do not fear, and do not let your heart be faint because of these two smoldering stumps of firebrands, at the fierce anger of Rezin and Syria and the son of Remaliah...
Isaiah 7:1-4

It doesn't take long before the servant who volunteered, "Here am I! Send me!" is indeed sent. And to whom? To one of the most immoral, idolatrous kings ever to rule over Judah, a man who had led his nation into apostasy and now was bearing the consequences, in facing an allied army of invaders.

The fear must have been palpable in Jerusalem, in those days, particularly in the heart of Ahaz, Judah's godless king. His father and grandfather had been good and righteous leaders, but Ahaz had purposefully strayed from his religious moorings, and plunged his country into new depths of depravity.

What will God's message be to the quivering king? In contrast to the judgment Ahaz deserves and probably expects to hear, the message Isaiah relates from God is one of grace and comfort—"calm down, do not fear, what they threaten is not going to happen." Tucked into the conclusion of this word of hope is a timeless truth God wants Ahaz to hear and heed: *"If you are not firm in faith, you will not be firm at all."* (Isa 7:9)

Unfortunately, the king ignores the gentle reminder that the faith of his fathers is his only hope for stability in life, and Ahaz continues to flail about in unrighteousness for the rest of his days, but at least he was told. In the time of his greatest fear, God sent him a fearless prophet. It's too bad Ahaz didn't make the connection between faith and courage.

Not Afraid

Revolutionary Fear

For the LORD spoke thus to me with his strong hand upon me, and warned me not to walk in the way of this people, saying: "Do not call conspiracy all that this people calls conspiracy, and do not fear what they fear, nor be in dread. But the LORD of hosts, him you shall regard as holy. Let him be your fear, and let him be your dread...." Isaiah 8:11-13

At a time when few are hearing from God, Isaiah is. And one of the things Isaiah is hearing from the Lord is the warning not to follow the crowd, not to adopt the assumptions or habits of those around him, and not to fear what they fear, but instead to fear Him.

God's servant is listening to God, not the crowd. God's servant is going God's way, not the crowd's way. God's servant isn't even afraid of the same things; he's only afraid of God, or of displeasing Him. If we're going to be God's servant, it means that much of the time, we'll not be on the same page as everyone else! We may as well get used to it.

"But the LORD of hosts, him you shall regard as holy. Let him be your fear, and let him be your dread."

I'm thinking of the level of holy fear I've observed among American Christians, lately. It's pitifully low. Fear of offending the Lord of the Universe seems to scarcely cross most people's minds. More apparent is the fear I've seen (and experienced) when it comes to the possibility of ticking off a cranky church member than the fear of sinning against the Creator Himself. I think of the times when I have feared man's anger more than God's, and I wince. The attitude I've seen —and occasionally practiced— which says, "God will forgive me, but so-and-so never will," has been used as an excuse for a lot of spiritual compromise and some outright sin. The casualness with which God is approached—when He is approached—is an indicator of the disturbing lack of respect many have for His power or wrath. God's forgiveness is taken for granted far too much of the time, as if the free gift of salvation was also free to God. It wasn't.

The message Isaiah was getting is one I still need, today: "Don't be afraid of anything, except offending God." That's the healthy fear which frees and revolutionizes my life. What could it do for our country?

Not Afraid

Anxiety-Free Witnessing

"And when they bring you before the synagogues and the rulers and the authorities, do not be anxious about how you should defend yourself or what you should say, for the Holy Spirit will teach you in that very hour what you ought to say." Luke 12:11-12

I'm noticing that He said, *"when* they bring you..., not *"if."* Hmm. Although it's obvious that, at least in America, not everyone claiming the name of Christ has been dragged before the rulers to account for our faith, things could change in a hurry. If (or should it be "when"?) they change, will we be ready? Jesus gives the calm assurance that we don't even need to be anxious about the whole episode—all we have to do is read off the teleprompter the Holy Spirit will provide for our turn in the hot seat. Something like that.

No need to be anxious? Really? Most people can't even get through an episode of friendly fire, such as high school speech class—no, that was a bad example—or let's say, a preacher speaking to his own congregation (Hmm, another bad example; forget the examples) without sick-bag-level nerves. And we're supposed to be able to face off with nasty bureaucrats and not lose any sleep over it?! I guess so!

How's it going to happen?

This is how it happened to those who heard Jesus say it, in person. When the time came for them to face public persecution, as so many of them did, what the public witnessed was not a trembling, cringing religious coward. What observers saw, again and again, was Jesus. The witness was crystal clear. They were not hearing the words of an uneducated fisherman or tax collector; it was as though Jesus had hopped inside that body and was now speaking once again, with unheard of authority. It wasn't them, it was Jesus. It's why the disciples didn't stay up late, huddled with their attorneys, crafting their defense in preparation for the trial of their life. In fact, when God answered the prayers of the Early Church and delivered Peter from prison, the angel had to smack him just to get him awake! Had it been me, I would have been making notes on a 3x5 card for what I was going to say. There's a time to prepare. And there's a time to just turn your tongue over to God, and see what He has to say through you.

July 15

Not Intimidated or Distracted
Bulldog Leadership

Now when Sanballat and Tobiah and Geshem the Arab and the rest of our enemies heard that I had built the wall and that there was no breach left in it (although up to that time I had not set up the doors in the gates), Sanballat and Geshem sent to me, saying, "Come and let us meet together at Hakkephirim in the plain of Ono." But they intended to do me harm. And I sent messengers to them, saying, "I am doing a great work and I cannot come down. Why should the work stop while I leave it and come down to you?" And they sent to me four times in this way, and I answered them in the same manner. Nehemiah 6:1-4

I'm a fan of Nehemiah. He has those leadership qualities I have often envied, one of them being "focus." Faced on all sides with intense and crafty opposition, Nehemiah refuses to be distracted from his God-given task of rebuilding Jerusalem's walls. His enemies pull out all the stops, but no amount of threatening or trickery can induce God's man to give up his mission. He won't be intimidated, he won't be swayed, he refuses to compromise. And he succeeds! The wall is completed in 52 days, despite incredible odds.

The entire book of Nehemiah is like a workshop on leadership. It abounds in lessons on that subject. One of them is that a good servant (or leader) will not be distracted or intimidated into abandoning his duties. He knows his mission, and won't be dissuaded. Like a bulldog, once he grabs on, he won't let go, except at the orders of his master. He won't bite on the temptations that are designed to get him to release his hold on the goal. His enemies can't get him to quit by threatening him, or by damaging his reputation through rumors, or by negotiating him to death (he won't even stop to negotiate!). A good servant will not let go of his assigned mission.

We all need a focus from God that gives us the courage to endure distractions, threats and temptations. When we know our goal is God-given and so is our role, like Nehemiah, we can become successfully stubborn in refusing to let go until we complete the task before us. And when, like Nehemiah, we refuse to be intimidated or distracted, we bring inspiration to our friends, fear to our enemies and glory to our God.

Who Asked You To Judge Your Brother?

Why do you pass judgment on your brother? Or you, why do you despise your brother? For we will all stand before the judgment seat of God, for it is written,
> *'As I live, says the Lord, every knee shall bow to me, and every tongue shall confess to God.'*

So then each of us will give an account of himself to God.

Therefore let us not pass judgment on one another any longer, but rather decide never to put a stumbling block or hindrance in the way of a brother.
Romans 14:10-13

"Why do you pass judgment on your brother?"

Good question. I'm trying to think of who it was that asked me to do that. I know it wasn't God. It seems that maybe it was this snake-looking kind of thing that suggested it, I don't remember. Anyway, passing judgment on my brother has been an interesting hobby, and one that helps me to feel better about my own relationship with the Father. Noticing the faults of others, which does have a way of helping me to despise them (the brothers, not the faults), keeps me from having to focus too much on my own faults. Plus, I have brothers who help to remind me of my faults, so I'm just returning the favor. And it's not that I usually tell my brother his fault, anyway. I just make note of it, and let him sink a little further into the "despised" column.

I'm forgetting something, when I engage in the sport of brother-judging. I'm forgetting that some day I will be standing before the judgment seat of God, and the account I'll be giving won't be of what my brother did, but of what I did. If I've spent my life judging people it was not my business to judge, and despising them for not following the rules according to me, I'm going to be in a lot of trouble if God starts judging me, using my standard. I'd better knock it off, and confess my own sins, and let God worry about my brother.

Not My Job

As for the one who is weak in faith, welcome him, but not to quarrel over opinions. One person believes he may eat anything, while the weak person eats only vegetables. Let not the one who eats despise the one who abstains, and let not the one who abstains pass judgment on the one who eats, for God has welcomed him. Who are you to pass judgment on the servant of another? It is before his own master that he stands or falls. And he will be upheld, for the Lord is able to make him stand.

One person esteems one day as better than another, while another esteems all days alike. Each one should be fully convinced in his own mind. The one who observes the day, observes it in honor of the Lord. The one who eats, eats in honor of the Lord, since he gives thanks to God, while the one who abstains, abstains in honor of the Lord and gives thanks to God. For none of us lives to himself, and none of us dies to himself. If we live, we live to the Lord, and if we die, we die to the Lord. So then, whether we live or whether we die, we are the Lord's. For to this end Christ died and lived again, that he might be Lord both of the dead and of the living.
Romans 14:1-9

It's not my job to critique God's other servants, or to straighten out their theology, or to decide whether or not they're true servants of God. It's just not. The irritation it causes God when I choose to do those things must be similar to what parents feel when their kids are continually squabbling and lobbing things at one another, then coming to tattle on the evil behavior of their siblings and to suggest possible punishments, which they would gladly help administer. It's not my job to pass judgment on a fellow servant! That's God's servant, not mine. He'll deal with it. My job is to be the best servant of God I can be, which includes not picking on the other servants.

July 18

When Faith Can Hurt Somebody

Do not, for the sake of food, destroy the work of God. Everything is indeed clean, but it is wrong for anyone to make another stumble by what he eats. It is good not to eat meat or drink wine or do anything that causes your brother to stumble. The faith that you have, keep between yourself and God. Blessed is the one who has no reason to pass judgment on himself for what he approves. But whoever has doubts is condemned if he eats, because the eating is not from faith. For whatever does not proceed from faith is sin. Romans 14:20-23

Here's one of the few times in scripture when we're asked to "keep our faith to ourselves." The "faith" to which it refers is the one that says, "I'm a strong enough Christian that I can watch this movie and it doesn't affect me; if you were a strong Christian, it wouldn't bother you, either." Their deal was eating food which had sat under a false god's nose for a few hours in a pagan temple, and which was now sold at discount in the marketplace. Explaining how there had been no chemical or spiritual change in perfectly good meat in its short tenure as idol food was not a particular blessing to the new Christian who used to serve in that temple. There was just way too much baggage. If his "mature" Christian friend convinces him to go ahead, because "it's just food," that nagging feeling in the pit of his stomach is going to turn into something more spiritually damaging. Every bite is going to feel like another step backward, into the painful past. There are connotations and temptations here of which the "free" Christian is completely unaware. It's Satan's trap. Why on earth should a Christian push his "faith" on someone, when it results in thrusting a brother back into the danger zone?

Our problem is not food offered to idols. Our problem is practically everything else. Entertainments, habits, ethical decisions... Don't let your baby follow you out into the street. What's relatively safe for you may be disastrous for him.

Serve God by helping your brother on his journey. Don't allow your "strength" to dare him into danger.

Not On the Same System

Now the Jews' Feast of Booths was at hand. So his brothers said to him, "Leave here and go to Judea, that your disciples also may see the works you are doing. For no one works in secret if he seeks to be known openly. If you do these things, show yourself to the world." For not even his brothers believed in him. Jesus said to them, "My time has not yet come, but your time is always here. The world cannot hate you, but it hates me because I testify about it that its works are evil. You go up to the feast. I am not going up to this feast, for my time has not yet fully come." After saying this, he remained in Galilee. John 7:2-9

I suppose Jesus' brothers were just trying to be helpful. It didn't make sense to them that He would do what He was doing, in a place off the beaten path. "If you're trying to become a public figure, why waste yourself on Galilee? If you're going to become well-known, it'll have to be in Judea. Go there, so you can accomplish what you want."

They didn't understand. The world never does understand. It's because those who serve God and those who operate under the world's standard are getting their direction from two completely different sources. For the one who operates by the methods of the world, pragmatism is the only thing that makes sense. "If it works, it must be right."

For the one who takes his cues from God, the leading that supercedes everything else is what comes from the Father. That even includes the timing. If the Father isn't leading us this way, we don't do it, no matter how logical it might seem to those around us. Let the rest of the world keep charging ahead, operating according to their own wisdom; we wait for God's signals and God's timing, because that's who it is we're serving.

For the servant of God, life is not about reaching our worldly goals through worldly ways; life is about serving God. If unbelieving friends and family don't understand, so be it. We're not on the same system.

Respectful Faithfulness

But Daniel resolved that he would not defile himself with the king's food, or with the wine that he drank. Therefore he asked the chief of the eunuchs to allow him not to defile himself. And God gave Daniel favor and compassion in the sight of the chief of the eunuchs, and the chief of the eunuchs said to Daniel, "I fear my lord the king, who assigned your food and your drink; for why should he see that you were in worse condition than the youths who are of your own age? So you would endanger my head with the king." Then Daniel said to the steward whom the chief of the eunuchs had assigned over Daniel, Hananiah, Mishael, and Azariah, "Test your servants for ten days; let us be given vegetables to eat and water to drink. Then let our appearance and the appearance of the youths who eat the king's food be observed by you, and deal with your servants according to what you see." So he listened to them in this matter, and tested them for ten days. At the end of ten days it was seen that they were better in appearance and fatter in flesh than all the youths who ate the king's food. So the steward took away their food and the wine they were to drink, and gave them vegetables. Daniel 1:8-16

As a young captive in Babylon, confronted with compromise in the situation regarding the food offered him, instead of pushing his way through, Daniel asks permission of those in authority over him, and gains their favor, and as a result, is able to serve God faithfully without getting himself martyred. His approach garners respect for his God, and also elevates Daniel in the kingdom of Babylon.

Daniel is one of the least obnoxious people in the Bible. At a tender age, he already has found that it's possible to serve God and show respect and concern for others at the same time. This winsomeness of service would characterize Daniel's lengthy career. He simply proved himself so invaluable, time and again, that he could maintain favor with nearly any king. Some magnificent inroads were gained by a persistent, faithful use of God-given gifts, combined with a respectful attitude. Daniel's life is a reminder that just because we're serving God doesn't mean we have to be a pain in the neck to everyone else!

Suffering as a Christian

Beloved, do not be surprised at the fiery trial when it comes upon you to test you, as though something strange were happening to you. But rejoice insofar as you share Christ's sufferings, that you may also rejoice and be glad when his glory is revealed. If you are insulted for the name of Christ, you are blessed, because the Spirit of glory and of God rests upon you. But let none of you suffer as a murderer or a thief or an evildoer or as a meddler. Yet if anyone suffers as a Christian, let him not be ashamed, but let him glorify God in that name. For it is time for judgment to begin at the household of God; and if it begins with us, what will be the outcome for those who do not obey the gospel of God? And

"If the righteous is scarcely saved, what will become of the ungodly and the sinner?"

Therefore let those who suffer according to God's will entrust their souls to a faithful Creator while doing good. 1 Peter 4:12-19

There's no glory in suffering because we were meddling. Ditto for stealing, murder and other acts of evil frowned upon by societies everywhere. Suffering is part of the bargain for a Christian, but it should be suffering for *being* a Christian, not suffering for being a criminal or a jerk!

Insults will come to us because we bear the name of Jesus. They will actually bring us blessing! The insults which don't bear blessing are those which are pretty much deserved due to our wretched behavior.

We're reminded to not be surprised at trials, suffering or persecution—it's part of being identified with Christ. We are also reminded to not bring upon ourselves needless suffering, caused only by our bad conduct. The bottom line is: Check to be sure we're not earning insults and persecution through obnoxious actions which only dishonor God, anyway. If we know we're suffering for the cause of Jesus Christ, and not our own foolishness, we are encouraged to just entrust our souls to God and keep on doing good.

Grace Instead Of a Lawsuit

As she continued praying before the LORD, Eli observed her mouth. Hannah was speaking in her heart; only her lips moved, and her voice was not heard. Therefore Eli took her to be a drunken woman. And Eli said to her, "How long will you go on being drunk? Put away your wine from you." But Hannah answered, "No, my lord, I am a woman troubled in spirit. I have drunk neither wine nor strong drink, but I have been pouring out my soul before the LORD. Do not regard your servant as a worthless woman, for all along I have been speaking out of my great anxiety and vexation." Then Eli answered, "Go in peace, and the God of Israel grant your petition that you have made to him." And she said, "Let your servant find favor in your eyes." Then the woman went her way and ate, and her face was no longer sad. 1 Samuel 1:12-18

The next time Hannah met up with Eli the priest, it was to present him with the son God had granted her in response to her prayer, and his blessing. Had a woman been falsely accused and reprimanded by her spiritual leader for drunkenness in America, these days, we might have expected their next encounter to have been in a courtroom, accompanied by their lawyers!

Hannah's firm but very polite correction and her subservient attitude toward Eli gives her well-meaning priest a chance to reverse course, gracefully, and turns a curse into a blessing: *"Go in peace, and the God of Israel grant your petition that you have made to him."* There's a time for humility: I think it's most of the time!

Hannah could have let this episode be the straw that broke the camel's back: "Not only am I barren, and ridiculed by my rival, but when I come to you, God, your priest chews me out for being drunken! I'm through with this!" It could have become a very deep-seated bitterness, and it also could have been used of Satan to damage or end Eli's ministry. Instead, partly due to her gentle spirit, she gets a blessing; Eli gets to keep his job even though he made a pretty bad mistake; and Hannah goes away happy, not bitter! Not bad, for what could have been a disastrous encounter! Not only that, but God's just getting started blessing Hannah. The barren woman becomes the mother of one of Israel's greatest leaders—Samuel, plus five more children!

She could have sued! She went away happy, instead. God is good.

The Place of God's Mercy

But David's heart struck him after he had numbered the people. And David said to the LORD, "I have sinned greatly in what I have done. But now, O LORD, please take away the iniquity of your servant, for I have done very foolishly." 2 Samuel 24:10

The account of the census taken by David strikes me as strange. In 2 Samuel 24 it says God incited him to do it because He was angry with Israel; in 1 Chronicles 21 it says Satan was the one who incited David to number the people. When even Joab, David's opportunistic, pragmatic and unholy general, begs him not to do this, it must have been a much greater sin than appears to modern eyes. The horrible punishment it brought upon Israel was proof that, for once, Joab was right about righteousness.

So what could possibly be wrong with taking a national census? The main thing I come up with is "pride." God wanted His people to take pride in Him, not in themselves. "National pride" is not always a good thing, particularly if it minimizes reverence for God.

Had "No Census" been a rule God made up on the spot, David's conscience would have left him alone, but David knew it was wrong, and didn't express the least bit of surprise when his seer, Gad, came to deliver an ominous message from the Lord. Three punishment alternatives are given to David, who wisely refers the choice back to God. One of David's strengths is that he is always more willing to depend on God than he is to depend on man. *"Let us fall into the hand of the LORD, for his mercy is great; but let me not fall into the hand of man."* (2 Sa 24:14)

David did well to lean on God's mercy. God's choice is the shortest of the three punishments, and that one is even further shortened when the angel working destruction reaches Jerusalem, and God gives the command, *"It is enough; now stay your hand." And the angel of the LORD was by the threshing floor of Araunuh the Jebusite.* (2 Sa 24:16) An altar is built at God's command on the threshing floor of Araunuh the Jebusite.

When it comes time to erect a temple in Jerusalem, where will it be built? The place of God's mercy. We worship a God of mercy! Even when we have offended Him, we're better off to throw ourselves upon His mercy rather than man's wisdom. *"Let us fall into the hand of the LORD, for his mercy is great; but let me not fall into the hand of man."* His mercy *is* great, and regardless of what we've done, there is a place for us, there.

Not a Quitter

Stubbornness in the Right Direction

Therefore, since we are surrounded by so great a cloud of witnesses, let us also lay aside every weight, and sin which clings so closely, and let us run with endurance the race that is set before us, looking to Jesus, the founder and perfecter of our faith, who for the joy that was set before him endured the cross, despising the shame, and is seated at the right hand of the throne of God.

Consider him who endured from sinners such hostility against himself, so that you may not grow weary or fainthearted. Hebrews 12:1-3

The servant of God is not a quitter.

The roll call of saints listed in Hebrews 11 doesn't include any quitters. It includes people like Noah, who heard from God and believed God, but who then had the unbelievable task of constructing an ark 450 feet long just to prove he believed God! I'm just finishing up a yard project for which I bought materials ten years ago; I'm trying to think how long it would take me to do an ark—*with* power tools! How did he do it? Simple. He never quit.

After he heard from God and believed God, there was a very long period of time in which he had to keep on working, in order to prepare for what God had promised. I guess that's all of us, in some ways.

Our Savior, Jesus, on the way to the cross, set His face toward Jerusalem and refused to turn back. He was marching to His death, and knew it, but nothing could stop Him. He was doing it for us.

We disciples of Jesus need a pretty good amount of stubbornness, when it comes to following Christ. There are going to be times when the mountaintop experience that got us started on this journey seems like a distant illusion. There will be times when we're not hearing anything from God, when we're weary and all of our friends are telling us to quit. We need to stubbornly refuse to give up. We need to keep following Jesus. Stubbornness is a good thing, if it's what keeps us from quitting on God.

Not a Quitter

A Bad Time to Quit

"I have said all these things to you to keep you from falling away. They will put you out of the synagogues. Indeed, the hour is coming when whoever kills you will think he is offering service to God. And they will do these things because they have not known the Father, nor me. But I have said these things to you, that when their hour comes you may remember that I told them to you." John 16:1-4

If we're going to get smacked, it helps to know it's coming, and why. Jesus told His followers about the coming persecutions so they wouldn't be caught off guard. As His present-day followers, some of us may have experienced very little persecution, but if and when it comes, we really shouldn't be surprised. More importantly, we shouldn't quit! It's only the fulfillment of scripture taking place within our very lives.

Why do people do things like this? *"Because they have not known the Father, nor me."* It's really pretty simple. If they don't know the Father, and don't accept the Son, they're going to be able to convince themselves they're doing the right thing in tormenting Christians for living out their faith. Atrocities will be rationalized by people serving a god created in their own image. We'd better get ready to stand firm. We've been warned. We also need to remind ourselves that we're not alone. Jesus has not deserted His Church; on the contrary, He has sent the Holy Spirit to empower us, comfort us, and convict a world of sin, righteousness and judgment. Our job? To love. God will take care of the matters of judgment. Vengeance is up to Him, too. Our task is to stand firm in His power, in the knowledge that we saw the enemy's onslaught coming. Our Lord told us, in advance. It may be their hour, now, but ours is coming! Now would be a really bad time to quit.

Not a Quitter

Enduring Faith

Also it was allowed to make war on the saints and to conquer them. And authority was given it over every tribe and people and language and nation, and all who dwell on earth will worship it, everyone whose name has not been written before the foundation of the world in the book of life of the Lamb that was slain. If anyone has an ear, let him hear:

If anyone is to be taken captive,
to captivity he goes;
if anyone is to be slain with the sword,
with the sword must he be slain.

Here is a call for the endurance and faith of the saints.
Revelation 13:7-10

For those trying to follow Christ in the midst of the scenario when the beast is in power, it looks like the emphasis is going to need to be on endurance and faith, rather than self-preservation. It appears that when captivity or death has already been decreed for individuals, efforts to alter that fate will prove fruitless.

So what is the answer? Endurance and faith, on the part of the saints! How do we develop endurance and faith? By practice.

Rather than spending a lot of energy plotting how to spare ourselves and our loved ones from persecution, or whimpering in a corner as we worry over the bad things which might beset us, we are called to increase in our endurance and faith, by utilizing it on a daily basis, even when times are relatively easy. Endurance and faith grow through practice, through use. It shouldn't take a beast on the throne to get me to exercise my faith; the more I exercise it and depend on my God, the more stamina I develop and the more determined I become to not give in or give up.

When the time comes, the saints will need all the endurance and faith which can be summoned! Actually, we need it now. We might as well be working on it.

Not a Quitter

Saints with a Long Shelf-Life

For when the horses of Pharaoh with his chariots and his horsemen went into the sea, the LORD brought back the waters of the sea upon them, but the people of Israel walked on dry ground in the midst of the sea. Then Miriam the prophetess, the sister of Aaron, took a tambourine in her hand, and all the women went out after her with tambourines and dancing. And Miriam sang to them:

> *"Sing to the LORD, for he has*
> *triumphed gloriously;*
> *the horse and his rider he has*
> *thrown into the sea."* Exodus 15:19-21

I'm glad they stopped to praise God on the other side of the Red Sea. (Too bad they didn't continue praising Him, instead of getting into the nasty habit of whining)! But at least for a short period of time, the Israelites were filled with wonder and gratitude. They were singing songs of praise to the LORD, exalting the One who had safely led them through the middle of the sea and vanquished their enemies before their eyes.

Leading the contingent of praising women is Miriam, who grabbed a tambourine and began to sing the refrain of God's glorious victory. Somehow, the idea of a lithe teen-ager, dancing and singing to God, comes to mind. Then I do the math. This is Miriam, sister of Moses and Aaron, right? No other sisters are mentioned in the Bible as far as I know, so assuming Miriam is their only sister, this would be the one who watched over baby Moses as he floated in a basket on the Nile River, awaiting his fate. This was the one with the wherewithal to arrange with Pharaoh's daughter to pay the mother to raise the son she was supposed to have killed! Smart girl.

The baby had grown up. Life in the palace had taken a sudden turn when good intentions backfired, and Moses became a fugitive. God's burning bush call brought his return to Egypt, in order to help free his people. How old was Moses, when they crossed the Red Sea? Eighty. That's no teen-ager out there praising God with a tambourine in her hand, singing God's praises at the head of the dancers. She has to be close to ninety. Maybe praise is a kind of fountain of youth. It's certainly a fountain of blessing.

Not a Quitter

Predictable Failure

"Simon, Simon, behold, Satan demanded to have you, that he might sift you like wheat, but I have prayed for you that your faith may not fail. And when you have turned again, strengthen your brothers." Peter said to him, "Lord, I am ready to go with you both to prison and to death." Jesus said, "I tell you, Peter, the rooster will not crow this day, until you deny three times that you know me." Luke 22:31-34

It's one thing to fail miserably; it's another thing to have someone warn us of the precise temptation, and still we fail miserably! Simon Peter's situation gives us a slight glimpse into the spiritual battles raging around us. On the same night Jesus will be arrested, Peter glibly promises to share a prison cell with his Master if need be, or even to die with Him. Meanwhile, Peter is oblivious to the campaign of total destruction Satan has plotted against him, or the fact that only Jesus' intercessory prayers prevent the devil from grinding the apostle into dust, permanently.

Peter will rise again as a disciple, but it won't be on his own strength; it will be on the grace, mercy and forgiveness of his Lord, gently granted him on the beach in Galilee, post-resurrection.

Peter was a strong man, and like most strong men, tended to rely on his own strength. His own strength was sufficient for commercial fishing and making bold promises, but when it came to battling Satan, Peter didn't have a prayer. The only thing that got him through this ordeal at all was Jesus. The Lord had enough strength and faith for both of them. The lessons Simon learned about whose strength was reliable were lessons he would never forget. When the restored disciple turned to help his fellow fallen, he had switched over to a greater power than he'd ever before known. With it came more humility, more grace, more empathy than anyone had dreamed could come out of the rough fisherman.

God really does work everything for the good, in the lives of those who continue to follow Him and love Him. God can even take predictable failure and turn it into powerful ministry! And look what He does with obedience!

Not a Quitter

It's Worth the Heat

Then I said to them, "You see the trouble we are in, how Jerusalem lies in ruins with its gates burned. Come, let us build the wall of Jerusalem, that we may no longer suffer derision." And I told them of the hand of my God that had been upon me for good, and also of the words that the king had spoken to me. And they said, "Let us rise up and build." So they strengthened their hands for the good work. But when Sanballat the Horonite and Tobiah the Ammonite servant and Geshem the Arab heard of it, they jeered at us and despised us and said, "What is this thing that you are doing? Are you rebelling against the king?" Then I replied to them, "The God of heaven will make us prosper, and we his servants will arise and build, but you have no portion or right or claim in Jerusalem."
Nehemiah 2:17-20

It will get much worse before it gets better. From the first day, Nehemiah encounters opposition from some fierce, dastardly enemies. Sanballat, Tobiah, and Geshem begin an immediate campaign of slander and derision, directed at the new Jewish leader who has come to rebuild Jerusalem's shattered walls. They try everything they can think of: Threats, tricks, ambushes, starting rumors, negotiation, intimidation. None of it pulls Nehemiah off task. He is determined to accomplish his purpose in Jerusalem. With God's help and the cooperation of some everyday heroes who simply have a mind to work, the wall is up in fifty-two days. It's to the glory of God!

Had Nehemiah chosen to remain in his comfortable position as cup-bearer to the king of Babylon, he would never have known the kind of attacks and challenges he would face in Jerusalem. He also would never have experienced the joys of seeing the miraculous take place, in answer to prayer and determined work. God's way is very often a way of conflict, of opposition. We draw heat unlike anything we've ever known, simply because we're engaged in Spirit-led activities which tear up Satan's kingdom. It's worth it! It's worth the heat. There's nothing on this earth quite like the experience of knowing we've been used of God to accomplish something to His glory. Sure, it draws fire. It's worth it.

Not a Quitter

Keep Swimming

*Therefore, brothers, since we have confidence to enter the holy places by
the blood of Jesus, by the new and living way that he opened for us through
the curtain, that is, through his flesh, and since we have a great priest over
the house of God, let us draw near with a true heart in full assurance of
faith, with our hearts sprinkled clean from an evil conscience and our bodies
washed with pure water. Let us hold fast the confession of our hope without
wavering, for he who promised is faithful. And let us consider how to stir
up one another to love and good works, not neglecting to meet together, as
is the habit of some, but encouraging one another, and all the more as you
see the Day drawing near.* Hebrews 10:19-25

Satan's tactics are many. Some of his most effective lies are the ones
which convince us that we are unwanted by God, unqualified to even talk to
Him, unworthy to be in His presence. In other words, we are on our own.
That's not an encouraging thought. It's also not an accurate one.

The very blood of our Savior, Jesus Christ, punched a way through to
the places where only the holy may enter, and with Jesus as our priest, we
are invited to come boldly into the presence of the Almighty. We have been
cleansed. We who were not worthy have been made worthy, by the blood
of the Lamb. There is not one thing Satan can do about it!

So, he bluffs. If he can con us into dropping our confidence, forego-
ing our faith, he can minimize the sense of freedom which is our birthright
in Christ, and thus limit our effectiveness as redeemed followers of Jesus.
This trick works by far the best in isolation, where there is no other believer
nearby to knock some sense into us in a kind sort of way. That's why Part
Two of Satan's plan is almost always to drive some kind of wedge between
believers and give them plenty of excuses to stay apart. That way they're
sure not to exchange notes and figure out the scam he's pulling on them.
If they develop the habit of encouraging one another and praying for one
another, it's basically all over for him, so he does his best to keep us apart,
forgetful of the privileges awarded us at Calvary, ignorant of the blessings
which would be ours if we just stayed with the body of believers. And the
closer we get to the final bell, the more important it is that we aren't falling
for a pack of lies, or avoiding the God who loves us.

July 31

Not a Quitter

The Incredible Non-Shrinking Faith

But recall the former days when, after you were enlightened, you endured a hard struggle with sufferings, sometimes being publicly exposed to reproach and affliction, and sometimes being partners with those so treated. For you had compassion on those in prison, and you joyfully accepted the plundering of your property, since you knew that you yourselves had a better possession and an abiding one. Therefore do not throw away your confidence, which has a great reward. For you have need of endurance, so that when you have done the will of God you may receive what is promised. For,

"Yet a little while,
and the coming one will come and will not delay;
but my righteous one shall live by faith,
and if he shrinks back, my soul has no pleasure in him."

But we are not of those who shrink back and are destroyed, but of those who have faith and preserve their souls. Hebrews 10:32-39

Non-shrinking faith is a good thing to have. Apparently, it doesn't come easily. I'm trying to imagine *"joyfully accepting the plundering of (my) property,"* maybe going around as thugs ransack my house, handing them things they might have missed, because "I've got more stuff than this in heaven—here, take it."

I can't quite get there in my mind. Maybe I never will. Property has always meant more to me than it probably should, and putting "losing things of importance to me" and "joyfully" in the same sentence is something I don't think I could do, yet. Maybe never.

Endurance, though, I think I understand a little more. "Joyfully" needs some work, for me, but the idea of persevering for the sake of Christ and not quitting, not shrinking back from the challenge—I guess that one feels more natural, because that one has been tested repeatedly, while the other one has not. It's nice to know we can still get the prize, just because we didn't quit, even if we never quite made it to "joyfully." We still made it. And our God is pleased.

Promises to Servants

Great Things Formerly Hidden

Call to me and I will answer you, and will tell you great and hidden things that you have not known. Jeremiah 33:3

At least there is some relief in this book! Even as the prophet Jeremiah receives this encouraging promise from God, he is shut up in the court of the guard. The prophecies given him to speak over Judah to this point have not been well-received! People are not going to like you when you tell them their daughters will starve to death, or that their future contains four choices: Pestilence, the sword, famine or captivity! (Jer 15 & 16) Needless to say, Jeremiah was not a popular guy. He suffered much for nothing more than faithfully delivering God's message to his people.

In the midst of persecution, Jeremiah receives direction and a promise from God:

Therefore thus says the LORD: "If you return, I will restore you, and you shall stand before me. If you utter what is precious, and not what is worthless, you shall be as my mouth. They shall turn to you, but you shall not turn to them. And I will make you to this people a fortified wall of bronze; they will fight against you, but they shall not prevail over you, for I am with you to save you and deliver you, declares the LORD. I will deliver you out of the hand of the wicked, and redeem you from the grasp of the ruthless." (Jer 15:19-21)

I get this picture of a lonely servant, hated by everyone, pleading with God to get him out of this job. Here comes God's promise: You shall be as my mouth. I will make you as tough as a bronze wall. I will rescue you from the grasp of the ruthless.

I would imagine that Jeremiah would still just as soon have skipped the whole deal, but since he didn't have a choice, God's promise must have been very comforting. Then here comes more: *Call to me and I will answer you, and will tell you great and hidden things that you have not known.* (Jer 33:3)

Fortunately, not all of us have painful prophecies to deliver to ungrateful leaders. But all of us have the opportunity to call upon a loving God who will answer us, and will tell us great and hidden things we have not known. When it comes to a listening, inquiring, trustworthy servant, that's all it takes for our great God to share with us great things formerly hidden.

Not a Quitter

Mud or Prosperity

...Jeremiah was saying to all the people, "Thus says the LORD: He who stays in this city shall die by the sword, by famine, and by pestilence, but he who goes out to the Chaldeans shall live. He shall have his life as a prize of war, and live. Thus says the LORD: This city shall surely be given into the hand of the army of the king of Babylon and be taken." Then the officials said to the king, "Let this man be put to death, for he is weakening the hands of the soldiers who are left in this city, and the hands of all the people, by speaking such words to them. For this man is not seeking the welfare of this people, but their harm." ... So they took Jeremiah and cast him into the cistern of Malchiah, the king's son, which was in the court of the guard, letting Jeremiah down by ropes. And there was no water in the cistern, but only mud, and Jeremiah sank in the mud. Jeremiah 38:1-4,6

It wouldn't have taken much imagination on Jeremiah's part to foresee the reaction to the message God had given him to preach. He knew this one wouldn't be popular! Famine, pestilence and death are never going to be favored sermon topics, when the catastrophes are being prophesied against the listeners! Jeremiah knew there would be an extreme response to this word of death; he just didn't know precisely what course it might take. Being lowered into a cistern to slowly starve in the mud probably didn't even crop up in his nightmares. Those who cringe at the truth God sends do have their ways of quieting the messenger! They couldn't get Jeremiah to quit obeying God, though. It was actually his stubborn obedience to God which landed this prophet in the mud.

There's a "health and wealth" gospel which says, "If you serve God, you'll always be happy and healthy and have everything you want." This philosophy sounds nice, but doesn't square with reality, especially when we're stuck in the mud because we obeyed God. Sometimes serving God means everyone turns against you, and they throw you down a cistern! Serving the Lord can result in job-loss, health loss, and every other kind of temporal loss imaginable. Discipleship may confine us to a prosperity-free existence for the rest of our days—our *earthly* ones. It's *still* better to serve God than it is to do anything else.

Not a Quitter

Quitting Is Not an Option

Now when Elisha had fallen sick with the illness of which he was to die, Joash king of Israel went down to him and wept before him, crying, "My father, my father! The chariots of Israel and its horsemen!" And Elisha said to him, "Take a bow and arrows." So he took a bow and arrows. Then he said to the king of Israel, "Draw the bow," and he drew it. And Elisha laid his hands on the king's hands. And he said, "Open the window eastward," and he opened it. Then Elisha said, "Shoot," and he shot. And he said, "The LORD'S arrow of victory, the arrow of victory over Syria! For you shall fight the Syrians in Aphek until you have made an end of them." 2 Kings 13:14-17

Elisha never quit. Even on his deathbed, he is making prophecies. *"The chariots of Israel and its horsemen,"* the king said of Elisha. That's what they had said about Elijah, too. God's Spirit did rest upon Elisha in double portion.

In times when I've found myself discouraged for no particular reason, I'm amused to think of Elisha grumping to God, telling Him some of the same things modern-day "servants" say:

"God, this is not fun, anymore. I don't think these people appreciate me!"

"I'm not feeling called to this place, anymore."

As if it was *ever* "fun"!

As if the people *ever* appreciated God's prophet!

As if you can leave, just because things aren't going well, anymore.

When you're God's servant, quitting is not an option.

We didn't start this journey in order to please ourselves, or even other people, so when we're discouraged or when others are disappointed in us, it's still no reason to quit, since self-fulfillment or the approval of others was not the reason we accepted this assignment, anyway.

Quitting is not an option, for God's servant. So, like Elisha, we persevere, going all the way to the finish line with God, not because we feel well or because of the accolades we're receiving or the fulfillment we're sensing, but because quitting never was an option. This is the kind of persevering, fierce obedience which leaves a wake of blessing in our path all the way to the grave, and beyond.

Not All the Same

And he gave the apostles, the prophets, the evangelists, the pastors and teachers, to equip the saints for the work of ministry, for building up the body of Christ, until we all attain to the unity of the faith and of the knowledge of the Son of God, to mature manhood, to the measure of the stature of the fullness of Christ, so that we may no longer be children, tossed to and fro by the waves and carried about by every wind of doctrine, by human cunning, by craftiness in deceitful schemes. Rather, speaking the truth in love, we are to grow up in every way into him who is the head, into Christ, from whom the whole body, joined and held together by every joint with which it is equipped, when each part is working properly, makes the body grow so that it builds itself up in love. Ephesians 4:11-16

In the past few years, I've heard a lot of "one-size-fits-all" leadership talk. A whole lot of us have been told, in many not-so-subtle ways, that we are not leadership material since we don't fit the "prototype" of a "leader" in temperament, ability or whatever. I'm really glad God doesn't see it that way. As I look through the Bible, I see all kinds of people being used of God. Although everyone is called to follow God, not everyone is called to be a "leader." In the Bible, leaders arise from all kinds of personality types, and they're not all the same!

Moses was a rescuer. He himself was rescued, when he was supposed to have been drowned in the Nile. He rescued a fellow Hebrew, killing an Egyptian in the process. The subsequent rescue of another Hebrew ended with Moses running for his life. He ended up in Midian, where he rescued Reuel's daughters from the other shepherds. Finally, God sent him to rescue the Israelites from Pharaoh. Rescuer. Moses even rescued the Israelites from God, when God was ready to judge them right out of existence!

Do we all have a God-given "identity" which belongs to us?

Some of God's servants are counselors (Solomon); some are administrators (Nehemiah); some are pioneers (Paul); some are poet/kings (David); some are fiery prophets (Elijah and John the Baptist); some are rescuers (Moses). The list goes on and on! Some of those people wouldn't have done very well, had they traded places with another of God's servants!

Lord, you have made me for a specific purpose. Please help me fulfill that purpose, and not covet another servant's position or abilities. Help me today to be the servant you have made *me* to be!

August 5

Not All the Same
Jesus Loves Martha—and Mary

Now as they were on their way, Jesus entered a village. And a woman named Martha welcomed him into her house. And she had a sister called Mary, who sat at the Lord's feet and listened to his teaching. But Martha was distracted with much serving. And she went up to him and said, "Lord, do you not care that my sister has left me to serve alone? Tell her then to help me." But the Lord answered her, "Martha, Martha, you are anxious and troubled about many things, but one thing is necessary. Mary has chosen the good portion, which will not be taken away from her."
Luke 10:38-42

I love this story. It deals with life on the daily level—the "doing dishes" level which seems to demand a verdict: "Who's right, here?" The response for which Martha was fishing was one which would justify her ire against her "lazy, good-for-nothing sister" who had abandoned her to throw a world-class spread on the table, single-handed, while she sat at Jesus' feet doing nothing. Martha assumed Jesus would put her sister in her place, especially when she played the "Don't you care?" card.

I like the way this conflict is so gently resolved, without anyone getting chewed out or publicly embarrassed, without any square pegs being crammed into round holes for the rest of their lives. Jesus acts as a firewall to protect the heart of a worshiper (Mary), while not demanding that Martha become like Mary, either. It's beautiful.

I understand Martha's allegiance to responsibility, and her frustration with what seems to be mutiny to that principle. In the farm family in which I was raised, responsibility trumped feelings pretty much every time. It developed people who excelled at work and struggled at play. Everything had to have a purpose to justify its own existence. What was the purpose of play, when there was work to be done? For some people, worship fits that same category of frivolity, particularly compared to practical endeavors. Then again, what is our purpose on this earth? "To love God and enjoy Him forever," says the creed. So worship has a purpose? The highest one of all. That's why Jesus wasn't about to jerk it out from under Mary, who braved Martha's disgust in order to concentrate on Him a few moments in what would prove to be the chance of a lifetime. Martha loved through service, Mary through listening. Jesus loved both.

Not All the Same

Beyond The Welcome Mat

For though I am free from all, I have made myself a servant to all, that I might win more of them. To the Jews I became as a Jew, in order to win Jews. To those under the law I became as one under the law (though not being myself under the law) that I might win those under the law. To those outside the law I became as one outside the law (not being outside the law of God but under the law of Christ) that I might win those outside the law. To the weak I became weak, that I might win the weak. I have become all things to all people, that by all means I might save some. I do it all for the sake of the gospel, that I may share with them in its blessings.
1 Corinthians 9:19-23

Not all servants are alike; neither are all *potential* servants. That's why, if we really care about them, we must be willing to adapt in order to reach them with the gospel. It's not just a matter of "I've gotta be me;" it's also a matter of "I'll do whatever it takes to reach you!" The depth of our compassion is illustrated by our willingness to forego our own personal preferences in order to match the needs and preferences of others, purely for their benefit.

I get the impression that Christ wants us to follow the pattern of His Incarnation, to a degree: He wants us to identify with lost people, in such a way that they can grasp His love. Sitting in our sanctuaries guarding the truth and expecting our "Welcome" sign out front to draw unsaved sinners in like a magnet to seek answers at our feet is not a plan which is working very well. I don't really think that's what Jesus had in mind, either. The impact of Christianity is felt when it comes through a disciple who has gone out of his or her way to identify with someone where they *are,* not where they should have been.

The idea of the Incarnation was that Emanuel ("God with us") would come to us, would become one of us, in order to save us. Salvation has been wrought by our Savior, Jesus—Emanuel. But in these days, we are the delivery system of that salvation. We have been entrusted with the Gospel, the truth about salvation. The truth will always be more effective if it's kindly delivered by people who care, as opposed to a "Come and get it" attitude. Not enough are crossing the river to get it; we need to swim over.

Not All the Same

Gifts as Weapons

Now there are varieties of gifts, but the same Spirit; and there are varieties of service, but the same Lord; and there are varieties of activities, but it is the same God who empowers them all in everyone. To each is given the manifestation of the Spirit for the common good. To one is given through the Spirit the utterance of wisdom, and to another the utterance of knowledge according to the same Spirit, to another faith by the same Spirit, to another gifts of healing by the one Spirit, to another the working of miracles, to another prophecy, to another the ability to distinguish between spirits, to another various kinds of tongues, to another the interpretation of tongues. All these are empowered by one and the same Spirit, who apportions to each one individually as he wills. 1 Corinthians 12:4-11

Why so much variety? Wouldn't it have been easier to just give everyone equal and similar gifts? Wouldn't it have decreased the bickering and jealousy? Naw. We'd still have it. We got variety for *"the common good."* Apparently God thought it better that we should have a little of many things which can then complement each other, rather than a surplus of one gift and an absence of everything else. Hence, variety: Varieties of gifts, varieties of service, varieties of activities. Same God and same Spirit.

I'm not sure why this is so difficult for us to accept, because the division which comes from gift warfare is some of the most non-productive energy the Church has ever spent. Then again, who is our foremost enemy? And what is his primary method of minimizing our effectiveness? Division. If the serpent can get us to flail each other over tongues, prophecies and knowledge, we won't have anything left to throw at him, and he wins.

The variety was intended to be a blessing, not a thorn. The Spirit-given manifestations are exactly that—*Spirit-given.* They're not ordered in according to our whims, like celestial take-out. It's God who does the choosing, God who determines the type and quantity. If we try to engineer the outcome, somewhere along the line it ceases to be a gift and becomes something closer to blackmail. If we badger people because their manifestation doesn't match ours, we're taking perfectly good gifts and turning them into perfectly good weapons—for the devil. Like t-ball, one of the first things we need to learn is, "Don't fight with your own team."

Not All the Same

Souvenirs from the Old Life

For just as the body is one and has many members, and all the members of the body, though many, are one body, so it is with Christ. For in one Spirit we were all baptized into one body—Jews or Greeks, slaves or free—and all were made to drink of one Spirit. 1 Corinthians 12:12-13

Part of what keeps us from effectiveness is a desire to retain at least a part of our original identity, souvenirs from the old life. What's the problem with this? It leads to a kind of hyphenated service: "Gentile-Christian," "Jewish-Christian," "slave-Christian," "free-Christian."

If it doesn't matter, once we're part of the Body, why do we insist on retaining the distinctiveness which preceded our baptism into the Body? Doesn't reminding others of our distinctive's simply encourage them to drag out theirs, as well? Of course.

Am I willing to go the route where it doesn't matter? When something becomes part of a body, it loses its distinctive qualities, and becomes part of something bigger than itself. Food doesn't keep its identity once it enters a body; it begins undergoing a process of transformation which is vital to the body's health but which soon makes it indistinguishable. Its former identity is literally absorbed, and it *becomes* the body.

Here's where it applies to me, as a Christian. Am I willing to let go of my distinctive identity, in order to become part of a larger whole where I will no longer even be identifiable, apart from Christ? This is not a theoretical question! Am I willing to be absorbed into the Kingdom, becoming part of a Body, where when people see me, they no longer see the individual "me," but just Christ?

There's not a lot I can do as an autonomous, "free, Gentile-Christian" body part, insistent upon carrying the badges and souvenirs of my previous life; there's a lot I can do as part of the Body. I just have to be willing to be absorbed. Will people not see my heritage and my individuality? Probably not. Instead, maybe they'll see the Body of our Lord Jesus.

Not All the Same

Accepting Our Ear-Ship

For the body does not consist of one member but of many. If the foot should say, 'Because I am not a hand, I do not belong to the body,' that would not make it any less a part of the body. And if the ear should say, 'Because I am not an eye, I do not belong to the body,' that would not make it any less a part of the body. If the whole body were an eye, where would be the sense of hearing? If the whole body were an ear, where would be the sense of smell? But as it is, God arranged the members in the body, each one of them, as he chose. If all were a single member, where would the body be? As it is, there are many parts, yet one body.
1 Corinthians 12:14-20

The implication of this scripture is that our problems are more a result of envy than of ostracism. Occasionally, people are put down because their role is considered inferior; more often, they put themselves down because their gifting doesn't find them on the platform, catching accolades.

The individual jostling for position is sometimes extended to entire denominations, who pride themselves on their "eye" or "ear" abilities and emphasis, to the exclusion of nearly everything else. It's as though the only thing which mattered in the church was the "eye" gift. "Ear" gifts are regarded as silly and unnecessary. And who would want a "nose" gift?

If we're an eye, it makes sense to focus on being the best eye we can be. We needn't go around trying to coax and guilt ears into seeing, either. The same applies to churches, denominations, etc.: We would do far better to develop an appreciation for other parts of the Body than to waste our time in preening: "Everyone knows that without the eyes, the body is blind." Interpreted, "We're the most important part of the body and we know it." Pride is not an important body part. We'd be better off without it.

When we decide to accept our "ear-ship," our "nose-ship" or whatever, we are agreeing that our God really is good, really does happen to know what He's doing, and can be trusted to grant gifts and assignments without our persuasive help. The less energy we waste in battling other Body parts or in pitying ourselves for our uniqueness, the better off are we, and the entire Church.

August 10

Not All the Same

All the Way to "Body"

The eye cannot say to the hand, 'I have no need of you,' nor again the head to the feet, 'I have no need of you.' On the contrary, the parts of the body that seem to be weaker are indispensable, and on those parts of the body that we think less honorable we bestow the greater honor, and our unpresentable parts are treated with greater modesty, which our more presentable parts do not require. But God has so composed the body, giving greater honor to the part that lacked it, that there may be no division in the body, but that the members may have the same care for one another. If one member suffers, all suffer together; if one member is honored, all rejoice together. 1 Corinthians 12:21-26

If one member is honored, all rejoice together. No, they don't. If one member is honored in the church, what often happens is that most of the other members go home and feel badly about it for the next few years! We're better at the *"if one member suffers, all suffer together"* part.

So what's the problem? The problem is we don't see ourselves as being part of a "body;" at best, we see ourselves being part of a "family," and when someone is honored in a family, to the exclusion of the others, it doesn't generate goodwill and brotherhood; it results in envy. By the same token, in a family, suffering is generally shared pretty well; it's honor that shakes things up.

We need to get past "family" mentality and get all the way to "body" mentality. In an actual *body*, Thanksgiving comes along, and it's not just the taste buds which rejoice, it's the whole calorie-laden body! The fat cells are doing hand-stands. In an actual *family*, Thanksgiving can produce the opposite of thankfulness; it can be just one more difficult holiday which tends to highlight the lack of true caring and unity present in that family. Instead of increasing gratitude, it can actually lessen it.

When we get all the way to "body," everyone's benefits become ours, though. Every triumph is our triumph. The blessings don't have to be parceled out, because there's just one body—bless the body in any one place, and the whole thing rejoices, because they're all connected, they're all on the same team. "I'm so glad I'm a part of the family of God"—but we really need to get to "Body." It's more fun, all the way around.

Not All the Same

Stuck On Gifts

Now you are the body of Christ and individually members of it. And God has appointed in the church first apostles, second prophets, third teachers, then miracles, then gifts of healing, helping, administrating, and various kinds of tongues. Are all apostles? Are all prophets? Are all teachers? Do all work miracles? Do all possess gifts of healing? Do all speak with tongues? Do all interpret? But earnestly desire the higher gifts.

And I will show you a still more excellent way. 1 Corinthians 12:27-31

"Do all...?" Paul's rhetorical question has way too often slipped past the church. His anticipated answer in each case to "Do all work miracles?", etc., is "No. Some do, but not everyone." Paul took an entire chapter to remind us that we're not all serving in the exact same manner, and we're not serving alone. God has gifted people in different ways for different kinds of service. The next chapter, 1 Corinthians 13, will explain to us that even more important than our service is our *love*.

So, how have so many gotten stuck on "gifts"? Take, for example, the question, "Do all speak with tongues?"

Depends. Is the church a "have-to," a "get-to" or a "better-not-do" church, when it comes to that issue? Whole denominations and movements have sprung up or declined around this question, but a churchman is expected to be on the right side of it and be appropriately adorned with or lacking the gift, in accordance with the thoughts of the rest of his group. Why?

How did we find ourselves pleading with God to gift us so we'd be like our friends and family, rather than as He sees fit? How did a gift of God move from the "gift" column to the litmus test column, and who moved it there? The original purpose of this particular gift was in uniting people who otherwise had difficulty understanding one another. Who managed to get it to be something which had the exact opposite effect on people—dividing them from those with whom they had formerly been united?! Does that sound like something engineered by the Holy Spirit, or by the enemy of our soul? How about if we left this one up to the Lord, and quit trying to referee Him over what He's going to do or not do with His own gifts? It takes two to tango, and I, for one, refuse to let this be an issue which separates me from a brother. Gifts are gifts, not "issues," and they're up to God, not me.

A Servant Checks with the Master

Stuck With the Gibeonites

So the men took some of their provisions, but did not ask counsel from the LORD. Joshua 9:14

Had the Gibeonites been living under the same code of ethics as the Israelites, they wouldn't have been able to get away with this deception, but it's an uneven playing field. The one chance Joshua and the Israelites had was to check with the LORD—and they didn't bother, this time. As a consequence, the Israelites ended up getting stuck with the Gibeonites for the rest of their lives.

The Gibeonites had come to the conquering Israelites, with a clever ruse about coming from a far country. They told enough lies to convince Joshua and the leaders to swear a peace covenant to them in the name of the LORD; only later did the Israelites realize they'd been duped. Back to the different standards: The Gibeonites can lie all they want, and get away with it; the Israelites are bound by the covenants they have made in God's name, even if they've been deceived into making them! Our only hope is in asking counsel from God!

God's help more than balances out the advantage those without morals may have in gaining the upper hand over us. When Joshua took things to the Lord, he was never disappointed or defeated; when he considers it too simple to bother taking to God, he consigns his people to be mired in a perpetual, irritating compromise. Five minutes of listening for God's direction would have saved the Israelites years of grief! Check with God! Please!

Joshua seems to have learned his lesson, though. By the next chapter, he is back to listening to God, and back to getting miraculous results. Yes, it's an uneven playing field—but greatly to our advantage!

Our God never loses. When we seek counsel from Him, listen carefully and obey fully, we can't lose, either.

August 13

A Servant Checks with the Master

A Very, Very Good Way to Live

Then said Abishai to David, "God has given your enemy into your hand this day. Now please let me pin him to the earth with one stroke of the spear, and I will not strike him twice." But David said to Abishai, "Do not destroy him, for who can put out his hand against the LORD's anointed and be guiltless?" And David said, "As the LORD lives, the LORD will strike him, or his day will come to die, or he will go down into battle and perish. The LORD forbid that I should put out my hand against the LORD's anointed. But take now the spear that is at his head and the jar of water, and let us go." So David took the spear and the jar of water from Saul's head, and they went away. No man saw it or knew it, nor did any awake, for they were all asleep, because a deep sleep from the LORD had fallen upon them. 1 Samuel 26:8-12

For the second time, all David has to do is say the word, and one of his lieutenants will dispose of the man who spends his time in nothing more than pursuing David to kill him. Not only that, but in all likelihood, David will then be crowned king of Israel, and God's promise to David will be fulfilled. Isn't this the end God has in mind? Ultimately, yes, but it's not the means to the end, and David knows it. David is sufficiently tuned in to God's leading and God's character to live in the realization that it isn't David's job to try to fulfill God's promises for him, particularly when it comes to resorting to tactics such as assassination! Sneaking around in the middle of Saul's camp in the darkness, they grab Saul's spear and water jar and depart, under cover of God's grace.

Saul's awakening produces another pledge of remorse, which David knows to be hollow. No matter. David is gliding along in the will of God, confident that the Almighty will take care of His own promises and figure out a way to remove any obstacles to them, without David's assistance. It's a very, very good way to live.

Abishai had meant well, and was only trying to advance the cause of his leader. But just because someone is our friend doesn't always mean they are right. I'm glad David chose to go with God's direction, rather than the urging of a friend. When push comes to shove, a servant of God chooses God, even over his friends. It's a very, very good way to live.

A Servant Checks with the Master

What's Really Risky

Then David said in his heart, "Now I shall perish one day by the hand of Saul. There is nothing better for me than that I should escape to the land of the Philistines. Then Saul will despair of seeking me any longer within the borders of Israel, and I shall escape out of his hand." So David arose and went over, he and the six hundred men who were with him, to Achish the son of Maoch, king of Gath. 1 Samuel 27:1-2

There's a weariness which accompanies living by faith. When we look all around, following another "close call," and listen to the advice of well-meaning friends, both our common sense and our relatives will come to a point of telling us, "One of these days, your luck will run out." Fatigue leads to panic—not always, but sometimes. That's how this entire chapter hits me.

David goes from absolute dependence on God to relying upon his own wits. For sixteen months, he lives among the Philistines, who seem to have amnesia regarding David's former attitude toward them. The dim-witted Achish is so convinced David is his best new friend that he wants to sign him on as bodyguard! This same David spends each day wiping out entire villages of Philistines, careful to never leave a single survivor, then reporting back to Achish that the pillaged places were in Israel.

How is this new campaign based on daily deceit, the murder of innocents and the silence of 600 malcontents less risky than simply depending on God?! It *feels* less risky to David, because *it's under his control.* He's depending on his own considerable strengths. Fueled by the rationalization, "You do what you have to do," David continues a lifestyle of lies. He steels himself to the inevitable consequences of what happens when a man relies on his own strength. He had told himself that his luck would eventually run out, so he'd better do something, when he wasn't living on luck at all, but on God's unerring grace. *Now, he's chosen to live on luck!* Sure enough, it will soon expire. David's legendary relationship with God? Psalm 18, written after God rescued him from Saul, is David's testimony to his confidence in God's delivering power; I can't find a single psalm he wrote while pretending to be Achish's buddy.

Yes, living by faith can see us grow weary and nervous, but if we want to try something *really* risky, all we have to do is depend on ourselves.

A Servant Checks with the Master

Fear Born Of Disobedience

When Saul saw the army of the Phlistines, he was afraid, and his heart trembled greatly. And when Saul inquired of the LORD, the LORD did not answer him, either by dreams, or by Urim, or by prophets. Then Saul said to his servants, "Seek out for me a woman who is a medium, that I may go to her and inquire of her." And his servants said to him, "Behold, there is a medium at En-dor."

So Saul disguised himself and put on other garments and went, he and two men with him. And they came to the woman by night. And he said, "Divine for me by a spirit and bring up for me whomever I shall name to you." ... Then the woman said, "Whom shall I bring up for you?" He said, "Bring up Samuel for me." When the woman saw Samuel, she cried out with a loud voice. And the woman said to Saul, "Why have you deceived me? You are Saul." 1 Samuel 28:5-8,11-12

The woeful ending of Saul's life mirrors the rest of his kingship. While David's reliance on his own wits rather than God's wisdom was temporary, Saul's was chronic. Now Saul is in a desperate situation, with the Philistines at the door. His sole spiritual advisor, Samuel, the man who anointed him king, is dead. Saul's attempts at getting answers from God are being met with stony silence. In his heart, Saul knows why: Disobedience. Time and again, he had directly disobeyed the LORD's orders, always altering the plan according to his own fashion. Samuel had told him straight out that God had rejected him as king.

Now Saul's desperation to know his future drives him to yet another sin. In disguise, he seeks out a medium to try to contact the dead prophet Samuel. This whole scenario is so typical of Saul and his methods—"If God won't do it your way, find another way." Deceit, disguise, whining—that's Saul. All he gets for his extreme efforts is a short-term (and accurate) prophecy that he'll be dead, too, within 24 hours. It's an ignoble and sad ending to a tragic life. It all could have been so very different, had Saul ever come to a point where he was willing to follow God's orders, rather than always barging ahead on his own.

Listen to God, and obey Him!

August 16

A Servant Checks with the Master
A Better Plan than This

*Now the Philistines had gathered all their forces at Aphek. And the
Israelites were encamped by the spring that is in Jezreel. As the lords of
the Philistines were passing on by hundreds and by thousands, and David
and his men were passing on in the rear with Achish, the commanders of
the Philistines said, "What are these Hebrews doing here?" And Achish
said to the commanders of the Philistines, "Is this not David, the servant
of Saul, king of Israel, who has been with me now for days and years, and
since he deserted to me I have found no fault in him to this day." But the
commanders of the Philistines were angry with him. And the commanders
of the Philistines said to him, "Send the man back, that he may return to
the place to which you have assigned him. He shall not go down with us to
battle, lest in the battle he become an adversary to us. For how could this
fellow reconcile himself to his lord? Would it not be with the heads of the
men here? Is not this David, of whom they sing to one another in dances,
'Saul has struck down his thousands,
and David his ten thousands'?"* 1 Samuel 29:1-5

There had to have been a better plan than this! What David is doing
makes me nervous when I read it, and I even know how it's going to turn
out! To me, it's only God's great grace that rescues David from this thing.
It looks to me like this could have been the biggest blunder, yet, for God's
anointed—going to war against his own people as a Philistine bodyguard!
Knowing David, he probably would have done exactly what the Philistine
lords suspected, had they not relieved him of the option and sent him away,
but I still can't believe that this plan of David's originated with God in the
first place. It seems to me that had David consulted the Lord on this whole
deal, God would have come up with a better plan!

The reason they ever made up songs about David in the first place
was because he trusted in God, instead of himself. During this episode of
his life, David's reliance on God seems to be pretty slim, compared to his
dependence upon his own cleverness and acting ability. I liked it much
better when it was obvious that God was leading the way! Yes, David will
survive all of this and wear the crown God promised, but it's not because
he was so smart; it's because of God's grace.

A Servant Checks with the Master

Unstoppable

Now when David and his men came to Ziklag on the third day, the Amalekites had made a raid against the Negeb and against Ziklag. They had overcome Ziklag and burned it with fire and taken captive the women and all who were in it, both small and great. They killed no one, but carried them off and went their way. And when David and his men came to the city, they found it burned with fire, and their wives and sons and daughters taken captive. Then David and the people who were with him raised their voices and wept until they had no more strength to weep. David's two wives also had been taken captive, Ahinoam of Jezreel and Abigail the widow of Nabal of Carmel. And David was greatly distressed, for the people spoke of stoning him, because all the people were bitter in soul, each for his sons and daughters. But David strengthened himself in the LORD his God. 1 Samuel 30:1-6

Now it *definitely* seems God must have had a better plan! David and his men come back to find that the Amalekites (who are only still around due to Saul's disobedience) had burned their village and kidnaped their families.

David has no one to turn to but God: His family is gone, his own men are talking of stoning him. He "strengthened himself in the LORD his God." Afterward, he knows what to do.

Once again, David is checking with God.

And David inquired of the LORD, "Shall I pursue after this band? Shall I overtake them?" He answered him, "Pursue, for you shall surely overtake and shall surely rescue." (1 Sam 30:8)

Every time David *ever* checks with God, he gets a good answer. I don't think David had checked with God about this whole Philistine adventure. I think in that case he just got tired and scared, and decided that his luck was going to eventually run out, so he went to Philistia.

A change is coming. David is at the end of his resources, with nowhere to turn but God. Once again, he's ready to rely totally on God, willing to obey any and all orders. He really did "strengthen himself in the LORD his God"! This is a major turning point in David's life, because it's the day he switches back over to God's power and wisdom. When he's running on God's strength, God's man is unstoppable—then, and now.

August 18

A Servant Checks with the Master

Twelve for Twelve

After this David inquired of the LORD, "Shall I go up into any of the cities of Judah?" And the LORD said to him, "Go up." David said, "To which shall I go up?" And he said, "To Hebron." So David went up there... And the men of Judah came, and there they anointed David king over the house of Judah. 2 Samuel 2:1-2,4

The presents sent from David to his friends in Judah probably had not even arrived, yet, when Israel was left without a king. David has only been back in Ziklag three days when a messenger arrives to tell him about the deaths of Saul and Jonathan.

It seems a foregone conclusion what David should do, now, but he checks with God, anyway. I like the way David seeks guidance step by step, without trying to manipulate the outcome. First of all, he asks if he should go up to *any* of the cities of Judah. Then, when the answer is "Yes," he simply asks which one. I love it that David doesn't make assumptions, but allows himself to be guided by God. I think God loved it, too!

I come up with 12 recorded times over the course of his life that David specifically checks with God and asks for direction. Unfortunately, he doesn't do it as regularly after he becomes king (seven times prior, five times after). Nevertheless, *every single time David asks God what to do, he gets it right. Every time.*

Meanwhile, David must continue to be patient, because his kingship extends only over Judah, and Saul's son Ish-bosheth has the rest of Israel. It stays that way for seven years! David manages to maintain the same posture of dependence on God throughout the period, despite the murderous actions of his supposed friends. David stays above the fray by refusing to "help" God along with His promise! That attitude must have added to his sense of satisfaction when, in God's time, the promise comes true, and the king anointed long ago is at last on the throne of all Israel. David was wise enough to do things God's way, and to ask God before acting. And he was smart enough to notice that when he checked with the LORD, God was twelve for twelve.

A Servant Checks with the Master

Note To Self: Check With God

When the Philistines heard that David had been anointed king over all Israel, all the Philistines went up to search for David. But David heard of it and went out against them. Now the Philistines had come and made a raid in the Valley of Rephaim. And David inquired of God, "Shall I go up against the Philistines? Will you give them into my hand?" And the LORD said to him, "Go up, and I will give them into your hand." And he went up to Baal-perazim, and David struck them down there....

And the Philistines yet again made a raid in the valley. And when David again inquired of God, God said to him, "You shall not go up after them; go around and come against them opposite the balsam trees. And when you hear the sound of marching in the tops of the balsam trees, then go out to battle, for God has gone out before you to strike down the army of the Philistines." And David did as God commanded him, and they struck down the Philistine army from Gibeon to Gezer. And the fame of David went out into all lands, and the LORD brought the fear of him upon all nations. 1 Chronicles 14:8-11,13-17

This was not a fluke event in David's life, but a familiar pattern with an amazing outcome: Every single time David is recorded as having checked with God about something, God gave Him unerring guidance, and David was successful. Not only that, but God caused David's fame, and a fear of him, to spread throughout all the lands.

Why would a newly minted king who finally got his promised crown bother to ask God about something as elementary as, "Shall I go up against the Philistines?" After all, they were already in the country. Isn't this just self-defense? Why *wouldn't* David take his army and respond to the challenge? Because this man wants to be God's man, and God's man does what God wants, not what he wants. God always honors that!

God's man also doesn't rely on assumptions, like the one that says, "If it worked last time, why not do it again?" For the second encounter with the Philistines, David's inquiry brings a detailed battle plan from God, who inserts a heavenly host to make sure His guy wins(!)—which is what always happens whenever God's servants inquire of Him, rather than heading off on their own. I need to remember this, and never forget it: Check with God!

A Servant Checks with the Master

Serious Instructions

And they carried the ark of God on a new cart and brought it out of the house of Abinadab, which was on the hill. And Uzzah and Ahio, the sons of Abinadab, were driving the new cart, with the ark of God, and Ahio went before the ark....

And when they came to the threshing floor of Nacon, Uzzah put out his hand to the ark of God and took hold of it, for the oxen stumbled. And the anger of the LORD was kindled against Uzzah, and God struck him down there beside the ark of God. And David was angry because the LORD had burst forth against Uzzah... 2 Samuel 6:3-4,6-8

David was upset at God because David didn't understand what he'd done to offend God. He had made a presumption that everything was OK, and hadn't checked the scriptures for what was right; otherwise he would have realized that the way they were doing things was offensive to God. Had they bothered to look it up, there was no mystery involved in how God wanted the holy things representing His presence to be treated. Numbers 4 contains specific directives as to how and by whom the ark was to be transported, along with the warning that to even touch the holy things was to invite death.

So what did the Israelites do to offend the LORD? They took the ark of the covenant, symbol of God's presence and holiness, and treated it as an unholy thing. As casually as if they were transporting furniture across town, they put it on an oxcart (It was to be covered with a special veil, and carried by certain priests on foot, using the special poles designed to transport it without humans ever touching it). Uzzah may have thought he was being heroic when he incautiously reached out his hand to steady the ark of God's presence, after the oxen which should have never been used in the first place stumbled; instead, it represented the last straw. God chose it as the time to reinforce how serious He was about humans respecting His holiness.

David's first response is anger; his second is to have a theological autopsy conducted, to figure out what had gone wrong. The answers were there all along, had someone bothered to look them up. The next time, they get it right. God has already told us how to avoid tragedy. All we have to do is look.

A Servant Checks with the Master
Blowing Past the Signs

It happened, late one afternoon, when David arose from his couch and was walking on the roof of the king's house, that he saw from the roof a woman bathing; and the woman was very beautiful. And David sent and inquired about the woman. And one said, "Is this not Bathsheba, the daughter of Eliam, the wife of Uriah the Hittite?" 2 Samuel 11:2-3

I really don't like this chapter, yet I'm so very glad it's in the Bible! The sad story of how God's man falls into temptation, and then in the process of the cover-up, becomes a murderer, a liar, and all the rest.... it's such a disappointment! *"But the thing that David had done displeased the LORD."* (2 Sam 11:27) I'm not the only one disappointed in this story.

O.K., where did God's man go wrong?

Was he supposed to have been at the battle? The implication is there: *"The time when kings go out to battle..."* (2 Sam 11:1) This king didn't go out. Somehow I don't think he checked with God about whether or not he should, this time. He also obviously didn't check with God about what to do before or after he sinned with Bathsheba. He blows past three huge warning signs all in one sentence, any one of which should have stopped him cold in his tracks: *"Is this not Bathsheba, the daughter of Eliam, the wife of Uriah the Hittite?"*

The daughter of Eliam. In 2 Samuel 23, the list is given of "The Thirty," David's most elite bodyguard. These are his very best guys. Eliam is a name on that list. Warning number one.   *The wife of.* As in, "not your wife, David—somebody else's wife." Warning number two.

The wife of Uriah the Hittite. The final name in the list of The Thirty is Uriah's name. These are the men who not only *would* give their life for you; they've demonstrated it on more than one occasion. You're contemplating adultery with the wife of one of your most trusted, loyal soldiers, and the daughter of another one. What are you thinking, David?! In a short span of time, David loses the trust of his family and his subjects, and disappoints His God. It takes a messenger from God before David begins to get back on track. Not only did David purposely neglect to check with God; he ignored all the warnings along the way. We can still see the scars.

A Servant Checks with the Master

Save Me, O King

And Joab sent to Tekoa and brought from there a wise woman and said to her, "Pretend to be a mourner and put on mourning garments. Do not anoint yourself with oil, but behave like a woman who has been mourning many days for the dead. Go to the king and speak thus to him." So Joab put the words in her mouth.

When the woman of Tekoa came to the king, she fell on her face to the ground and paid homage and said, "Save me, O king." And the king said to her, "What is your trouble?" 2 Samuel 14:2-4

Her "trouble" was made up, designed by Joab to deceive the king. David's trouble was that he was king, making him more susceptible to thinking he was also savior. There's nothing like a loyal subject on her face saying, "Save me, O king," telling you that you have wisdom "like the wisdom of the angel of God to know all things that are on the earth" (2 Sam 14:20), to disarm you of any residual wisdom you might possess and turn you into a quite ordinary person who just wants to make their appreciative subject happy.

Kings (and leaders) get to make lots of decisions. The more you make, the easier it gets to just make them, and the harder it is to interrupt someone's flattery to let them know you need to check with God, first, and get back to them! Just use your wonderful wisdom, man! Hmmm. Once again, it turned out to be not-that-wonderful. We remember why it was that we started checking with God in the first place.

Reading 2 Samuel, I miss the good old days when it was impossible to fool David, because he took all his decisions before God. Now that he's been king for a long time, it's become more of a rarity. This little decision looks easy; the reason it's easy is because it's a trap. David fell for it, Joab got his way, God was left out of the equation, altogether. It doesn't have to be that way, but with kings—and other would-be saviors, it too often is.

When we check with God, we're as invincible as we will ever be; when we play savior, relying on our own wisdom, all it takes to fool us is a little flattery. It's less humiliating to just admit that whatever wisdom we have comes from God and we ask Him about everything, than it is to face the consequences of trying to be a savior when we're not.

"Save me, O king." That should be *my* line, because He will.

A Servant Checks with the Master

Modern-Day Parallels

After this Absalom got himself a chariot and horses, and fifty men to run before him. And Absalom used to rise early and stand beside the way of the gate. And when any man had a dispute to come before the king for judgment, Absalom would call to him and say, "From what city are you?" And when he said, "Your servant is of such and such a tribe in Israel," Absalom would say to him, "See, your claims are good and right, but there is no man designated by the king to hear you." Then Absalom would say, "Oh, that I were judge in the land! Then every man with a dispute or cause might come to me, and I would give him justice." And whenever a man came near to pay homage to him, he would put out his hand and take hold of him and kiss him. Thus Absalom did to all of Israel who came to the king for judgment. So Absalom stole the hearts of the men of Israel.

And at the end of four years Absalom said to the king, "Please let me go and pay my vow, which I have vowed to the LORD, in Hebron. For your servant vowed a vow while I lived at Geshur in Aram, saying, "If the LORD will indeed bring me back to Jerusalem, then I will serve the LORD.'" The king said to him, "Go in peace." 2 Samuel 15:2-9

Modern-day politics isn't so modern. Neither is modern-day parenting. The king's spoiled son is siphoning off David's kingdom, one man at a time, with promises and kisses, coupled with negative campaigning, and of course, it's working. David thinks his son is at last getting straightened out with God, which pleases him, when in fact Absalom is headed for Hebron to declare a coup!

Where did the son pick up such "talents" of lying and deception? Sorrowfully, he seems to have gotten some of it from his father, a man he had seen practice deception on more than one occasion. Meanwhile, David seems to be completely disengaged when it comes to his own family—another modern-day characteristic far too common. Absalom had experienced his father's anger and his love, but it seems he rarely, if ever, had experienced his father's involved discipline. Here's a kid who seems to have never been corrected. Now he's taking over, even if he has to kill his father in order to do it. I wonder if David ever checked with God along the way, when it came to how to raise a family. Another modern-day parallel, I'm afraid.

A Servant Checks with the Master

Journey from Jerusalem

And all the land wept aloud as all the people passed by, and the king crossed the brook Kidron, and all the people passed on toward the wilderness.
...So Zadok and Abiathar carried the ark of God back to Jerusalem, and they remained there.
But David went up the ascent of the Mount of Olives, weeping as he went, barefoot and with his head covered. And all the people who were with him covered their heads, and they went up, weeping as they went. And it was told David, "Ahithophel is among the conspirators with Absalom." And David said, "O LORD, please turn the counsel of Ahithophel into foolishness." 2 Samuel 15:23,29-31

It's all there. Crossing the book Kidron, ascending the Mount of Olives in mass grief, a confidant turned conspirator in an act of brazen betrayal. The address is the second book of Samuel, but the picture fits the Lord Jesus as well as it fit His ancestor. What is so shockingly different is the reason for the journey. In one case, a despairing father is only reaping the consequences of his own sins from years back; in the other case, the Sinless One makes the same journey that He might break the curse of sin, forever.

There are two sons of David in this enlarged story which repeats itself centuries later, on the same turf. David's bitter son, Absalom, sought to grasp a kingdom for himself; Jesus, Son of David, sought to give a Kingdom to others. One son is attempting to disgrace and destroy his father; the other is attempting to honor and obey His Father by bringing salvation to the world.

And what of the earthly, broken father, King David, fleeing from his son and the others who have betrayed him and rebelled against him? David turns where he always turns, in times of trouble: Toward God. Finally, David is praying, again! It's been too long. This is the first recorded instance of David praying in a while. But now that David is once again looking to God for help, rather than relying on his own wisdom or his advisors, it will be O.K. It always is, when we seek God. That's why we need to just seek Him, first. It spares us *so much trouble!*

A Servant Checks with the Master

Check with God!

Therefore David inquired of the LORD, "Shall I go and attack these Philistines?" And the LORD said to David, "Go and attack the Philistines and save Keilah." 1 Samuel 23:2

That was the first recorded time of David checking with God, but there were more. David checked with God—not once, but twelve recorded times throughout his lifetime. I suspect there were many more times which were not recorded. I suspect the results were identical to these twelve times:

1 & 2. Shall I attack the Philistines at Keilah? (1 Sa 23:1-5) Yes. Are you sure? Yes. Result: Success.
3. Will Saul come down to Keilah? (1 Sa 23:6-11) Yes. Result: Success.
4. Will Keilah surrender me to Saul? (1 Sa 23:12-14) Yes. Result: Success.
5. Shall I pursue the Amalekites who raided Ziklag? (1 Sa 30) Yes. Result: Success.
6 & 7. (After Saul's death) Shall I go up to any of the cities of Judah? (2 Sa 2:1-4) Yes. Which one? Hebron. Result: Success.
8. Shall I go up against the Philistines? Will you give them into my hand? (2 Sa 5:17-21) Yes and yes. Result: Success.
9. (Philistines, again) What do I do? (2 Sa 5:22-25) Here's the plan. Result: Success.
10. (Absalom's attempted coup) "O LORD, please turn the counsel of Ahithophel into foolishness." (2 Sa 15:31) Result: Success.
11. Why do we have this famine? (2 Sa 21:1-14) Here's why. Result: Success.
12. (Post-census) (2 Sa 24:10) "O LORD, please take away the iniquity of your servant, for I have done very foolishly." Result: Mercy and Success.

What can I say? The theme that pounds at me from the life of David is, "Check with God!" *Every single time he does it, David gets it right. Every time!* When he neglects to check with God, David becomes more of an ordinary man, with the flaws to prove it. When he checks with God, David is unbeatable. *Check with God!*

Trustworthy With His Glory

It's All Worship Time

And three of the thirty chief men went down and came about harvest time to David at the cave of Adullam, when a band of Philistines was encamped in the Valley of Rephaim. David was then in the stronghold, and the garrison of the Philistines was then at Bethlehem. And David said longingly, "Oh, that someone would give me water to drink from the well of Bethlehem that is by the gate!" Then the three mighty men broke through the camp of the Philistines and drew water out of the well of Bethlehem that was by the gate and carried and brought it to David. But he would not drink of it. He poured it out to the LORD and said, "Far be it from me, O LORD, that I should do this. Shall I drink the blood of the men who went at the risk of their lives?" Therefore he would not drink it. These things the three mighty men did. 2 Samuel 23:13-17

The intensity of the devotion to David displayed by his "three mighty men" is only overshadowed by the devotion David displays toward his God. What must it be like to have people risk their lives for you, breaking into an enemy stronghold, just to get you a drink of water from your favorite well?! When shown that sort of allegiance, it is only a very small step to despotism for most men. David refuses to take the step. Rather, he seems embarrassed that he made a passing comment which triggered such an act of reckless devotion among followers willing to do absolutely anything for him, when the expected reaction of a leader in these circumstances would have been to congratulate his men on their bravery and himself on his popularity, while his ego expanded by several sizes.

David's reaction, instead, is so typical of him. Instead of grinning and reveling in the glory of adulation, David denies himself, pouring the water out as a sacrifice to God, without so much as a sip for himself. His astonished men, rather than being offended, stand in awe of the dedication David has for the LORD, which is even greater than their dedication to David.

This is an opportunity for David to experience a little glory for himself (along with the resulting pride); he turns it into worship. Is this "worship" time?! Isn't it time to exult in the fruit of well-deserved loyalties? The temptation toward pride is turned instead into an act of worship. How? When David is at his best, it's *all* worship time.

Trustworthy With His Glory

Mentality of Mercy

Then David came to the two hundred men who had been too exhausted to follow David, and who had been left at the brook Besor. And they went out to meet David and to meet the people who were with him. And when David came near to the people he greeted them. Then all the wicked and worthless fellows among the men who had gone with David said, "Because they did not go with us, we will not give them any of the spoil that we have recovered, except that each man may lead away his wife and children, and depart." But David said, "You shall not do so, my brothers, with what the LORD has given us. He has preserved us and given into our hand the band that came against us. Who would listen to you in this matter? For as his share is who goes down into the battle, so shall his share be who stays by the baggage. They shall share alike." And he made it a statute and a rule for Israel from that day forward to this day.

When David came to Ziklag, he sent part of the spoil to his friends, the elders of Judah, saying, "Here is a present for you from the spoil of the enemies of the LORD." 1 Samuel 30:21-26

David's God-guided exploit of taking 600 men and chasing the Amalekites who had raided their city, Ziklag, saw a pursuit so strenuous that 200 of his men had to be left behind, too exhausted to continue. When the victorious band returns, having recovered everything taken in the raid plus much more, David encounters the graceless spirit of some of his warriors, who insist on penalizing those left behind, so they can have the rest for themselves. David will have none of it. David gives the credit to God, then applies God's mercy. Good servant!

Not only does David keep the allegiance of the weaker portion of his army; he capitalizes on this unexpected windfall by sharing it with the elders of Judah and sending out a bunch of presents. This is *not* going to hurt him, when, in a matter of days, the political landscape of Israel changes drastically.

Throughout David's career, he tries to be fair and merciful to people under his authority. There is a parallel between being a good steward of God's glory and a good steward of human power. If a person does well with one, he's probably ready for the other. And if not, probably not.

Trustworthy With His Glory

A Servant Can Be Trusted with God's Glory

Therefore Daniel went in to Arioch, whom the king had appointed to destroy the wise men of Babylon. He went and said thus to him, "Do not destroy the wise men of Babylon; bring me in before the king, and I will show the king the interpretation."

Then Arioch brought in Daniel before the king in haste and said thus to him: "I have found among the exiles from Judah a man who will make known to the king the interpretation." The king said to Daniel, whose name was Belteshazzar, "Are you able to make known to me the dream that I have seen and its interpretation?" Daniel answered the king and said, "No wise men, enchanters, magicians, or astrologers can show to the king the mystery that the king has asked, but there is a God in heaven who reveals mysteries, and he has made known to King Nebuchadnezzar what will be in the latter days. Your dream and the visions of your head as you lay in bed are these: ..." Daniel 2:24-28

A death sentence turned into an amazing promotion, thanks to God's intervention and Daniel's obedience. Nebuchadnezzar had determined to execute the entire cadre of wise men and astrologers in Babylon if they didn't tell him what his dream had been, as well as the interpretation. Ill-equipped for anything on this level, the magicians whined and made out their wills, and it was left to God's man, Daniel, the Hebrew captive, to rise to the occasion and get the answer through prayer.

God came through, and so did Daniel. The dream, the interpretation, everything was there when it was needed. Suddenly Daniel finds himself catapulted to a position of political power and honor, a place he would retain throughout much of his long life. Daniel, from beginning to end, is careful to give glory to God, and to thank Him. He tells the king that it is not because of superior wisdom that he knows; it's because God revealed it to him. Daniel gives God the glory, and ends up ruler over the province of Babylon, along with his friends!

Serving God faithfully means that He can trust you with His glory (and you're not going to grab it for yourself, or turn it into some kind of road show). Help me to be trustworthy with your glory, Lord.

Trustworthy With His Glory
The Message before the Message

In those days I, Daniel, was mourning for three weeks. I ate no delicacies, no meat or wine entered my mouth, nor did I anoint myself at all, for the full three weeks. On the twenty-fourth day of the first month, as I was standing on the bank of the great river (that is, the Tigris) I lifted up my eyes and looked, and behold, a man clothed in linen, with a belt of fine gold from Uphaz around his waist. His body was like beryl, his face like the appearance of lightning, his eyes like flaming torches, his arms and legs like the gleam of burnished bronze, and the sound of his words like the sound of a multitude. And I, Daniel, alone saw the vision, for the men who were with me did not see the vision, but a great trembling fell upon them, and they fled to hide themselves. So I was left alone and saw the great vision, and no strength was left in me. My splendor was changed to ruin, and I retained no strength. Then I heard the sound of his words, and as I heard the sound of his words, I fell on my face in deep sleep with my face to the ground.

And behold, a hand touched me and set me trembling on my hands and knees. And he said to me, "O Daniel, man greatly loved, understand the words that I speak to you, and stand upright, for now I have been sent to you." Daniel 10:2-11

God's servant doesn't have to be forced in order to engage in spiritual disciplines. A three-week partial fast? He does these kinds of things just because he feels a need, or because he wants to, not because he has to. The reward God sends is likewise—just because He wants to. Daniel is not asking for a vision, but the Lord knows He can trust Daniel with one, so here it comes, through the appearance of a heavenly being. It will be a long, detailed and incredibly accurate prophecy for the future of Daniel's people, but before the message is even delivered, comes the honor: *"O Daniel, man greatly loved,..."*

What kind of greeting is that? That's not just a greeting; that's part of the message! *God loves you, Daniel—you are greatly loved by Him.* Wow.

The message before the message was the same one heard by Jesus when the Father spoke from heaven saying, "This is my Son, whom I love!" It's the message we can—and will—hear, too, when we listen: God's love, His favor. How do we get God to love us like that? Too late. He already does.

Trustworthy With His Glory

The Pursuit of Godly Wisdom

And behold, a hand touched me and set me trembling on my hands and knees. And he said to me, "O Daniel, man greatly loved, understand the words that I speak to you, and stand upright, for now I have been sent to you." And when he had spoken this word to me, I stood up trembling. Then he said to me, "Fear not, Daniel, for from the first day that you set your heart to understand and humbled yourself before your God, your words have been heard, and I have come because of your words."
Daniel 10:10-12

God notices it all. The first day that Daniel set his heart upon understanding his God better, he got an answer, and the answers never stopped. The pursuit of Godly wisdom is a noble and rewarding pursuit!

God knew that Daniel could be entrusted with visions of the future, and Daniel would relate them faithfully, without grandstanding or embellishment. Nor would he let the experience go to his head. Daniel was a trustworthy servant, even with some of the weightiest things imaginable. God knew He could count on Daniel.

"From the first day that you set your heart to understand and humbled yourself before your God,"... There are two things which always get God's attention and favor! A heart set on understanding, listening, paying attention to God—learning—that is a heart which will be rewarded very soon! And nothing speeds up the process like humility. A bigger obstacle than the "prince of the kingdom of Persia" (Daniel 10:13) is our pride. God dare not share anything of great importance with us, because of what we will let it do to us. Momentous messages from God and pride don't mix! There seem to be few who can be trusted with God's glory, especially when it comes to prophecy. But when that rare individual sets their mind on hearing from God, understanding His Word, and maintaining a spirit of true humility, which is the key to being trustworthy with His glory, heaven notices *immediately.* The angels will literally fight their way to us, to bring the message that our prayers have been heard and accepted by God.

Humility before God. Seeking to understand what He is saying to us. What a good direction to set our hearts! When we do, all the princes of darkness put together couldn't keep us from our reward.

August 31

Reflecting It, Not Capturing It

Now the Lord is the Spirit, and where the Spirit of the Lord is, there is freedom. And we all, with unveiled face, reflecting the glory of the Lord, are being transformed into the same image from one degree of glory to another. 2 Corinthians 3:17-18

Whether it's Moses on Mount Sinai, glimpsing God's glory and forgetting to spend the rest of his life bragging about it, or Daniel receiving visions that are millennia into the future, just because he prayed and fasted, God's servants can be trusted with His glory. When they worship, they're not doing it in order to feel better or to get a sermon; they're doing it because their whole life is about worshiping God. God's glory is safe in their hands, because they don't try to make it their own glory.

Am I trustworthy with God's glory? It is obvious that in the ministry of the Holy Spirit, every believer is invited to behold and reflect the glory of the Lord. We not only get to see His glory; we are being transformed by it!

I must ask again, though: Am I trustworthy with His glory? Is His glory safe in my hands, or will I attempt to shave off a little for myself? The temptation is always there to "capture" just a little of God's glory, or let the exalted status of my perceived intimate relationship with the God of the Universe push me a little further up the ladder of comparison that always seems to be handy. What can be done to magnify *me?* That's the odious question which lurks around every thrilling encounter with the Divine. Who will get the glory? Will I get a cut of it, or is it my job to see that I keep none of the glory for myself, but faithfully deliver it all back to its rightful owner?

God is not stingy at all with His glory, but He seems to entrust it only to those bent on reflecting it to a world desperately needing to see it, rather than loaning it to those who wish to capture and keep it.

Is God's glory safe with me? I surely hope so. The best reflection is when I don't stop looking toward Him, and don't even realize that others see Him in me. If my face is shining from His presence, it's probably best that I not even know. The surest way to keep His glory safe is if I just keep my eyes on Jesus.

Promises to Servants

The Reason for Revelation

The revelation of Jesus Christ, which God gave him to show to his servants the things that must soon take place. He made it known by sending his angel to his servant John, who bore witness to the word of God and to the testimony of Jesus Christ, even to all that he saw. Revelation 1:1-2

Revelation is not written to scare people or to answer the questions of curious non-believers; it's to *"show to his servants the things that must soon take place."* This book is for His servants!

Revelation contains many promises. Again and again, the promise is "to the one who conquers." Jesus expects His servants to overcome, to "conquer" their inner passions and the obstacles of Satan, to serve Him effectively in whatever our situation might be. And there is a reward:

"The one who conquers and who keeps my works until the end, to him I will give authority over the nations, and he will rule them with a rod of iron, as when earthen pots are broken in pieces, even as I myself have received authority from my Father. And I will give him the morning star." (Rev 2:26-28)

Authority over the nations? Talk about responsibility! God has pretty big plans for His servants! The promises go on and on for *"the one who conquers:"* *"To eat of the tree of life, which is in the paradise of God"* (Rev 2:7); *"not be hurt at all by the second death"* (Rev 2:11); to be given *"hidden manna"* and *"a white stone, with a new name written on the stone"* (Rev 2:17); clothed in white garments, name never blotted out of the book of life, name confessed before the Father and the angels (Rev 3:5); *"I will make him a pillar in the temple of my God. Never shall he go out of it, and I will write on him the name of my God, and the name of the city of my God, the new Jerusalem, which comes down from my God out of heaven, and my own new name."* (Rev 3:12-13); last of all: *"The one who conquers, I will grant him to sit with me on my throne, as I also conquered and sat down with my Father on his throne."* (Rev 3:21) These promises are to encourage us to keep going.

At the end of Revelation, the message of the beginning is repeated: *"These words are trustworthy and true. And the Lord, the God of the spirits of the prophets, has sent his angel to show his servants what must soon take place."* (Rev. 22:6) God wanted His servants to know in advance.

Trustworthy As a Steward

The Acid Test of Stewardship

This is how one should regard us, as servants of Christ and stewards of the mysteries of God. Moreover, it is required of stewards that they be found trustworthy. 1 Corinthians 4:1-2

A steward is one who takes care of things which don't belong to him. A servant is someone who works for someone else, not for himself. These two identities fit together so well that they are nearly interchangeable. *This is how one should regard us, as servants of Christ and stewards of the mysteries of God*—our identity in a sentence. But do we really take this identity seriously?

"Steward-ship" is being a steward of things which don't belong to us. It's a part of servanthood. If the money and possessions God has placed in our care do not really belong to us, but instead really belong to Him, it shouldn't hurt to spend the money on what God tells us to spend it on, since it's not our money! It's all supposed to be at God's complete disposal. Where did we get the idea that we could maybe pay off God with 10%, and do whatever we wished with the rest, with the idea that the 90% is ours? I'm getting the impression that *none* of it is really ours! That's why Jesus could require of the rich young ruler that he sell everything. If he became a disciple, it was no longer his, anyway, and Jesus could do what He wanted with His own possessions.

The acid test of stewardship is how trustworthy I am with what is entrusted to me, and if I still regard the Master's resources as the Master's, not mine. *Moreover, it is required of stewards that they be found trustworthy.* How much can He put in my care before I begin to think those resources are mine? Am I a trustworthy steward? Am I a faithful servant of Christ, who refuses to embezzle even a small portion of a small portion, but who insists on properly stewarding everything entrusted to me, big or small? If the Lord finds me to be a trustworthy steward, I'm pretty sure I will never be lacking in resources placed in my care.

The bottom line is: Whose money is this? Whose resources are these? And can the Lord put them in the hands of this servant, knowing that when He gives directions regarding what to do with them, I'll remember they are His? "Trustworthy steward"—I want that to be me.

Trustworthy As a Steward

Handling or Owning

And he began to speak to them in parables. "A man planted a vineyard and put a fence around it and dug a pit for the winepress and built a tower, and leased it to tenants and went into another country. When the season came, he sent a servant to the tenants to get from them some of the fruit of the vineyard. And they took him and beat him and sent him away empty-handed. Again he sent to them another servant, and they struck him on the head and treated him shamefully. And he sent another, and him they killed. And so with many others; some they beat, and some they killed. He had still one other, a beloved son. Finally he sent him to them, saying, 'They will respect my son.' But those tenants said to one another, 'This is the heir. Come, let us kill him, and the inheritance will be ours.' And they took him and killed him and threw him out of the vineyard. What will the owner of the vineyard do? He will come and destroy the tenants and give the vineyard to others..." Mark 12:1-9

The story of the tenants was a pointed parable aimed directly at the Pharisees who were soon to kill Jesus, but it is also an indictment against all those who refuse to give God what is rightfully His. God is serious about stewardship—not just of money, but of everything of value entrusted to us.

Bank tellers don't make much money. However, they *handle* enormous amounts of it! What would we call a bank employee who diverted that money for their own purposes? A criminal. Why? Because that's not their money.

How is it any different if what God has given us to handle is used for selfish purposes, rather than that for which He intended it? Does it become ours, just because God has allowed us to handle it? Handling it and owning it are two different things, just like at the bank. God has given us resources to handle, but that doesn't mean the resources become ours. And if we choose to be unfaithful with what is entrusted to us, we should be prepared to face the consequences of that unfaithfulness.

The good news is that the Lord has promised to reward the faithful servant, the one who can be entrusted with little or much, the one who has figured out the difference between handling and owning, who correctly handles God-entrusted resources, and surrenders them easily, never allowing them to become a "possession."

Trustworthy As a Steward
Careful With the Down Payment

Follow the pattern of the sound words that you have heard from me, in the faith and love that are in Christ Jesus. By the Holy Spirit who dwells within us, guard the good deposit entrusted to you. 2 Timothy 1:13-14

We have been given something of incredible value. The "good deposit entrusted to you" represents so many things: The gift of salvation; spiritual resources and gifts; material blessings; relationships; opportunities and power. The list could go on and on.

All of this represents not the culmination of God's blessings and gifts toward us, but the "good deposit." That means there is infinitely more to come!

Since God ultimately has so much for us, why would we need to be careful with the down payment? After all, there's more where that came from! Why "guard" it? Why treat what He has placed with us as a "trust"?

For one thing, because of the price. Our salvation was not inexpensive; rather, each of us was bought with a price—the price of God's own Son, Jesus! That would be reason alone to guard what has been entrusted to us.

Another aspect of God's character is that He never wastes anything. Jesus' command to gather up leftovers which amounted to many times more than the original five loaves and two fish was accompanied by the admonition, "Let nothing be wasted." If you can multiply food by just blessing it, why not just make more, rather than working to utilize every last crumb? Something in God's character focuses on the small and insignificant, bringing redemption to and out of every little thing.

It goes back to His whole purpose with mankind. Wouldn't it be easier to just create new, perfect humans, rather than going to such incredible lengths to salvage the fallen ones? We know He can do it. After all, He made Adam and Eve; it wouldn't be too tough to make some more sinless ones, instead of entrusting His Holy Spirit to those with inherited sin tendencies. But our Heavenly Father is into *redemption.* He rescues the broken, the discarded, the useless. In place of brokenness, He grants life and eternal redemption. When we approach stewardship of everything entrusted to us in the same way He approaches us, it shows we are getting it. We are becoming like our Father. No wonder He would want us to guard what He has given us.

September 5

Seeing the End Zone

Therefore, since we are surrounded by so great a cloud of witnesses, let us also lay aside every weight, and sin which clings so closely, and let us run with endurance the race that is set before us, looking to Jesus, the founder and perfecter of our faith, who for the joy that was set before him endured the cross, despising the shame, and is seated at the right hand of the throne of God. Hebrews 12:1-2

Football season is upon us. What if I didn't know what football was, had never seen a game, so I asked, "What is football?" and got this response: "Football is exercising all the major muscle groups without resting, while at the same time experiencing pain and possible lifelong injury."

Would I sign up?

I would at least need to be able to envision myself scoring the winning touchdown, being a front page hometown hero, being swarmed by grateful fans, before I ever would have considered subjecting myself to the obvious suffering football entails. If I didn't know what this was all about, I would need a pretty good picture of what victory in the end zone looked like before I would think the pain and effort might be worthwhile.

Too many times when folks ask "What does it mean to be a Christian?" what they're hearing is something like this: "Being a Christian means you don't get to do anything fun, plus you're ridiculed in public, people think you're narrow-minded, and you have to spend all your weekends in church. Oh, and they want 10% of your income."

"Hey! Sign me up!"

Jesus endured the cross because He saw the end zone. We need to see it, too. What does the end zone look like, for servants of God?

What does it mean, to be a Christian?

It means being on a team which will triumph over *all of history.* It means sitting at the table of glory at a place with our name on it, in the presence of the Creator of the Universe and the greatest Hero ever. It means getting to live in a perfect world forever, with the God who loves us as His own child, surrounded by family, friends and heroes of the ages. It's hearing the words, "Well done, faithful servant," from the lips of the One who gave His life to provide a place for us with Him at the victory table.

Beat that!

That's what it means to be a Christian! It's worth it. Sign me up.

What a Servant Does

Living In a New Kingdom

And so, from the day we heard, we have not ceased to pray for you, asking that you may be filled with the knowledge of his will in all spiritual wisdom and understanding, so as to walk in a manner worthy of the Lord, fully pleasing to him, bearing fruit in every good work and increasing in the knowledge of God. May you be strengthened with all power, according to his glorious might, for all endurance and patience with joy, giving thanks to the Father, who has qualified you to share in the inheritance of the saints in light. He has delivered us from the domain of darkness and transferred us to the kingdom of his beloved Son, in whom we have redemption, the forgiveness of sins. Colossians 1:9-14

I love the part about being *delivered from the domain of darkness and transferred... to the kingdom of his beloved Son.* That pretty well sums it up! Now that we've gotten a divine transfer, we need a new lifestyle to go with it! We shouldn't be continuing in ungodly pursuits, living like we were still trapped in darkness, once we've been delivered by the Son.

So what does a servant in this new kingdom do, actually?

Even within these few short verses, there's a laundry list of pursuits befitting a servant sprung from captivity and now basking in the kingdom of light. The servant is:

Praying

Learning

Bearing fruit in every good work

Increasing in the knowledge of God

Increasing in God's strength

Thankful

Qualified, because God has made him qualified

Forgiven, and living like it.

If the things on this list have no part in our life, we are living like those who have not yet been freed, which is tragic—and needless.

What should a servant in this new kingdom do? I think we could start anywhere on that list, and do O.K.

September 7

What a Servant Does

Doers of the Word

But be doers of the word, and not hearers only, deceiving yourselves. For if anyone is a hearer of the word and not a doer, he is like a man who looks intently at his natural face in a mirror. For he looks at himself and goes away and at once forgets what he was like. But the one who looks into the perfect law, the law of liberty, and perseveres, being no hearer who forgets but a doer who acts, he will be blessed in his doing.

If anyone thinks he is religious and does not bridle his tongue, but deceives his heart, this person's religion is worthless. Religion that is pure and undefiled before God and the Father is this: to visit orphans and widows in their affliction, and to keep oneself unstained from the world.
James 1:22-27

The whole book is like this. James is the Simon Cowell of the Bible, the guy who just blurts it out. "You are deceiving yourself, and your religion is worthless." It sounds like something the notorious judge on "American Idol" would say, were he judging would-be disciples instead of would-be singers. Sometimes it's exactly the kind of thing we need to hear. Subtle suggestions intended to kindly steer us in the right direction are too often ignored, and smugly forwarded on to others who "need this;" not a problem to James! He just uses a sledge hammer. With one sentence he levels us, then moves on to the next subject!

It's almost always instructive, too. In the book of James there is not much about what we *believe;* it's mostly about what we *do.* For James, it just makes sense. Belief will always result in action; otherwise we're showing that we don't really believe something, we just say we do. So, under the inspiration of the Holy Spirit, James writes out short little principles and statements which give direction to our actions: "Want pure and undefiled religion? Visit orphans and widows, and stay out of the mud. Now that you've heard the word, put it into practice; be a doer of the word."

Simplicity is good. The whole Bible isn't like the book of James, but then again, when the story of the Early Church was written, they didn't call it "The Beliefs of the Apostles" or "The Plans of the Apostles;" it was appropriately termed "The *Acts* of the Apostles." They were a bunch of "doers of the Word." *Applied* religion is never worthless.

What a Servant Does

Faith in Action

What good is it, my brothers, if someone says he has faith but does not have works? Can that faith save him? If a brother or sister is poorly clothed and lacking in daily food, and one of you says to them, "Go in peace, be warmed and filled," without giving them the things needed for the body, what good is that? So also faith by itself, if it does not have works, is dead.

But someone will say, "You have faith and I have works." Show me your faith apart from your works, and I will show you my faith by my works...

For as the body apart from the spirit is dead, so also faith apart from works is dead. James 2:14-18,26

That last verse reminds me of the story of three guys discussing the things they wanted people to be able to say of them as they lay in a casket at their own funeral. The first man wanted people to say how spiritual he had been. The second wanted them to say he had been a good family man. The third one said that what he wanted people to say at his funeral as they gazed in his casket was, "Look, he's still moving!"

A nice epitaph doesn't make up for the fact that we're dead, especially if being alive is still an option! And when it comes to my faith, rather than a postmortem on how impressive it appeared to be when I still had it, I'd much prefer observers to be able to say, "Look, it's still moving!"

People shouldn't be forced to guess at our faith. Our trust in Christ shouldn't lie there motionless, blending in with the surroundings like one of those lizards that looks like a leaf. People shouldn't have to peer closely at our faith, trying to distinguish if it's real or not. They ought to see the mercy and kindness of God flowing through our lives like a rushing stream, then they won't have to ask if we believe in God. If we pull a Mother Theresa, resign from the world's perks and journey off to invest our lives in friendless lepers because that's what we believe Christ would have us to do, we no longer have to convince folks we're serious about our faith. Nothing shows off faith like works done solely because of it.

Is our faith alive? If it's still moving, that's a really good sign.

What a Servant Does

Faith Followed By Obedience

What good is it, my brothers, if someone says he has faith but does not have works? Can that faith save him? If a brother or sister is poorly clothed and lacking in daily food, and one of you says to them, "Go in peace, be warmed and filled," without giving them the things needed for the body, what good is that? So also faith by itself, if it does not have works, is dead. James 2:14-17

James is good at pointing out the places where we like to deceive ourselves. One of them is in defending the cherished tenet that, since we are saved by faith alone, that's also a good place to stop. It isn't. Obedience to God's commands doesn't show a lack of faith ("You're trying to be saved by works!"); rather, it helps prove that we have faith. It shows that we believe God not only exists, but that He expects us to respond when He tells us something. Faith which is not followed by obedience is not really faith, "saving" or otherwise.

For as the body apart from the spirit is dead, so also faith apart from works is dead. (James 2:26)

Is it really a body, when the spirit is gone? Yes. A dead body. We needn't be expecting much out of it!

So, faith without works. Technically, we could still call it "faith," but sadly, it's a dead faith. Obedience would have kept it alive and shown that faith to be vibrant, but the absence of any response to the stimuli of God's commanded Word shows it to be lifeless and worthless. True faith will respond in obedience when God summons—not flawless obedience, of course—but at least an attempt to comply with the wishes of the Master.

Works cannot gain us the Kingdom of Heaven; no, that requires God's grace. Salvation is a free gift, generously bestowed upon every sinner willing to humble himself enough to receive it. But faith without obedience is not a living faith. In order to do the works God has prepared in advance for us to do, faith must be alive. Obedience proves that it is.

September 10

What a Servant Does

Garaged Faith

Count it all joy, my brothers, when you meet trials of various kinds, for you know that the testing of your faith produces steadfastness. And let steadfastness have its full effect, that you may be perfect and complete, lacking in nothing. James 1:2-4

Obedience is the chance to prove that our faith is alive, that it's real. James began his book by telling us to "count it all joy, my brothers" when we get a chance to try out our faith. When our faith is tested, it will grow stronger and so will we. Untested faith is tenuous faith, nervous faith. Nothing removes doubts as well as a successful trial run! And once again, God is doing us a favor. He's letting us try out the faith He's given us.

Faith without the opportunity to act on it must be like being the owner of a new sports car we don't get to drive (Not that it's ever happened to me). A speedometer that goes up to 150 mph, and we can't even back it out of the garage so the neighbors can see it, much less drive it. A sports car confined to the garage. What a waste that would be—and feel like.

That must be what it would feel like to have to "believe in God," and say "Yes" to all the creeds, etc., but know that we never get to try out our faith, at all. It just sits there, blending in with the boring surroundings. From the outside, it doesn't look a bit different from "non-faith," or any better. Until we get a chance to step on the gas, what good does it do to have "faith that would move mountains," when we don't use it to so much as mow the lawn?!

Sports cars and faith were not meant to be kept in the garage. In both cases, in order to appreciate what we have, we need the opportunity to get out and see what she'll do. So, the next time a trial comes my way, instead of moaning or whining I'm to get excited! Here comes the chance to get my faith out of the garage, and show off God's grace a little.

Gentlemen, start your engines!

September 11

What a Servant Does

Omitted Obedience

So whoever knows the right thing to do and fails to do it, for him it is sin. James 4:17

Omitted obedience is disobedience.

As a young child, our firstborn, compliant by nature, would never tell us "No," or exhibit open defiance, but when it came to actually doing what she was told to do, there were many times when she pleasantly disobeyed by simply not obeying. She would allow herself to get distracted, she would "forget," she would proceed so slowly that someone else would end up doing it for her. Smiling, cute disobedience. It was still disobedience, because she didn't do what she understood she was supposed to do! I've seen many an adult operate this way, too, including me. Way too many times, me.

I rarely tell God "No;" I know better than that. I also know that it's still disobedience, even if I skipped smarting off to Him when I skipped my specific assignment.

Omitted obedience is disobedience.

God tells us things for a reason. My Dad used to try to couch his commands in the language of suggestion: "You want to go and ____?" It was gently put, but we both knew it to be a command, and we both knew that the only choice I was being given was between a reluctant "Yes" and a cheerful one. Obedience was not optional in our home, nor did my father waste his time on suggestions; he only made his commands sound like them to soften them. Underneath, they were still commands.

When I know perfectly well what the Father would have me do, but instead of obedience I've been offering excuses and "forgetting" to obey, my omission of obedience results in the sin of omission.

Meanwhile, the enemy of our souls is always looking for opportunities to pile on a little more guilt to my already guilt-ridden life. It doesn't help that I've always been able to think up more things that I "should" be doing than were humanly possible, then carry the (false) guilt of not accomplishing my self-imposed goals. When I think about it, I realize that any time I knew it was God who was requiring my obedience, the assignment was always specific and achievable, never vague. And just like my Dad, never optional.

Serving God   261

September 12

What a Servant Does

Waiting Patiently

Be patient, therefore, brothers, until the coming of the Lord. See how the farmer waits for the precious fruit of the earth, being patient about it, until it receives the early and the late rains. You also, be patient. Establish your hearts, for the coming of the Lord is at hand. Do not grumble against one another, brothers, so that you may not be judged; behold, the Judge is standing at the door. As an example of suffering and patience, brothers, take the prophets who spoke in the name of the Lord. Behold, we consider those blessed who remained steadfast. You have heard of the steadfastness of Job, and you have seen the purpose of the Lord, how the Lord is compassionate and merciful. James 5:7-11

Judging from the fact that in the space of five verses he mentions it four times, I'd say that God wants His servants to "be patient." Servanthood is not non-stop activity; sometimes, the most important thing a servant can be doing is waiting, patiently.

It's hard enough to wait, let alone to do it patiently, without grumbling and grousing at one another. Patient waiting as an assignment? Four times in five verses.

I remember seeing the guards in London. Talk about an exercise in patience! That seemed to be the principal challenge: How long can this man stand here, motionless and imperturbable, under the unending and sometimes purposeful distraction of tourists hoping to make him move? Patience. His assignment is to remain as still as a statue for his entire shift, until a merciful replacement comes to continue the assignment of waiting, patiently.

When we think "soldiers," the tendency is to think of violent action—activity. Those who have served their country in the military know there is a lot more waiting than fighting. Willing and ready to fight? Yes. But the actual service—and perhaps the hardest service—is most often "waiting patiently," without grumbling, without going AWOL, without letting people or events pull us off-task.

In the Lord's service, an awesome sight to observe is a servant of Christ, eyes straight forward, oblivious to chaos or confusion, patiently awaiting His next command. Pretty impressive. And useful.

September 13

What a Servant Does

Empowered To Sit

And he called to him his twelve disciples and gave them authority over unclean spirits, to cast them out, and to heal every disease and every affliction.

These twelve Jesus sent out, instructing them,... John 10:1,5

The disciples weren't being trained to sit! I'm trying to picture myself as one of the Twelve, taking notes as Jesus gives instructions for this first "Faith Field Trip."

"Just go among your own people. It's not time for the Samaritans or Gentiles, yet."

"Check. Good idea."

"Here's the message: 'The kingdom of heaven is at hand.'"

"Good. Short. Easy to remember."

"Heal the sick."

I write down, "Heal the sick."

"Raise the dead."

Huh? I write down, "Raise the dead!"

"Cleanse lepers."

I'm still writing.

"Cast out demons."

This is unreal. I'm thinking, "Anything else impossible you want me to write down, Lord?!"

"Don't take anything with you, even if you already own it. I want you to see what it's like to live by faith, in my power."

I've stopped taking notes, as Jesus continues to give a chapter's worth of specific, detailed instructions and explanations regarding various scenarios. He's serious about this. We're not in a class, studying theology or theory; we're about to be sent out to do the impossible, and then come back and report to Him about it!

And that's exactly what happened, to their amazement. It happened again, when a larger group was subsequently sent out. They were sent out, followed Jesus' specific instructions, and returned with joy (Lk 10:17)!

Jesus empowered and sent out the Twelve; the same with the 72; but now when Jesus instructs His disciples, He just tells us to sit. Right?

September 14

What a Servant Does
The Ministry Of Receiving

"Whoever receives you receives me, and whoever receives me receives him who sent me. The one who receives a prophet because he is a prophet will receive a prophet's reward, and the one who receives a righteous person because he is a righteous person will receive a righteous person's reward. And whoever gives one of these little ones even a cup of cold water because he is a disciple, truly, I say to you, he will by no means lose his reward."
Matthew 10:37-42

It stands to reason that someone functioning as a prophet should get some kind of reward. After all, when we browse through the pages of the Old Testament, we come across people called "prophets" faced with some pretty grim circumstances! When they have to stand before kings and tell them things kings don't like to hear, there ought to be something more than death to look forward to, I would think! Obviously, there is.

But I hadn't taken this passage to heart, before, about *other* people getting in on a prophet's reward, simply for receiving him as a prophet. It just stands to reason, though—everyone can't be a prophet. Who would the audience be?! If everybody just hears from God on their own, what's the purpose of having any prophets at all? Just read the Memo from God.

Notwithstanding the presence of the Holy Spirit in each believer, there continues to be a place for prophets, according to scripture (Eph 4:11). Consequently, there also continues to be a ministry of *receiving* prophets. Jesus says the prophet and the receiver get the same reward! I think that's because, when it comes down to it, they have the same job: Believing. The prophet's job is to believe that what he has heard is a message from God which has been given him to deliver. The receiver's job is to believe that what he is hearing (from the prophet) is a message from God, to treat it as such and to act on it, accordingly.

It's basically the same job: Believe God. When the prophet faithfully delivers the message from the Lord, and the receiver faithfully receives the words of the prophet as having been passed on from God, they are both just believing that God speaks *to* people and *through* people. Whichever end we may be on, the reward is the same: The reward God grants to those who exercise faith and obedience, whether they are a messenger or a receiver.

September 15

What a Servant Does

What to Do With Hypocrites

Then Jesus said to the crowds and to his disciples, "The scribes and the Pharisees sit on Moses' seat, so practice and observe whatever they tell you—but not what they do. For they preach, but do not practice. They tie up heavy burdens, hard to bear, and lay them on people's shoulders, but they themselves are not willing to move them with their finger. They do all their deeds to be seen by others. For they make their phylacteries broad and their fringes long, and they love the place of honor at feasts and the best seats in the synagogues and greetings in the marketplaces and being called rabbi by others. Matthew 23:1-7

Jesus is just getting started. Seven times in this chapter He pronounces woes on the scribes and Pharisees, whom He addresses as "hypocrites," "blind guides" and "a brood of vipers," among other things.

Hatred toward Jesus had long been brewing among the brood He described, and this particular speech only fueled the fire. It was all for a purpose. One of those purposes was to instruct us concerning what to do with hypocrites.

Hypocrites grab at glory and authority, and fairly often get it, which means that many people will face each day answering in some way to a person of bloated ego and diminutive character. Jesus sketches out the fine line we are to follow, in these situations: Show respect for those in authority, even when it is undeserved, but reserve your ultimate respect for God and His law. Many times what a hypocrite says will actually be right and true; the example they set is where the rub comes. If what they're saying is appropriate, we follow their instruction, while ignoring their hypocritical behavior. If a hypocrite's preaching is good, follow their words, but not their example. Jesus is asking us to ignore hypocrisy in others, as we serve Him.

And once again, here comes the command to take an entirely different track than the world usually offers: *"The greatest among you shall be your servant. Whoever exalts himself will be humbled, and whoever humbles himself will be exalted."* (Mt 23:11-12) Our personal target is humility and service, not self-aggrandizement. The first defense against hypocrites is to not *be* one. If we head toward humility, we encounter (A) The fewest hypocrites wanting our seat, and (B) The greatest blessings of God.

September 16

What a Servant Does

Hot Potato Talents

"For it will be like a man going on a journey, who called his servants and entrusted to them his property. To one he gave five talents, to another two, to another one, to each according to his ability. Then he went away.
...

He also who had received the one talent came forward, saying, 'Master, I knew you to be a hard man, reaping where you did not sow, and gathering where you scattered no seed, so I was afraid, and I went and hid your talent in the ground. Here you have what is yours.' But his master answered him, 'You wicked and slothful servant! You knew that I reap where I have not sowed and gather where I scattered no seed? Then you ought to have invested my money with the bankers, and at my coming I should have received what was my own with interest. So take the talent from him and give it to him who has the ten talents. For to everyone who has will more be given, and he will have an abundance. But from the one who has not, even what he has will be taken away. And cast the worthless servant into the outer darkness. In that place there will be weeping and gnashing of teeth.'" Matthew 25:14-15,24-30

Being given a "talent" was no little deal. It represented the amount of money a working man would make in *twenty years!* Five talents—a century's worth of income for a laborer—were given to one servant, who doubled the money over time, was blessed by his returning master, and told, *"Well done, good and faithful servant. You have been faithful over a little; I will set you over much. Enter into the joy of your master."* (Mt 25:21) If 100 years' wages is what God calls "a little thing," it makes me wonder what He would call "much"!

The point, of course, is not that God is into us making money for Him, particularly since it holds no value for Him. The point is about us becoming responsible, faithful servants, who can be trusted with little or much, who will *do* something with whatever is entrusted to us, to the glory of God, rather than wasting time on excuses. We're supposed to *do* something with what has been given to us! That's the difference between the wicked, slothful servant and the good and faithful servant. And it's not the amount which matters; it's the faithfulness. Every resource in my possession is there for a reason. When He returns, I don't want to be just holding it.

What a Servant Does

Crystal Clear Commission

And Jesus came and said to them, "All authority in heaven and on earth has been given to me. Go therefore and make disciples of all nations, baptizing them in the name of the Father and of the Son and of the Holy Spirit, teaching them to observe all that I have commanded you. And behold, I am with you always, to the end of the age." Matthew 28:18-20

Our purpose for remaining on earth is crystal clear. The Great Commission was given us by the One possessing all authority in heaven and on earth! Plus, that One is still with us, and promised that He always will be. What in the world holds us back?!

We really can't plead ignorance. This is not a foggy mission statement. We can't say we don't know if we're supposed to or not. Jesus reminds His followers that *all* authority belongs to Him, and follows it up with *"Go therefore." "All authority," * plus *"Go"* is not very ambiguous.

"Where" is clear, also: *"All nations."*

"What?" *"Make disciples," "baptize," "teach them to observe all that I have commanded you."*

"What if we have questions or problems?" *"And behold, I am with you always, to the end of the age."*

I think I'm out of excuses.

In my lifetime, I've observed the Church in America emphasize fad after fad, each one harked as the latest "key" to church growth and effectiveness, each one disappointing in its long-term results, each one failing to turn around a culture bent on decay, even as mission efforts around the world produced astonishing growth.

There's hope. In my own denomination, the complex mission statement too often ignored through the years was recently reduced to seven words: "To make Christlike disciples in the nations." It's hard to go wrong with that one! Now it's just a matter of doing it.

Jesus' final instructions to His disciples were not meant to be debated or even merely crafted into new mission statements to be subsequently ignored. With all authority in heaven and earth backing them, and the Savior Himself present to empower us, these instructions were given us *to be carried out.* No more excuses. We can't say we don't know what to do.

What a Servant Does

Unbelievable Doors

"This is my commandment, that you love one another as I have loved you. Greater love has no one than this, that someone lays down his life for his friends. You are my friends if you do what I command you. No longer do I call you servants, for the servant does not know what his master is doing; but I have called you friends, for all that I have heard from my Father I have made known to you. You did not choose me, but I chose you and appointed you that you should go and bear fruit and that your fruit should abide, so that whatever you ask the Father in my name, he may give it to you. These things I command you, so that you will love one another." John 15:12-17

Love was not a suggestion or an ideal presented to the disciples by Jesus, but a command. It was always a command. All the other commands He gave hinged on that one: *"Love one another as I have loved you."* It was to be our best way of showing we were obedient. It was the way to show we belonged to Him. It was the best way of demonstrating that we love God with all our heart, soul, mind and strength, the greatest commandment of all.

It all revolves around love—not the sticky, whimsical "luv" of modern culture, but the rugged, self-sacrificial love exemplified in our Lord. That love is based on choice, not attraction. The kind of love with which Christ loved us is relentless, impervious to response, strong and selfless. This love is governed by an attitude of the will, independent of emotions.

"Love one another as I have loved you." That is a very hard act to follow! It is, however, an act, not a feeling. It's a series of actions, a chosen lifestyle pursuit of loving one another after the model of Christ's example.

"Love one another as I have loved you" is a door-opening commandment. When we follow it, it greatly increases our intimacy, not only with one another, but with God. We go from "command-keeping servant" to "friend." When our goal is synchronized with God's—"Love these people"—He entrusts us with information only given to those who share a mission of the heart. We are never "helping" God more than when we love! We are never closer to His heart. We are never truer to our purpose in life. What an honor it is to be given a commandment which shows more clearly than anything else His mark on our lives, and which opens so many wonderful doors!

What a Servant Does

It Couldn't Be Clearer

When they had finished breakfast, Jesus said to Simon Peter, "Simon, son of John, do you love me more than these?" He said to him, "Yes, Lord; you know that I love you." He said to him, "Feed my lambs." He said to him a second time, "Simon, son of John, do you love me?" He said to him, "Yes, Lord; you know that I love you." He said to him, "Tend my sheep." He said to him the third time, "Simon, son of John, do you love me?" Peter was grieved because he said to him the third time, "Do you love me?" and he said to him, "Lord, you know everything; you know that I love you." Jesus said to him, "Feed my sheep. Truly, truly, I say to you, when you were young, you used to dress yourself and walk wherever you wanted, but when you are old, you will stretch out your hands, and another will dress you and carry you where you do not want to go." (This he said to show by what kind of death he was to glorify God.) And after saying this he said to him, "Follow me."

Peter turned and saw the disciple whom Jesus loved following them, the one who had been reclining at table close to him and had said, "Lord, who is it that is going to betray you?" When Peter saw him, he said to Jesus, "Lord, what about this man?" Jesus said to him, "If it is my will that he remain until I come, what is that to you? You follow me!"
John 21:15-22

"*Simon, son of John, do you love me more than these?*"....
"Feed my lambs."
"....Do you love me?"
"Tend my sheep."
"....Do you love me?"
"Feed my sheep."
"*FOLLOW ME.*"

What more instruction does a pastor need?!

"But Lord, what about John?!"....
"*What about him? If it is my will that he remain until I come, what is that to you? You follow me!*"
How clear can it be? If we really love Jesus, what is it that He would have us to do? *Feed my sheep. Follow me.* It couldn't be clearer.

September 20

What a Servant Does

As Smart As an Ant

Go to the ant, O sluggard; consider her ways, and be wise. Without having any chief, officer, or ruler, she prepares her bread in summer and gathers her food in harvest. How long will you lie there, O sluggard? When will you arise from your sleep? A little sleep, a little slumber, a little folding of the hands to rest, and poverty will come upon you like a robber, and want like an armed man. Proverbs 6:9-11

This was the passage my younger brother liked to quote right before jumping on top of me in bed to wake me, in the rare day on the farm when I was trying to sleep in. We both had plenty to do, but both of us put together would never compare to our father. "Hard-working" seemed way too trite a term for him!

But rather than being a burden, being taught to work hard turned out to be one of the greatest blessings ever conferred upon us by our Dad. Countless doors have opened for each of the four of us raised in a household where we learned to work and pray. The ability to exercise self-discipline, foresight, determination, skill and planning, self-denial—the ability to apply oneself to a task with a focused stubbornness that refuses to quit until success is achieved—it makes me smile to think that all of this and more was purposely passed down to us by earthly parents who looked at work not as a necessary evil but as a blessing from God.

And so it is. The "Protestant work ethic" is not an unnatural burden passed down from one repressive generation to another, but a blessing from God. What was it Jesus said about His Father? *"My Father is working until now, and I am working."* (Jn 5:17) In God's eyes, work is a good thing! Work was how all of Creation was formed. God did it because He wanted to, not because anyone could force Him. It is His nature to work, creatively and wonderfully. He wanted His creation to share in His nature, so He blessed mankind with the gift of work. It is a blessing, not a burden. It's another opportunity to be like our Father.

Wisdom is realizing that what God calls "good" is always good, and that everything He has given us is for our benefit, including the gift of work. When we understand that, we're at least as smart as an ant.

What a Servant Does

Walking In Good Works

For by grace you have been saved through faith. And this is not your own doing; it is the gift of God, not a result of works, so that no one may boast. For we are his workmanship, created in Christ Jesus for good works, which God prepared beforehand, that we should walk in them.
Ephesians 2:8-10

There it is. In a short passage of three verses, Paul puts grace, faith and works in their place.

Saved? *By grace...through faith.*

By your own doing? No. *It is the gift of God.*

Saved as a result of? *Grace.* We already said that. Salvation is *not a result of works, so that no one may boast.* God knew us really well, didn't He? If even one person managed to get into the Kingdom through his works, we'd hang a medal on him and everybody would be trying to match his feat. *No one* gets in by works! There's no need to try.

This does *not* mean that no one needs to work! On the contrary— Why were we created? As a work of God, *his workmanship.*

For what? *For good works, which God prepared beforehand, that we should walk in them.*

Like handy "Make-a-Dent-in-Life" kits, carefully arranged before us with our name tags fluttering from them, God has prepared for each of us *good works,...that we should walk in them.* Good works aren't what get us in to the Kingdom; good works are what we do once we're in.

It's all coming together. This isn't Paul versus James, or some such nonsense; this is Paul explaining how faith, grace and works fit together perfectly, with no tension at all between them.

We're saved by grace, through faith, so that we can walk in the good works God has prepared in advance for each of us to do.

God knew we could never qualify for His Kingdom through our works, so He gave us salvation by grace through faith. And God knew how excited we would be in a Kingdom we got into for free where we would have absolutely nothing to do but sit around and be thankful we missed hell, so through Christ Jesus He prepared good works, that we should walk in them.

This isn't really that complicated, is it?

What a Servant Does

Bless God

I will extol you, my God and King,
and bless your name forever and ever.
Every day I will bless you
and praise your name forever and ever.
Great is the LORD, and greatly to be praised,
and his greatness is unsearchable.

One generation shall commend your works to another,
and shall declare your mighty acts.
On the glorious splendor of your majesty,
and on your wondrous works, I will meditate.
They shall speak of the might of your awesome deeds,
and I will declare your greatness. ...

My mouth will speak the praise of the LORD,
and let all flesh bless his holy name forever and ever.
Psalm 145:1-6,21

Part of the job of a servant is to "bless God." We are to be good advertisements for His glory and goodness. That's why it was good for David to say to the Lord and to himself: *"My mouth will speak the praise of the LORD."* Like a press agent for God, our job is to talk about His goodness and to let people know of His faithfulness, His love, and His greatness.

So many people don't seem to know that God is good! They pass judgment on Him, based on their own experiences, coming to the conclusion that either He doesn't really exist, or that He does in some form, but cannot be trusted. Bitter personal history with fathers or church people, inexplicable tragedies, their view of God is tainted by a worldview of general mistrust. This is why one of the crucial things a servant does is to bless God. People who don't know the Father desperately need to hear the heartfelt praise and thanksgiving of His children, proclaiming that He is unimaginably *good.* They don't know that. They need to. Because it is so very true! *Every day I will bless you... My mouth will speak the praise of the LORD.*

September 23

What a Servant Does

Dispensing God's Grace

For this reason I, Paul, a prisoner for Christ Jesus on behalf of you Gentiles—assuming that you have heard of the stewardship of God's grace that was given to me for you, how the mystery was made known to me by revelation, as I have written briefly. When you read this, you can perceive my insight into the mystery of Christ, which was not made known to the sons of men in other generations as it has now been revealed to his holy apostles and prophets by the Spirit. This mystery is that the Gentiles are fellow heirs, members of the same body, and partakers of the promise in Christ Jesus through the gospel.

Of this gospel I was made a minister according to the gift of God's grace, which was given me by the working of his power. To me, though I am the very least of all the saints, this grace was given, to preach to the Gentiles the unsearchable riches of Christ, and to bring to light for everyone what is the plan of the mystery hidden for ages in God who created all things, so that through the church the manifold wisdom of God might now be made known to the rulers and authorities in the heavenly places.
Ephesians 3:1-10

Paul knew he had been given something special. He had been divinely commissioned to preach God's grace to the Gentiles, welcoming them into God's Kingdom as fellow-heirs. Undeserving as Paul felt about this honor, he took the responsibility even more seriously. Proclaiming God's grace to those who had never even heard it was the focal point of his life, a sacred trust.

A phrase which stands out to me in the opening verse of this passage is *"the stewardship of God's grace."* It was not just the apostle Paul who has been granted God's grace; every believer has been granted grace, not only for ourselves, but to extend toward others. It's as though God's grace has been given to us as a "resource," which we are to generously steward.

Just as we are stewards of various material things which don't really belong to us, but to God, and we are expected to manage them in accordance with God's will, so we are stewards of His grace, dispensing it to people who don't realize that God's grace is for them, too. What a treasure we have! And what a responsibility—to be dispensers and stewards of the grace of God. And how delightful it is to "steward" a resource which never runs out!

Serving God   273

What a Servant Does

A Conduit of Joy

Have you not known? Have you not heard?
The LORD is the everlasting God, the Creator of the ends of the earth.
He does not faint or grow weary; his understanding is unsearchable.
He gives power to the faint, and to him who has no might he increas-
es *strength.*
Even youths shall faint and be weary,
and young men shall fall exhausted;
but they who wait for the LORD shall renew their strength;
they shall mount up with wings like eagles;
they shall run and not be weary;
they shall walk and not faint. Isaiah 40:28-31

When we come to the end of chapters like this one—so beautiful, so powerful and so joyful—we know it came from God. And instead of saying, "What a writer!" we say, "What a God!"

Isaiah's prophetic role once took him to the bedside of a king. There he delivered the somber news that Hezekiah was soon to die. The king's tears prompted God to grant him a fifteen year extension on his life, and Isaiah was sent back to announce the reprieve.

Isaiah's prophecies of the future are some of the key passages concerning the Christ. They are beautiful, exquisitely fashioned predictions which found exact fulfillment in Jesus of Nazareth. It was so important that these prophecies were written down and preserved, hundreds of years prior to the birth of the Messiah.

Sometimes the prophet's role was to faithfully deliver a message from God, whether to a bedridden ruler or to generations yet unborn. And sometimes the role of the prophet was simply to be a mouthpiece of praise, a conduit of joy. Sometimes what the world needs to hear is not what will happen next, or in the distant future, but the astonishing truth that God is good—that He is beautiful and magnificent and can be trusted. There is a joy which resides in God. At times, the most significant thing we can do is to be a channel for God's joy to be manifest on earth.

Lord, help me to be a conduit of your joy and power and beauty, today.

What a Servant Does

The People at the Gate

"There was a rich man who was clothed in purple and fine linen and who feasted sumptuously every day. And at his gate was laid a poor man named Lazarus, covered with sores, who desired to be fed with what fell from the rich man's table. Moreover, even the dogs came and licked his sores. The poor man died and was carried by the angels to Abraham's side. The rich man also died and was buried, and in Hades, being in torment, he lifted up his eyes and saw Abraham far off and Lazarus at his side. And he called out, 'Father Abraham, have mercy on me, and send Lazarus to dip the end of his finger in water and cool my tongue, for I am in anguish in this flame.' But Abraham said, 'Child, remember that you in your lifetime received your good things, and Lazarus in like manner bad things; but now he is comforted here, and you are in anguish...'" Luke 16:19-25

This has never been one of my favorite parables, probably because it's not hard to figure out to which of the two men my life circumstances most closely compare! In fact, if nice clothes and plenty to eat qualifies us as rich, that would include most of the population of my country. Even the guy who stands at the intersection hitting people up for money is quite a ways from Lazarus.

Is it a sin to be rich? Come to think of it, Abraham easily fit that category, and it was God who gave it to him! *Now Abram was very rich in livestock, in silver, and in gold.* (Gen 13:2) Abraham was also generous, merciful and obedient, qualities obviously lacking in the rich man in Jesus' parable. So, it must not be a sin to be rich, but it is a sin to be selfish? Sounds right.

How does this apply to the servant of God, who has been blessed with more than enough food and clothing, not to mention what's in the two-car garage and spilling out into the driveway? It's a reminder that we are not here to serve ourselves and sit around enjoying our luxuries; there's a responsibility to those at our gate. The servant of God, especially the rich one, is supposed to share, not grudgingly, but willingly. There is a place of comfort coming even for the rich, if they choose to use riches to bless and comfort those around them, now. But if we think God's not serious about us learning to show mercy, like the rich man, we are sadly mistaken.

What a Servant Does

Prayer on the Go

In the month of Nisan, in the twentieth year of King Artaxerxes, when wine was before him, I took up the wine and gave it to the king. Now I had not been sad in his presence. And the king said to me, "Why is your face sad, seeing you are not sick? This is nothing but sadness of the heart." Then I was very much afraid. I said to the king, "Let the king live forever! Why should not my face be sad, when the city, the place of my fathers' graves, lies in ruins, and its gates have been destroyed by fire?" Then the king said to me, "What are you requesting?" So I prayed to the God of heaven. And I said to the king, "If it pleases the king, and if your servant has found favor in your sight, that you send me to Judah, to the city of my fathers' graves, that I may rebuild it." And the king said to me (the queen sitting beside him), "How long will you be gone, and when will you return?" So it pleased the king to send me when I had given him a time. Nehemiah 2:1-6

Quick prayers and being prepared! What a combination! When Artaxerxes asks Nehemiah what's wrong, Nehemiah tells him, and when the question comes, "What are you requesting?" Nehemiah quickly prays, then makes a very specific, reasonable, well-thought-out request, which indicates that this servant makes thorough preparations for everything. I like this balance: He thinks things through and thoroughly prepares, yet depends on God and prays through everything! It's a good combination of faith and reason. It also works!

When the time came to reply to the king, Nehemiah had all the answers the king needed, because he had already prayed and thought this thing through, so he wasn't saying, "I don't know" to anything. In one fateful day, it all happened and came together! *And the king granted me what I asked, for the good hand of my God was upon me.* (Neh 2:8)

Here's lesson one from Nehemiah: Be prepared, and never stop praying. That philosophy served well the man who was cupbearer to the king of an empire, but who rebuilt the walls of Jerusalem and greatly helped his people. God hears the quick prayers, too—especially when it's just one more prayer in a never-ending series, as we always go to Him, first, even as we prepare.

What a Servant Does

The Constant Commandment

For this is the message that you have heard from the beginning, that we should love one another.

By this we know love, that he laid down his life for us, and we ought to lay down our lives for the brothers. But if anyone has the world's goods and sees his brother in need, yet closes his heart against him, how does God's love abide in him? Little children, let us not love in word or talk but in deed and in truth. 1 John 3:11,16-18

It's always going to come back to love, isn't it? There's a lot more where this passage came from! It's everywhere in the Book. Our job is to love. The Lord gives it to us in about every conceivable manner, hoping that somehow we'll get it, take it into our hearts, and actually fulfill this greatest of all commandments. We're supposed to love. He has built us for that purpose, commissioned us to do it, set the greatest example possible, tucked the commandment into scripture after scripture.... Now the Lord waits, to see if we're serious about being people after His heart. If we are, we'll love. There's just no getting past this commandment!

It's the message we've *heard from the beginning.* It's the message we'll hear 'til the end. Love. Lay down your life for your brother. Bolster up all the mercy within you, and open up your heart to the needs of people besides yourself. Don't just talk about love, but let it seep into your actions.

What does a servant of God do? He loves. What about "obedience?" When it comes to serving God, "love" and "obedience" are the same thing. There's just no getting around it.

What a Servant Does

The Unavoidable Lesson

Beloved, let us love one another, for love is from God, and whoever loves has been born of God and knows God. Anyone who does not love does not know God, because God is love. In this the love of God was made manifest among us, that God sent his only Son into the world, so that we might live through him. In this is love, not that we have loved God but that he loved us and sent his Son to be the propitiation for our sins. Beloved, if God so loved us, we also ought to love one another. No one has ever seen God; if we love one another, God abides in us and his love is perfected in us. 1 John 4:7-12

Again. We could easily spend a month on nothing more than "What does a servant do? He loves." There's plenty of ammunition! It is the key, though. Love for one another is the sign that we've been in contact with the one true God, who loved the world so much that He sent His only Son to save it. I've noticed that it's missing in all of the cults. The messengers trying to straighten out our worldview or theology are big on what they think is "truth," but their god is never a loving God who would come down to earth and save us; he's always something different. And the "love for one another" part generally appears to be either missing or skewed. Many times, it smacks of commiseration, rather than an actual desire to be together.

Yet, as I think of it, I've just described the Church, more often than I'd like to think! How many Christians have I encountered who somberly professed "love" for Christ, and fellowship with one another, but who exhibited little or no evidence of either? Way too many. And I've been there, too, plenty of times. We have work to do on this commandment.

John makes it clear that we're not going to see God, face to face; we already knew that. But he also reminds us that the world isn't going to see God at all, until they see people who love Him and who choose to love one another, because of Him. This is where we come in! Love is the unavoidable lesson. But once we learn it, the world gets a front-row seat to what God is all about.

Beloved, let us love one another, for love is from God, and whoever loves has been born of God and knows God. We can't get away from it.

What a Servant Does

Retained Disciples

Therefore let us leave the elementary doctrine of Christ and go on to maturity, not laying again a foundation of repentance from dead works and of faith toward God, and of instructions about washings, the laying on of hands, the resurrection of the dead, and eternal judgment. And this we will do if God permits. Hebrews 6:1-3

"Going on" is part of the education process. No one I know aspires to spend two or three years in third grade, although it sometimes happens. Why do kids get retained? Because, before we're ready for Grade Four, we need to have somewhat of a handle on Grade Three, or things will just get worse.

Likewise in the Christian life. We may be engrossed with thoughts of becoming a big-time prophet, sharing our wisdom about Revelation far and wide, but if we haven't gotten past our "times tables" yet, we can forget it, and prepare for another fun-filled year in third grade.

Retaining children in school is not something anyone likes, but reality makes it a necessity, at times. Pretending that we're ready when we're not isn't to anyone's advantage. Nor is settling down to some form of pseudo-contentment, when no progress is being made.

God doesn't like to retain us at our present level, either. He would much rather that we learn, grow and go on. But if we think that we've arrived, and we refuse to try to learn any more, even though we're still at "elementary" levels, how is God ever going to get us to maturity? He can either allow us to fake our way through, in experiences where we're sure to be crushed, or He can "retain" us at our present level, until we finally grasp the vital truths and skills we're going to need in the next "grade." What will a loving Father do?

If we recognize the marks on our desk from last year, and the teacher wears a very familiar face, rather than grousing at God for leaving us behind as our friends proceed to new challenges, maybe we should just settle down and learn this stuff. And thank God that He loves us enough to retain us, rather than letting us drown in water too deep for us.

Maturity. That's the goal, and He'll get us there. But we don't go on to the next level until He says we're ready.

What a Servant Does

Sluggish Servants

For land that has drunk the rain that often falls on it, and produces a crop useful to those for whose sake it is cultivated, receives a blessing from God. But if it bears thorns and thistles, it is worthless and near to being cursed, and its end is to be burned.

Though we speak in this way, yet in your case, beloved, we feel sure of better things—things that belong to salvation. For God is not so unjust as to overlook your work and the love that you showed for his sake in serving the saints, as you still do. And we desire each one of you to show the same earnestness to have the full assurance of hope until the end, so that you may not be sluggish, but imitators of those who through faith and patience inherit the promises. Hebrews 6:7-12

The first-glance picture presented by this passage isn't pretty, and might tend to make us think, "What's the use? I guess I'm just 'bad land,' with no hope." But the promises of which the writer speaks are promises about "whosoever" believes in Christ, and don't have anything to do with natural talent or station in life. The point being, anyone who wants to be "good land" only has to put himself at God's disposal and is guaranteed a "crop." The only one with anything to fear is the "sluggish"servant, who insists on bearing thorns and thistles (sinning), despite the fact that he has received all the "rain" needed to produce the fruit of righteousness.

God lets us choose what kind of "land" we will be. He has promised that if we abide in Christ, we can't help but produce fruit (Jn 15). He has also warned that *"apart from me you can do nothing."* (Jn 15:5). It's totally up to us, whether or not we bear fruit, based on the position we choose for ourselves. "In Christ" equals fruitful. "Apart from Christ" equals nothing. Those of us who choose "in Christ" inherit all the promises which attend such a life. We proceed with faith and patience, and in the end, no one is disappointed. *All* our work is rewarded, with love shown to others once again representing the greatest "work" of all.

There's no need for any of us to be a "sluggish" servant. Since following Christ is the only road leading to fruitfulness, there's no sense in being indecisive about that choice, or lagging behind once we've made it. It's time to aggressively pursue the promises God has for us, and not look back.

October 1

A Crown like Paul's

For I am already being poured out as a drink offering, and the time of my departure has come. I have fought the good fight. I have finished the race. I have kept the faith. Henceforth there is laid up for me the crown of righteousness, which the Lord, the righteous judge, will award to me on that Day, and not only to me but also to all who have loved his appearing.
2 Timothy 4:6-8

I'm trying to see the apostle Paul's face, as he writes the final page of correspondence the world will ever see from him. It's written to a beloved son in the faith, Timothy. The short epistle is sincere, passionate, hopeful, yet calmly realistic.

Paul's face is calm. In fact, everything he has penned is reflected in his countenance. The hope of eternal life, of a reward which will more than compensate for every trial. The satisfaction of having done absolutely everything in his power to win a world for Christ. The raw determination to see this race through to the very end, letting nothing stop him from crossing the finish line. The resignation that he is at last nearing the point where he will surrender what's left of his earthly body, in exchange for a glorified one.

There is no fear in Paul's face, and no regret. There is only hope. And there is no way that our Father in heaven will let His servant enter His presence unheralded or without reward! A crown bearing his name awaits Paul. Yet, Paul's gaze is not fixed on the crown he will receive, but on the Savior who called him on the Damascus road and who has guided his every step since that day. The reward isn't the crown, it's Jesus.

The hope the apostle held wasn't for him alone, but to all of us *"who have loved his appearing."* Paul calls the prize *"the crown of righteousness."* It doesn't just go to famous and highly esteemed apostles; we get it, too. It's really something to think about—we get the same crown as the apostle Paul! The crown of righteousness is not just awarded to "Most Valuable Player's" who make an incredible showing for the cause of Christ, here on earth. The crown goes to *"all who have loved his appearing."*

It's like the Super Bowl. On the winning team, everybody gets a ring. The star player and the guy who never left the bench both get the same ring. I want to finish this race. A crown just like Paul's awaits me.

What a Servant Does

God's Favorite Sacrifices

Through him then let us continually offer up a sacrifice of praise to God, that is, the fruit of lips that acknowledge his name. Do not neglect to do good and to share what you have, for such sacrifices are pleasing to God.

Obey your leaders and submit to them, for they are keeping watch over your souls, as those who will have to give an account. Let them do this with joy and not with groaning, for that would be of no advantage to you.

Pray for us, for we are sure that we have a clear conscience, desiring to act honorably in all things. I urge you the more earnestly to do this in order that I may be restored to you the sooner. Hebrews 13:15-19

It's never hard to find things to do, when we read the Bible. Mentioned here in a few brief verses are some of God's favorite sacrifices: Praise, Doing good, Sharing, Obedience, Intercession.

In each case, there are times when this particular action might be easy and natural—such as praising God when a totally wonderful event has just taken place—and times when to do this is nothing other than a sacrifice.

A life of sacrifice is a life which pleases God. The servant who praises God when he is sick or times are bleak, as well as when things are good, is a servant who knows the "sacrifice of praise." Likewise for the servant who shares with others not out of his excess, but sacrificially, who prays earnestly for the needs of others, who obeys leaders who aren't very good leaders but does it as a sacrifice to God. God is pleased with such sacrifices. One of the themes of the book of Hebrews is that the animal sacrifices are no longer necessary, since the perfect sacrifice of Jesus Christ atoned for our sin. His blood purchased our salvation once and for all. But that doesn't mean we can't bring a sacrifice of love to our Father, as an act of worship. What would He have us bring? The sacrifice of praise is always appropriate. Doing good—He smiles at that offering, especially when we're sharing with others. Praying for others—it's a sacrifice pleasing to Him. And being a cheerful, cooperative follower of the leaders He has placed over us blesses our boss and our God. Sometimes it's a sacrifice, but whatever we do out of love for God is acceptable in His sight. There's plenty to do. We don't have to (and can't) "sacrifice" our way into the Kingdom, but God is pleased when we bring a sacrifice He likes "just because."

October 3

What a Servant Does

A Choice Made In Public

"Now therefore fear the LORD and serve him in sincerity and in faithfulness. Put away the gods that your fathers served beyond the River and in Egypt, and serve the LORD. And if it is evil in your eyes to serve the LORD, choose this day whom you will serve, whether the gods your fathers served in the region beyond the River, or the gods of the Amorites in whose land you dwell. But as for me and my house, we will serve the LORD."
Joshua 24:14-15

Joshua assembles the leaders and elders of Israel and recites to them their history. He recounts God's promises, reminds them that it was *God* and not their own strength that got them here, then concludes with a very serious challenge: He tells them to make a choice. They need to choose their God.

There are times when we need to renew the covenant. It's not enough to struggle on, bouncing between tradition and scripture and cultural undertow and confusion; there are times when we need to say it out loud, in the presence of witnesses: "We will serve the LORD!"

Joshua gave the Israelites that opportunity. Had he not done it in that way, I think the outcome for his generation would have been different. Instead of remaining faithful to the LORD as they did, I think many of them would have drifted into pluralism or whatever without even giving it much thought. Their leader didn't give them that choice. He *made* them choose, after clearly revealing his own decision. The public commitment made to Yahweh by the Israelite leaders lasted them the rest of their generation.

It's only too bad that the torch didn't get transferred. The lights went out on the people who had witnessed God's miraculous provision and power, and the younger generation still hadn't gotten it: *And all that generation also were gathered to their fathers. And there arose another generation after them who did not know the LORD or the work that he had done for Israel.* (Judges 2:10)

Why not? Why didn't they know the LORD? I think it's because people didn't take the time or trouble to publicly express their gratitude to Him, or to consciously and openly renew their covenant with Him in the presence of their children. Until the baton is passed, our work is not finished.

What a Servant Does

Trained In Godliness

If you put these things before the brothers, you will be a good servant of Christ Jesus, being trained in the words of the faith and of the good doctrine that you have followed. Have nothing to do with irreverent, silly myths. Rather train yourself for godliness; for while bodily training is of some value, godliness is of value in every way, as it holds promise for the present life and also for the life to come. The saying is trustworthy and deserving of full acceptance. For to this end we toil and strive, because we have our hope set on the living God, who is the Savior of all people, especially of those who believe.

Command and teach these things. Let no one despise you for your youth, but set the believers an example in speech, in conduct, in love, in faith, in purity. Until I come, devote yourself to the public reading of Scripture, to exhortation, to teaching. Do not neglect the gift you have, which was given you by prophecy when the council of elders laid their hands on you. Practice these things, devote yourself to them, so that all may see your progress. Keep a close watch on yourself and on the teaching. Persist in this, for by so doing you will save both yourself and your hearers.
1 Timothy 4:6-16

The kind of discipline exercised by players in professional sports is the kind of discipline God desires of disciples. Hours spent in training camp pay off when the season arrives; every spiritual discipline we apply to our lives helps us in training ourselves for godliness. Training in sports only yields a return in this life; training in godliness offers benefits both for now and eternity. Even a little discipline produces a much more useful servant.

The minister receives special instructions: Be an example. Focus on these things and devote yourself to them. Watch yourself! Practice the basics. Something as simple as the public reading of scripture produces constant benefits (particularly in a culture where few had access to scripture and many were illiterate). Discipline yourself in the fundamentals, but above that, take the gift you have been given, and do something with it. Train yourself for godliness, knowing that everything *counts.* Coaches go with well-conditioned players; God gives special assignments to those who have trained themselves in godliness, who keep showing up for practice.

What a Servant Does

Healthy In Faith

But as for you, teach what accords with sound doctrine. Older men are to be sober-minded, dignified, self-controlled, sound in faith, in love, and in steadfastness. Older women likewise are to be reverent in behavior, not slanderers or slaves to much wine. They are to teach what is good, and so train the young women to love their husbands and children, to be self-controlled, pure, working at home, kind, and submissive to their own husbands, that the word of God may not be reviled. Likewise, urge the younger men to be self-controlled. Show yourself in all respects to be a model of good works, and in your teaching show integrity, dignity, and sound speech that cannot be condemned, so that an opponent may be put to shame, having nothing evil to say about us. Slaves are to be submissive to their own masters in everything; they are to be well-pleasing, not argumentative, not pilfering, but showing all good faith, so that in everything they may adorn the doctrine of God our Savior. Titus 2:1-10

An interesting alternate translation occurs three times in this paragraph: "Sound" may also be translated "healthy." "Sound" doctrine becomes "healthy" doctrine, being "sound in faith" means being "healthy in faith" and "sound speech" is "healthy speech." Not bad. God is interested in His people being "healthy," including their speech, faith and what they teach.

This revealing substitute translation also helps us to veer away from a dead-end road for Christians, the misconstrued notion that all that counts is being "right," "sound doctrine" too often merely associated with alignment with somebody's idea of theological correctness. "Sound doctrine" deserves a better place than that. It deserves the place of "healthy doctrine," meaning "healthy teaching"—the place where society observes with amazement people whose actions make their God look so appealing and kind. Healthy doctrine makes for a healthier society, complete with healthier, more uplifting speech and a healthy faith which thrives in spite of society's inequities.

It's interesting also that when the Bible talks "doctrine," it's scarcely ever about what we believe; mostly it's about what we do. What we do shows pretty clearly what we believe. And healthy faith is easier to detect in a marriage than in a theological textbook.

What a Servant Does

In The Present Age

For the grace of God has appeared, bringing salvation for all people, training us to renounce ungodliness and worldly passions, and to live self-controlled, upright, and godly lives in the present age, waiting for our blessed hope, the appearing of the glory of our great God and Savior Jesus Christ, who gave himself for us to redeem us from all lawlessness and to purify for himself a people for his own possession who are zealous for good works.

Declare these things; exhort and rebuke with all authority. Let no one disregard you. Titus 2:11-15

Two phrases really stand out to me in this passage. The first is *"in the present age."* Why is that a big deal? Look at what it's talking about: *"training us to renounce ungodliness and worldly passions, and to live self-controlled, upright, and godly lives <u>in the present age,</u>..."*

In my travels amongst churches I've often heard a "Nobody's perfect, so why try?" philosophy/theology expressed; what has been more rare has been to encounter groups of believers who assumed that this verse was true, and that God is in the business of training us to not live like the world but to live *"godly lives in the present age"*—as in, *now.* It makes me uncomfortable to think of how few times I have witnessed modern-day Christians in America renouncing ungodliness and worldly passions—I mean in themselves, not in others! It's very clear in this passage and others like it that God is wanting us to pursue holiness of heart and life, *now,* not later. We needn't get hung up on "perfection," either; that's not what He's asking of us. What He's asking of us is to turn away from ungodliness and act like people who are *his own possession who are zealous for good works.* Simply put, He wants us to act like we belong to Him rather than the world! Is that so hard? (Yes, sometimes).

<u>*"A people for his own possession."*</u> Us? It should be. Others should see that, not because they immediately notice some sort of perfect life, but because they see a zeal for good works born out of love for God. They will see people who are more interested in godliness than they are in imitating the world or satisfying their own passions. They will observe self-control—one of the habits of holiness. They will see a person being purified day by day, by the grace of God. And they will see it *now,* right before their eyes, *"in the present age."*

What a Servant Does

Saved and Fruitful

Remind them to be submissive to rulers and authorities, to be obedient, to be ready for every good work, to speak evil of no one, to avoid quarreling, to be gentle, and to show perfect courtesy toward all people. For we ourselves were once foolish, disobedient, led astray, slaves to various passions and pleasures, passing our days in malice and envy, hated by others and hating one another. But when the goodness and loving kindness of God our Savior appeared, he saved us, not because of works done by us in righteousness, but according to his own mercy, by the washing of regeneration and renewal of the Holy Spirit, whom he poured out on us richly through Jesus Christ our Savior, so that being justified by his grace we might become heirs according to the hope of eternal life. The saying is trustworthy, and I want you to insist on these things, so that those who have believed in God may be careful to devote themselves to good works. These things are excellent and profitable for people. ...

And let our people learn to devote themselves to good works, so as to help cases of urgent need, and not be unfruitful. Titus 3:1-8,14

"Saved by grace, appointed to good works." It makes sense to me! Apparently it did to Paul, too, who promotes being devoted to good works three times in the final sentences of his letter to Titus, even as in the same passage he reiterates the fact that works do not bring about our salvation. Saved by the goodness and loving kindness of God, and nothing else! Devoted to good works in the name of Christ! Those two statements are not in tension with one another; in fact, they are incomplete without one another. No amount of attempted righteousness on our part would get us into the Kingdom of God; it's grace and mercy on God's part—always has been, always will be. But why would we want to be in a kingdom where we had nothing to do?

God knew we would never be content to sit idly by; He has given us meaningful things to do, and wants us to devote ourselves to doing these good works, so we won't be unfruitful (and thus, unsatisfied). Good works are *"excellent and profitable for people."* We're not saved by good works, but (as a favor to us) we're commanded to do them. God knew we would not only want to be saved; we'd want to be fruitful, too.

What a Servant Does

Sacrificing the Right to Die

I appeal to you therefore, brothers, by the mercies of God, to present your bodies as a living sacrifice, holy and acceptable to God, which is your spiritual worship. Romans 12:1

We're starting out in a chapter which in itself is a sort of comprehensive theology of what a servant should do. It starts out with presenting our bodies to God as a *living sacrifice*. This is in direct contrast to our natural tendency to offer ourselves as martyrs or nothing.

"Sure, God, I'd give my life for You—unless I don't get to die!"

God likes His sacrifices still alive.

That is the hard part, after all. Martyrdom is easy, at least in theory: The good part of martyrdom is, if you do it well once, you never have to do it, again!

A living sacrifice is the same thing, except we don't get to die. A living sacrifice means we *sacrifice* our right to die, as part of the sacrifice! We go on the altar still alive! And once our body has been presented to God in this way, we don't get to either die or jump up and resume our former life, according to God's preference. Rather, we rise from the altar still living, still breathing, but without the right to our former existence. Something did die on that altar: My old life, complete with its ambitions, sins, everything.

But the body still lives. What am I to do with it? Anything He wants. Now that it's swept clean and empty, my body can be useful for whatever purpose my Lord assigns it. He wanted not another dead sacrifice, but a living one, holy and acceptable to Him, to be used exclusively for His purposes. Yes, it would have been easier for me to just die and get it over with, but this is much more to everyone's advantage! I am rid of my life of sin (Praise God, because it died when the old "me" died!), and this old, still-living body now has a new Master, a much better one. What could He not do with a living body given totally over to Him, for His exclusive personal use?

The sacrifice is real. It's still death, to self. God merely says, "Don't kill the body. Give it to me to use, every day, for the rest of your life."

With a "living sacrifice" arrangement, I show up each new day God has granted me with the same question: "What do you want me to do, today, with this body which now belongs to you?" That's a living sacrifice. Harder than martyrdom, but also much better!

October 9

What a Servant Does

The Last Piece on the Altar

Do not be conformed to this world, but be transformed by the renewal of your mind, that by testing you may discern what is the will of God, what is good and acceptable and perfect.

For by the grace given to me I say to everyone among you not to think of himself more highly than he ought to think, but to think with sober judgment, each according to the measure of faith that God has assigned.
Romans 12:2-3

As difficult as it is to give over our bodies to the Lord as a living sacrifice, it is even more difficult to relinquish to Him our mind. I have seen people try to be committed Christians, who have given God everything *except* their mind. Nearly always, these were individuals who prided themselves on their intellect and had but little use for the body, anyway. Giving God their body wasn't that big of a deal. Relinquishing control of the mind? That was different!

Yet, offering our bodies as living sacrifices while at the same time withholding our brain from the bargain is equivalent to giving away a television while hanging on to the remote. How can our bodies be at God's complete disposal when we still have the control?

Are we talking lobotomy, here? Is that what God wants—Brainless, non-thinking Christian robots who accomplish His desires? No. He's after renewed minds, which lead to transformed actions. Instead of being just one more creature of the world, spit out in the same mold as millions of others who think and act alike in their ungodliness, God is after renewed, sanctified people, who have given their minds to Him as completely as they have given their bodies. That's a mind with which God can work! That's also a mind which will be tuned to a proper estimation of itself, and not constrained by the pride which kills creativity and relationships.

This also is the most exciting part of the "living sacrifice" picture. When we contemplate Creation, we have a glimpse of the intelligence of our Heavenly Father. What will He do when we give Him our mind, to renew in whatever way He sees fit? Is there any way we would become *less* intelligent by presenting our minds to One like this?

Serving God

289

What a Servant Does

Not Clean, but Complete

For as in one body we have many members, and the members do not all have the same function, so we, though many, are one body in Christ, and individually members one of another. Having gifts that differ according to the grace given to us, let us use them: if prophecy, in proportion to our faith; if service, in our serving; the one who teaches, in his teaching; the one who exhorts, in his exhortation; the one who contributes, in generosity; the one who leads, with zeal; the one who does acts of mercy, with cheerfulness. Romans 12:4-8

This is so simple, and so hard. Doesn't it just make sense that God would not make everyone the same, or assign us all the same role? Yet I look around at churches and see nearly everyone frustrated over this topic. Pastors flounder because they are only gifted in three things, not five! What kind of absurdity is it to expect anyone with a call to preach to also excel in everything else, too? The same goes for all the gifts. Having too many gifts is actually a problem! Who would have time to use all of them?

So it's clear: The gifts are *supposed* to differ, and the gifts are *supposed* to be used. When people use their God-given abilities with grace and a good attitude, they soar. They find satisfaction. What a servant does is to find his gift and put it into play, with passion and focus. A really useless pursuit is to shelve our own gifts and spend our life in griping over what we don't have! These gifts are like tools: Useful if used, worthless if not.

Then, too, it's back to "body." It's hard in our individualistic culture to truly grasp truths like being *"one body in Christ, and individually members one of another."* I've worked pretty hard at not needing other people. Here God is reminding me that I'm part of a body (which makes "leaving" no longer an option), and that my life is even less my own than I had come to think! Just about the time I'm finally resigned to the fact that I belong to Christ and I'm part of His Body, He reinforces the verdict that in the Church (which is just another name for His "Body"), we actually are *members one of another.* So much for independence! I belong to Christ; I belong to all the other believers, plus they're stuck belonging to me. But when we add up the gifts, nothing is missing, plus we have Jesus! It's not "clean," but it's complete.

October 11

What a Servant Does
Twenty-Seven Ways to Win

Let love be genuine. Abhor what is evil; hold fast to what is good. Love one another with brotherly affection. Outdo one another in showing honor. Do not be slothful in zeal, be fervent in spirit, serve the Lord. Rejoice in hope, be patient in tribulation, be constant in prayer. Contribute to the needs of the saints and seek to show hospitality.

Bless those who persecute you; bless and do not curse them. Rejoice with those who rejoice, weep with those who weep. Live in harmony with one another. Do not be haughty, but associate with the lowly. Never be conceited. Repay no one evil for evil, but give thought to do what is honorable in the sight of all. If possible, so far as it depends on you, live peaceably with all. Beloved, never avenge yourselves, but leave it to the wrath of God, for it is written, 'Vengeance is mine, I will repay, says the Lord.' To the contrary, "if your enemy is hungry, feed him; if he is thirsty, give him something to drink; for by so doing you will heap burning coals on his head." Do not be overcome by evil, but overcome evil with good.
Romans 12:9-21

I simply love the passages in the Bible which occur every so often where the instructions are written in short, blunt, practical sentences. The faithful application of this chapter alone would create one of the most phenomenal Christians ever! Even putting a couple of the habits into consistent practice would make a huge difference. For instance, *"Outdo one another in showing honor."* I've watched plenty of people try to outdo one another, but I've rarely witnessed competitive honor. It would have to be a most godly challenge. Maybe I should try it! Or for that matter, any of the other 26 tips for how to live a practical Christian life contained in just two paragraphs!

God never wanted us to be beaten down or bewildered. So why are we? When we have page after page of specific instructions of what to do when confronted by evil, why do we act as if we didn't know what to do? Why do we accept defeat, and forfeit entire days of the calendar to the power of the enemy? Our Lord has shown us what to do with evil: Overcome it with good. How? In just two paragraphs alone, we have 27 ways to win!

October 12

What a Servant Does

Civil Servants, God's Servants

Let every person be subject to the governing authorities. For there is no authority except from God, and those that exist have been instituted by God. Therefore whoever resists the authorities resists what God has appointed, and those who resist will incur judgment. For rulers are not a terror to good conduct, but to bad. Would you have no fear of the one who is in authority? Then do what is good, and you will receive his approval, for he is God's servant for your good. But if you do wrong, be afraid, for he does not bear the sword in vain. For he is the servant of God, an avenger who carries out God's wrath on the wrongdoer. Therefore one must be in subjection, not only to avoid God's wrath but also for the sake of conscience. For the same reason you also pay taxes, for the authorities are ministers of God, attending to this very thing. Pay to all what is owed to them: taxes to whom taxes are owed, revenue to whom revenue is owed, respect to whom respect is owed, honor to whom honor is owed.
Romans 13:1-7

In this chapter, "servant of God," or even "minister of God" are terms applied to ruling civil authorities. We are explicitly told to give them the consideration due them, even when it's obvious they are not lovers of God. There is still the tension of "We must obey God rather than men," and times when civil disobedience may be necessary, but for the most part, in order to be a good Christian, we ought to be a good citizen, too. God's servants ought to be some of the favorite servants of civil servants. Our cooperation level, cheerfulness and overall ease of being governed should be head and shoulders above others.

Much of the concept of submission to earthly authorities is directly tied in with the idea of God's authority. God, having ultimate authority, has delegated some of it to governments and governing leaders. If we thumb our nose at the person God has placed in that station, we are actually rebelling against God! This chain of authority is so important that God is willing to refer to governing officials as His "ministers," even though they may lack allegiance to anyone but themselves. Civil servants are God's servants. Part of what a servant of Christ Jesus does is to try to make their job as easy as possible, by being a responsible, respectful, tax-paying, cooperative citizen.

What a Servant Does

Daytime Living

Owe no one anything, except to love each other, for the one who loves another has fulfilled the law. The commandments, 'You shall not commit adultery, You shall not murder, You shall not steal, You shall not covet, and any other commandment, are summed up in this word: 'You shall love your neighbor as yourself.' Love does no wrong to a neighbor; therefore love is the fulfilling of the law.

Besides this you know the time, that the hour has come for you to wake from sleep. For salvation is nearer to us now than when we first believed. The night is far gone; the day is at hand. So then let us cast off the works of darkness and put on the armor of light. Let us walk properly as in the daytime, not in orgies and drunkenness, not in sexual immorality and sensuality, not in quarreling and jealousy. But put on the Lord Jesus Christ, and make no provision for the flesh, to gratify its desires. Romans 13:8-14

I love the Bible. We can start virtually anywhere in it, and find something helpful, practical and personal. It's more than a book of wisdom; God's words contain life, for us!

This chapter, like the one preceding it, is chock-full of concise directions for a great life. I'm glad that so many specifics are mentioned, both here and in many other places in scripture. Yet it always comes down to just one word, a word on which all of the other commandments are based: Love. If we love one another, we are assured that we are fulfilling the law. If there's a "one-word-fits-all" philosophy in scripture, it would be the word, "love." If we love our neighbor, we're pretty much there, when it comes to fulfilling God's expectations of us.

The only way to walk in the way of Christ's love, though, is to put aside the ways of darkness. This must be done deliberately; they cling. That's why Paul's term for ridding ourselves of them is forceful: *"So then let us cast off the works of darkness ..."* The works of darkness need to be unsympathetically booted out of our lives. It's the only way they will go. And to prevent them from reestablishing themselves in our lives (which they will definitely attempt to do), our defense is to *"put on the armor of light."* That's what happens when we kick out the old life, and invite Jesus Christ in. We quit living in darkness, and we start living in light.

October 14

What a Servant Does
Whatever He Tells Us

Blessed is that servant whom his master will find so doing when he comes. Luke 12:43

Doing what? The context is that of a faithful manager doing his master's bidding, but it can simply be extended to all of us, regardless of our assignment. What does the servant do? *Whatever the Master tells us.*

I could stop right here, and it would be pretty accurate. The number one thing a servant does is *obey the Master's commands.* What has the Lord asked of me? The commands might be general in nature, or very specific, but either by scripture or through the Holy Spirit, I know this is what the Father would have me do. Now, it's just a matter of obedience. What does the servant do? Whatever his Master says.

Very often that obedience entails utilizing the gifts and resources entrusted to us. There's even considerable creativity involved, when it comes to figuring out how best to fulfill our role. When we're commanded to love one another and to serve one another (a couple of default commands always appropriate, regardless of situation), there's a lot of leeway. In the parable of the talents, the stewards are not given specifics as to exactly what they are to do with their master's money, but it's clear they are to do *something* with it which will please their master.

And attitude counts, as does character. Our Master is not fishing for mechanical compliance. He desires us to not only follow His instructions, but to do it out of an eager love, not a begrudging submission. The point is hardly ever our completion of some task, but the development of a soul which more and more resembles Christ. It's not only *what a servant does* that matters; it's *who the servant is—and what he's becoming.*

What a servant does: It's simple, really—a servant of God serves God. All of his resources go toward that; all of his time goes toward that; it's his only true ambition; he doesn't go beyond serving God to include his own personal agenda; he is not only faithful in service, he is joyful in service, going beyond the minimum requirements to make service worship. To be a "good and faithful servant" of God is the highest honor a human being can reach. How do we get there? We just cheerfully do whatever He tells us.

October 15

The Servant's Faith Is in God, Not in Himself

What's Scarier than Faith?

But Caleb quieted the people before Moses and said, "Let us go up at once and occupy it, for we are well able to overcome it." Then the men who had gone up with him said, "We are not able to go up against the people, for they are stronger than we are." Numbers 13:30-31

Then all the congregation raised a loud cry, and the people wept that night. And all the people of Israel grumbled against Moses and Aaron. The whole congregation said to them, "Would that we had died in the land of Egypt! Or would that we had died in this wilderness! Why is the LORD bringing us into this land, to fall by the sword? Our wives and our little ones will become a prey. Would it not be better for us to go back to Egypt? And they said to one another, "Let us choose a leader and go back to Egypt."...

And the LORD said to Moses, "How long will this people despise me? And how long will they not believe in me, in spite of all the signs that I have done among them?" Numbers 14:1-4,11

The disastrous reaction to the report of the spies indicated where the faith of the people lay—in themselves. They still had not learned to trust the God who had brought them out of Egypt; in fact, they wanted to choose a new leader and go back to Egypt! If they had merely put their faith in God, they would have known the joys of living in the land of promise. Instead, they refused to believe God's promises, and, since they knew they couldn't do it on their own strength, shrank back into despair, only to spend the rest of their lives in that despair. They would have been far better off to have died in battle, had they been mistaken in a belief that God would help them, than to have died in the desert because they refused to have faith. The children they thought would suffer if they exercised faith, instead suffered greatly because they *didn't* exercise it! What's scarier than faith? Lack of it!

Sometimes statistics are a bad deal, particularly if we are willing to arrange our whole life around the "odds," when we could instead choose to arrange it around a God who doesn't *do* odds—just miracles. Those who put their trust in God are not disappointed, while those who trust in themselves spend their years in a spin cycle of fear and failure. When we check history and look around a bit, it's actually scarier to *not* trust God, when we see what happens to folks who only have their statistics, and only trust themselves.

October 16

The Servant's Faith Is in God, Not in Himself

Only the Promise

And say to the people, 'Consecrate yourselves for tomorrow, and you shall eat meat, for you have wept in the hearing of the LORD, saying, "Who will give us meat to eat? For it was better for us in Egypt." Therefore the LORD will give you meat, and you shall eat. You shall not eat just one day, or two days, or five days, but a whole month, until it comes out at your nostrils and becomes loathsome to you, because you have rejected the LORD who is among you and have wept before him, saying, "Why did we come out of Egypt?"' " But Moses said, "The people among whom I am number six hundred thousand on foot, and you have said, 'I will give them meat, that they may eat a whole month!' Shall flocks and herds be slaughtered for them, and be enough for them? Or shall all the fish of the sea be gathered together for them, and be enough for them?" And the LORD said to Moses, "Is the LORD's hand shortened? Now you shall see whether my word will come true for you or not."

So Moses went out and told the people the words of the LORD.
Numbers 11:18-24

When the Israelites complain about not having meat, God instructs Moses to tell them they will have enough meat for a month, until they are sick of it. Moses reminds God of how many people there are and how much it would take to feed them; God reminds Moses of His power. How much faith would it take to tell that crowd they were going to have a month's worth of meat when you didn't know from where any of it would come? But Moses' faith was in God, not in himself. He gave the message when he didn't even know what God's plan was, only His promise. For the servant, that's enough.

Is that enough for me? I don't know what God's plan is, either; only His promises. One of His promises is:

"For I know the plans I have for you, declares the LORD, plans for wholeness and not for evil, to give you a future and a hope." (Jer 29:11)

As long as God knows His plans, I guess I don't have to. If we have His promise, we don't even have to know His plan.

Lord, thank you for your promises! They're all true.

The Servant's Faith Is in God, Not in Himself

What We Tell Our Hearts

"Take care lest you forget the LORD your God by not keeping his commandments and his rules and his statutes, which I command you today, lest, when you have eaten and are full and have built good houses and live in them, and when your herds and flocks multiply and your silver and gold is multiplied and all that you have is multiplied, then your heart be lifted up, and you forget the LORD you God, who brought you out of the land of Egypt, out of the house of slavery, who led you through the great and terrifying wilderness, with its fiery serpents and scorpions and thirsty ground where there was no water, who brought you water out of the flinty rock, who fed you in the wilderness with manna that your fathers did not know, that he might humble you and test you, to do you good in the end. Beware lest you say in your heart, 'My power and the might of my hand have gotten me this wealth.' You shall remember the LORD your God, for it is he who gives you power to get wealth, that he may confirm his covenant that he swore to your fathers, as it is this day." Deuteronomy 8:11-18

Success is a hotbed for pride. The Lord knew that when the Israelites were no longer dependent upon manna from heaven, when they were comfortable in their own houses and well-fed and prosperous, they would begin to believe it was their own industry and savvy which had accomplished all this. Through Moses, He warns them of the danger facing them when they switch over from a lifestyle based entirely upon God's direct provision to one based upon God's indirect provision. The inclination would be to forget God, rely on themselves and give themselves the glory for the wealth and success they were enjoying. (At least they *started* with God-dependence)!

It starts with what we tell ourselves: *Beware lest you say in your heart, 'My power and the might of my hand have gotten me this wealth.'* Pride, like bitterness, only needs permission to take root—and the permitted seed becomes an overpowering plant almost overnight. We need to be really, really careful what we tell our hearts. Sometimes gratitude is spontaneous; more often, it is a discipline, an on-purpose decision to say to our hearts, "This came from God, not me, and I choose to gratefully acknowledge that." Setting a guard over what we tell our hearts is the kind of discipline which brings great reward, and keeps a lid on damaging pride.

October 18

The Servant's Faith Is in God, Not in Himself

Faith for the Sabbath

The LORD spoke to Moses on Mount Sinai, saying, "Speak to the people of Israel and say to them, When you come into the land that I give you, the land shall keep a Sabbath to the LORD. For six years you shall sow your field, and for six years you shall prune your vineyard and gather in its fruits, but in the seventh year there shall be a Sabbath of solemn rest for the land, a Sabbath to the LORD. You shall not sow your field or prune your vineyard. You shall not reap what grows of itself in your harvest, or gather the grapes of your undressed vine. It shall be a year of solemn rest for the land...

"Therefore you shall do my statutes and keep my rules and perform them, and then you will dwell in the land securely. The land will yield its fruit, and you will eat your fill and dwell in it securely. And if you say, 'What shall we eat in the seventh year, if we may not sow or gather in our crop?' I will command my blessing on you in the sixth year, so that it will produce a crop sufficient for three years. When you sow in the eighth year, you will be eating some of the old crop; you shall eat the old until the ninth year, when its crop arrives... Leviticus 25:1-5,18-22

The whole concept of "Sabbath" is based on faith in God, whether it be the weekly Sabbath of the Ten Commandments or the year-long Sabbaths prescribed by God to the Israelites in the seventh and fiftieth years. It comes down to, "Do we trust God to take care of us?"

It would take an incredible faith in God for *everyone* to live by faith for an entire year as the planting and harvest seasons came and went, trusting that God would provide for the whole nation, but it would have been a lesson for the whole country. As God commanded a blessing to accompany their obedience, they would have experienced a year-long revival, I think. What a pity that it seems the Israelites never even once did it!

Each time the nation experienced a Sabbath year, a new generation would have learned dependence on God, and an older generation would have been reminded of His faithfulness. What a national witness it would have been! The world would have marveled at how God cared for His people, and how they trusted Him.

What of us? Are we off the hook? God still wants His people to learn to trust in Him, not ourselves. He still commands a blessing on the obedient.

The Servant's Faith Is in God, Not in Himself

Miraculous Protection

As soon as all the kings of the Amorites who were beyond the Jordan to the west, and all the kings of the Canaanites who were by the sea, heard that the LORD had dried up the waters of the Jordan for the people of Israel until they had crossed over, their hearts melted and there was no longer any spirit in them because of the people of Israel.

At that time the LORD said to Joshua, "Make flint knives and circumcise the sons of Israel a second time." So Joshua made flint knives and circumcised the sons of Israel at Gibeath-haaraloth...

When the circumcising of the whole nation was finished, they remained in their places in the camp until they were healed. And the LORD said to Joshua, "Today I have rolled away the reproach of Egypt from you."
Joshua 5:1-3,8-9

This plan would have had a difficult time making it past any battle-hardened generals! A strategy which calls for crossing into enemy territory with women, children and livestock, then simultaneously rendering every man in the nation helpless for a few days while a flooded river blocks retreat, is not the sort of undertaking to be approved at military school. They didn't even stagger the procedures so that at least part of the army might be able to defend them while the other part healed—this was complete, mass vulnerability in a place of extreme danger, and complete, mass obedience to a God who had promised to provide for them and protect them.

A new generation of Israelites put their faith in God by undergoing circumcision right after they crossed the Jordan into enemy territory! In theory, they were helpless. In reality, they had never been safer. God held their enemies at bay while they healed, with nothing more than the miracle of their crossing. God had provided not just a way across the river, but divine protection at the same time; it took the heart right out of their enemies! Their protection was God's miraculous power. They were very safe.

As long as the Israelites trusted in God enough to obey Him fully, they were always absolutely safe. It was only when they relied on their own intelligence and strategy that they failed. Funny. That seems to be the pattern in our lives today, too. When are we going to learn? We are never safer than when we obey.

The Servant's Faith Is in God, Not in Himself

How to Lose a Kingdom

At the end of the days I, Nebuchadnezzar, lifted my eyes to heaven, and my reason returned to me, and I blessed the Most High, and praised and honored him who lives forever,...

At the same time my reason returned to me, and for the glory of my kingdom, my majesty and splendor returned to me. My counselors and my lords sought me, and I was established in my kingdom, and still more greatness was added to me. Now I, Nebuchadnezzar, praise and extol and honor the King of heaven, for all his works are right and his ways are just; and those who walk in pride his is able to humble. Daniel 4:36-37

These are unusual words, coming from a ruler of the world's largest empire, but not every king spends seven years in insanity, driven from men and eating grass like an ox, only to resume his reign, this time with humility!

The king of Babylon was first warned in a dream he had, which predicted precisely what would happen to him (Dan 4). The dream had been interpreted by Daniel, who pled with the king to try a little righteousness and humility.

It worked for a while, but twelve months later, a little rooftop crowing triggered its fulfillment:

All this came upon King Nebuchadnezzar. At the end of twelve months he was walking on the roof of the royal palace of Babylon, and the king answered and said, "Is not this great Babylon, which I have built by my mighty power as a royal residence and for the glory of my majesty?" (Dan 4:28-30)

That was all it took. This time it isn't a dream, but a voice from heaven, pronouncing the commencement of the king's lesson, *"until you know that the Most High rules the kingdom of men and gives it to whom he will."* (Dan 4:32)

What a lesson. Would that kings and wannabe kings everywhere could learn what Nebuchadnezzar learned the hard way: It's not by our own strength or intelligence that we become king; it's by God's design. Don't put your faith in yourself, and don't become proud of what you've built and what you've done. *"Those who walk in pride he is able to humble."* Well said, Nebuchadnezzar. Presidents, legislators, judges, pastors? Take heed.

October 21

The Servant's Faith Is in God, Not in Himself

Stubborn Devotions

When Daniel knew that the document had been signed, he went to his house where he had windows in his upper chamber open toward Jerusalem. He got down on his knees three times a day and prayed and gave thanks before his God, as he had done previously. Then these men came by agreement and found Daniel making petition and plea before his God. Then they came near and said before the king, concerning the injunction, "O king! Did you not sign an injunction, that anyone who makes petition to any god or man within thirty days except to you, O king, shall be cast into the den of lions?" The king answered and said, "The thing stands fast, according to the law of the Medes and Persians, which cannot be revoked." Then they answered and said before the king, "Daniel, who is one of the exiles from Judah, pays no attention to you, O king, or the injunction you have signed, but makes his petition three times a day."
Daniel 6:10-13

Daniel's jealous rivals comprise a law to trap him. Using King Darius' vanity against him, they trick the king into an executive order which will cause him to lose his most trusted administrator to some hungry lions. The well-known account ends with Daniel's delivery and his accusers' demise.

While God's stubborn faithfulness toward His servants is always consistent, man's faithfulness is usually spotty at best, making Daniel's bravery wonderfully stand out. All he would have had to do was lie low for a month, and he would have been fine! Plenty of rationalizations were available to prevent him from stepping into this obvious trap, but Daniel ignored the law as well as the instinct of self-preservation. He boldly, blatantly had his devotions, as usual, in public, in full view of his accusers, and allowed them to take the evidence he had given them to a king who would spend the night fasting and praying for the man he had unwittingly sentenced to death. Daniel's stubborn devotional life is richly rewarded. They were God's lions. Daniel's choice to put his faith in God, rather than compromising to try to save his own life, reminds me of my favorite Bible verse, 2 Chronicles 16:9: *For the eyes of the LORD run to and fro throughout the whole earth to give strong support to those whose heart is blameless toward him.* A man who refuses to compromise, whose trust is totally in God, is just the kind of man for whom God is looking. Stubborn faith will be rewarded!

The Servant's Faith Is in God, Not in Himself

How to Repent For Your Nation

In the first year of Darius the son of Ahasuerus, by descent a Mede, who was made king over the realm of the Chaldeans—in the first year of his reign, I, Daniel, perceived in the books the number of years that, according to the word of the LORD to Jeremiah the prophet, must pass before the end of the desolations of Jerusalem, namely, seventy years.

Then I turned my face to the LORD God, seeking him by prayer and pleas for mercy with fasting and sackcloth and ashes. I prayed to the LORD my God and made confession, saying, "O Lord, the great and awesome God, who keeps covenant and steadfast love with those who love him and keep his commandments, we have sinned and done wrong and acted wickedly and rebelled, turning aside from your commandments and rules. We have not listened to your servants the prophets, who spoke in your name to our kings, our princes, and our fathers, and to all the people of the land...."
Daniel 9:1-6

This chapter could be entitled, "How to Repent for Your Nation." First, Daniel begins by studying the scriptures, a sure way to get enlightenment from God regarding all kinds of matters.

Second, Daniel applies himself wholeheartedly to seeking God's face in regard to his nation. This is not a trivial attempt. Daniel is quite serious! He fasts, wearing sackcloth and ashes, praying and pleading with God on behalf of his nation. Rather than pointing fingers at others, he shoulders the blame himself. The message throughout Daniel's prayer is consistent: *We* have sinned, *we* have done wrong. Daniel is not reluctant to specify the sins or accept responsibility for them, even when it is obvious that his part in that particular sin was minimal or non-existent. I'm thinking that part of intercession is accepting responsibility for sins we did not commit.

Daniel's prayer for his nation is so effective and sincere that God sends the angel Gabriel to bring him answers, an unsolicited vision for the future, and the awesome assurance that Daniel is "greatly loved." (Dan 9:23)

It is tempting to think that the key to turning a nation around is to gain and use political power and influence. Sometimes, but not often. I'm pretty sure God prefers the way Daniel did it. If any Jew had political influence, it was Daniel. Yet, when it came to trying to change his nation, Daniel depended not on his political power, but on seeking God. God answered.

October 23

The Servant's Faith Is in God, Not in Himself

Prayers God Wants To Answer

And behold, a hand touched me and set me trembling on my hands and knees. And he said to me, "O Daniel, man greatly loved, understand the words that I speak to you, and stand upright, for now I have been sent to you." And when he had spoken this word to me, I stood up trembling. Then he said to me, "Fear not, Daniel, for from the first day that you set your heart to understand and humbled yourself before your God, your words have been heard, and I have come because of your words..."
Daniel 10:10-12

This is one of my favorite passages in the Bible. Daniel had access to the accumulated knowledge of mankind, as he occupied a place of power in the dominant empire of the world, but he chose to focus instead on the wisdom and word of God. The angel's message to Daniel tells us this is one of the best ways to gain the approval of God: *"Fear not, Daniel, for from the first day that you set your heart to understand and humbled yourself before you God, your words have been heard, and I have come because of your words."*

This attitude of humility is too often missing. If we approach God or His Word like some laboratory specimen to be dissected, analyzed and categorized, we should not be surprised to find frustration and a lack of faith as our reward. God is not trifled with, no matter how many Ph.D.'s we may be packing.

What God loves is a humble spirit, seeking to learn, willing to engage and believe. Skeptics get nowhere; humble seekers get angels from heaven! (Or at least, Daniel did).

We may not get an angel-gram reporting on how pleased the Lord is with our progress, but I am convinced that every serious seeker after wisdom from God will get exactly what he needs, and the peace and approval to go along with it. Every time someone sets their heart on understanding, and humbling themselves before God, they are noticed!

The attitude of Daniel's heart was that God had the answers, and Daniel wanted to understand God's wisdom. He was ready to learn.

In a world awash in knowledge, in the age of information, may the focus of my heart be to humbly seek after the wisdom only God can give. I won't be sorry.

The Servant's Faith Is in God, Not in Himself

Seeing With Different Eyes

When the servant of the man of God rose early in the morning and went out, behold, an army with horses and chariots was all around the city. And the servant said, "Alas, my master! What shall we do?" He said, "Do not be afraid, for those who are with us are more than those who are with them." Then Elisha prayed and said, "O LORD, please open his eyes that he may see." So the LORD opened the eyes of the young man, and he saw, and behold, the mountain was full of horses and chariots of fire all around Elisha. And when the Syrians came down against him, Elisha prayed to the LORD and said, "Please strike this people with blindness." So he struck them with blindness in accordance with the prayer of Elisha. And Elisha said to them, "This is not the way, and this is not the city. Follow me, and I will bring you to the man whom you seek." And he led them to Samaria.

As soon as they entered Samaria, Elisha said, "O LORD, open the eyes of these men, that they may see." So the LORD opened their eyes and they saw, and behold, they were in the midst of Samaria. 2 Kings 6:15-19

Elisha, the prophet of God, had repeatedly foiled the plans of the Syrian king by relaying the details of his every move to the king of Israel. He was getting his information from God. In exasperation, the king of Syria found out Elisha was in the city of Dothan and sent an army to seize him. When Elisha's servant awoke early to find the city surrounded by hostile forces, he was more than a little alarmed! Elisha wasn't. Why? While Elisha's servant only had eyes to see the physical, Elisha had eyes to see both the physical and the spiritual. The prophet had long since chosen to focus his attention on the things of God, rather than the things of man. The result was an incredible depth of spiritual discernment, and basically a one-man defense system for Israel. Elisha posed such a threat to invaders that an army had been dispatched to try to contain him!

When threatened, Elisha immediately falls back on the method by which he deals with all problems—he prays. He first prays for his servant, who is unable to see into the spiritual realm until his eyes have been opened. Then he proceeds to bring an army into total submission through nothing more than prayer. Throughout the course of Elisha's life, his faith grew because he relied consistently on God, not armies or spies. Good plan.

October 25

The Servant's Faith Is in God, Not in Himself

The Keys to Heaven and Earth

*"Let not your hearts be troubled. Believe in God; believe also in me.
In my Father's house are many rooms. If it were not so, would I have told
you that I go to prepare a place for you? And if I go and prepare a place
for you, I will come again and will take you to myself, that where I am you
may be also. And you know the way to where I am going." Thomas said
to him, "Lord, we do not know where you are going. How can we know
the way?" Jesus said to him, "I am the way, and the truth, and the life.
No one comes to the Father except through me. If you had known me, you
would have known my Father also. From now on you do know him and
have seen him."*

*Philip said to him, "Lord, show us the Father, and it is enough for us."
Jesus said to him, "Have I been with you so long, and you still do not know
me, Philip? Whoever has seen me has seen the Father. How can you say,
'Show us the Father'? Do you not believe that I am in the Father and the
Father is in me? The words that I say to you I do not speak on my own
authority, but the Father who dwells in me does his works. Believe me that
I am in the Father and the Father is in me, or else believe on account of
the works themselves.*

*"Truly, truly, I say to you, whoever believes in me will also do the works
that I do; and greater works than these will he do, because I am going to
the Father. Whatever you ask in my name, this I will do, that the Father
may be glorified in the Son. If you ask me anything in my name, I will do
it."* John 14:1-14

The world of today speaks frequently of faith, but nearly always that
faith is in oneself, not faith in a God who loves us, whom we can personally
know. It is this connection with God that Jesus is encouraging His disciples
to have. Incredible promises are linked to nothing more than the belief that
Jesus is the Son of God; that He is in the Father and the Father is in Him;
that the works the Father has done through the Son are the same kind of
works He is willing to do through us, if we come to the Father through the
Son; that the only way to the Father is through the Son, but once we believe
in Jesus, we are in line with possibilities beyond our comprehension. It's
not just "believing in ourselves"—that's a hollow business. It's believing in
Jesus—and suddenly we find ourselves with the keys to heaven, and earth.

The Servant's Faith Is in God, Not in Himself

His Name, Not Mine

But Peter said, "I have no silver and gold, but what I do have I give to you. In the name of Jesus Christ of Nazareth, rise up and walk!" And he took him by the right hand and raised him up, and immediately his feet and ankles were made strong. And leaping up he stood and began to walk, and entered the temple with them, walking and leaping and praising God. And all the people saw him walking and praising God, and recognized him as the one who sat at the Beautiful Gate of the temple, asking for alms. And they were filled with wonder and amazement at what had happened to him.

While he clung to Peter and John, all the people ran together to them in the portico called Solomon's, astounded. And when Peter saw it he addressed the people: "Men of Israel, why do you wonder at this, or why do you stare at us, as though by our own power or piety we have made him walk? The God of Abraham, the God of Isaac, and the God of Jacob, the God of our fathers, glorified his servant Jesus,...

"And his name—by faith in his name—has made this man strong whom you see and know, and the faith that is through Jesus has given the man this perfect health in the presence of you all." Acts 3:6-13,16

"Men of Israel, why do you wonder at this, or why do you stare at us, as though by our own power or piety we have made him walk?" It's interesting that these early apostles were so quick to divert the credit for their faith, while some modern-day folks are so quick to capitalize on it ("Actually, it *was* my own power and piety, and especially my incredible faith...") And the "no silver and gold" thing is pretty much out the window, too. So is the humility. According to my television, real people of faith are never broke, but according to the Bible, a couple of pretty genuine apostles seemed short on cash at the same time they possessed plenty of faith. Go figure.

Peter wanted it to be known that it's not just "faith in something," or "faith in the power of faith," but it's the name of Jesus, and faith in His name, that made the miraculous difference. How have so many people managed to miss that? It's not faith in ourselves that makes the difference, it's faith in Him. It's not our own piety or power, it's His. It's not our credit, it's His. And when it comes to "Who has faith?" I'll go with the people who reach out to the lame to help them leap in Jesus' name, then give Him credit.

The Servant's Faith Is in God, Not in Himself

More Like Him, Less Like Us

Now there were in the church at Antioch prophets and teachers, Barnabas, Simeon who was called Niger, Lucius of Cyrene, Manaen a member of the court of Herod the tetrarch, and Saul. While they were worshiping the Lord and fasting, the Holy Spirit said, "Set apart for me Barnabas and Saul for the work to which I have called them." Then after fasting and praying they laid their hands on them and sent them off.

So, being sent out by the Holy Spirit, they went down to Seleucia, and from there they sailed to Cyprus. Acts 13:1-4

All through the book of Acts, it's obvious that it's the Holy Spirit calling the shots, rather than man. From the Day of Pentecost on, it's a continual orchestration of revivals, miracles and breakthrough's, none of it planned out by man, not even the missionary movement. The times when God puts it in man's responsibility to figure out the plan seem to be few.

The lack of any kind of strategic plan in the book of Acts is shocking, in light of our day. How are you supposed to get anywhere without a plan?

They did have a plan—it was God's plan. Pieces of it were revealed to them along the way, as needed; whenever the disciples listened to the Holy Spirit, they got it right and obeyed. The Gospel spread, thousands of people were saved, and there was astounding power evident in the Early Church.

Fastforward to the American church of today. We're brimming with plans, strategies, equipment, books and buildings, but for the most part, sadly lacking in power and new converts. Yet we put a lot of faith in ourselves. Why? The Early Church seemed to put nearly all their faith in Christ, and hardly any in themselves. They didn't seem to schedule many planning seminars or great conventions to come up with strategy, yet the Church flourished in the midst of incredible persecution. They trusted in the Holy Spirit to guide them. Sometimes He did it through their leaders, sometimes not. By modern standards, they didn't have much of a system, but theirs worked.

Modern day believers, especially in America, sometimes seem incapable of functioning without a thick notebook stuffed with man-made plans. If we depended more on the Holy Spirit, and less on ourselves, it seems the results we'd witness would be more like the Holy Spirit and less like ourselves, too.

October 28

The Servant's Faith Is in God, Not in Himself

Enough Faith for Everybody

When neither sun nor stars appeared for many days, and no small tempest lay on us, all hope of our being saved was at last abandoned.

Since they had been without food for a long time, Paul stood up among them and said, "Men, you should have listened to me and not have set sail from Crete and incurred this injury and loss. Yet now I urge you to take heart, for there will be no loss of life among you, but only of the ship. For this very night there stood before me an angel of the God to whom I belong and whom I worship, and he said, 'Do not be afraid, Paul; you must stand before Caesar. And behold, God has granted you all those who sail with you.' So take heart, men, for I have faith in God that it will be exactly as I have been told. But we must run aground on some island."
Acts 27:20-26

I always thought captains were supposed to be in charge of the ship! And soldiers were supposed to be in charge of the prisoners, who don't give orders. Before long, the whole ship will be taking their commands from Paul. Only one problem. Paul is a prisoner! How did he get to be in charge?! After all, they have a captain; a Roman centurion and soldiers are on board, along with experienced sailors. Why would they listen to a prisoner?

Because he's the one who is hearing from God. He is also the one who has chosen to believe in God, and to trust His Word more than he trusts his own intellect or instincts, or the prognostications of others. The apostle/ missionary/prisoner Paul has become an expert because of where he decided to put his faith. Why believe Paul? Because he's the one who has faith in God, who has heard from God and communicates that message to the others. The sailors trusted in luck and their own skill, and they were done; the soldiers trusted in the sailors (who would try to desert them); Paul trusted in God, who told him everything would be all right. God's man doesn't have to be a meteorologist or a professional sailor to get through the storm; God's man only needs to know and have faith in God. It's what separates the men from the boys, when it comes to faith. When you hear from God, suddenly you become an authority, if you believe. Paul did. *"So take heart, men, for I have faith in God that it will be exactly as I have been told."*

Paul had enough faith for everybody. His faith in God encouraged the whole ship! "Who cares if he's a prisoner? The guy heard from God."

October 29

The Servant's Faith Is in God, Not in Himself

Snake-Proof Disciples

After we were brought safely through, we then learned that the island was called Malta. The native people showed us unusual kindness, for they kindled a fire and welcomed us all, because it had begun to rain and was cold. When Paul had gathered a bundle of sticks and put them on the fire, a viper came out because of the heat and fastened on his hand. When the native people saw the creature hanging from his hand, they said to one another, "No doubt this man is a murderer. Though he has escaped from the sea, Justice has not allowed him to live." He, however, shook off the creature into the fire and suffered no harm. They were waiting for him to swell up or suddenly fall down dead. But when they had waited a long time and saw no misfortune come to him, they changed their minds and said that he was a god.

Now in the neighborhood of that place were lands belonging to the chief man of the island, named Publius, who received us and entertained us hospitably for three days. It happened that the father of Publius lay sick with fever and dysentery. And Paul visited him and prayed, and putting his hands on him healed him. And when this had taken place, the rest of the people on the island who had diseases also came and were cured. They also honored us greatly, and when we were about to sail, they put on board whatever we needed. Acts 28:1-10

Paul lets nothing stop him! Shipwreck? A viper? He just goes on with his business—being a blessing to the islanders, starting with healing everybody on the island! Talk about taking risks! God is standing by, giving Paul every miracle he needs. The islanders gratefully respond.

I love the theme of faith in the book of Acts. This is not about a bunch of people, each doing their own thing, building their own empire or "ministry." This is a book about the acts of the Holy Spirit, who is leading the Church in marvelous ways, doing miracles through the hands of ordinary men. The plans we read about are His plans, not the plans of man. There is very little that takes place in Acts that is not God-generated, either directly or indirectly. Would that describe the Church in America? I'm afraid not.

But it could. Same Holy Spirit, right? If we determined to be Spirit-led rather than putting our trust in ourselves or other mortals, wouldn't that same God show Himself strong through us? Or, we could keep our kingdoms.

The Servant's Faith Is in God, Not in Himself

Whose Power Is This?

For what we proclaim is not ourselves, but Jesus Christ as Lord, with ourselves as your servants for Jesus' sake. For God, who said, "Let light shine out of darkness," has shone in our hearts to give the light of the knowledge of the glory of God in the face of Jesus Christ.

But we have this treasure in jars of clay, to show that the surpassing power belongs to God and not to us. 2 Corinthians 4:5-7

Whose power is this? It's God's. It's very, very important to remember that. Whom are we proclaiming? Jesus, not ourselves. Again—very important.

The light God has placed in our hearts is not to spotlight our own magnificence or power, but to enlighten the world to the glory of the Son of God. Even being a reflection of that light and love is plenty for us! We mess everything up when we try to capitalize on our role as a container for God's glory. This is why our "container" is made of clay, and crumbling clay at that. If the focus begins to be on the wrapper instead of the treasure inside, things are amiss. *The surpassing power belongs to God and not to us.* We need to remember that!

While we may be a channel of God's power, it's not "ours," in the sense of being able to do with it whatever we want. *The surpassing power belongs to God and not to us.*

The "surpassing" part is true, too. This is the same power which spoke the world into being, creating light from darkness with a word! Yet He dwells in us!

A treasure beyond measure resides in an ordinary clay vessel. The vessel is not the source of the power, nor is it the master of the power; it's only the vessel. But the power within is real.

May the world around us know that the power reflected in our lives is more than adequate for every challenge, including theirs. May the world know that this surpassing power would also invade their lives, if they open their heart to Christ. May the world understand that *the surpassing power belongs to God and not to us.* And when they notice that this great treasure is camped out in a pretty shabby, ordinary vessel, may they realize it's not about the vessel, but about a God willing to inhabit clay.

The Servant's Faith Is in God, Not in Himself

Harmless Faith

To you, O LORD, I lift up my soul.
O my God, in you I trust;
let me not be put to shame;
let not my enemies exult over me.
Indeed, none who wait for you shall be put to shame;
they shall be ashamed who are wantonly treacherous.

Make me to know your ways, O LORD;
teach me your paths.
Lead me in your truth and teach me,
for you are the God of my salvation;
for you I wait all the day long. Psalm 25:1-5

This psalm of David is one of many which testify to the source of his strength. Although an extremely capable individual, David instinctively relied on the Lord, especially at the first sign of trouble. Contrast that to his predecessor, King Saul. How many times do we know of when Saul humbled himself before God and chose to wait on Him, rather than barging ahead with his own agenda? I can't think of any.

You can tell where a person puts their faith by where they turn in a crisis. Saul always relied on himself, especially under pressure; David relied on God, particularly in crisis situations, but also as a habit of life. One of David's terrific character strengths was his propensity to go toward God, instead of just trusting in himself. Saul's opposite tendency made him virtually worthless when it came to being a spiritual leader.

The servant's faith is in God, not in himself. The ongoing spiritual battles around us are won when we trust in God, lost when we trust in ourselves. When we place our faith in the God who can do anything, Satan trembles. It's when we put our faith in ourselves that we become harmless.

Too often we trust in our own knowledge and education, rather than the power of God's Spirit. Our faith is harmless when it's placed in our buildings, programs, reputation or income. But when our trust is in God, devil beware! When a crisis arises, we show our faith by where we put our trust. The strongest servant is the one who can be counted on to go to God first.

November 1

The Wages of Faithfulness

"Who then is the faithful and wise servant, whom his master has set over his household, to give them their food at the proper time? Blessed is that servant whom his master will find so doing when he comes. Truly, I say to you, he will set him over all his possessions. But if that wicked servant says to himself, 'My master is delayed,' and begins to beat his fellow servants and eats and drinks with drunkards, the master of that servant will come on a day when he does not expect him and at an hour he does not know and will cut him in pieces and put him with the hypocrites. In that place there will be weeping and gnashing of teeth." Matthew 24:45-51

Dire warnings. Unbelievable promises. Interspersed throughout the prophecies and parables of Matthew 24 and 25 are both warnings and promises, all having to do with the Second Coming of Christ. The underlying theme in each pronouncement or story is, "Let Him find you ready when He returns." "Being ready" means "being responsible" in the Kingdom of God. This is an important concept easily overlooked. Through the years I have encountered so many people whose only interest in things spiritual was a kind of "market timing" strategy of wanting to know when "it" will happen, thinking they could somehow slide in to God's Kingdom at the last second, gripping their heavenly pass, having outfoxed God into letting a smart sinner live out his preferred lifestyle, only to "repent" at the last second and make heaven. Something like that.

Others don't seem to even care about heaven; their main deal is earthly survival, and their goal is to escape Armageddon, so they'd like to know when it will be and which direction to head or hide.

Of course, the theme of these scriptures is fortunately not at all helpful to those wanting to outsmart God, since the theme is "Be ready by faithfully carrying out your responsibilities." While not being a popular idea with "market timing" types, this is the surefire way to get God's approval, plus being of value to His kingdom in the process. And look at the little promise tucked away for the responsible servant who keeps doing what he was told: *"He will set him over all his possessions."* What kind of promise is that?! I'm thinking, "a good one," worth every bit of waiting it requires. Faithfulness brings *lots* of favor, *lots* of blessing, *lots* of opportunities.

November 2

The Servant's Faith Is in God, Not in Himself

Forgotten Faith

Therefore do not throw away your confidence, which has a great reward. For you have need of endurance, so that when you have done the will of God you may receive what is promised. For,

> *"Yet a little while,*
> *And the coming one will come and will not delay;*
> *But my righteous one shall live by faith,*
> *and if he shrinks back, my soul has no pleasure in him."*

But we are not of those who shrink back and are destroyed, but of those who have faith and preserve their souls. Hebrews 10:35-39

And without faith it is impossible to please him, for whoever would draw near to God must believe that he exists and that he rewards those who seek him. Hebrews 11:6

Remember your leaders, those who spoke to you the word of God. Consider the outcome of their way of life, and imitate their faith. Jesus Christ is the same yesterday and today and forever. Hebrews 13:7-8

I think we need to more closely imitate the faith of the apostles and early disciples. After all, *Jesus Christ is the same yesterday and today and forever!* So, why do we regard Him as if He somehow changed, and is different than He was during His earthly ministry? Did the Lord take back His miracle-working power from earth when the original Twelve disciples were gone? Did the dispensation of God wanting His children to live by faith somehow end in the second or third century? It seems to me that *"my righteous one shall live by faith"* was for *all* the centuries.

Our faith needs to be in Christ, not ourselves or in "our faith." And if that faith is truly in a Christ who is exactly the same One worshiped by the disciples, that puts a whole different light on our resources. It puts us in a level of expectancy that is different from what most of us have ever experienced, before. That expectancy alone could help to trigger revival! We need to go for it. I'll bet we're closer than we think.

November 3

The Servant's Faith Is in God, Not in Himself

Now, Not Later

Then I saw another beast rising out of the earth. It had two horns like a lamb and it spoke like a dragon. It exercises all the authority of the first beast in its presence, and makes the earth and its inhabitants worship the first beast, whose mortal wound was healed. It performs great signs, even making fire come down from heaven to earth in front of people, and by the signs that it is allowed to work in the presence of the beast it deceives those who dwell on earth, telling them to make an image for the beast that was wounded by the sword and yet lived. And it was allowed to give breath to the image of the beast, so that the image of the beast might even speak and might cause those who would not worship the image of the beast to be slain. Also it causes all, both small and great, both rich and poor, both free and slave, to be marked on the right hand or the forehead, so that no one can buy or sell unless he has the mark, that is, the name of the beast or the number of its name. This calls for wisdom: let the one who has understanding calculate the number of the beast, for it is the number of a man, and his number is 666. Revelation 13:11-18

It becomes obvious in Revelation that sides are clearly chosen, and the only ones who will ultimately survive all that is coming upon the earth are those whose faith is in God. During the Tribulation, it will not be possible to "fit in" with the rest of society. The choice will be to take the mark of the beast or the mark of the Savior. One means that you can buy and sell on earth; the other means that you are spared from the wrath of God and will be welcomed into heaven! Those who are here will have to choose. The choice will be for eternity. Faith in anything other than God will mean eternal disaster.

Also, it is made clear that things like captivity and death are preordained, and will not be avoided, despite people's cautions and compromises (Rev 13:10). It's not like, "If you just plan well enough, you can avoid all of this." However, we do need to plan ahead by choosing to serve and put our trust in the Savior, no matter what. We need to choose that *now*, not later. We'd better decide ahead of time not to be deceived by any counterfeit "savior" sent from Satan, or lured into compromise in order to try to avoid hardship. Our faith must be in Almighty God and nothing else, because nothing else will stand, in the last days. Or these days.

November 4

Faith and Courage Required

Then I saw a new heaven and a new earth, for the first heaven and the first earth had passed away, and the sea was no more... And he who was seated on the throne said, "Behold, I am making all things new." Also he said, "Write this down, for these words are trustworthy and true." And he said to me, "It is done! I am the Alpha and the Omega, the beginning and the end. To the thirsty I will give from the spring of the water of life without payment. The one who conquers will have this heritage, and I will be his God and he will be my son. But as for the cowardly, the faithless, the detestable, as for murderers, the sexually immoral, sorcerers, idolaters, and all liars, their portion will be in the lake that burns with fire and sulfur, which is the second death."
Revelation 21:1,5-8

The water of life is a free gift given to all who thirst for righteousness—it's obvious once again that God desires all of His children to be saved—but it's also obvious once again that not everyone will be. The reason we are warned in so many scripture passages is so we *won't* go to hell. Yet, if we persist in idolatry, sexual immorality and the like, our "portion" will be in the lake that burns with fire and sulfur, and it won't be God's fault.

There are some unnerving adjectives on the list of those who go to hell. "Faithless" makes the list. So does "cowardly." Is faith that important? Apparently so! Courage? That, too. According to passages like this, we won't get to opt out of hell on the excuse that we suffer from a delicate temperament and "courage deficiency," or that we didn't believe in hell in the first place and therefore should be exempt from its reality!

Salvation is a free gift, available to all! But it requires some faith and courage to accept this free gift. It takes a spirit willing to go from being a wimp or a victim to become a disciple and an overcomer. It takes a person willing to leave behind a life of sin before we can even look forward to a world without it. It stands to reason that heaven will not be populated by unrepentant murderers; what takes a little more thought is to realize that God's not kidding when He says that heaven's gates will also be closed to those who couldn't even seem to muster the faith or courage required to accept His free gift of salvation, and trade an empty life for an eternal one.

November 5

The Servant's Faith Is in God, Not in Himself
With Us or Without Us

"Abide in me, and I in you. As the branch cannot bear fruit by itself, unless it abides in the vine, neither can you, unless you abide in me. I am the vine; you are the branches. Whoever abides in me and I in him, he it is that bears much fruit, for apart from me you can do nothing." John 15:4-5

I still remember the kind rebuke. I was thinking of the church I was pastoring, and about a friend of mine who has had phenomenal success in ministry. I thought to myself, "If he were pastoring this church, it would grow. What would he do? He'd figure it out, he'd pray it through, he'd get the right answer and then do it, and it would grow."

Suddenly my own thoughts were interrupted by thoughts I knew came from God: "You have more faith in him than you do in Me."

"How so?"

"You believe that he could grow a church anywhere, but you don't believe that I could, using you. Your lack of confidence is not only in yourself; it's a lack of confidence in Me, too, that thinks it's the tool which determines whether or not I can accomplish my work. What tools did I need to form the Universe? What tools do you suppose I need, in order to make a church grow? Put your faith in Me, not in yourself. I can accomplish all things *without* you; do you think I can't win *with* you on my team?"

I wrote down my response to the Lord's gentle rebuke:

"O.K., God, several dozen "leadership" books written by outstanding people just went out the window. "Everything rises and falls on leadership." Not in the Church. Everything rises and falls on God, who uses leaders willing to have faith in Him and follow Him. Lord, you don't need me, in order to build anything, but if I follow you, and my faith is in you, rather than my own cleverness, there has never been anything you couldn't do. Never. And that's 'with me' or 'without me.' Help me to put my faith in you, not in my own leadership abilities, or the abilities of others."

I was reminded that day that it's not the abilities of the branch which produce the fruit; it's the fact that it's connected to the vine. I've tried harder to put my faith in God rather than my own abilities. My friend and I are both still abiding. His branch still sports more fruit than mine, but we're both connected to a God who can do anything, with us or without us.

November 6

The Servant's Faith Is in God, Not in Himself

It's Just a Stick

The LORD said to him, "What is that in your hand?" He said, "A staff." Exodus 4:2

"And take in your hand this staff, with which you shall do the signs." Exodus 4:17

It's just a stick, really, a simple tool used by shepherds. Suddenly, that has changed, along with Moses' entire life plan. From being an outcast shepherd far from home, Moses is commissioned by God to lead the Israelites out of the grip of Pharaoh and into a Promised Land. What will he use? A stick!

Moses had not chosen his staff on the basis of its miracle propensities or fantastic powers. How is he supposed to do miracles with it?!

God did not give Moses a magic staff; He gave Moses a promise: I'll back you. Just do what I say, and you'll work miracles through this staff. Moses' faith was never in his staff; it was in the God who spoke to him from a burning bush. Does holding a stick out over a sea usually make it form into walls of water on either side, with a dry path down the middle?! The power wasn't in the stick. This wasn't one of those "genie in the lamp" things, where whoever's got the lamp gets to boss the genie around. Had Pharaoh managed to steal Moses' stick, he would have been wasting his time trying to open or close seas with it—it wasn't very powerful by itself. Even Moses hadn't done any miracles with it, prior to hearing from God in a burning bush.

It's just a stick.

And Moses is just a shepherd who once had been a prince.

Until God gets a hold of them.

Then, it's the *Servant of God*, taking the *Rod of God*— and performing miracles at God's command.

The power? *It's all God.*

The faith? *It's all in* God, not the stick, not the education or the background, not in himself. It is faith in God that parts seas, not faith in sticks or shepherds.

The servant's faith is in a God who can use a wooden stick to rescue a nation, or a wooden cross to save a world.

November 7

The Servant's Faith Is in God, Not in Himself

The Discipleship Benefit Package

And he called to him his twelve disciples and gave them authority over unclean spirits, to cast them out, and to heal every disease and every affliction...

These twelve Jesus sent out, instructing them, "Go nowhere among the Gentiles and enter no town of the Samaritans, but go rather to the lost sheep of the house of Israel. And proclaim as you go, saying, 'The kingdom of heaven is at hand.' Heal the sick, raise the dead, cleanse lepers, cast out demons. You received without paying; give without pay. Acquire no gold nor silver nor copper for your belts, no bag for your journey, nor two tunics nor sandals nor a staff, for the laborer deserves his food. And whatever town or village you enter, find out who is worthy in it and stay there until you depart."... Matthew 10:1,5-11

Unencumbered by their own resources, the Twelve set out on a faith field trip. Jesus sent His disciples out without health insurance! Instead, He gives them instructions to "heal the sick" and "raise the dead"?! Wallets are to be left home, along with all the spare "What if?" items they might be tempted to bring. With a clear mission and boundaries, no reservations, no itinerary and no back-up plan, the disciples set out. God will provide. This little adventure will change their lives forever. Never again will they have to convince themselves that it's *possible* to live by faith—they will *know*. Each one will have faith stories they will treasure for the rest of their lives.

The question which comes to every disciple, at some point: Is Jesus enough for me? Is He sufficient for my needs, or do I need something else along with Jesus, before I could hope to quell my fears? Jesus and health insurance? Jesus and money? Jesus and earthly security? Jesus and a plan?

The times when our faith grows by leaps and bounds are times when it's pure faith in God, without benefit of human arms underneath, "just in case." It's never going to be comfortable to launch out on impossible missions with nothing more than God's Word and whatever authority He has granted us for our assignment. There's also no other way to experience the true benefit package of a disciple—knowing in our heart that it's totally safe to trust God.

November 8

The Cost of Servanthood

Rights Set Aside

We put no obstacle in anyone's way, so that no fault may be found with our ministry, but as servants of God we commend ourselves in every way: by great endurance, in afflictions, hardships, calamities, beatings, imprisonments, by purity, knowledge, patience, kindness, the Holy Spirit, genuine love, by truthful speech, and the power of God; with the weapons of righteousness for the right hand and for the left; through honor and dishonor, through slander and praise. We are treated as impostors, and yet are true; as unknown, and yet well known; as dying, and behold, we live; as punished, and yet not killed; as sorrowful, yet always rejoicing; as poor, yet making many rich,: as having nothing, yet possessing everything.

We have spoken freely to you, Corinthians; our heart is wide open.
2 Corinthians 6:3-11

American citizens lay claim to a Bill of Rights. Where's the Bill of Rights for servants of God?

Servants of God don't need "rights;" we have God. The assignment we are given to represent Him is a tough one, though, because one of the things it requires of us is that, like Jesus, we relinquish our "rights" in order to pursue our ministry. Philippians 2 details what Jesus did with His "rights" in order to save us, and what we should do with ours:

Have this mind among yourselves, which was also in Christ Jesus, who, though he was in the form of God, did not count equality with God a thing to be grasped, but made himself nothing, taking the form of a servant, being born in the likeness of men. And being found in human form, he humbled himself by becoming obedient to the point of death, even death on a cross. (Php 2:5-8)

I've read this passage many times before; it still hits me hard. The Son of God set aside everything, to be born as a man. He relinquished all of His rights, that He might win us to Himself. Christ set us the example of how to truly minister to people: You set aside your rights, and open your heart. The person who does this is the one God exalts. Being exalted by the Father is a lot better than "rights."

November 9

The Cost of Servanthood

Servants of God, Armed to the Teeth

We put no obstacle in anyone's way, so that no fault may be found with our ministry, but as servants of God we commend ourselves in every way: by great endurance, in afflictions, hardships, calamities, beatings, imprisonments, by purity, knowledge, patience, kindness, the Holy Spirit, genuine love, by truthful speech, and the power of God; with the weapons of righteousness for the right hand and for the left; through honor and dishonor, through slander and praise. We are treated as impostors, and yet are true; as unknown, and yet well known; as dying, and behold, we live; as punished, and yet not killed; as sorrowful, yet always rejoicing; as poor, yet making many rich,; as having nothing, yet possessing everything.

We have spoken freely to you, Corinthians; our heart is wide open.
2 Corinthians 6:3-11

As servants of God, we may have set aside our rights, but we are not without weapons! Yet, these *weapons of righteousness* bear little resemblance to the weapons with which the world is familiar. What's a "weapon of righteousness" look like, anyway, and what will it do?

An entire arsenal is listed here—things like purity, patience, kindness. These are *weapons?!* They are in the hands of righteous people! Any one of the weapons listed is totally overwhelming to the enemy. A weapon like genuine love or truthful speech easily slices through Satan's lies and lust.

I picture the stereotypical bandoleero—drawn guns in each hand, cartridge belts slung over both shoulders, a knife at his belt, guns in his boots—armed to the teeth, and ready for anything. That's how I think the soldier of Jesus Christ is supposed to look, except that instead of mere firearms, he's supposed to be bristling with *weapons of righteousness.* What a formidable sight it must be in the spiritual realms to see a devoted servant of the Lord packing purity, knowledge, truthful speech and the power of God! He is ready, and God's going to use him!

Regretfully, not enough Christians present a very imposing spiritual threat to Satan or his hirelings. Too many try to timidly slip through spiritual battlefields, unarmed, when effective weapons of righteousness have been provided for our victory. I want to be a servant of God, armed to the teeth!

November 10

Dangerous Journey to a Safe Place

Are they servants of Christ? I am a better one—I am talking like a madman—with far greater labors, far more imprisonments, with countless beatings, and often near death. Five times I received at the hands of the Jews the forty lashes less one. Three times I was beaten with rods. Once I was stoned. Three times I was shipwrecked; a night and a day I was adrift at sea; on frequent journeys, in danger from rivers, danger from robbers, danger from my own people, danger from Gentiles, danger in the city, danger in the wilderness, danger at sea, danger from false brothers; in toil and hardship, through many a sleepless night, in hunger and thirst, often without food, in cold and exposure. And, apart from other things, there is the daily pressure on me of my anxiety for all the churches. Who is weak, and I am not weak? Who is made to fall, and I am not indignant?

If I must boast, I will boast of the things that show my weakness. The God and Father of the Lord Jesus, he who is blessed forever, knows that I am not lying. At Damascus, the governor under King Aretas was guarding the city of Damascus in order to seize me, but I was let down in a basket through a window in the wall and escaped his hands.
2 Corinthians 11:23-33

I'm looking for the benefit package here, in being an apostle! To think that someone who had been through this list for the cause of Christ would have to defend his record to fellow believers! Wow.

As I solemnly review Paul's hardships, I can't find a single place where my record of hardship or endurance for the cause of Christ is on a level with his. When I became a pastor, I got a salary and health insurance; the first missionary was beaten with rods!

One of the wonderful things about being a servant of Christ is that we don't have to be imprisoned for our faith or beaten nearly to death before we are welcomed into His Kingdom. While my suffering for Jesus has been minuscule compared to Paul, we both entered the Kingdom of God the same way: By faith in Jesus. The requirement was the same for each of us: Everything. We had to let go of our old life, repent of our sins, trust in Christ for a new life and follow Him. That journey took Paul down a more dangerous, difficult path than the one I've been on, so far, but they both end up at the same place: Safe with our Lord, in heaven.

The Cost of Servanthood

Everything

"So therefore, any one of you who does not renounce all that he has cannot be my disciple." Luke 14:33

There's more where that came from.

The cost of discipleship is very simple, and always has been: Everything. It will cost us everything.

Meanwhile, God reassures us that everything will be made up to us, both in this life and the life to come, and He lets us know that His strength is actually shown to be most perfect in our weakness, but the cost is the same: Everything. It's always been everything.

Along the way, there are some bridges that need to be burned, to keep us from going back to the old life, when it gets tough. We need to approach this like soldiers enlisting for war, paying attention to every aspect of our armor, and knowing that this is not just a drill; we're going to see combat with the enemy, and the stakes are eternal. We *will* be shot at, we *will* face persecution, it *will* be hard at times. Endure, like a good soldier. That's part of the cost of being a disciple.

One more thing. Forget this "happiness" stuff. Soldiers are not recruited with the idea that they are going to be "happy;" neither are disciples. Jesus isn't calling people to be "happy;" He's calling them to be disciples. Disciples follow their Master. Sometimes that leads to the fulfillment of dreams and desires; sometimes it leads into the teeth of unimaginable hardships and pain. Jesus never gives us one of those little cards asking us if we enjoyed our experience and are satisfied with His leadership. This isn't about "happy." It's about obedience, which usually also involves sacrifice.

What I hear God saying to me is, "Don't look for whatever you think is going to make you happy—do what you know I want you to do, and choose to enjoy it. Choose contentment and joy." Peace, contentment and joy are about as close as we come to "rights" as disciples. The cost of servanthood never goes up or down, though. It's always been "everything." It's still a great deal.

November 12

The Cost of Servanthood

Content with Weaknesses

So to keep me from being too elated by the surpassing greatness of the revelations, a thorn was given me in the flesh, a messenger of Satan to harass me, to keep me from being too elated. Three times I pleaded with the Lord about this, that it should leave me. But he said to me, "My grace is sufficient for you, for my power is made perfect in weakness." Therefore I will boast all the more gladly of my weaknesses, so that the power of Christ may rest upon me. For the sake of Christ, then, I am content with weaknesses, insults, hardships, persecutions, and calamities. For when I am weak, then I am strong. 2 Corinthians 12:7-10

How do you get a Type A personality like Paul to be "content with weaknesses"? You give him no choice. That's about the only way I know of to do it, and apparently God felt the same way!

Paul enjoyed his marvelous revelations from God; he despised the "thorn." The apostle was not about to be "content" with such a bothersome affliction until his repeated requests of God garnered him a message of solace for all time: *"My grace is sufficient for you, for my power is made perfect in weakness."*

All it took for Paul to switch from pleading for relief to being "content with weaknesses" was the assurance from God Himself that the weaknesses were O.K.—that in fact what was occurring was an even greater display of God's power because of them. When Paul got the message that his weaknesses and tribulations were actually advancing the Kingdom rather than holding him back, he was able to make a huge jump in his response to affliction. Rather than fighting it, he chose to be content with it. Only a person wired like this could appreciate what a miracle of grace such an attitude shift would be!

All of this moves so much in the opposite direction of "demanding my rights," at the same time I'm trying to be a servant of God. What rights? There is no greater manifestation of His power than when it is displayed through a weak servant who so loves his Master that he would choose to be content with weaknesses and all that goes with them, if that's what advances the Kingdom.

A person content with weaknesses is a spectacle of God's grace.

The Cost of Servanthood

Burning the Right Bridges

So he departed from there and found Elisha the son of Shaphat, who was plowing with twelve yoke of oxen in front of him, and he was with the twelfth. Elijah passed by him and cast his cloak upon him. And he left the oxen and ran after Elijah and said, "Let me kiss my father and my mother, and then I will follow you." And he said to him, "Go back again, for what have I done to you?" And he returned from following him and took the yoke of oxen and sacrificed them and boiled their flesh with the yokes of the oxen and gave it to the people, and they ate. Then he arose and went after Elijah and assisted him. 1 Kings 19:19-21

I like the way Elisha goes at things wholeheartedly. First of all, in a one or two-ox country, he's plowing with 12 yoke! Yet, when Elijah calls him, all he's interested in is letting his folks know where he's going, and the next step is to sacrifice the oxen, and use the yokes for fuel! He's not going back. Elisha shows how God's servant needs to burn some bridges. He didn't burn the bridges between him and his parents; he burned the bridge that would make it easy for him to go back to being a farmer. Elisha burned the right bridges.

It's interesting to me that in this Old Testament story, the new prophet's apprentice understands that following God is not to be a part-time pursuit, done in the off-season. He realizes that procrastinating is not going to be wise, so he acts immediately on the call of God, before someone can talk him out of it. Another wise tactic Elisha uses is to burn his bridges publicly. The "bridge burning" Elisha does is to turn his farming equipment into a big feast for the relatives and friends! The oxen are sacrificed and fed to the crowd; what does he use for fuel but the wooden yokes he would be needing should he decide to resume farming. He could have just used some brush for firewood, but this was all about proving a point: He wasn't going back. This was no experiment, but a definitive, public answer to a call of God. Sometimes, to make it stick, it just needs to be public.

Elisha went after being a prophet of God the same way he went after farming: Wholeheartedly. And when it came time for Elijah to go to heaven, his protege received, once again, the cloak first laid on his shoulders by the prophet, along with a double portion of his spirit. It was only fitting.

November 14

The Cost of Servanthood

Straight Ahead For Jesus

When the days drew near for him to be taken up, he set his face to go to Jerusalem. And he sent messengers ahead of him, who went and entered a village of the Samaritans, to make preparations for him. But the people did not receive him, because his face was set toward Jerusalem. And when his disciples James and John saw it, they said, "Lord, do you want us to tell fire to come down from heaven and consume them?" But he turned and rebuked them. And they went on to another village.

As they were going along the road, someone said to him, "I will follow you wherever you go." And Jesus said to him, "Foxes have holes, and birds of the air have nests, but the Son of Man has nowhere to lay his head." To another he said, "Follow me." But he said, "Lord, let me first go and bury my father." And Jesus said to him, "Leave the dead to bury their own dead. But as for you, go and proclaim the kingdom of God." Yet another said, "I will follow you, Lord, but let me first say farewell to those at my home." Jesus said to him, "No one who puts his hand to the plow and looks back is fit for the kingdom of God." Luke 9:51-62

Like a guy with a new golf driver, James and John wanted to try out a little divine power at Samaritan expense. Rather than rebuking the villagers, Jesus rebuked His disciples, and walked on.

Repeatedly, Jesus made clear the cost of being a disciple. This was not to be a part-time occupation! It was also not something a person got to pursue on their own terms. It was all the way, or nothing. I don't recall Jesus ever changing that standard!

It's also clear that it's not just about a "willingness" to leave everything behind—Jesus was serious! The implications of discipleship, as Jesus described it, are quite real. Like a surgeon explaining to a patient exactly what will happen prior to the operation, Jesus lays it out. I need to understand that in choosing to follow Him, I am giving up my "right" to have a home, my "right" to live in proximity to my family. In matters where the wishes of others conflict with the orders of my Master, I'll have to go with God. And if I insist on spending half my time in looking back on what I've given up for Jesus, I'd better just stay away from the plow. Hard? Yes. But I can't say He didn't tell me. Straight ahead for Jesus.

A Priority List of One

But whatever gain I had, I counted as loss for the sake of Christ. In-deed, I count everything as loss because of the surpassing worth of knowing Christ Jesus my Lord. For his sake I have suffered the loss of all things and count them as rubbish, in order that I may gain Christ and be found in him, not having a righteousness of my own that comes from the law, but that which comes through faith in Christ, the righteousness from God that depends on faith—that I may know him and the power of his resurrection, and may share his sufferings, becoming like him in his death, that by any means possible I may attain the resurrection from the dead.

Not that I have already obtained this or am already perfect, but I press on to make it my own, because Christ Jesus has made me his own. Brothers, I do not consider that I have made it my own. But one thing I do: forget-ting what lies behind and straining forward to what lies ahead, I press on toward the goal for the prize of the upward call of God in Christ Jesus.
Philippians 3:7-14

Modern life often leaves us feeling like sluggish rats on an exercise wheel, huffing and puffing. As Christians, we attempt to "prioritize" our lives with these little models, arranging the pieces in the "proper" order: God, family, work, church, etc. The many pieces scarcely fit on the page! Are they in the right order? Are there supposed to be this many? Is the order static or does it change?

I've thought of faith heroes of the past, and how they coped with things like priority management. What would the apostle Paul have said, anyway? I'm picturing myself in the privileged position of getting to ask him.

"Paul, could you please show me what your priority list looks like? I need to know what goes first, and how you arrange all of these things, as a disciple of Jesus. If you would be so kind as to write it out for me, I would be most grateful. Just show me your priority list, please."

For some reason the brilliant apostle has a perplexed look on his face. He studies my face to assure himself that I'm serious. He asks a couple questions to better understand what a "priority list" might be, a concept obviously foreign to him. At last realizing that I am asking him to write down the list of things which govern his life, in a sort of pecking order of importance, he nods, and without another word, takes a piece of parchment and writes out his list for me.

He hands it to me. Paul's entire list consists of one word: Jesus.

A Priority List of One

Could This Work?

Not that I have already obtained this or am already perfect, but I press on to make it my own, because Christ Jesus has made me his own. Brothers, I do not consider that I have made it my own. But one thing I do: forgetting what lies behind and straining forward to what lies ahead, I press on toward the goal for the prize of the upward call of God in Christ Jesus.
Philippians 3:12-14

One word: Jesus. That's what Paul's priority list would have looked like. Jesus wasn't just at the top of the list; Jesus was the *whole* list!

The simplicity with which Paul approached life was what enabled him to manage the incredible responsibilities facing him, continually. His life was pressured from all sides. Thousands of people were counting on him; dozens of churches, but Paul enjoyed the freedom experienced when we have just one Master to serve, and that Master is Jesus. *"One thing I do"*—that one thing was to follow Jesus.

Maybe our main problem with priorities is that we have too many of them in the first place! It's not so much that they're in the wrong order; it's that there are so many of them that they won't even fit on the page, in *any* order! Would it really be possible to live off a priority list of one?

Does this work in daily life? It sounds really spiritual, but how does it work? I think it's simpler than it sounds. Would Jesus have me to love and care for my family? That would be in keeping with His priorities for me, wouldn't it? Would Jesus have me to provide for myself and my loved ones by some sort of work? Would Jesus have me love other people and minister to them in some way? He said that was one of the greatest commandments of all. I'm realizing that if Jesus is my only priority, He will faithfully point me in the direction of the responsibilities which matter most to Him, and in fulfilling those assignments, I will actually be serving my one Master. Rather than suffering, my family (and other things God values) will actually benefit.

Instead of trying to juggle a too-long priority list and make it all fit, would it work to have *just one Master?* Would it work to basically have only one word *on* my priority list? The more I consider it, the more I think it may be the only way that *does* work.

A Priority List of One
Life on Overload

"Come to me, all you who are weary and burdened, and I will give you rest. Take my yoke upon you and learn from me, for I am gentle and humble in heart, and you will find rest for your souls. For my yoke is easy, and my burden is light." Matthew 11:28-30

Of all the findings of this study, now in its sixth year, the idea of having "a priority list of one" strikes me as the most controversial. I'm not sure why. Perhaps it's because I've struggled so much with priorities, myself. Maybe it's because nearly every person I know is overburdened, weary and plagued with feelings of guilt regarding their schedule. That includes many retirees I know! Is it supposed to be this hard for everybody? I don't think so!

Jesus promised His followers a "light burden." When I look at what most folks are dragging around, "light" is not a term which comes to mind! What does come to mind is "life on overload." Apparently, it's not a new problem. The solution has been around for a couple thousand years, too: *"Come to me, all you who are weary and burdened, and I will give you rest."* For relief from a life on overload, Jesus says, *"Come to me; take my yoke upon you and learn from me."* The promise when we do that? *"Rest for your souls."*

Relief from priorities! How did Jesus approach the many demands of life? Quite simply. He only did one thing: He pleased His Father. Doing the will of the Father was not *at the top* of Jesus' priority list; it was the *only* thing on it. He expressed that very philosophy of life to His disciples on more than one occasion. He wanted them to understand that He was living life with just one Master, and one agenda. How else could Jesus possibly have carried out His Father's wishes, were He trying to juggle His own agenda while at the same time being the perfectly obedient Son of God?

It's looking like if I want relief from "priorities," what I have to do is narrow life down to one Master—Jesus, then be willing to accept the yoke He gives me. That means all other yokes come off! That's the scary part. I have to trust Him, that He knows what He's doing, that freedom from the tyranny of private ambitions and priorities is worth the cost, that only in following just one Master do I find the promised rest for my soul.

November 18

Too Many Good Things

"As for what was sown among thorns, this is the one who hears the word, but the cares of the world and the deceitfulness of riches choke the word, and it proves unfruitful." Matthew 13:22

The explanation offered by Jesus for His parable of the sower fits very well with the actualities of modern-day life, strangled by the pursuit of wealth and the false assumption that the many options before us are all needs. Who among us has not felt the implanted Word grow limp within us as we strive to not miss out on the good things offered by the world?

Our usual approach to priorities reminds me of a train. We concern ourselves with getting all the cars in just the right order, only to find out we don't have enough power to move *any* of them! Too many cars for the engine to pull; too many priorities for the time and resources available to us. Some cars are going to need to be released before this thing will budge!

It's not easy cutting cars loose, when they represent long-cherished ambitions and expectations, but neither is it fun to see thorns overcoming our immobile train, just because we couldn't let go of some priorities.

I need to let God go through my life, cutting loose every car He doesn't want me trying to pull. If I expect this to be a light load, and if I expect to be able to move it, I can no longer see a complicated, long list of priorities being the way He would have me to operate. If Jesus is not alone on my priority list, not only will life's load not be "light;" I won't be able to move it. The thorns will grow up around it and choke out what could have been fruitful if I'd had the courage to jettison everything else but what God had instructed me to carry.

We have to get it down to one Master. Jesus never offered to be a "part" of our lives; it's always been about being *Lord* of our lives. Total lordship doesn't leave room for a priority list, even when we place Him at the top of the list. Total lordship is a "priority list" of One.

If we trust Him, we can be assured He won't forget the family He gave us, or the job, or the resources He placed under our stewardship. We can also trust Him not to forget His promise of a yoke that fits, and a light load. The hard part is unhooking all those rail cars, and not looking back. But at least now we're moving!

A Priority List of One

Not a License for Laziness

But if anyone does not provide for his relatives, and especially for members of his household, he has denied the faith and is worse than an unbeliever. 1 Timothy 5:8

Well, there went the idea that maybe we can make "a priority list of One," quit our jobs, and just sit around and love Jesus until He returns! Yes, I did resign from my pastorate, but it was at the Lord's direction, rather than a sudden desire to live without a steady paycheck or medical insurance! It was a release from that particular position, but not a license for laziness.

I'm so glad passages like this are in the scriptures! Sometimes it takes something pretty strong to get my attention, and having the Bible inform me that if I don't take care of my family, I'm worse than an unbeliever definitely gets my attention!

This is also a reminder that God is never going to lose track of the responsibilities with which He has entrusted me. I can trust Him enough to put Him on my priority list all by Himself, knowing for sure that He wants me to provide for my family, love my wife and children, etc., etc., and will direct my attention to all these matters of importance without my having to remind Him of their needs. Even though the Lord is all by Himself on my priority list, I can trust Him to not require of me all of my time and resources to be focused "directly" upon Him; on the contrary, when I tell Him I love Him, the first thing He says to me is, "Feed my sheep." (Jn 22:15-17) My Father loves those little lambs (like my children) more than I do; if I wish to be obedient to Him, I ought to make sure they have food on the table, provided by my own labor, prompted by both my love for them and the love for my Father which requires obedience.

This seems like a lot to write, just to say, "Don't be a lazy, good-for-nothing bum and call it 'being spiritual.'" I'm just glad it's in here. I have enough innate laziness in me that I need to stumble across an occasional scripture which says, "Even unbelievers at least try to take care of their families' needs! Don't try to fool yourself into thinking lazy living is the same thing as being spiritual, because it's not." A safe assumption to make is that God wants me to provide for my family. A wrong assumption is that He would ever want me to be lazy!

A Priority List of One

Slippery Hearts

But as for you, O man of God, flee these things. Pursue righteousness, godliness, faith, love, steadfastness, gentleness. Fight the good fight of the faith. Take hold of the eternal life to which you were called and about which you made the good confession in the presence of many witnesses. I charge you in the presence of God, who gives life to all things, and of Christ Jesus, who in his testimony before Pontius Pilate made the good confession, to keep the commandment unstained and free from reproach until the appearing of our Lord Jesus Christ, which he will display at the proper time—he who is the blessed and only Sovereign, the King of kings and Lord of lords, who alone has immortality, who dwells in unapproachable light, whom no one has ever seen or can see. To him be honor and eternal dominion. Amen. As for the rich in this present age, charge them not to be haughty, nor to set their hopes on the uncertainty of riches, but on God, who richly provides us with everything to enjoy. They are to do good, to be rich in good works, to be generous and ready to share, thus storing up treasure for themselves as a good foundation for the future, so that they may take hold of that which is truly life. 1 Timothy 6:11-19

"*O man of God, flee these things!*" Excellent advice. It's just really difficult (impossible?) to truly serve God, and to also be caught up in building some kind of earthly kingdom. It's best to not even get started down that road. Serve God, and be content with what He provides!

The charge to those "rich in this present age" covers most Americans. I love the practicality of it, and how it zones in on the attitude, rather than merely telling us to divest ourselves of all material goods and try to live as poor people. Poor people can be just as caught up in the love of money as rich people! It's all in the attitude. A person who doesn't have money can be as much in love with it as someone trying to hang on to great wealth. The love of money seeks to grip every heart, possession not a requirement for greed.

And what should we do when we find ourselves rich? Use it as an opportunity to share, to do good, to generously build in the lives of others. When we keep our hope in God and see ourselves as a dispenser of blessings rather than a hoarder of riches, we develop a slippery heart. Money has a hard time getting a grip on it.

A Priority List of One

Greedy Priorities

*When one of those who reclined at table with him heard these things,
he said to him, "Blessed is everyone who will eat bread in the kingdom of
God!" But he said to him, "A man once gave a great banquet and invited
many. And at the time for the banquet he sent his servant to say to those
who had been invited, 'Come, for everything is now ready.' But they all
alike began to make excuses. The first said to him, 'I have bought a field,
and I must go out, and see it. Please have me excused.' And another said,
'I have bought five yoke of oxen, and I go to examine them. Please have me
excused.' And another said, 'I have married a wife, and therefore I cannot
come.' So the servant came and reported these things to his master. Then the
master of the house became angry and said to his servant, 'Go out quickly
to the streets and lanes of the city, and bring in the poor and crippled and
blind and lame.' And the servant said, 'Sir, what you commanded has been
done, and still there is room.' And the master said to the servant, 'Go out
to the highways and hedges and compel people to come in, that my house
may be filled. For I tell you, none of those men who were invited shall taste
my banquet.' "* Luke 14:15-24

Here's the story of what happens when we have our own agenda, and
we try to fit God into our "priority list." Does this sound like our culture?
"Save me a spot at the banquet, in case I might want to come!" But when
it comes right down to it, almost anything is more important than actually
following through on that commitment. "I'm trying to work God into my
priority list." I'm beginning to think that the only thing that works is when
God is all alone on our priority list! If He's not, whatever else is on there
always seems to crowd Him out. Priorities are greedy. They resent being
dropped further down the list, even temporarily, so they have a way of
sabotaging the success of other priorities. Career priorities think families
are O.K., as long as they don't get in the way of the career; families like
the money a job brings in and resent the time it takes out; volunteer-fed
organizations are ravenous. Meanwhile, God still refuses to be on some
list where He gets crowded out by a soccer game, a new boat or even a new
wife! The whole "priority list" thing doesn't seem to work. The priorities
argue and refuse to share. Once again, I'm back to Paul's priority list: Jesus.
Period. At least it's peaceful.

November 22

A Priority List of One

My Only Option

*Now great crowds accompanied him, and he turned and said to them,
"If anyone comes to me and does not hate his own father and mother
and wife and children and brothers and sisters, yes, and even his own life,
he cannot be my disciple. Whoever does not bear his own cross and come
after me cannot be my disciple. For which of you, desiring to build a
tower, does not first sit down and count the cost, whether he has enough to
complete it? Otherwise, when he has laid a foundation and is not able to
finish, all who see it begin to mock him, saying, "This man began to build
and was not able to finish." Or what king, going out to encounter another
king in war, will not sit down first and deliberate whether he is able with ten
thousand to meet him who comes against him with twenty thousand? And
if not, while the other is yet a great way off, he sends a delegation and asks
for terms of peace. So therefore, any one of you who does not renounce all
that he has cannot be my disciple.*

*Salt is good, but if salt has lost its taste, how shall its saltiness be re-
stored? It is of no use either for the soil or for the manure pile. It is thrown
away. He who has ears to hear, let him hear."* Luke 14:25-35

I think that for most of my life, I have heard a gospel that begged people
to "accept Jesus," but which stopped there, in terms of the commitment
required of a disciple. A lot of it has even skipped the step of repentance,
much less included hard passages like the one above that basically says,
"Unless you're willing to renounce even your own family and yourself,
don't bother to apply!" My generation has not counted the cost, because
it's been emphasized over and over and over again that there *is* no cost, that
salvation is a free gift which cannot be earned. I still think that *salvation*
is a free gift, but *discipleship* sure doesn't look to be one!

Salvation is free; discipleship isn't. Discipleship—following Christ—is
consistently billed in the Bible as costing everything which a person has.
The cross is also mentioned on numerous occasions! In light of passages
like this, it's no wonder that our "priority list" style of discipleship doesn't
work. Discipleship was never intended to be a "prioritized" thing; Jesus
made it clear that if we weren't willing to completely clear the list, except
for Him, we need not apply. A priority list of One is looking like my only
option.

November 23

A Priority List of One
I Can't Have It All?

And a ruler asked him, "Good Teacher, what must I do to inherit eternal life?"...

When Jesus heard this, he said to him, "One thing you still lack. Sell all that you have and distribute to the poor, and you will have treasure in heaven; and come, follow me." But when he heard these things, he became very sad, for he was extremely rich. Jesus, looking at him with sadness, said, "How difficult it is for those who have wealth to enter the kingdom of God! For it is easier for a camel to go through the eye of a needle than for a rich person to enter the kingdom of God." Those who heard it said, "Then who can be saved?" But he said, "What is impossible with men is possible with God." And Peter said, "See, we have left our homes and followed you." And he said to them, "Truly, I say to you, there is no one who has left house or wife or brothers or parents or children, for the sake of the kingdom of God, who will not receive many times more in this time, and in the age to come eternal life." Luke 18:18,22-30

"What do you mean, I can't have it all?!" This story isn't very popular among those who have been trained that they can "have it all" in this world and have Jesus, too. That's definitely not the way Jesus is portraying discipleship, here! It's a choice: Jesus or the world. The choice is not "both."

In the case of the rich ruler, we see the bar of discipleship for what it is: A call to complete obedience and commitment. The bar wasn't raised for the rich ruler; that's basically what Jesus was requiring of others who wanted to be His disciple, too.

It's not like God doesn't notice the sacrifice of a servant! Not only do we receive eternal life, but we also receive many times more in *this* time! Hey, be a servant! You get to keep what you get, then!

November 24

A Priority List of One

What I Love Most

Do not love the world or the things in the world. If anyone loves the world, the love of the Father is not in him. For all that is in the world—the desires of the flesh and the desires of the eyes and pride in possessions—is not from the Father but is from the world. And the world is passing away along with its desires, but whoever does the will of God abides forever.
1 John 2:15-17

In the establishment of the "priority list," are we not sometimes asking God to rank the degree of love we should have for something which is *against* Him? If we are not to *"love the world or the things in the world,"* how high on a priority list should the things of the world be?! The main contenders—*desires of the flesh, desires of the eyes, pride in possessions*—are all, according to the Bible, *not from the Father,* but *from the world.* We have a problem, here, and I think it is a key when it comes to the failure of our "priority list" thinking. We are asking God to shuffle priorities for us which He never intended should even make the list. Where would He put "pride in possessions," for example?! The lusts of the flesh and the eyes drive all kinds of activities, all of them worldly. Where should they be on the list? Nowhere. So how did they get on my list?

Priority lists are love-driven, especially when I'm talking about what I *do,* as opposed to what I *say* I'll do. I may *say* that God is first on my list, or even all alone, but when push comes to shove, as it always eventually does, the winner will be whatever I love the most. If the pride I have in my possessions outranks my love for the Father, possessions will usually win, no matter where I said God was on the list. The same thing for everything else: What I love most will win.

So why try to live life with a list of warring desires as my guide?! If God has to share a spot on my "priority list" with the various contenders for my soul who represent the love of the world, I'm setting myself up for failure. Is God content to be on the list with other loves, who grab at the top slot at every opportunity? No. Are the desires of the flesh satisfied with second or third place? No. If I seriously love God, I need to leave off of my list *every rival* to that love. The only way to bring peace to the "list" is to remove from it all but my first love. Once again, I'm down to one word: Jesus.

A Priority List of One

Contentment, Now

Keep your life free from love of money, and be content with what you have, for he has said, "I will never leave you nor forsake you." So we can confidently say,
> *"The Lord is my helper;*
> *I will not fear;*
> *what can man do to me?"*

Hebrews 13:5-6

If we are able to clear from our priority list the pursuit and love of money, the battle is half-won. The reason the Bible describes it as *"Keep your life free from love of money"* is because love of money is something which controls us, once it gains a foothold in our lives. It represents a bondage from which we need to be freed.

The answer? Contentment. We need to purposefully choose contentment as a replacement for greed. *Greed?* Who thinks they're greedy?! Not me! It's just an appreciation for money and the things money will buy, that's all. It's not really "love" of money.

It's not contentment, either. Am I really, truly content with what I have? Almost! If I had just a little bit more...

Contentment never really comes into play until we are freed from love of money. We don't even have to call it "greed;" all we have to do is look at where our time and energy go, as we strive after possessions and financial security. We will faithfully, wholeheartedly serve the Master—once we have enough to be "comfortable." Yeah, right.

How do we gain freedom from the love of money? We choose to replace it with contentment. Instead of aiming for a certain standard of living, which is maddeningly (always) just out of reach, I choose to be content with what I have, *now.* Instead of relying on my accumulated resources for security, I choose to rely on the great God who promised to never leave me or forsake me. Instead of being fearful of loss of possessions or other "What if's," I'll choose faith in Christ, and pursue Him as my first love.

A life and priority list where "love of money" has been replaced with "contentment" is a big step in the right direction.

A Priority List of One

Righteous Wealth

"One who is faithful in a very little is also faithful in much, and one who is dishonest in a very little is also dishonest in much. If then you have not been faithful in the unrighteous wealth, who will entrust to you the true riches? And if you have not been faithful in that which is another's, who will give you that which is your own? No servant can serve two masters, for either he will hate the one and love the other, or he will be devoted to the one and despise the other. You cannot serve God and money."
Luke 16:10-13

Here again is the reference to "unrighteous wealth." It's only money, just man-made currency, unrighteous and of no value to God. If we're not even faithful with *that*, why would God entrust to us something that's actually worth something?! There are lessons in here about tithing, about generosity, about accountability. We have to be proven trustworthy in these areas, first, or we're not ready to go on to things that really matter. I'm picturing God holding up a $100 bill, saying, "If I can't trust you with a piece of paper, why would I trust you with something that's really valuable?"

If money is considered an example of "unrighteous wealth," the implication is strong that there must also be "righteous wealth." Our stewardship of one is preparation for stewardship of the other.

How do we get ready for righteous wealth? Once again, I think the first step is settling on just one Master. In this, one of the defining passages in the whole Bible concerning servanthood, Jesus reminds us *"No servant can serve two masters."* It won't happen! I experienced the reality of that principle when I worked for a few months in a retail establishment owned by 50/50 partners—who hated each other! We low-level employees would trudge from one task to another, building a display for one owner, then tearing it down because the other owner didn't like it, etc., etc.

What was my job? It depended on which one had spoken to me, last! Trying to please one of these guys was hard enough; pleasing both was impossible. *"No servant can serve two masters."* Right, Jesus!

Back again to the priority list. It's not just a matter of keeping the list in the right order. The problem with a priority list is that we end up with too many masters. It's too crowded, too complicated, everybody ends up frustrated and losing. A priority list of One!

A Priority List of One

How Do You Get To Be A Man Of God?

Now Elisha came to Damascus. Ben-hadad the king of Syria was sick. And when it was told him, "The man of God has come here," the king said to Hazael, "Take a present with you and go to meet the man of God, and inquire of the LORD through him, saying, "Shall I recover from this sickness?" 2 Kings 8:7-8

A king from a foreign (and hostile) country recognizes Elisha as "the man of God." *"The man of God has come here..."*

What does it take before a person has that kind of credibility? I think it takes a call of God—you don't just elevate yourself to this status by wanting it; more than that, I think it takes pure obedience. Elisha is no "part-time prophet" who serves God in his spare time. Elisha, like many prophets before him, seems to have no other agenda than just carrying out God's will.

When you have someone who does nothing except what God has instructed him to do, and he's done it faithfully for decades, it's not surprising that even foreigners would say of him, *"The man of God has come here."*

How do I get to be a "man of God"? By being a servant of God, with no other agenda. Credibility is tied to track record; the longer we serve God faithfully, the more credibility our lives have. It may reach a point where even unbelievers regard us with respect, for the mere fact that they see the mark of God on our lives. If our only agenda in life is to serve God, the longer we are consistent in that direction, the more people can't help but notice that we are a man or woman of God. Faithfulness over the years makes "man of God" not a title, but an observation. If we set the course of our lives to serve God, and stay on that course, God takes care of the reputation part. The Spirit who dwells in us makes people think of God whenever they see one of His servants show up.

Lord, help me be a man of God. When people see me, I want them to think of You.

A Priority List of One

The Checkbook Is Gone

And I tell you, make friends for yourselves by means of unrighteous wealth, so that when it fails they may receive you into the eternal dwellings. The Pharisees, who were lovers of money, heard all these things, and they ridiculed him. And he said to them, "You are those who justify yourselves before men, but God knows your hearts. For what is exalted among men is an abomination in the sight of God." Luke 16:9,14-15

I notice that it says "when" it fails, not "if." There's nothing eternal about unrighteous wealth. The dishonest manager in the parable Jesus told preceding this verse was shrewd enough to realize that if he was going to lose everything, anyway, he may as well make some friends with it as he was letting go! We have this parable, not to encourage dishonesty, but as a reminder that there will come a time when we all, like the dishonest manager, will be relieved of our possessions and our management. We won't be running a business anymore, or writing any checks. We'll be relieved of all our responsibilities and our earthly life. The question is, "What then? Are we preparing for that?" Since we're going to have to let go of all of it, anyway, why not use it to make friends while we're here? Why not put the resources into things that will outlast us, like ministry to people?

The parable of the dishonest manager, the admonition to be faithful with whatever we've been given, and the bold statement that *"what is exalted among men is an abomination in the sight of God"* all added up to even more disdain toward Jesus on the part of the Pharisees. None of us likes to be told that our value system is corrupt. Jesus informed the religious rulers of the day that the very things they prized were *"an abomination in the sight of God."* No wonder they weren't happy.

Here's the tough question, though: Did *"what is exalted among men"* suddenly gain favor with God in the intervening generations? Jesus didn't approve of the love of money which gripped the Pharisees, but He's O.K. with it if *we're* doing it? I would guess that the things which were an abomination to God a couple thousand years ago still are!

What is "exalted among men"? What does humanity think is great? Now, does God think it's great, too, or does He consider it an abomination?

Of all rival masters, money is greediest. One Master. One priority.

A Priority List of One

Mind Games

For those who live according to the flesh set their minds on the things of the flesh, but those who live according to the Spirit set their minds on the things of the Spirit. To set the mind on the flesh is death, but to set the mind on the Spirit is life and peace. For the mind that is set on the flesh is hostile to God, for it does not submit to God's law; indeed, it cannot. Those who are in the flesh cannot please God.

You, however, are not in the flesh but in the Spirit, if in fact the Spirit of God dwells in you. Anyone who does not have the Spirit of Christ does not belong to him. But if Christ is in you, although the body is dead because of sin, the Spirit is life because of righteousness. If the Spirit of him who raised Jesus from the dead dwells in you, he who raised Christ Jesus from the dead will also give life to your mortal bodies through his Spirit who dwells in you. Romans 8:5-11

How many of our struggles could be eliminated if we were willing to submit our minds to Christ, along with our bodies? Where did we get the notion that we can be servants of Christ, yet free to do whatever we please with our resources, our bodies and our minds?! Is that the way it is for slaves? They just do whatever they want, right? They do work for their masters, then they're free to go wherever they like, and do as they wish? Of course not. If you're a slave, you're a slave all the time! The master even controls your "free time."

I need to remember that not only is this not my body, to do with as I please, and these are not my resources, to spend as I see fit; this is *not my mind*, either. Rather than this being a degrading blow to my individuality, this is the best answer I have for each and every temptation I encounter! What should I do when tempted? Pray a simple prayer: "Lord, what do you want me to think about right now?" It's like putting my mind in four-wheel-drive! Jesus never leads me into more temptation or drives me in the ditch; every time I've found myself in the ditch it was always *me* doing the driving!

But we have the mind of Christ (1 Co 2:16). Letting the Spirit control the thoughts of that mind is infinitely better than allowing the mind to be controlled by the flesh. Out of temptation, along a blessed path, never in the ditch—that's the difference when my mind is Spirit-controlled.

A Priority List of One

Undivided Devotion

You were bought with a price; do not become slaves of men....
This is what I mean, brothers: the appointed time has grown very short.
From now on, let those who have wives live as though they had none, and
those who mourn as though they were not in mourning, and those who re-
joice as though they were not rejoicing, and those who buy as though they
had no goods, and those who deal with the world as though they had no
dealings with it. For the present form of this world is passing away.
I want you to be free from anxieties. The unmarried man is anxious
about the things of the Lord, how to please the Lord. But the married man
is anxious about worldly things, how to please his wife, and his interests
are divided. And the unmarried or betrothed woman is anxious about the
things of the Lord, how to be holy in body and spirit. But the married
woman is anxious about worldly things, how to please her husband. I say
this for your own benefit, not to lay any restraint upon you, but to promote
good order and to secure your undivided devotion to the Lord.
1 Corinthians 7:23,29-35

Undivided devotion to the Lord. That's what this is about. We are
needing to learn to live in transition, because the world we inhabit is in
transition—*For the present form of this world is passing away.* Hence, it
makes sense to live as though whatever we are experiencing, mourning or
rejoicing, will soon be over. The worldly demands which cause us anxiety
now will one day cease.

The cautions in this passage are several: Do not become slaves of men
(since we belong to Christ); don't let possessions or emotions or worldly
pursuits control your life; it's not wrong to marry, but it does divide our
interests.

It goes back to eternity. Since believers have heaven to look forward
to, we needn't be trapped by the things of this world; we would be wise to
hold all of them loosely and to live focused on Jesus and the eternal life
He has promised, rather than allowing our energies to be scattered amongst
trivial and temporal pursuits, not to mention living as anxious heathen rather
than hopeful Christ-followers.

Undivided devotion to the Lord. We must have dealings with this fad-
ing world, but we need not be captivated by it. One priority: Jesus.

December 1

Promises to Servants

Peace-Backed Promises

At my first defense no one came to stand by me, but all deserted me. May it not be charged against them! But the Lord stood by me and strengthened me, so that through me the message might be fully proclaimed and all the Gentiles might hear it. So I was rescued from the lion's mouth. The Lord will rescue me from every evil deed and bring me safely into his heavenly kingdom. To him be the glory forever and ever. Amen.
2 Timothy 4:16-18

Four more sentences of personal greetings and he's done. This is Paul's final written communication in our possession. Like Jesus, Paul knew the pain of abandonment, as well as suffering of every kind. Like his Master, Paul chose forgiveness and grace over bitterness, and experienced divine power when his own strength was completely gone.

Here is the faith and trust of a servant who has been through it all, and knows his Lord. There is a calmness here that comes from God. It's good in every situation, and it's good even when everybody knows this is not going to turn out the way we're hoping it will. Anyone can have peace when things are peaceful, but it's the one who trusts in the Lord who is able to have peace when surrounded by chaos and impending doom. The reason is that God shows up! In the worst of situations, that's all it takes to bring peace. This is the peace to which Jesus was referring when He promised His disciples, *"Peace I leave with you; my peace I give to you. Let not your hearts be troubled, neither let them be afraid."* (Jn 14:27) Millions of disciples, including Paul and myself, have found this promise to be so true!

The trust is not in God rescuing me from every peril and always helping me to escape suffering; the trust is that He will bring me safely into His heavenly kingdom. We have to remember that!

"The Lord will rescue me from every evil deed and bring me safely into his heavenly kingdom." (2 Tim 4:18)

With exception of his final greetings, these are the last recorded words of the apostle Paul. He's telling us what is going to happen—not the details or the sequence, but the conclusion. What a good statement of faith! The declaration itself is evidence of the peace dwelling within. We can know for sure that the Lord will bring us safely home. *"To him be the glory...!"*

December 2

A Priority List of One

The Only Thing That Counts

It is those who want to make a good showing in the flesh who would force you to be circumcised, and only in order that they may not be persecuted for the cross of Christ. For even those who are circumcised do not themselves keep the law, but they desire to have you circumcised that they may boast in your flesh. But far be it from me to boast except in the cross of our Lord Jesus Christ, by which the world has been crucified to me, and I to the world. For neither circumcision counts for anything, nor uncircumcision, but a new creation. And as for all who walk by this rule, peace and mercy be upon them, and upon the Israel of God.

From now on let no one cause me trouble, for I bear on my body the marks of Jesus.

The grace of our Lord Jesus Christ be with your spirit, brothers. Amen.
Galatians 6:12-18

A weary apostle tells his would-be accusers to back off, even as he offers grace to fellow believers and a clear perspective on what, for them, had been a thorny issue.

The solution to the circumcision dilemma is that it doesn't even matter! Like many dilemmas, it is man-made and the real question has to do with who gets to be proud rather than biblical principles supposedly being at stake. Paul shines the light on it and reminds us all that there's really nothing besides the cross which matters. When Paul was confronted with the cross, the world died for him, along with its rules and demands. He ultimately made a decision of the heart that the only boasting he would do would be in the cross; he had died to the world, too.

The *Israel of God* is how Paul identifies the family of believers, circumcised and uncircumcised, Jew and Gentile, who have also died to the world and allowed Christ Jesus to raise them up as a new creation. The new creation is the only thing that counts.

The world has been crucified to me, and I to the world. The old life is over, rules and all. The world no longer cares what we do when we're dead to it; we no longer care what the world does, either. The only thing that counts is our new life in Christ. My life is marked by Jesus. Buzz off, world.

A Priority List of One

One Priority to Shuffle

"I can do nothing on my own. As I hear, I judge, and my judgment is just, because I seek not my own will but the will of him who sent me."
John 5:30

The words of Jesus have such an impact. *I can do nothing on my own.* He makes it so clear that He has no other agenda other than to accomplish the will of the Father. Jesus lived with a priority list of one: The Father.

Still, this may be the most radical concept in this book. The idea of "a priority list of One" seems to fit the Bible, but it definitely doesn't fit our cultural mindset. I still think it's right, though. God knows about the responsibilities He's entrusted to me. He knows about my family, and my physical needs. I can trust Him, and I can trust Him *totally.* In order to truly be an effective servant, I need to quit trying to juggle this big priority list of important things, and I need to focus on serving God *alone;* He's already said that serving Him is to serve others.

I realize that in practical reality, I will still have a kind of priority list of what matters and what doesn't matter as much, and there will still be many decisions to make. However, just the mere idea that I have only one priority in life is so freeing! This, I can do!

"But what about my family?" God has done a census, and He knows how many people are in my family. It tells me in the Bible that He even keeps track of the sparrow population! It tells me in the Bible that He has even done a census of the hairs on my head! (For some people, it didn't take Him long). He is absolutely and totally aware of my relationships and my responsibilities and everything else. The thing that complicates all of this, immensely, is when I take the priority of "God," and add to that priority a bunch of my own ambitions, plus the perceived expectations of others, and try to juggle all of them together, with the assumption that it can or should be done that way. It doesn't work. No one can serve two masters. You end up wishing one of them would just bug off and leave you alone. One of the masters always wins, and when it's not always the same one, or it's the same one but it's the wrong one, you're in trouble!

One Master. One Lord. One priority. This sounds like a workable plan, to me. It also agrees with the scripture. A priority list of One.

Servants God Commends

The Patient Champion

The LORD said to Satan, "From where have you come?" Satan answered the LORD and said, "From going to and fro on the earth, and from walking up and down on it." And the LORD said to Satan, "Have you considered my servant Job, that there is none like him on the earth, a blameless and upright man, who fears God and turns away from evil?" Then Satan answered the LORD and said, "Does Job fear God for no reason? Have you not put a hedge around him and his house and all that he has, on every side? You have blessed the work of his hands, and his possessions have increased in the land. But stretch out your hand and touch all that he has, and he will curse you to your face." And the LORD said to Satan, "Behold, all that he has is in your hand. Only against him do not stretch out your hand." So Satan went out from the presence of the LORD.
Job 1:7-12

And the LORD said to Satan, "Have you considered my servant Job, that there is none like him on the earth, a blameless and upright man, who fears God and turns away from evil?" (Job 1:8)

When God is able to boast about His servant to the devil himself, that's a servant! The resulting challenge issued by Satan garners a response from God only because God knows His servant will not falter even though stripped of every blessing he has ever received; this servant is a champion.

At stake in this contest is Job's attitude toward God. Satan contends that as soon as Job's riches are gone, he will curse God to His face. God knows better. Satan later whines that Job's health is the key to him turning his back on God, but that proves also to be a fallacious assumption. The key is that there *is* no key! When faced with simultaneous, full-force attacks from Satan himself resulting in unbelievable suffering, rather than cursing God as the devil predicted, Job's response remains, *"Though he slay me, I will hope in him;"* (Job 13:15)

Even when his grieving, embittered wife prods Job to "Curse God and die," Job's gentle response to her is, *"Shall we receive good from God, and shall we not receive evil?"* (Job 2:10) At every turn, Satan's attempts to turn Job against God failed. God had a champion in Job. The servant whom God knows to be serving Him because of faithful love, rather than accumulated blessings, is a servant who can and will triumph over Satan himself.

Servants God Commends

My Servant Job

After the LORD had spoken these words to Job, the LORD said to Eliphaz the Temanite: "My anger burns against you and against your two friends, for you have not spoken of me what is right, as my servant Job has. Now therefore take seven bulls and seven rams and go to my servant Job and offer up a burnt offering for yourselves. And my servant Job shall pray for you, for I will accept his prayer not to deal with you according to your folly. For you have not spoken of me what is right, as my servant Job has." So Eliphaz the Temanite and Bildad the Shuhite and Zophar the Naamathite went and did what the LORD had told them, and the LORD accepted Job's prayer. Job 42:7-9

In four sentences, God refers four times to *"my servant Job."* What an identity! What kind of servant does God commend? One who speaks of Him what is right, for one thing. It turns out that God is rather particular about theology, after all! He wasn't impressed with the doctrines being tossed around by Job's three friends, and let them know who was correct and who wasn't: *My anger burns against you and against your two friends, for you have not spoken of me what is right, as my servant Job has.* (Job 42:7)

Not only does God rebuke Job's well-meaning accusers and correct their theology; He sets Job up as their priest, requiring them to bring sacrifices to him so he can offer intercessory prayer for them, that they might not receive what their folly deserves! They fancied themselves counselors and theologians, there to set their friend straight; God reversed the roles, assuring the others that He would do whatever Job requested Him to do with them! Once again, theology is the issue, as for the second time God remands: *"For you have not spoken of me what is right, as my servant Job has."* (Job 42:8)

The kind of servant God commends is one who does his best to give an accurate portrayal of the LORD to others, who speaks of God "what is right," who refuses to let his faith be demolished by circumstances, false accusations, screwy theology or even the bitter suggestions of his closest companions or the full-frontal attack of Satan himself. When a servant gets to the point where the attitude of life is, *"Though he slay me, I will hope in him,"* (Job 13:15) that's an impenetrable faith, smiled upon by God.

December 6

The Servant God Doesn't Commend

The word of the LORD came to Samuel: "I regret that I have made Saul king, for he has turned back from following me and has not performed my commandments." And Samuel was angry, and he cried to the LORD all night. 1 Samuel 15:10-11

When God's prophet Samuel catches up with the anointed king, Saul has just set up a monument in his own honor. I have a feeling that Saul's approval ratings were just now at an all-time high—except with God.

Samuel's job had been to "king" Saul in the first place; now his job was to "un-king" him! It's not always fun to be a prophet. The sensitive prophet cries out to God all night. He's sad, angry—all that potential gone to waste! Saul continues to do his own thing, leaving behind him a trail of self-centered pride and disobedience, which he quickly tries to justify and spiritualize, when God's man catches up to him for what will be their final confrontation. The reply he gets back from God's servant is timely for every generation:

"Has the LORD as great delight in burnt offerings and sacrifices, as in obeying the voice of the LORD?

Behold, to obey is better than sacrifice, and to listen than the fat of rams.

For rebellion is as the sin of divination, and presumption is as iniquity and idolatry.

Because you have rejected the word of the LORD, he has also rejected you from being king." (1 Sam 15:22-23)

It was God's fervent intention to bless King Saul beyond his biggest dreams, but a servant who will neither listen to nor obey his master's commands is a servant who cannot be commended. Saul was that kind of man. The only thing left to do was send a broken-hearted, true servant to deliver the message: God will never commend disobedience to Him, and He is pulling the plug on your kingship.

God is deadly serious about complete obedience to His commands! We can try all we want to gloss over incomplete obedience with religious platitudes and other rationalizations—we might even gain the favor of some people in the process, but with God, obedience outweighs "results," and rebellion against His commands will never be blessed.

Servants God Commends

Commendable Faith

Now a centurion had a servant who was sick and at the point of death, who was highly valued by him. When the centurion heard about Jesus, he sent to him elders of the Jews, asking him to come and heal his servant. And when they came to Jesus, they pleaded with him earnestly, saying, "He is worthy to have you do this for him, for he loves our nation, and he is the one who built us our synagogue." And Jesus went with them. When he was not far from the house, the centurion sent friends, saying to him, "Lord, do not trouble yourself, for I am not worthy to have you come under my roof. Therefore I did not presume to come to you. But say the word, and let my servant be healed. For I too am a man set under authority, with soldiers under me: and I say to one, 'Go,' and he goes; and to another, 'Come,' and he comes; and to my servant, 'Do this,' and he does it." When Jesus heard these things, he marveled at him, and turning to the crowd that followed him, said, "I tell you, not even in Israel have I found such faith." And when those who had been sent returned to the house, they found the servant well. Luke 7:2-10

A servant who understands authority! Jesus is thrilled that someone gets the concept of authority, and how faith works along with it. Servants do what they're told. The centurion knows that and expresses that. So, it makes sense to him that all Jesus has to do is to just say the word, and the centurion's servant will be healed. He's right.

Jesus jumps on the chance to commend the centurion's faith. He absolutely delights in finding someone who so trusts Him that, having never even seen Jesus, He still expresses total confidence in Jesus' authority and His willingness to use it as grace. Jesus marveled, and enjoyed the marveling. It turns out that all we have to do to bring a smile to the Lord's face is just to believe in Him, totally—and act like it!

Lord, help me to do just that. Help me to be the kind of servant who has so much faith in you that you don't have to come and put on a big show, in order for me to believe you. I don't want to have to see you in person before I'll believe that you'll come through with what is needed. Thank you for all those times when you "said the word," and miracles happened, for me! Help me to be a person of commendable faith.

December 8

Trading With God

And he sat down opposite the treasury and watched the people putting money into the offering box. Many rich people put in large sums. And a poor widow came and put in two small copper coins, which make a penny. And he called his disciples to him, and said to them, "Truly, I say to you, this poor widow has put in more than all those who are contributing to the offering box. For they all contributed out of their abundance, but she out of her poverty has put in everything she had, all she had to live on."
Mark 12:41-44

The total value of the widow's offering wasn't much in monetary terms, yet garnered Jesus' attention to the extent that He rounded up the disciples to give them a speech about it. Obviously, it wasn't the amount of money which was impressive; it was the faith, the sacrifice, the absolute trust. These are the things which always receive God's attention. (Should we be surprised that our Creator is not enamored with pieces of metal, but always picks up on noble things His children do, especially when we're exhibiting love and trust toward Him)?

It was an offering of faith. The insignificant widow with the inconsequential contribution was saying, through her offering, "I am totally dependent upon your mercy, O God. I am giving my all. I have nothing left but you. I trust you completely."

It reminds me of the time when our five-year-old son was praying desperately for his twelve-year-old sister in the hospital, who had been there for weeks as the result of a ruptured appendix. His un-coached bedtime prayer was "Lord, please, please, please heal my sister, and I'll give you all my strength." I think our kind Heavenly Father received those words from a five-year-old boy and basically said, "How about if we trade? You give me all your strength, and I'll give you all of mine." Our daughter was suddenly healed within days of that prayer, in a turnaround which only took minutes. God had "said the word" for her, in response to the prayers of thousands, including a little boy willing to give Him "all his strength."

Whenever we're willing to give our all, whatever that might be, it never fails to get the attention of a loving Father in heaven who is willing to do the same.

December 9

Friend-Making Money

*He also said to the disciples, "There was a rich man who had a manager,
and charges were brought to him that this man was wasting his possessions.
And he called him and said to him, 'What is this that I hear about you? Turn
in the account of your management, for you can no longer be manager.'
And the manager said to himself, 'What shall I do, since my master is taking
the management away from me? I am not strong enough to dig, and I am
ashamed to beg. I have decided what to do, so that when I am removed from
my management, people may receive me into their houses.' So, summoning
his master's debtors one by one, he said to the first, 'How much do you owe
my master?' He said, 'A hundred measures of oil.' He said to him, 'Take
your bill, and sit down quickly and write fifty.' Then he said to another,
'And how much do you owe?' He said, 'A hundred measures of wheat.' He
said to him, 'Take your bill, and write eighty.' The master commended the
dishonest manager for his shrewdness. For the sons of this world are more
shrewd in dealing with their own generation than the sons of light. And I
tell you, make friends for yourselves by means of unrighteous wealth, so
that when it fails they may receive you into the eternal dwellings."* Luke
16:1-9

Here's a slick new principle, for our times! *Use money to make friends,
don't use friends to make money.*

Rather than promoting dishonesty, the parable is promoting the idea of
using worldly resources in order to achieve eternal results.

"Unrighteous wealth." I don't know if that means all wealth is "unrighteous," or if just some of it is, but either way, Jesus is encouraging us to
utilize it in order to attain a higher end. Rather than living for the wealth,
we need to think about what is coming, and plan accordingly. I notice that
Jesus, referring to wealth, says, "*when* it fails," not "if." It *will* fail, eventually. And the servant who planned ahead, thinking about the future, is the
one who had a place to stay and even earned the respect of his master.

Jesus concludes: *"One who is faithful in a very little is also faithful in
much, and one who is dishonest in a very little is also dishonest in much. If
then you have not been faithful in the unrighteous wealth, who will entrust to
you the true riches?"* (Lk 16:10-11) If we do a good job with "unrighteous
wealth," we get to find out what "true riches" are like!

December 10

Sudden Promotions

He said therefore, "A nobleman went into a far country to receive for himself a kingdom and then return. Calling ten of his servants, he gave them ten minas, and said to them, 'Engage in business until I come.' But his citizens hated him and sent a delegation after him, saying, 'We do not want this man to reign over us.' When he returned, having received the kingdom, he ordered these servants to whom he had given the money to be called to him, that he might know what they had gained by doing business. The first came before him, saying, 'Lord, your mina has made ten minas more.' And he said to him, 'Well done, good servant! Because you have been faithful in a very little, you shall have authority over ten cities.' And the second came, saying, 'Lord, your mina has made five minas.' And he said to him, 'And you are to be over five cities.' Then another came, saying, 'Lord, here is your mina, which I kept laid away in a handkerchief; for I was afraid of you, because you are a severe man. ...' Luke 19:12-21

Here is the last speech of Jesus before the Triumphal Entry. It's a reminder that, whether anybody likes it or not, Jesus *will* be the King, and He *will* reign. He expects His servants to *do something* with what He's placed in their care! That's what I'm trying to do. It's not enough to "not lose" what He's given us; we're supposed to do something with it.

Here again is the principle of the kind of servant God commends and the kind He does not commend. The sniveling servant facing the master with nothing but excuses is shown no pity; he is condemned by his own words and relieved of all responsibilities. The industrious servants who have done their best, with varying success, are granted authority beyond their dreams. Given the equivalent of three months' wages in cash to invest, they now find their disciplined faithfulness in managing it has earned them not only their master's approval, but the privilege of being in charge of entire *cities!* From being a money manager of an account which manages to grow tenfold under his care, a servant suddenly finds himself responsible for eleven cities!

This is a *hint* of the kind of responsibilities and privileges God wishes to bestow on His faithful servants—and how serious He is about us learning to be faithful and trustworthy with His resources. Bottom line: It's a *really, really* good thing to be a faithful servant of the King!

The Authority of a Servant

"Truly, I say to you, whatever you bind on earth shall be bound in heaven, and whatever you loose on earth shall be loosed in heaven. Again, I say to you, if two of you agree on earth about anything they ask, it will be done for them by my Father in heaven. For where two or three are gathered in my name, there am I among them." Matthew 18:18-20

In this morning's corporate prayer time, we talked about the power of walking in unity: There are certain things which can be accomplished individually; there are other things which can only be accomplished together.

Passages like this are like being handed God's credit card. It's not an isolated teaching, either! Again and again, Jesus gives His followers instructions, then encourages them to *ask*.

I picture it like a general contractor overseeing a giant building project. The contractor has secured credit everywhere it's needed. He instructs all of the workers according to their particular role in the project so that everyone knows precisely what they are to do. Then, again and again, he stresses, "Whatever you need in order to accomplish my mission for you, *ask*. It will be given to you. All you need is my name. Just tell them it's for me, and you'll get what you need. As an extra safeguard, so they know this is a legitimate request, we'll have two people sign every check or work order. O.K., you know what to do! Go do it, and whatever you need, just ask for it in my name. When I come to check on you, don't be giving me any excuses about not having what you needed to do the job! Everything you need is available to you. Two of you agree together on what it is, then charge it to my account. You have all the authority you need to fulfill the assignment I have for you. No excuses, now. Use this authority to accomplish what I've told you to do."

We have far more authority as servants of Christ than we realize! Not only are we holding God's credit card; we have His presence, too! *For where two or three are gathered in my name, there am I among them.* Is the "quorum" to keep us from beginning to think that *we're* God, and as a safeguard for this incredible authority? I think so. One person with a crazy amount of authority can (and usually does) quickly go astray; a second person adds accountability, balance and confidence to the situation. I think God wants us to think it through, together. Then we make our request, knowing that to ask Him for what we need to accomplish His purposes for us is actually *obedience*.

December 12

The Authority of a Servant

Beyond The Battle Cry

And David rose early in the morning and left the sheep with a keeper and took the provisions and went, as Jesse had commanded him. And he came to the encampment as the host was going out to the battle line, shouting the war cry. And Israel and the Philistines drew up for battle, army against army. And David left the things in charge of the keeper of the baggage and ran to the ranks and went and greeted his brothers. As he talked with them, behold, the champion, the Philistine of Gath, Goliath by name, came up out of the ranks of the Philistines and spoke the same words as before. And David heard him.

All the men of Israel, when they saw the man, fled from him and were much afraid. ...

And David said to the men who stood by him, "What shall be done for the man who kills this Philistine and takes away the reproach from Israel? For who is this uncircumcised Philistine, that he should defy the armies of the living God?" 1 Samuel 17:20-24,26

For 40 long days the same humiliating scenario had repeated itself. The battle lines were drawn and the Israelites shouted the "war cry." ("I'm too young to die!")? Anyway, that was apparently the highlight of the day for them, because everything which followed was humiliation. Goliath stepped forward, the trash talking began, the Israelites ran in fear, and there was no battle. The next day was the same. After the first week, they were considering it *normal* to shout the battle cry, then run!

It took someone fresh from the presence of Almighty God to see the ridiculousness of the situation and be able to pick out the possibilities. Full of faith, it all looked easy to David. It was. After having faced bears and lions in singlehanded combat, a dim-witted, slow-moving nine-foot giant who had just defied God was hardly a challenge! A single well-placed stone dropped Goliath, and the Israelites finally got to do something about their "war cry"—like engage in an actual fight!

The present-day church in America resembles the Israelites, shouting the war cry, but not engaging in the spiritual battle. How long are we going to put up with the intimidation of the devil, without responding? For people of faith, with so much at stake, the war cry is not a good place to stop.

The Authority of a Servant

A Fortified City

"And I will declare my judgments against them, for all their evil in forsaking me. They have made offerings to other gods and worshiped the works of their own hands. But you, dress yourself for work; arise, and say to them everything that I command you. Do not be dismayed by them, lest I dismay you before them. And I, behold, I make you this day a fortified city, an iron pillar, and bronze walls, against the whole land, against the kings of Judah, its officials, its priests, and the people of the land. They will fight against you, but they shall not prevail against you, for I am with you, declares the LORD, to deliver you." Jeremiah 1:16-19

Prior to receiving any pronouncements to make from the Lord, Jeremiah is given some vital information, contained in the first few verses of the book which bears his name:

(1) *"Before you were born, I consecrated you; I appointed you a prophet to the nations."* (Jer 1:5)

(2) *"Do not be afraid of them, for I am with you to deliver you, declares the LORD."* (Jer 1:8)

(3) *Then the LORD put out his hand and touched my mouth. And the LORD said to me, "Behold, I have put my words in your mouth. See, I have set you this day over nations and over kingdoms, to pluck up and to break down, to destroy and overthrow, to build and to plant."* (Jer 1:9-10)

It's important that the prophet understands his role, before going up against royal opposition! Jeremiah the priest became Jeremiah the prophet because of the word of the Lord coming to him. With that word he realizes a foreordained destiny, the backing of God Himself, and an incredible authority directly from God. Jeremiah's mission? Simple. Say whatever God tells him to say, and don't be dismayed by them.

Before even the first message is delivered, Jeremiah already knows that he will face opposition, but that God has made him strong enough to prevail. Conscious of his identity, God's message and God's reassuring presence, Jeremiah embarks on a path of destiny, faithful to the end, while proclaiming an exceedingly unpopular message. The only thing which saves Jeremiah is that his message is from God, who grants His servants all the authority they need, who makes His prophets a "fortified city."

December 14

The Authority of a Servant

The Protected and Hidden Messenger

The word of the LORD came to me, saying, "Go and proclaim in the hearing of Jerusalem, Thus says the LORD,

"I remember the devotion of your youth, your love as a bride,
how you followed me in the wilderness, in a land not sown.
Israel was holy to the LORD, the firstfruits of his harvest.
All who ate of it incurred guilt;
disaster came upon them, declares the LORD."

Hear the word of the LORD, O house of Jacob, and all the clans of the house of Israel. Thus says the LORD:

"What wrong did your fathers find in me
that they went far from me,
and went after worthlessness, and became worthless?"
Jeremiah 2:1-5

Jeremiah's first message to deliver is something else! When you start out calling the fathers of your hearers "worthless," then proceed from there to name each societal sin, bringing the blame squarely upon those listening, you'd better have really good authority behind you! Jeremiah did: God.

His only protection was the fact that this message was not original with him at all: He was merely the messenger. When God's message is delivered faithfully, the messenger is protected and hidden by its power.

When we are delivering our own message, people focus on the sermon and the messenger, and though they may like it or dislike it, it's not really about God; it's about the messenger. When the message is truly from God, it doesn't make much difference who is delivering it, and in fact, people may tend to forget that there even *was* a messenger!

Lord, may my preaching be like that! May it be a powerful message that came right from you, which could be delivered by a rock and would still be powerful and effective! I want to be used of you to communicate your message to people. Help me to be a faithful messenger, Lord, hidden and protected by your power.

December 15

The Authority of a Servant

The Command to Engage

Finally, be strong in the Lord and in the strength of his might. Put on the whole armor of God, that you may be able to stand against the schemes of the devil. For we do not wrestle against flesh and blood, but against the rulers, against the authorities, against the cosmic powers over this present darkness, against the spiritual forces of evil in the heavenly places. Therefore take up the whole armor of God, that you may be able to withstand in the evil day, and having done all, to stand firm. Stand therefore, having fastened on the belt of truth, and having put on the breastplate of righteousness, and as shoes for your feet, having put on the readiness given by the gospel of peace. In all circumstances take up the shield of faith, with which you can extinguish all the flaming darts of the evil one; and take the helmet of salvation, and the sword of the Spirit, which is the word of God, praying at all times in the Spirit, with all prayer and supplication. To that end keep alert with all perseverance, making supplication for all the saints, and also for me, that words may be given to me in opening my mouth boldly to proclaim the mystery of the gospel, for which I am an ambassador in chains, that I may declare it boldly, as I ought to speak. Ephesians 6:10-20

There is no reason for a soldier to wear his armor unless there is the potential of battle. The Bible reminds us that as long as Satan is on the loose, that's all the time. We must always be prepared for warfare.

The weapons with which Christ-followers fight are different, because the conflict is different. Swords made of metal can be effective if wielded properly against a fleshly opponent; spiritual adversaries require a different kind of sword: The Word of God. On down the list, Paul replaces the armor of the flesh with the armor of the Spirit. There is an assumption running throughout this passage which is vital to its meaning: The assumption is that we are willing to fight. I've read that one of the most frequent problems in the military is the reluctance of soldiers to engage in battle. Getting them to fire their weapon is one of the biggest challenges faced by commanders.

Back to the Church. There's a reason we wear this armor and carry the sword of God's Word. It's to use. We have not only permission to engage with the powers of darkness, but the command.

December 16

The Authority of a Servant

Called, Equipped, Sent

And he called the twelve together and gave them power and authority over all demons and to cure diseases, and he sent them out to proclaim the kingdom of God and to heal. And he said to them, "Take nothing for your journey, no staff, nor bag, nor bread, nor money; and do not have two tunics. And whatever house you enter, stay there, and from there depart. And wherever they do not receive you, when you leave that town shake off the dust from your feet as a testimony against them." And they departed and went through the villages, preaching the gospel and healing everywhere.
Luke 9:1-6

The Faith Field Trip was not the idea of the Twelve, but of the Lord. He called them together and laid out the plan for this mission.

It started with authority—*major* authority—at least that's what I would call *"power and authority over all demons and to cure diseases"*! At the same time, Jesus systematically rummages through each of their backup systems, stripping away everything except what will come to them in response to their faith. He even gives them the answer to some of their "What if?" questions: "What if we get a better offer, somewhere?" "What if they don't receive us?"

What Christ wished His disciples to learn was that if they had His power and authority, it was all they needed! Along with that, they were to realize that Jesus never issued authority or spiritual power without a commission which would necessitate its use; power was not to play with, it was to use for godly purposes. At the same time, they were beginning to understand that God doesn't commission people to do things without also equipping them.

So, here were the disciples—called, equipped and sent. This would be a faith venture, from beginning to end. It would help them prove to themselves that faith was not simply esoteric, but a reliable way of approaching life. Jesus wanted His disciples to learn to rely on Him and live by faith. O.K., when did He ever change His mind about that approach?

The Authority of a Servant

Anything Can Happen

In the morning, as he was returning to the city, he became hungry. And seeing a fig tree by the wayside, he went to it and found nothing on it but only leaves. And he said to it, "May no fruit ever come from you again!" And the fig tree withered at once.

When the disciples saw it, they marveled, saying, "How did the fig tree wither at once?" And Jesus answered them, "Truly, I say to you, if you have faith and do not doubt, you will not only do what has been done to the fig tree, but even if you say to this mountain, 'Be taken up and thrown into the sea,' it will happen. And whatever you ask in prayer, you will receive, if you have faith." Matthew 21:18-22

This was one interesting day in the life of Jesus! As soon as they get to the temple, the challenges will start, in what will be one of the most aggressively challenging days in Jesus' life. The chief priests and elders will attack His teaching, asking Him where He got the authority to do these things. The Pharisees and Herodians try to trap Him with a question about whether to pay taxes to Caesar. The Sadducees come up with the dumb question of the day, the one about the woman who was married to seven brothers in sequence, each of whom died, leaving her to the next one. (I would think that after losing about three brothers to this gal, the survivors would be getting nervous)! Finally the woman herself mercifully dies. The question? "In the resurrection, whose wife will she be?" The answer? Who cares!

Jesus' real response to the Sadducees was to simply tell them they were wrong because they didn't know the scriptures or the power of God. For any scribes and Pharisees not yet offended by the Galilean, by day's end He has publicly pronounced seven "woe's" against them for their hypocrisy. It was quite a day, all starting with the cursing of a fig tree!

I don't think I've ever needed to move a real mountain, and I don't recall even seeing a fig tree, much less needing to curse one, but there have been many, many times when I needed to pray, have faith and not doubt. That's a routine not just for the tough days, but for every day. Prayer links us to One who has authority over all creation, even the big chunks of it. If we pray, have faith and don't doubt, anything can happen!

December 18

The Authority of a Servant

Set Apart, but Sent

"They are not of the world, just as I am not of the world. Sanctify them in the truth; your word is truth. As you sent me into the world, so I have sent them into the world. And for their sake I consecrate myself, that they also may be sanctified in truth.

I do not ask for these only, but also for those who will believe in me through their word, that they may all be one, just as you, Father, are in me, and I in you, that they also may be in us, so that the world may believe that you have sent me. The glory that you have given me I have given to them, that they may be one even as we are one, I in them and you in me, that they may become perfectly one, so that the world may know that you sent me and loved them even as you loved me." John 17:16-23

The word translated "sanctified" or "consecrated" means literally, "set apart." This important prayer of Jesus, prayed in the presence of His disciples just prior to His betrayal, occupies a whole chapter of scripture, and emphasizes unity and separation at the same time. The separation part is from the world—we are to be set apart, different, distinct from the world. The unity part comes back repeatedly to the union we are to have with one another and with God.

It's clear that we are to be sanctified—set apart as holy and special to God—but that we are not to hide. *As you sent me into the world, so I have sent them into the world.* We have been sent by our Master, just as He was sent. His prayer is that we would be one—not just with each other, but one in Him, and that the love of the Father for the Son would also be in us. Set apart, but sent. Sanctified, but sent. Into the world! We are Christ's representatives, and continuing proof that He was here, and that He is in us!

There are two options which are not available to the follower of Jesus Christ. One is to live a life which blends in with the belief and value systems of the world. The call is to holiness. If we don't act like Christ, we should drop the name "Christian."

The other option we don't have is to disengage from the world, trying to maintain a society of purity which isolates the love of Jesus from a society desperately in need of it. We are called to be set apart, holy to God; He then sends us into a world needing to see what God's love looks like.

December 19

The Authority of a Servant

Living Proof

Then he stretched himself upon the child three times and cried to the LORD, "O LORD my God, let this child's life come into him again." And the LORD listened to the voice of Elijah. And the life of the child came into him again, and he revived. And Elijah took the child and brought him down from the upper chamber into the house and delivered him to his mother. And Elijah said, "See, your son lives." And the woman said to Elijah, "Now I know that you are a man of God, and that the word of the LORD in your mouth is truth." 1 Kings 17:22-24

The widow's son dies. She is angry, and blames Elijah (and God). Elijah prays and the child revives. The widow's response: *"Now I know that you are a man of God, and that the word of the LORD in your mouth is truth."*

This is what the world needs to know! They need to know that the "prophets" they see are not just blowing smoke, or keeping their TV program on the air—they are actually men and women of God, with the word of the LORD in their mouths, which is truth!

Is that what people see when they look at ministers of the Gospel? It seems to me that all too often they hear words, but instinctively know that those words didn't come from God. It's not even that the words are bad, or theologically off-base; they just didn't come from God. How do we know? No power. God's truth has power to it, authority.

When God's power is applied, anything can happen! In this case a dead boy was delivered back to his grateful mother, the result of nothing more than the fervent prayer of a man of God. The widow had believed Elijah to be a "man of God" even before this episode, but there's nothing like living proof to move people from "believing" to "knowing." God's power makes all the difference!

The authority accessed by the prophet Elijah was not man's authority. What the grieving widow saw was a clear demonstration of the power of God. That's why she could say of Elijah, *"Now I know that you are a man of God, and that the word of the LORD in your mouth is truth."* W h e n what is in our mouths is only God's truth, and the world sees living proof of God's authoritative power, we don't have to convince people we are men or women of God.

December 20

The Authority of a Servant

No Time to Ad-Lib

"The LORD your God will raise up for you a prophet like me from among you, from your brothers—it is to him you shall listen—just as you desired of the LORD your God at Horeb on the day of the assembly, when you said, 'Let me not hear again the voice of the LORD my God or see this great fire any more, lest I die.' And the LORD said to me, 'They are right in what they have spoken. I will raise up for them a prophet like you from among their brothers. And I will put my words in his mouth, and he shall speak to them all that I command him. And whoever will not listen to my words that he shall speak in my name, I myself will require it of him. But the prophet who presumes to speak a word in my name that I have not commanded him to speak, or who speaks in the name of other gods, that same prophet shall die.' And if you say in your heart, 'How may we know the word that the LORD has not spoken?'—when a prophet speaks in the name of the LORD, if the word does not come to pass or come true, that is a word that the LORD has not spoken; the prophet has spoken it presumptuously. You need not be afraid of him." Deuteronomy 18:15-22

Moses' prophecy pointed straight to Jesus, but the qualifications of any prophet of God are similar: The prophet says what God has put in his mouth. This is not a free lance position! We should not "presume" to speak a word in God's name that He has not commanded us to speak, or we may be paying the consequences for it.

Here again the truth comes through—a prophet or messenger of God does not have authority in himself—all his authority is tied to the fact that the message is from God. If the message is not from God, there is no authority whatsoever! This is why the treatment of false prophets is so harsh; they have deceived people by leading them to believe that their words had come from God, when in fact they hadn't. The resulting fiasco when these words are believed, yet are contrary to truth, is damaging to faith.

God wants people to be able to believe His messengers. This is why it is so vitally important that His servants only speak words in His name which they are sure originated with Him. There may be times to ad-lib, but speaking prophetically in the name of the Lord is not one of them!

December 21

The Authority of a Servant
Supernatural Powers

Are they not all ministering spirits sent out to serve for the sake of those who are to inherit salvation? Hebrews 1:14

The entire first chapter of Hebrews downplays the importance of angels, while magnifying the importance of Christ. The final verse sums up the position of angels: *Are they not all ministering spirits sent out to serve for the sake of those who are to inherit salvation?*

Why would the writer of Hebrews feel the need to spend so much time on the topic of angels? The first century disciples must have had their own share of angel-mania, as we continue to experience from time to time in the present era.

Angels are magnificent beings, but they hold absolutely no comparison to the risen Christ! Angels are here to help us, but we aren't to worship them.

So what is the place of angels, again? *"Are they not all ministering spirits sent out to serve for the sake of those who are to inherit salvation?"*

It's rather humbling to think that the God of the Universe would send out ministering spirits with supernatural powers whose purpose was to serve us! This is not some "genie in the bottle" deal, though; these messengers are not here to obey our every whimsical command. In fact, we will only very rarely, if ever, be aware of their presence or of their intervention. Rather than commanding them, we seldom even know they are there.

Their commander is God Himself. The "guardian angels" referred to in scripture (Mt. 18:10) are not at the command of parents or of children, but of God. He commands them *concerning us*. He sends them out to serve... *us!* Imagine that.

There are movies made ad nauseum about superheroes with superhuman powers and abilities. Of course, it's all fiction. When it comes to actually confronting the forces of evil in real life, special effects aren't very adequate.

God has not stranded us to be at the mercy of those who come against us! Supernatural power is available! It comes in the form of invisible angels, *ministering spirits sent out to serve for the sake of those who are to inherit salvation.* Only God could come up with something this good!

December 22

Signing Off On a Miracle

And the angel said to her, "Do not be afraid, Mary, for you have found favor with God. And behold, you will conceive in your womb and bear a son, and you shall call his name Jesus..."
And Mary said to the angel, "How will this be, since I am a virgin?"
And the angel answered her, "The Holy Spirit will come upon you, and the power of the Most High will overshadow you; therefore the child to be born will be called holy—the Son of God..."
And Mary said, "Behold, I am the servant of the Lord; let it be to me according to your word." And the angel departed from her.
Luke 1:30-31, 34-35, 38

God entrusts the future of the world to a teenage girl, whose only duty, for now, is to believe Him. After clarifying that this is indeed miracle territory, her response to God's angel is, *"Let it be to me according to your word."* Soon after the angelic visitation, Mary, perhaps herself a descendant of the psalmist David, writes a beautiful poem of her own (Lk 1:46-55) magnifying God and praising Him for the fulfillment of His promises. The catch is, Mary wrote The Magnificat *before* Jesus was born—and possibly before she would have even had evidence that she was pregnant! She really did *believe* God. No wonder He picked her!

Her relative Elizabeth, pregnant with her own miracle from God (John the Baptist) pays tribute to Mary's faith: *"And blessed is she who believed that there would be a fulfillment of what was spoken to her from the Lord."* (Lk 1:45)

Mary's initial task was to believe—just believe. Her response to God's message was full of faith and joy. Her blessing was sure, and she knew it. That blessing is available to *all* of us who simply believe that what has been spoken to us from the Lord will be fulfilled—who say back to Him, *"Let it be to me according to your word."*

The Witness of Joyful Submission

In the sixth month the angel Gabriel was sent from God to a city of Galilee named Nazareth, to a virgin betrothed to a man whose name was Joseph, of the house of David. And the virgin's name was Mary....

And Mary said to the angel, "How will this be, since I am a virgin?"

And the angel answered her, "The Holy Spirit will come upon you, and the power of the Most High will overshadow you; therefore the child to be born will be called holy—the Son of God. And behold, your relative Elizabeth in her old age has also conceived a son, and this is the sixth month with her who was called barren. For nothing will be impossible with God." And Mary said, "Behold, I am the servant of the Lord; let it be to me according to your word." And the angel departed from her. Luke 1:26-27,34-38

Gabriel is busy, this year. He has a lot of good news to announce! What impresses me is the response he gets from people like Mary, a young woman probably barely in her teens, who chooses to believe the "impossible" message, and totally submit to God. Mary's response says it all: *And Mary said, "Behold, I am the servant of the Lord; let it be to me according to your word."*

Even though she was young, Mary understood perfectly what it means to be a servant of the Lord. It means, *"Let it be to me according to your word."*

Your word, not mine. Your will, not mine. Your ideas, not mine. Have it your way, God. I totally submit to you. Not only do I submit to you; your way is the way I *want* it to be! Not only do you win, but I am thrilled just to be included in your plan! Fulfill your promises in me, just like you said. Have your way in my life. I totally belong to you.

Some servants must be prodded or cornered before anything much happens, and when they do proceed, it's only reluctantly, but willing servants make wonderful witnesses. A joyful, submissive servant of God, eager to be used of Him, always will be, and the blessing will endure for generations. Not only are true servants of God identifiable by those who witness their actions and attitudes; we can pick them out of the history books! And sometimes, even the Bible.

Angelic Greetings

And in the same region there were shepherds out in the field, keeping watch over their flock by night. And an angel of the Lord appeared to them, and the glory of the Lord shone around them, and they were filled with fear. And the angel said to them, "Fear not, for behold, I bring you good news of a great joy that will be for all the people. For unto you is born this day in the city of David a Savior, who is Christ the Lord...." Luke 2:8-11

It's in the first book of the Bible, it's in the last book, and in most of the books in between. It's the opening line of angels, and often of the Lord Jesus Himself. Why is this command important enough to be found in scripture 70 times? What is it?

"Fear not." "Do not be afraid." Usually accompanying this comforting pronouncement is some reason as to why courage is an option, but God could simply stop at "Do not be afraid," and let us fill in the rest of the blanks, ourselves, if He wanted to.

The point made consistently in the Bible is that a servant of the Most High God does not need to be afraid—ever. It could be a fiery furnace stoked just for us, or Armageddon, and the answer is the same: "Do not be afraid."

So how do we pull that off? It's not so much that a servant is never afraid; it's that he takes his fear to God. I like the quote that says, "Courage is fear that has said its prayers." The servant of God who has said his prayers can still be fearful, so long as he does what he's supposed to do. We needn't wait for all fear to vanish before we obey! We say our prayers, then do what needs to be done. And all the while, we can know there is not one circumstance we will ever encounter which negates the divine command, "Do not be afraid."

Life or Death Dreams

Now after Jesus was born in Bethlehem of Judea in the days of Herod the king, behold, wise men from the east came to Jerusalem, saying, "Where is he who has been born king of the Jews? For we saw his star when it rose and have come to worship him."...

And going into the house they saw the child with Mary his mother, and they fell down and worshiped him. Then, opening their treasures, they offered him gifts, gold and frankincense and myrrh. And being warned in a dream not to return to Herod, they departed to their own country by another way.

Now when they had departed, behold, an angel of the Lord appeared to Joseph in a dream and said, "Rise, take the child and his mother, and flee to Egypt, and remain there until I tell you, for Herod is about to search for the child, to destroy him." And he rose and took the child and his mother by night and departed to Egypt and remained there until the death of Herod...."
Matthew 2:1,11-15

In this high-suspense drama, it is *vital* that all of God's servants are paying attention; otherwise, Jesus will be killed. Fortunately, the people God has chosen as guardians for His Son are attentive, obedient and courageous.

The wise men wouldn't have come in the first place, had they not noticed the new star in the East and been so motivated they were willing to travel many miles in search of the new king. They were paying attention! God led them to the precise house where His Son lay. The wise men heed the dream warning them not to return to Herod. Once again, paying attention.

Now, there's Joseph. A dream from God had prompted Joseph to take Mary, already pregnant, as his wife; here is another dream, with an urgent warning. I so much like Joseph! Instant obedience, based on nothing more than a dream!

But it's a dream he knows is from God. God chose the right man to be Jesus' earthly father. Before dawn's light hits the floor, they are on their way. I have a mental picture of Roman soldiers sealing the perimeter around Bethlehem just minutes after God's tiny Son is slipped past into safety.

When God's servants pay attention, God makes sure they get it right.

Trustworthy Servants

Now when they had departed, behold, an angel of the Lord appeared to Joseph in a dream and said, "Rise, take the child and his mother, and flee to Egypt, and remain there until I tell you, for Herod is about to search for the child, to destroy him." And he rose and took the child and his mother by night and departed to Egypt,.... Matthew 2:13-14

It's not every servant who is willing to wake up his family and leave during the night for a foreign country, based on a dream he just had! For Joseph, God's leading through dreams has almost become routine! So has Joseph's obedience. God could trust Joseph for rapid obedience, even though the stakes were as high as they could possibly be.

We can always trust God, but can He trust us? Is He able to count on us when there is no back-up plan?

Joseph is only one example among many, in scripture, of faithful servants who could be trusted to obey God, even when it didn't make sense.

Philip is willing to leave the revival he just started, to journey alone into the desert. (Acts 8) Why? Nothing but obedience. That obedience led to a rendezvous with an Ethiopian eunuch, whom Philip introduced to Christ. The little cloud of dust was the Gospel heading for Africa.

Ananias is such a trustworthy disciple that God is able to tell Saul a man named Ananias is coming, prior to notifying Ananias! All Ananias needs is a vision from God, and he is willing to march up to the door of the most feared Christian-persecutor in the world, and tell him, "Brother Saul, the Lord Jesus...sent me..." (Acts 9)

I want God to do significant things through me, but the bottom line is: Can He trust me? If He gives me an important assignment, will I instantly obey, or procrastinate? Will I finish the task given to me, even though I get tired or discouraged, or will I greet Him with excuses upon His return?

If a manager has two employees, one faithful and reliable, one requiring constant prodding and supervision, which one will be given the important tasks? If that's the way it is in the temporal, secular world, why would it not be that way in the eternal, spiritual world?

A servant must be proven trustworthy. Otherwise, he's of little value to the cause of his Master. May I be a trustworthy servant of God.

December 27

The Authority of a Servant
Talking To Trees

The apostles said to the Lord, "Increase our faith!" And the Lord said, "If you had faith like a grain of mustard seed, you could say to this mulberry tree, 'Be uprooted and planted in the sea,' and it would obey you." Luke 17:5-6

Jesus definitely wasn't saying this to His disciples in order to bait them; He was giving them a fact. So where's the breakdown? Do we have such pathetically small or non-existent faith? Is it because we not only don't have faith; we don't think to even ask? Or is part of our problem that we misdirect what faith or authority we do have?

On that last note, something which I think is consistent in all Jesus' sayings about faith, and transplanting trees and mountains, etc., is that He instructs us to talk to the tree, not the Father.

I'm thinking of numerous times when I've heard people "commanding" the Lord to do this or that; it's always made me very uncomfortable! I personally don't find it to ever be appropriate to try to tell God what to do!

On the other hand, here is one of several passages where Christ indicates that even a little faith gives us an authority over creation which we would find astounding. Why would Jesus say that we could speak to a tree and have it transplant itself in the ocean, were it not true? And all it takes is faith—and just a little faith, at that!

Yet, when it comes to the whole "faith scenario," I feel so totally inept at it that I wanted to just skip this blatant passage and go on to something "easier," something more in keeping with my experience, and the experiences of my peers.

It is true that all of the best things which have ever happened to me have all come by faith, in answer to prayer, so I don't think I'm a stranger to faith, but the faith which is directed toward creation as a use of authority? That one finds me very much a novice.

Someday I won't be. Someday the kind of faith of which Jesus speaks will be natural to me. But I don't think He wants us to wait until heaven! I think Jesus wants to increase our faith, now! And what I'm reminded of in this passage is that faith results in authority, but the authority is *from* God, never *over* Him. Mulberry trees, beware!

December 28

The Authority of a Servant

Desperate Tenacity

And he told them a parable to the effect that they ought always to pray and not lose heart. He said, "In a certain city there was a judge who neither feared God nor respected man. And there was a widow in that city who kept coming to him and saying, 'Give me justice against my adversary.' For a while he refused, but afterward he said to himself, 'though I neither fear God nor respect man, yet because this widow keeps bothering me, I will give her justice, so that she will not beat me down by her continual coming.' " And the Lord said, "Hear what the unrighteous judge says. And will not God give justice to his elect, who cry to him day and night? Will he delay long over them? I tell you, he will give justice to them speedily. Nevertheless, when the Son of Man comes, will he find faith on earth?" Luke 18:1-8

If He doesn't find much faith on earth, I think it will be because we have managed to not need it. The people in my country, even the Christians, will do nearly anything to avoid having to depend totally on God for something! We'll work, plan and borrow, and call the process "faith," but it's not the same. Much of the time, our "faith" is just asking God to bless our plans and make sure they work the way they're supposed to. Divine provision or intervention is welcomed, but optional. Sadly, that's the way we like it.

Which is easier? Living by faith or by a salary paycheck? Having done both, I can testify that living by faith is much more difficult. However, praying for provision is much easier when I'm living by faith! I'm highly motivated to ask God and keep asking, when my only source of income is whatever He directs people to send to my ministry. It's also a lot easier to be genuinely grateful living by faith than it was when a routine salary check was available.

And when it comes to persistence in asking the Father, nothing encourages tenacity in prayer like pure desperation! If the widow had other options, such as finding herself a different judge, she would have given up on this one. Since she had no choice, she relied on persistence, and it paid off.

We are going to find it much easier to persist in prayer if we allow ourselves to be in a position where we have no choice but to appeal to our good Father. If a helpless widow can get what she needs from an uncaring magistrate, how much better will we do with a caring God? Don't give up.

December 29

The Authority of a Servant
Not Here To Hide

On the evening of that day, the first day of the week, the doors being locked where the disciples were for fear of the Jews, Jesus came and stood among them and said to them, "Peace be with you." When he had said this, he showed them his hands and his side. Then the disciples were glad when they saw the Lord. Jesus said to them again, "Peace be with you. As the Father has sent me, even so I am sending you." And when he had said this, he breathed on them and said to them, "Receive the Holy Spirit. If you forgive the sins of anyone, they are forgiven; if you withhold forgiveness from anyone, it is withheld." John 20:19-23

There it is, again! Jesus wants all of Him to be in all of us—and just as He has been sent, He is sending us. We're not here to hide. Isn't it interesting that when He gives them the commission to go, they are hiding?

Jesus wants His disciples to be equipped. *Peace be with you.* Twice! *Receive the Holy Spirit.* We have the peace and we have the Presence; now the authority: *If you forgive the sins of anyone, they are forgiven; if you withhold forgiveness from anyone, it is withheld.*

Peace. The Holy Spirit. Authority. We have everything we need, and we have been sent.

The forgiveness part I don't fully understand. I'm going back to the statement made by the scribes and Pharisees, *"Who can forgive sins but God alone?"* (Lk 5:21) after Christ had proclaimed forgiveness to the paralyzed man let down through the roof. Jesus' reply was *"But that you may know that the Son of Man has authority on earth to forgive sins"* (Lk 5:24), followed by the immediate and miraculous healing of paralysis.

There are a couple ways to look at this, both of them leading to the same conclusion. One is that, yes, only God can forgive sins, but when we receive the Holy Spirit, God is in us, and it is He who is actually doing the forgiving. The other way of looking at it is that the Son of Man has authority on earth to forgive sins, and He has chosen to delegate authority to His disciples to do the same.

Conclusion? It's either delegated authority, or it's not even us, but the Holy Spirit dwelling in us; either way, we have it! And either way, we have been *sent.* I guess it's time to unlock the doors and go.

Serving God

"You did not choose me, but I chose you and appointed you that you should go and bear fruit and that your fruit should abide, so that whatever you ask the Father in my name, he may give it to you." John 15:16

That's my ordination verse. Years ago, when I was ordained into the ministry, the ordination candidates were asked to bring their Bibles with them to the altar where we would be ordained. My hands were resting on this passage in my open Bible as the Church gathered around me and bestowed upon me the highest affirmation they could give in recognition of a call of God upon my life. Honestly, the ceremony didn't hold a candle to the call. The "call" to which I refer is the one which began with my mother's dream, before I was even born, the prompting of His Spirit upon my heart for as long as I can remember, my response to that prompting beginning at age five, and several years of an increasingly intense call to preach, to which I surrendered at the age of sixteen after a lengthy struggle.

One thing about it. I never questioned if my call was real! I had spent months trying everything I could think of to make it go away, without success. God is relentless! Serving God wasn't the problem—I was happy to do that; I just didn't want to be a preacher! I had a long list of excuses which I felt got me off the hook. But He had chosen me for a purpose. Life became increasingly miserable as I tried to wriggle out from under the call.   Finally, at teen camp, in the presence of newfound friends, I decided to surrender. One morning, the camp speaker invited everyone with "a call to fulltime Christian service," as he put it, who wanted to say "Yes" to that call, to come forward and kneel at the altar. Some of my friends went forward. I did, too. Something really wonderful happened that morning, with a simple act of obedience. When I said to God, "O.K., I'm in," He suddenly changed my heart! When I arose from that altar, I had a desire to be a pastor, or anything else He wanted me to be. I've never wanted to be anything else since.

The greatest joy in my life has been to get to serve God. Making the choice to serve Him was the best decision I ever made, one which has been followed by blessings beyond number. Every good thing in my life points straight back toward Him. This study on what the Bible says about serving God has only been a reminder: *There is <u>nothing</u> like serving God!*

Why Stand Looking?

So when they had come together, they asked him, "Lord, will you at this time restore the kingdom to Israel? " He said to them, "It is not for you to know times or seasons that the Father has fixed by his own authority. But you will receive power when the Holy Spirit has come upon you, and you will be my witnesses in Jerusalem and in all Judea and Samaria, and to the end of the earth." And when he had said these things, as they were looking on, he was lifted up, and a cloud took him out of their sight. And while they were gazing into heaven as he went, behold, two men stood by them in white robes, and said, "Men of Galilee, why do you stand looking into heaven? This Jesus, who was taken up from you into heaven, will come in the same way as you saw him go into heaven." Acts 1:6-11

They didn't stand looking very long. Back to Jerusalem they went, just as Jesus had instructed. When the promised Holy Spirit came upon them on the Day of Pentecost, it was as if an explosion had occurred, and the Church was born. Before long the skeptics were shaking their heads, muttering something about the world being turned upside down. They were just getting started. The Early Church blazed a trail of holy fire across the Roman Empire and beyond. It was just like the Lord had said: "The gates of hell shall not prevail against it." (Mt 16:18)

A lot of time and history have passed since the day on which the apostles squinted into heaven and tried to catch just one more glimpse of their Lord. I'm glad they stopped looking and got to work, writing the book of Acts with their Spirit-filled lives.

Church in America, why do we stand looking at the book of Acts, wishing this were us? It is! We worship exactly the same Jesus they did. His power is undiminished. His love is the same as it was then. The same Holy Spirit who came to live in them has come to live in us who believe. What are we doing, standing around looking into heaven? And why would we treat the God of the Scriptures almost as if He were a different God than the one currently presiding over us, as in, "Of course He did that for them, because they were the apostles and the early believers, but He wouldn't do that for us"?

The same Christ who left behind a band of followers on a Galilean mountaintop will be returning for us. It's going to be Him, not some modern-day version of Him. I want to be ready! The same Jesus is coming back.

Serving God

INDEX

Serving God

Dave Ness has been a pastor for over 30 years, and a student of the Word since childhood. In 2005, he founded Servant Connection, a non-profit ministry dedicated to the spiritual transformation of America. Dave currently pastors North Seattle Church of the Nazarene, in Seattle, Washington.

Servant Connection
Website: PrayingforAmerica.org

Correspondence
or to purchase additional copies
of *Answers for Today* or *Serving God:*

Dave Ness
13130 5th Ave. NE
Seattle, WA 98125

Email
SCJForever@centurylink.net

Donations
Servant Connection
P.O. Box 1747
Longview, WA 98632

North Seattle Church of the Nazarene
13130 5th Ave. NE
Seattle, WA 98125

NorthSeattleNazarene.org

Pray for America.